Cryptography and Information Security

Second Edition

V.K. PACHGHARE
Associate Professor
Department of Computer Engineering and Information Technology
College of Engineering, Pune
(An Autonomous Institute of Government of Maharashtra)

PHI Learning Private Limited
Delhi-110092
2015

₹ 350.00

CRYPTOGRAPHY AND INFORMATION SECURITY, Second Edition
V.K. Pachghare

© 2015 by PHI Learning Private Limited, Delhi. All rights reserved. No part of this book may be reproduced in any form, by mimeograph or any other means, without permission in writing from the publisher.

ISBN-978-81-203-5082-3

The export rights of this book are vested solely with the publisher.

Fifth Printing (Second Edition) ... ... **January, 2015**

Published by Asoke K. Ghosh, PHI Learning Private Limited, Rimjhim House, 111, Patparganj Industrial Estate, Delhi-110092 and Printed by Mudrak, 30-A, Patparganj, Delhi-110091.

*To
my parents,
my wife Archana
and
my daughter Samiksha*

Contents

Preface .... *xv*
Acknowledgements .... *xix*

1. **Introduction** 1
   1.1 Security *1*
   1.2 Elements of Information Security *2*
       1.2.1 Confidentiality *2*
       1.2.2 Integrity *2*
       1.2.3 Availability *2*
   1.3 Security Policy *3*
   1.4 Security Techniques *3*
   1.5 Steps for Better Security *4*
   1.6 Category of Computer Security *5*
   1.7 The Operational Model of Network Security *6*
   1.8 Security Services *6*
   1.9 Basic Network Security Terminology *7*
       1.9.1 Cryptography *7*
       1.9.2 Hacking *8*
       1.9.3 Encryption *8*
       1.9.4 Decryption *8*
       1.9.5 Cryptanalysis *9*
   1.10 Security Attacks *9*
       1.10.1 Passive Attack *9*
       1.10.2 Active Attack *10*
   Summary 12
   Exercises 12
   Multiple Choice Questions 13

2. Data Encryption Techniques 14

- 2.1 Introduction **14**
- 2.2 Encryption Methods **15**
  - 2.2.1 Symmetric Encryption **15**
  - 2.2.2 Asymmetric Encryption **16**
- 2.3 Cryptography **17**
- 2.4 Substitution Ciphers **17**
  - 2.4.1 The Caesar Cipher **17**
  - 2.4.2 Monoalphabetic Ciphers **18**
  - 2.4.3 Playfair Cipher **19**
  - 2.4.4 The Hill Cipher **22**
  - 2.4.5 Polyalphabetic Ciphers **26**
  - 2.4.6 One-time Pad or Vernam Cipher **28**
- 2.5 Transposition Ciphers **29**
  - 2.5.1 Single Columnar Transposition **30**
  - 2.5.2 Double Columnar Transposition **31**
- 2.6 Cryptanalysis **32**
  - 2.6.1 Enumerate All Short Keywords **32**
  - 2.6.2 Dictionary Attacks **33**
- 2.7 Steganography **34**
  - 2.7.1 Applications **34**
  - 2.7.2 Limitations **35**

Solved Problems **35**
Summary **44**
Exercises **44**
Multiple Choice Questions **45**

3. Data Encryption Standards 47

- 3.1 Indrodution **47**
- 3.2 Block Ciphers **47**
- 3.3 Block Cipher Modes of Operation **48**
  - 3.3.1 Electronic Code Book (ECB) Mode **48**
  - 3.3.2 Cipher Block Chaining (CBC) Mode **49**
  - 3.3.3 Feedback Mode **51**
  - 3.3.4 Counter Mode **54**
- 3.4 Feistel Ciphers **56**
- 3.5 Data Encryption Standard **57**
  - 3.5.1 Working of DES **58**
  - 3.5.2 Cracking DES **64**
- 3.6 Triple DES **64**
  - 3.6.1 Working of Triple DES **64**
  - 3.6.2 Modes of Operation **65**
- 3.7 DES Design Criteria **65**
  - 3.7.1 Design of S-box **65**
- 3.8 Other Block Ciphers **66**
- 3.9 Differential Cryptanalysis **66**

3.10 Linear cryptanalysis **67**
3.11 Weak Keys in DES Algorithms **67**
Summary **70**
Exercises **70**
Multiple Choice Questions **71**

4. Advanced Encryption Standard 72

4.1 Introduction **72**
4.2 Advanced Encryption Standard (AES) **73**
4.3 Overview of Rijndael **73**
4.4 Key Generation **74**
    4.4.1 Round Constant **76**
4.5 Encryption **77**
    4.5.1 Initial Round **78**
    4.5.2 Round 1 **79**
4.6 Decryption **84**
    4.6.1 Initial Round **84**
    4.6.2 Round 1 **84**
4.7 Galois Field of Multiplication **86**
4.8 Advantages of AES **88**
4.9 Comparison of AES with Other Ciphers **89**
Solved Problems **89**
Summary **95**
Exercises **95**
Multiple Choice Questions **96**

5. Symmetric Ciphers 97

5.1 Introduction **97**
5.2 Blowfish Encryption Algorithm **97**
    5.2.1 Key Expansion **98**
    5.2.2 Encryption **99**
    5.2.3 Blowfish Architecture **101**
    5.2.4 Cryptanalysis of Blowfish **102**
5.3 RC5 **102**
    5.3.1 Characteristics of RC5 **103**
    5.3.2 Parameters **104**
    5.3.3 Cipher Modes in RC5 **105**
5.4 RC4 **106**
    5.4.1 Design **106**
    5.4.2 Characteristics **106**
    5.4.3 Algorithms **106**
5.5 RC6 **107**
    5.5.1 Parameters of RC6 **108**
    5.5.2 Basic Operations **108**
    5.5.3 Working of RC6 **109**
5.6 Comparison between RC6 and RC5 **109**

5.7 IDEA *110*
    5.7.1 Working of IDEA *111*
    5.7.2 Decryption *114*
    5.7.3 Security *115*
Solved Problems *115*
Summary *128*
Exercises *128*
Multiple Choice Questions *129*

6. Number Theory 130

6.1 Introduction *130*
6.2 Prime Numbers *130*
    6.2.1 Relative Prime Numbers *131*
6.3 Modular Arithmetic *131*
    6.3.1 Properties *132*
6.4 Fermat's Theorem *134*
    6.4.1 An Application of Fermat's Little Theorem and Congruence *136*
6.5 Euler's Theorem *138*
    6.5.1 The General Formula to Compute $\Phi(n)$ *139*
6.6 Euclidean Algorithm *143*
    6.6.1 Extended Euclidean Algorithm *145*
6.7 Primality Test *151*
    6.7.1 Naïve Methods *151*
    6.7.2 Probabilistic Tests *152*
    6.7.3 Fermat Primality Test *152*
    6.7.4 Miller–Rabin Primality Test *153*
    6.7.5 Agrawal, Kayal and Saxena Primality Test (AKS Test) *153*
6.8 Chinese Remainder Theorem *154*
6.9 Discrete Logarithms *158*
    6.9.1 Index Calculus Algorithm *159*
Summary *160*
Exercises *160*
Multiple Choice Questions *161*

7. Public Key Cryptosystems 162

7.1 Introduction *162*
7.2 Public Key Cryptography *163*
    7.2.1 Authentication, Secrecy and Confidentiality *165*
    7.2.2 Key Length and Encryption Strength *168*
    7.2.3 Applications of Public Key Cryptography *168*
    7.2.4 Strength and Weakness of Public Key *169*
    7.2.5 Comparison of Asymmetric Encryption and Symmetric Encryption *169*
7.3 RSA Algorithm *169*
    7.3.1 Working of RSA *169*
    7.3.2 Key Length *172*
    7.3.3 Security *172*

       Solved Problems   *173*
       Summary   *176*
       Exercises   *177*
       Multiple Choice Questions   *177*

8. Key Management 178

   8.1   Introduction   *178*
   8.2   Key Distribution   *178*
           8.2.1   Public Announcement   *179*
           8.2.2   Publicly Available Directory   *179*
           8.2.3   Public Key Authority   *180*
           8.2.4   Public Key Certificates   *181*
   8.3   Diffie–Hellman Key Exchange   *182*
           8.3.1   Description   *183*
           8.3.2   Security   *185*
           8.3.3   Man-in-the-Middle Attack   *185*
           8.3.4   Authentication   *186*
   8.4   Elliptic Curve Arithmetic   *186*
           8.4.1   Elliptic Curve Groups Over Real Numbers   *187*
           8.4.2   Elliptic Curve Addition: A Geometric Approach   *187*
           8.4.3   Elliptic Curve Addition: An Algebraic Approach   *190*
           8.4.4   Elliptic Curve Groups over F_P *190*
           8.4.5   Arithmetic in an Elliptic Curve Group over F_P *191*
           8.4.6   Elliptic Curve Groups over $F_2 n$ *192*
           8.4.7   Arithmetic in an Elliptic Curve Group over $F_2 m$ *192*
   8.5   Elliptic Curve Cryptography (ECC)   *193*
           8.5.1   Elliptic Curve Diffie–Hellman   *193*
           8.5.2   Key Establishment Protocol   *193*
   8.6   Elliptic Curve Security and Efficiency   *194*
   8.7   Zero-Knowledge Proof   *195*
           8.7.1   Cave Story   *196*
       Solved Problems   *198*
       Summary   *200*
       Exercises   *201*
       Multiple Choice Questions   *201*

9. Authentication 202

   9.1   Introduction   *202*
           9.1.1   Objectives   *202*
           9.1.2   Measurements   *203*
   9.2   Authentication Methods   *204*
           9.2.1   Password-based Authentication Method   *204*
           9.2.2   Two-factor Authentication Method   *206*
           9.2.3   Biometric Authentication Method   *206*
           9.2.4   Extensible Authentication Protocol (EAP)   *208*
   9.3   Message Digest   *210*
           9.3.1   MD2   *210*

         9.3.2   MD4   *211*
         9.3.3   MD5   *211*
         9.3.4   SHA-1   *218*
         9.3.5   HMAC   *222*
         9.3.6   RIPEMD-160   *224*
   9.4   Kerberos   *225*
         9.4.1   Basics of Kerberos   *226*
         9.4.2   Kerberos Ticket-granting Approach   *228*
         9.4.3   Ticket-Granting Server   *229*
         9.4.4   Kerberos Third-party Authentication Model   *230*
         9.4.5   Kerberos Authentication Model: Definitions and Notational Conventions   *231*
         9.4.6   Kerberos Authentication Model   *232*
         9.4.7   Cross-Realm Authentication   *233*
         9.4.8   Kerberos and Public Key Cryptography   *235*
         9.4.9   Advantages of Kerberos   *235*
         9.4.10   Weaknesses of Kerberos   *236*
         9.4.11   Attacks on Kerberos   *236*
         9.4.12   Applications and Limitations of Kerberos   *236*
         9.4.13   Comparisons of Kerberos with SSL   *237*
   9.5   X.509 Authentication Service   *237*
   Summary   *239*
   Exercises   *239*
   Multiple Choice Questions   *240*

10. Digital Signatures ... 241

   10.1 Introduction   *241*
         10.1.1   Implementation of Digital Signatures   *243*
         10.1.2   Association of Digital Signatures and Encryption   *243*
         10.1.3   Using Different Key Pairs for Signing and Encryption   *245*
   10.2 Algorithms for Digital Signature   *245*
         10.2.1   Digital Signature Algorithm (DSA)   *246*
         10.2.2   ElGamal Signature   *248*
         10.2.3   Elliptic Curve Digital Signature Algorithm (ECDSA)   *249*
   10.3 Digital Signature Standard (DSS)   *250*
         10.3.1   Applications of Digital Signature   *250*
   10.4 Authentication Protocols   *251*
   Summary   *251*
   Exercises   *252*
   Multiple Choice Questions   *252*

11. Electronic Mail Security ... 253

   11.1 Introduction   *253*
   11.2 Pretty Good Privacy (PGP)   *253*
         11.2.1   Need of PGP   *254*
         11.2.2   Working of PGP   *255*

        11.2.3 PGP Encryption Applications   *259*
        11.2.4 PGP: Backdoors and Key Escrow   *259*
        11.2.5 PGP Security Quality   *261*
　 11.3 MIME   *261*
        11.3.1 MIME Headers   *261*
        11.3.2 MIME Transfer-Encoding Header Field   *266*
　 11.4 S/MIME   *267*
        11.4.1 History of S/MIME   *267*
        11.4.2 Working of S/MIME   *268*
        11.4.3 Applications of S/MIME   *269*
　 11.5 Comparison of PGP and S/MIME   *269*
Summary   *269*
Exercises   *270*
Multiple Choice Questions   *270*

12. IP Security 272

　 12.1 Introduction   *272*
　 12.2 IP Security Architecture   *272*
        12.2.1 Strengths of IPsec   *272*
        12.2.2 Applications of IPsec   *273*
        12.2.3 Benefits of IPsec   *274*
        12.2.4 Overview of IPsec   *274*
        12.2.5 Working of IPsec   *275*
　 12.3 IPv6   *275*
　 12.4 IPsec, IPv4, and IPv6   *279*
　 12.5 IPsec Protocols and Operations   *280*
　 12.6 Authentication Header (AH) Protocol   *281*
        12.6.1 AH Transport Mode   *282*
        12.6.2 AH Tunnel Mode   *283*
　 12.7 Encapsulating Security Payload (ESP) Protocol   *283*
        12.7.1 ESP Transport Mode   *285*
        12.7.2 ESP Tunnel Mode   *286*
        12.7.3 Cryptographic Algorithms   *286*
        12.7.4 Usage   *286*
　 12.8 ISAKMP Protocol   *288*
        12.8.1 Overview   *288*
        12.8.2 Terms and Definitions   *289*
        12.8.3 Security Association Negotiation   *289*
        12.8.4 ISAKMP Payloads   *289*
        12.8.5 ISAKMP Exchange Types   *293*
　 12.9 Oakley Key Determination Protocol   *296*
        12.9.1 Overview   *296*
　 12.10 Key Exchange Protocol   *297*
　 12.11 Virtual Private Network   *298*
Summary   *301*
Exercises   *302*
Multiple Choice Questions   *302*

13. Web Security 304

- 13.1 Introduction *304*
- 13.2 Secure Socket Layer *304*
- 13.3 SSL Session and Connection *306*
- 13.4 SSL Record Protocol *307*
- 13.5 ChangeCipher SpecProtocol *308*
- 13.6 Alert Protocol *308*
- 13.7 Handshake Protocol *308*
- 13.8 Secure Electronic Transactions *311*
  - 13.8.1 Importance of SET *312*
  - 13.8.2 SET Mechanism *312*
  - 13.8.3 Key Elements of SET *313*
  - 13.8.4 Strengths of SET *314*
  - 13.8.5 Weaknesses of SET *315*

Summary 315
Exercises 315
Multiple Choice Questions 316

14. Intrusion 317

- 14.1 Introduction *317*
- 14.2 Intrusion Detection *318*
- 14.3 Intrusion Detection System *319*
  - 14.3.1 Need for Intrusion Detection Systems *320*
  - 14.3.2 Intrusion Detection Method *321*
- 14.4 Anomaly-based Intrusion Detection Systems *322*
  - 14.4.1 Statistical Approach *323*
  - 14.4.2 Immune System Approach *323*
- 14.5 Misuse-based intrusion Detection Systems *323*
  - 14.5.1 Expression Matching *324*
  - 14.5.2 State Transition Analysis *324*
  - 14.5.3 Genetic Algorithm *324*
- 14.6 Distributed Intrusion Detection System *324*
  - 14.6.1 Overview *325*
  - 14.6.2 Advantages of a dIDS *326*
  - 14.6.3 Incident Analysis with dIDS *327*
  - 14.6.4 Analysis Using Aggregation *327*
- 14.7 Base Rate Fallacy *328*
  - 14.7.1 Basic Frequency Assumptions *328*
  - 14.7.2 Honeypots *328*
- 14.8 Password Management Practices *329*
- 14.9 Limitations of Intrusion Detection Systems *334*
- 14.10 Challenges of Intrusion Detection *335*

Summary 337
Exercises 337
Multiple Choice Questions 337

15. Malicious Software 339

    15.1 Introduction   *339*
    15.2 Malicious Code   *339*
    15.3 Viruses   *340*
        15.3.1 Types of Viruses   *340*
        15.3.2 Working of Antivirus Software   *341*
        15.3.3 Methods to Avoid Detection   *343*
    15.4 Worms   *345*
        15.4.1 Historical Background   *346*
        15.4.2 Different Types of Computer Worms   *346*
        15.4.3 Protecting against Computer Worms   *347*
        15.4.4 Symptoms of a Computer Worm   *347*
    15.5 Trojans or Trojan Horses   *348*
        15.5.1 Features of Trojan Horse Virus   *348*
    15.6 Spyware   *349*
    15.7 Bots   *349*
    15.8 Best Practices   *350*
    15.9 Digital Immune System   *350*
        15.9.1 Behaviour Blocking   *351*
    15.10 Attacks   *351*
        15.10.1 Hoax   *351*
        15.10.2 Backdoor Attack   *352*
        15.10.3 Brute Force Attack   *352*
        15.10.4 Dictionary Attack   *352*
        15.10.5 Spoofing Attack   *353*
        15.10.6 Denial-of-Service Attack (DoS Attack)   *354*
        15.10.7 Distributed Denial-of-Service Attack   *355*
        15.10.8 Man-in-the-middle Attack   *356*
        15.10.9 Spam   *356*
        15.10.10 E-mail Bombing and Spamming   *356*
        15.10.11 Sniffer   *356*
        15.10.12 Timing Attack   *357*
    Summary   *358*
    Exercises   *358*
    Multiple Choice Questions   *359*

16. Firewall 361

    16.1 Introduction   *361*
    16.2 Characteristics of a Firewall   *362*
    16.3 Types of Firewall   *362*
        16.3.1 Packet Filtering Firewall   *362*
        16.3.2 Application Level Gateways   *364*
        16.3.3 Circuit Level Gateways   *366*
    16.4 Benefits of a Firewall   *366*
    16.5 Limitations of a Firewall   *366*

16.6 Firewall Architectures *366*
    16.6.1 Dual-Homed Host Architecture *366*
    16.6.2 Screened Host Architecture *367*
    16.6.3 Screened Subnet Architecture *368*
16.7 Trusted System *371*
    16.7.1 Trusted Systems in Policy Analysis *371*
16.8 Access Control *372*
    16.8.1 Objectives of Access Control *372*
    16.8.2 Types of Access Control *372*
Summary *373*
Exercises *373*
Multiple Choice Questions *374*

17. Computer Forensics ... 375

17.1 Introduction *375*
17.3 Areas of Application of Computer Forensics *379*
    17.3.1 Public Sector *379*
    17.3.2 Private Sector *379*
17.4 Understanding the Suspects *379*
    17.4.1 Electronic Evidence *379*
    17.4.2 E-mail Review *381*
17.5 Examples of Computer Forensics *381*
17.6 Free Space and Slack Space *382*
17.7 Incident Response *382*
17.8 Weaknesses *383*
Summary *384*
Exercises *384*
Multiple Choice Questions *385*

Bibliography ... *387*

Index ... *389*

Preface

Cryptography and information security has moved from the confines of academia to all users of computer all over the world. Computer security is a science as well as an art. It is an art because no system can be considered secure without an examination of how it is to be used. It is a science because its theory is based on mathematical constructions, analyses, and proofs. It has increasingly become obvious to everybody that something needs to be done in order to secure our network as well as personal computers. This field of security is a challenging field as technology changes every day. Thus, there is a need to secure computers and networks from the hackers by developing new algorithms. This book introduces the different areas of security in simple and clear terms. In this text, I have tried to put together the basics of computer security in a compact and concise manner.

The book discusses the importance of using information and the security of that information. The aim of this book is to fulfil the need for a quality textbook on cryptography and information security for the students of Information Technology, Computer Science and Engineering, and Master of Computer Applications. As the government is concentrating more on infrastructure security and to create awareness about information security among the people, there is a clear need to include practitioners and students of other disciplines. This book serves their purpose as well. It also contains advanced topics such as computer forensics.

The book is divided into 17 chapters and attempts to introduce the students to the essentials of cryptography and information security.

Chapter 1 discusses security, its importance, elements of security and the operational model of network security. Various encryption methods, their comparisons, and the cipher techniques used in the cryptography and information security are described in Chapter 2. Chapter 3 deals with different ciphers, DES, 3DES, side channel attacks, differential cryptanalysis, and linear cryptanalysis. Solved problems on DES are also given. Chapter 4 describes the RijnDael, and comparison of AES with DES and 3DES. Chapter 5 dwells on various encryption algorithms such as Blowfish, RC4, RC5, RC6 and IDEA.

Chapter 6 concentrates on the mathematical background required for cryptography and information security. It describes prime number, Fermat's theorem, Euler's theorem, primality test, Chinese remainder theorem, and discrete logarithms. Chapter 7 provides an introduction to public key encryption, the RSA algorithm, and timing attacks, besides solved problems on RSA. Chapter 8 focuses on key distribution, the Diffie–Hellman key exchange, elliptic curve and zero knowledge proof systems. Chapter 9 describes the authentication methods, message digest such as MD4, MD5, RIPEMD, SHA and Kerberos, X.509 authentication service. Digital signatures, algorithms, standards and authentication protocols are taken up in Chapter 10.

Chapter 11 introduces the reader to electronic mail security, pretty good privacy (PGP), S/MIME, MIME, and gives a comparison of PGP and S/MIME. Chapter 12 explains IP Security architecture, IPsec, IPv4, IPv6, the authentication header (AH) protocol, the encapsulating security payload (ESP) protocol, the ISAKMP protocol, the OAKLEY key determination protocol, and the key exchange protocol. Secure socket layer, SSL session and connection, the SSL record protocol, secure electronic transactions are explained in Chapter 13.

Chapter 14 describes intrusion detection system, anomaly detection systems, misuse detection system, rule-based intrusion detection, distributed intrusion detection, base-rate fallacy, and password management best practices. Different malicious software is discussed in Chapter 15. Firewall, types of firewall, firewall architecture, and trusted system are explained in Chapter 16. Chapter 17 discusses computer forensics, computer forensics investigations, the areas in which computer forensics are applied, and its drawbacks.

New to the Second Edition

There is a continuous innovations and improvements in the field of cryptography and information security. This edition of the book tries to capture these changes. These changes are more substantial and comprehensive. In this edition, the effort is taken to improve the pedagogy and user friendliness and incorporates MCQs with their answers in each chapter. There have been major substantive changes in the book. These include:

Security attacks: Attacks are the important components in information security. The material on these are completely rewritten.

Cryptanalysis: The strength of the algorithm is known using cryptanalysis. The cryptanalysis for different data encryption standards are newly added in this edition.

Solved problems: Different algorithms are explained with many solved numerical problems.

Weak keys: DES algorithm is suffered by brute force attack. There are many weak keys for DES which are discussed in this book.

AES algorithm: This topic is completely rewritten with solved problems on key generation and encryptions.

IDEA algorithm: It is rewritten with solved problems using simplified IDEA algorithm.

Number theory: This chapter is completely rewritten with lots of solved problems on different methods which is helpful to understand the concepts. Chinese remainder theorem and extended Euclidean algorithm are important for numerous cryptographic applications. This book provides a clear idea about all these algorithms.

RSA algorithm: Many solved problems are incorporated on RSA algorithm.

Diffie–Hellman algorithm: The algorithm and many solved problems are included to explain the key distribution mechanisms.

Authentication methods: This chapter is completely rewritten which makes it easy to understand the concepts.

Hashing algorithms: MD5 and SHA-1 are rewritten so that readers can get the proper working of these algorithms.

PGP: The working of PGP is rewritten in a simple way so that the reader can understand the concepts clearly.

IP security: This is an important concept in network security. In this book, IPv4 and IPv6 are explained in a simple manner.

Virtual Private Network (VPN): This topic is most important so it is newly added in this book.

SSL protocol: This topic is rewritten which discusses the detail working of each phase of SSL protocol.

Intrusion detection: This book discusses different types of intruders and types of IDS.

Malicious software: In this, many types of attacks are discussed.

Firewall: This chapter is rewritten. The material on firewall is expanded and the illustrations are redrawn for better clarity.

V.K. Pachghare

Acknowledgements

I express my heartfelt gratitude to my wife Archana, as always, for her positive attitude, full support, and encouragement in my writing endeavours. Thanks to my lovely daughter Samiksha for her continuous support and patience throughout the writing process.

I also wish to thank the editorial and production staff of PHI Learning for their careful processing of the manuscript.

I would like to thank my colleagues and students for their feedback without which it would not have been possible for me to complete this book. Many people have contributed directly or indirectly to this book in a variety of ways. I thank each of them.

Any constructive criticism for the improvement of the book is most welcome.

V.K. Pachghare

CHAPTER 1

Introduction

1.1 SECURITY

Today most of the time we use the word security in our day to day life. This word security indicates the state or the quality of being secure. It means particular object, software or system is to be free from any hazard. It means to be protected from attackers who would do harm, may be intentionally or unintentionally. In case of network security, the word security means protection of our network and allow only the authorised people to access the network. To protect the operation of any organisation and provide the security to the organisation, the following security layers are needed:

- *Physical security layer:* The security layer which provides the security to physical objects. It includes the access control to unauthorised person to physical devices such as pen drive, hard disk, CD/DVD, or computer.
- *Private security:* This layer provides the security to the individual or a group.
- *Project security:* When we provide the security to the details of any project such as design, code etc. then it is called *project* or *operational security*.

Today, the use of computer with internet is increasing rapidly. At the same time security challenges are also increasing. A number of software tools are available which help the attackers to attack easily without much knowledge of computer field. Therefore, today's information security is an emerging field which helps to protect the computer from various attacks and also provides the awareness about security among the common people. Information security supports to protect the information from unauthorised persons.

Information security not only confined to computer security but it includes the security of data or information in different forms. We use computer for various applications so it is very important to protect our computer so that unauthorised person cannot access our system and modify or delete or read the data. This modification can be happened in storage, processing or transit of information. Many times the attackers make the system busy so that the authorised users are unable to get the service. At the same time unauthorised users may access the information. This type of attack is called *denial of service attack*. Information security can be defined in various ways depending upon the usages or applications. Some people assume that the computer security and information security are the same. There are different terminologies used by different people for information security. Nomenclatures may be different but the ultimate goal is to secure our computer system and information from attackers. Information security field includes not only the security of information but it covers the security of all infrastructures related to computer system and internet.

No one can claim that the methods or mechanisms used for the security of the system or information is perfect. No one can ever get rid of all risks from the unauthorised use of the system or information, though they sue the proper mechanism to protect their system. This happens due to the new challenges in information security emerging day-to-day. One of the challenges is no prior knowledge about hacking is required to the attacker as a number of tools are freely available. The degree of security depends upon the importance of the information. Another challenge is that many people ignore or hesitate to use the security measures.

1.2 ELEMENTS OF INFORMATION SECURITY

The information security provides services such as confidentiality, integrity and availability to the user. Each of them is discussed here.

1.2.1 Confidentiality

The most important service of information security is confidentiality. It makes sure that only authorised user can access the data. The data should not be accessible to unauthorised person or group of unauthorised persons. Confidentiality can be defined as the protection of data from unauthorised disclosure.

1.2.2 Integrity

Another important service of information security is integrity. The validity of the data is checked by integrity. Integrity gives the information whether there is any change in the data or not. Integrity means assurance that data received are exactly as sent by an authorised sender, i.e., in transmission there is no change happens in the data. This modification or change includes deletion, modification and creation of new information in the data.

1.2.3 Availability

The next service of information security is availability. It is the measure to which a system or information is accessible and usable upon request by an authorised user at any particular time. Availability means a functioning condition of a system at any particular instance. For example, the access to a system or information should not be prevented to the legitimate users.

Initially at the end of the 20th century, the most significant elements of cryptography and network security were confidentiality. The next importance is given to the integrity of the information. As compared to above two services, availability considered as low priority element in information security. But in the first decade of the 21st century, these priorities had changed and the availability is treated as the most important service in information security. The *Information Security Model* gives us the guarantee of security. Assurance is the main element which helps to achieve various objectives of information security. Assurance also helps to achieve confidentiality of the information. This helps to secure the information and the system. It also provides the services like integrity and availability.

1.3 SECURITY POLICY

Information security or computer security is concerned with the control of threats related to the use of information or computer. To achieve this objective, we should develop a secure computing platform so that we can restrict the users to perform only particular actions that is permitted to him or her. For this secure environment should be created. Here computer security is related to the security of computer systems. It is the subpart of security engineering. Security engineering is a broad term which focuses on broader issues in computer, network, information and internet security. We can permit only the authorised users of any particular system to use that system. At the same time restrict these users to misuse their rights to use the system. That is called *access control*.

As per the requirement of system's security status, different techniques have to be used to provide the necessary security. Any particular technique cannot provide the full fledge security to a system. This may happens due to some fundamental flaws present in the system.

The security to the information or computer system can be provided by using following approaches:

1. External approach
2. Internal approach

Suppose the computer system is secure from attackers. In this case we should protect the system from external attacks. For this, necessary measures are applied. This approach is called *external approach*. In the second case, if the internal environment and the system itself is not secure so necessary measures have to be applied to protect from internal attacks then this is called *internal approach*.

1.4 SECURITY TECHNIQUES

Strong security to the system or information is provided by using cryptography and authentication techniques. We know that the channel which is used for transmission of information is not secure. We can provide the security to our information by using various cryptographic techniques. This helps from modification of data in transit. Another technique used for strong security is authentication technique. It can be used to guarantee that communication endpoints, i.e., sender and receiver are the parties who they claim.

The security of the computer system can be provided by using secure techniques. Some of the secure techniques are:

1. *Series of confidence:* This ensures that all software use has been authentic.
2. *Access control:* The access to the data or computer is controlled. If the user misuses the privileges given to him/her then the access to such user is denied. For example, suppose you gave access to your friend of your own computer by giving him/her separate user account. But you found out that your friend misuse your system by some other activities then as an administrator of your computer you can delete that user account so that he cannot access your computer any more.
3. *Ability to detect unpatched known flaws:* When an application provides no way to scrap already known security flaws, in such condition do not use it.
4. *Backup of data:* We can secure our data by taking regular backup. We can secure our data by storing another copy of data at another location. Today number of devices are available for storage which are portable. This provides security to our data.
5. *Antivirus software:* Number of antivirus software are available which provide the security to our system from malicious software.
6. *Firewalls:* Firewall is used to protect the internal network from external attacks. Firewall observes the traffic coming from the outside network and if any attacks find out block it there. It is acting like a security door to our network.
7. *Encryption:* It is the cryptographic technique used to protect the information. There are different techniques for encryption. We will learn later on these techniques. Encryption allows only authorised users to read the data. There are two methods of encryption, i.e., symmetric and asymmetric encryptions.
8. *Intrusion-detection systems (IDS):* It helps to detect the internal as well as external attacks on a computer or a network. There are two types of IDS, i.e., misused-based and anomaly-based IDS. Also IDS can be classified as host-based and network-based IDS. IDS just detect the attack and sends the alarm to the system administrator. It cannot protect the system or network from attack directly.
9. *Information security awareness:* It educates the people about the use of computer and internet, and precaution taking while using internet. Also educate the people about the use of social sites. These awareness help to avoid the damage to individual or organisation while using internet.

1.5 STEPS FOR BETTER SECURITY

Security is the most important aspect of computer world. For better security, we should follow the following steps:

- *Assets:* The first step is to identify what data and computer is to be protected. Identify the important information which need to be protected.
- *Risks:* After the information or assets to be protected have been identified then identify the threat, attacks, vulnerabilities and risks to the information.
- *Protections:* Next step is to find out the solution for the protection of the information.
- *Tools and techniques:* Select the appropriate tools and techniques for the protection of the information.
- *Priorities:* Decide the order of the tools and techniques for the protection of the information.

1.6 CATEGORY OF COMPUTER SECURITY

Computer security can be categorised into the following:

Cryptography also called secret writing which is used to hide the original message. Cryptography is simply the mathematical "scrambling" of data. Only the person having the necessary information (i.e., key) can read the information. Actually, the cryptography is used from ancient time for sending the information in the secret form. The original message is called *plaintext*. This plaintext is converted into some meaningless text called *ciphertext*. This conversion of plaintext to ciphertext is called *encryption*. Julius Caesar around 100 BC was known to use the technique for hiding information is the first cipher. But during 16th century Vigenere designed a cipher which was used a key for encryption.

Data security refers to the protective measures which ensure that data or computer is kept safe from modification or corruption. It also prevents unauthorised access to data or computer. Thus, data security helps to provide privacy to the data. Thus, data security and privacy help the organisation to prevent data breaches, ensure the integrity of data and protect the important information from disclosure.

Computer security models are the formal description of security policies. It refers to the underlying computer architectures, specifications, protection mechanisms, security issues, and formal models that provide the framework for information systems security policy.

Network security means protection of data on the network during transmission. It consists of different policies and provisions adopted by the administrator. It involves the authorisation and access control of the network. Network administrator is responsible for the proper implementation of access control and authentication to provide the security.

Computer security includes the protection, prevention and detection of unauthorised use of computer systems as well as data stored in the computer.

Security exploit is related to computer security vulnerabilities and their exploits. It is an unintended and unpatched flaws in the software which helps the attackers or hackers for attack. Security exploit includes hacking of computer, various types of attacks, viruses, worms, Trojan horses etc.

There are many measures available to provide the security to the computer system. Some of the security software used on large scale are Firewall, Intrusion Prevention System and Antivirus Software.

1.7 THE OPERATIONAL MODEL OF NETWORK SECURITY

It is a well-known thought that "Prevention is better than cure". The same thought was assumed in case of computer security. That is, if we prevent somebody from accessing our computer then our computer is secure. This is partially true as the reality is that though we apply various security measures to protect our system, it cannot give us 100% guarantee of the security of computer systems. Therefore, protection of the computer system, i.e., access control does not mean prevention of the computer system. So, we should provide the necessary protection to our data by using different security mechanisms such as encryption.

Secure transmission of the data can be done by using secure algorithm for transmission of the data. We can use some passwords, keys can be used to provide the security to the data. There are different algorithms such as Diffie-Hellman, available for key distribution. Using these algorithms we can transmit our data securely.

Figure 1.1 shows the working model of network security. From Figure 1.1, suppose sender A wants to communicate with B. He writes some message and hand over it to a person to give it to B. The message is open (assume it is like a postcard). Before the postcard is delivered to B, any third person including the person who transfer this postcard from A to B can read it. Now we want to avoid this, so we can use envelop instead of postcard and sealed it with our signature. Now, any third person cannot read the message. If he/she tries to do it, he/she has to break the seal. But in this case, B knows that somebody already read the message. The same process we can apply to send the digital information by encrypting the original message by some password which is known to A and B only. Any third party cannot decrypt the message as the password is not known to them. Here this password is known as key.

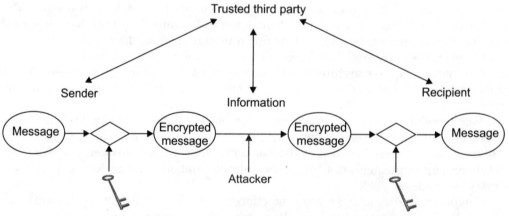

Figure 1.1 Operational model of network security.

1.8 SECURITY SERVICES

There are different security services which help to provide the strong security. Some of them are authentication, data confidentiality, access control, integrity and non-repudiation. We will discuss these services one by one.

- **Authentication:** It is the process of confirming or verifying that someone is who he claim he is. In cryptography and network security, digital signature of the user is used for authentication. Most general and most widely used method of authentication in our daily life is password.
- **Data confidentiality:** It is the process of protection of data or information from unauthorised disclosure. It ensures that information is accessible only to the authorised person. In cryptography and network security data, confidentiality is done by using encryption techniques.
- **Access control:** This ensures that privileged access is withdrawn when privileges are revoked. For example, deleting a user account should also stop any processes that are running with that user's privileges.
- **Integrity:** Integrity means assurance that data received are exactly as sent by an authorised sender, i.e., in transmission there is no change happens in the data. This modification or change includes deletion, modification and creation of new information in the data. We can use Hashing algorithms like MD5, SHA to check the integrity of the message.
- **Non-repudiation:** It is the assurance against denial by one of the parties in a communication. When a message is sent, the receiver can prove that the message was in fact sent by the alleged sender. When a message is received, the sender can prove that the message was in fact received by the alleged receiver. Digital signature can be used for this purpose.
- **Availability:** It is the measure to which a system or information is accessible and usable upon request by an authorised user at any particular time. Availability means a functioning condition of a system at any particular instance. For example, the access to a system or information should not be prevented to the legitimate users.

Initially at the end of the 20th century, confidentiality was the most significant element of information security. The next importance is given to the integrity of the information. As compared to confidentiality and integrity, availability considered as low priority element in information security. But in the first decade of 21st century, these priorities had changed and the availability is treated as the most important service in information security. The Models for Information Security gives us the guarantee of security. Another element of security is assurance. It helps to achieve various objectives of information security. Assurance helps to achieve confidentiality of the information. This helps to secure the information and the system. It also provides the services like integrity and availability.

1.9 BASIC NETWORK SECURITY TERMINOLOGY

1.9.1 Cryptography

It is the science of using mathematics to encrypt and decrypt data. Cryptography is the art of secret writing. The user can secure his/her message using different techniques of cryptography. He/she can securely store or transmit the message using these techniques.

1.9.2 Hacking

It is the most frequently used term in day-to-day life. A hacker is a person or a group of persons who creates, deletes and/or modifies software and hardware of the computer. Hacker uses different tools to break the security of the computer system. These tools are readily available online. The hackers break the security for different purposes. Hacking is of two types depend upon the purpose, i.e., ethical hacking and unethical hacking.

Types of Hackers

Hackers are of three types such as white hat, black hat and grey hat. We learn each of these type in brief as follows.

- *White hat:* This type of hacker is also called *ethical hacker*. They use their knowledge for the best of the society. For example, if we forget our password of our computer. In this case, a hacker helps us to break the password. In software company, before the release of the software, the security of the software is checked by the experts. This is also called *white hat hacker*.
- *Black hat:* This type of hacker is also known as *cracker*. They break the security of the computer for wicked intention.
- *Grey hat:* A hacker who is a combination of both white hat and black hat is known as *grey hat*.

1.9.3 Encryption

Encryption is a technique of translation of data (plaintext) into a secret code (ciphertext). This can be done by using secret key or keys. Using encryption, we can achieve more security to the data.

Depending upon the number of keys used for encryption and decryption, there are two types of classical encryption techniques:

1. Symmetric encryption (only one key for encryption and decryption)
2. Asymmetric encryption (also called public-key encryption)

In symmetric encryption, only one key is required. The same key is used for encryption as well as decryption of the data. There are many symmetric encryption algorithms. Some of them are DES, AES, IDEA, and 3DES.

In asymmetric encryption, two different keys are required. These keys are mathematically related to each other. These keys are called *public key* and *private key*. The key which is publically available for all are called *public key* whereas the key which is known to the owner of the key is called *private key*. There are many asymmetric encryption algorithms. Some of them are Diffie-Hellman, RSA, and Elliptic Curve Cryptography (ECC).

1.9.4 Decryption

Decryption is a technique of translation of decoded data (ciphertext) into original data (plaintext). A secret key is used for decryption. This can be done by using secret key or keys.

1.9.5 Cryptanalysis

It is the art of deciphering the encrypted message/data without knowing the key used for encryption. There are different techniques for cryptanalysis. Some of them are chosen plaintext attack, known plaintext attack, and man in the middle attack.

- *Chosen plaintext attack:* Here the key is not known to the attacker. He/she assumes some plaintext and try to encrypt it to get the desired ciphertext. The purpose of this attack is to get the key. Example of known chosen plaintext attack is differential cryptanalysis which is used against block ciphers.
- *Known plaintext attack:* In this, the attacker knows or guess about some part of the plaintext (original message). He uses this information to decrypt rest of the ciphertext. Example of known plaintext attack is linear cryptanalysis which is used against block ciphers.
- *Ciphertext only attack:* In this, the attacker does not have any information about the original message. He/she only have ciphertext. Using this ciphertext, the attacker tries to find out the original message called plaintext. In practise, it is possible to make guesses about the plaintext using the frequency analysis technique. But this frequency analysis technique not work well against modern ciphers. Modern ciphers are not weak against this attack.
- *Man in the middle attack:* This attack is related to key transmission. Suppose two parties A and B are trying to communicate to each other. In this attack, the attacker place himself between two parties A and B. Then the attacker captures the data which A and B transfer to each other. Then attacker performs key exchange separately with A and B. A and B use the different keys sent by the attacker. The attacker now able to decrypt any message send by two parties A and B.

1.10 SECURITY ATTACKS

In the last 35 years, use of computers and internet have increased significantly which result in increase in threats to the security of the computer system. Number of tools are easily available for attackers which make easy to create new vulnerabilities. These tools require very little or no prior knowledge to use. *Security attack* can be defined as any action that compromises the security of computer systems or the information.

Types of Attack

Attacks are classified into two categories as:
1. Passive attack
2. Active attack

1.10.1 Passive Attack

The attacks in which the attacker tries to learn something from the data or to make use of information from the system. Passive attack does not harm the information or computer system. The attacker captures the data or information during transition of data. This type of attacks are made by Eavesdropping (Figure 1.2). Eavesdropping means unauthorised listening of the private communication of others without their consent. Private communication includes phone call, instant message, videoconference etc. It also includes monitoring the flow of information during transmission to obtain message contents.

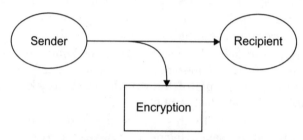

Figure 1.2 Passive attack.

Passive attacks are of two types, i.e., release of message contents and traffic analysis.

- *Release of message contents:* In this type of passive attack, the attacker captures the contents of a message without the knowledge of the sender and the recipient. Encryption can be used to protect the message from this type of attack.
- *Traffic analysis:* The attacker observes the pattern of flow of information during transmission. Using this observation, the attacker draws the conclusion about the flow of traffic. This attack can be done even if messages are encrypted. So the solution for this attack is masking and use of strong encryption algorithm.

It is difficult to detect the passive attack as there is no modification or changes in the original message.

1.10.2 Active Attack

The attacks in which the attempts are made to alter, change or modify the data or information. This is a direct attack of the users. In this attack, the attacker either done the modification of information or data during transmission, or he/she may create false data or information and send it to recipient.

Active attacks are classified into four categories:

- Masquerade
- Message replay
- Message modification
- Denial of service

Masquerade

When one entity pretends to be a different entity then it is a masquerade active attack. The solution for this attack is authentication. Suppose two friends A and B are in communication with each other. In this, the attacker communicate with B by saying that he is A (Figure 1.3).

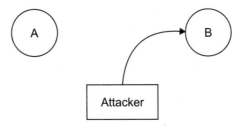

Figure 1.3 Active attack masquerade.

Message Replay

When messages or information or data is captured during transit. Then replay or retransmit the previous messages (Figure 1.4).

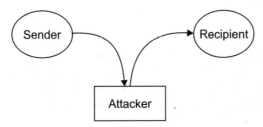

Figure 1.4 Active attack-message replay.

Message Modification

In this type of attack the messages are modified during transmission. In this attack, like message reply attack, first capture the message then modify it and retransmit or resend the modified message.

Denial of Service Attacks (DoS)

In this attack, the server is overloaded by sending number of false request to the server. This prevent legitimate or authorised users of the server to use the system resources or services of the server.

Classification of attack is shown in Figure 1.5.

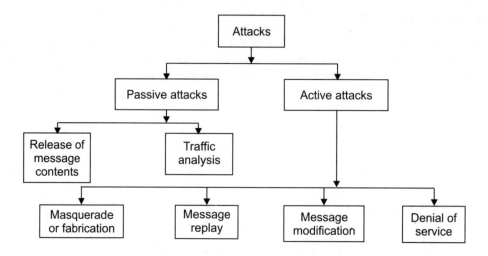

Figure 1.5 Attack classification.

SUMMARY

Hopefully, you are now convinced of the importance of security. Security indicates the quality or state of being secure. Security is good for computer and the data. It is also necessary to protect the information system against the denial of service to the authorised users. The resources must be available to the legitimate users whenever necessary. Security means doing what you can to protect, or at least to avoid damage, the network and computers used by yourself and others. The growth of e-commerce and the pervasive personal and business uses of the internet have created a demand for security. In this chapter, you learnt about the security services which are more important to keep our information secure.

EXERCISES

1.1 What is information security and explain the need of information security?
1.2 What are the different security services? Explain each in brief.
1.3 Explain the following terms with respect to Information Security:
(a) Access control (b) Risk assessment (c) Non-repudiation (d) Authorization (e) Confidentiality (f) Integrity (g) Encryption and (h) Decryption.
1.4 Explain the security model with block diagram.
1.5 What is authentication and authorisation?
1.6 What are the different types of attack? Explain each in brief.
1.7 What is eavesdropping?
1.8 What are the different types of passive attacks? Explain in brief.
1.9 What is man in the middle attack?

MULTIPLE CHOICE QUESTIONS

1.1 Which of the following is a passive attack?
   (a) Modify
   (b) Masquerade
   (c) Denial of Service (DoS)
   (d) Traffic analysis

1.2 _____ service ensures that a message was received by the receiver from the actual sender and not from an attacker.
   (a) Confidentiality
   (b) Access control
   (c) Non-repudiation
   (d) Authentication

1.3 Which of the following is an active attack?
   (i) Release of message contents
   (ii) Traffic analysis
   (iii) Modify
   (iv) Denial of service
   (a) (i) and (ii)
   (b) (i) and (iii)
   (c) (iii) and (iv)
   (d) (ii) and (iv)

1.4 Which of the following attacks is not a threat to the integrity of data?
   (a) Replay
   (b) Snooping
   (c) Masquerade
   (d) Modification of message contents

Answers

1.1 (d)   **1.2** (a)   **1.3** (c)   **1.4** (b)

CHAPTER 2

Data Encryption Techniques

2.1 INTRODUCTION

In today's world nothing is secure. Nobody gives you the guarantee of 100% security. So, there is a need to protect our computer and data from the attackers. Due to rapid increase in the use of internet, every individual as well as his/her information is having a threat from the attackers. Some information which is beneficial to an individual or a group may be used against them by the attacker. In the companies or business organisations due to huge competition, the security measures are very important to protect the data/information. These security measures include authentications, encryptions, access control, confidentiality, etc.

Encryption is the process of converting the original information which is in meaningful and readable form (in cryptography we called it as plaintext) into unreadable form (in cryptography we called it as ciphertext). Encryption process requires a key for this conversion. The process of converting the ciphertext into plaintext is called *decryption*. Decryption is the reverse process of encryption. Decryption process also uses a key for conversion. There are a number of algorithms available for encryption. Depending upon the number of key/keys used encryption is divided into two types:

1. Symmetric encryption
2. Asymmetric encryption

We will discuss these methods in detail in the next section. A model used for encryption and decryption process is called a *cryptosystem*. The area of study in which one can study various techniques of encryption is known as *cryptography*. There are various techniques available to derive the plaintext or decrypt the ciphertext without much knowledge about the key and plaintext. This process is called *cryptanalysis* or *breaking the code*. The areas of cryptography and cryptanalysis together are called *cryptology*. Figure 2.1 explains encryption and decryption process.

```
Sender  --Plaintext-->  Encryption  --Ciphertext-->  Decryption  --Original plaintext-->  Recipient
```

Figure 2.1 Encryption and decryption.

2.2 ENCRYPTION METHODS

The encryption algorithms are comparatively simple. The same encryption algorithm can be used for decryption but the subkeys should be used in reverse order. Encryption algorithms are classified into two types:

1. Symmetric encryption
2. Asymmetric encryption also called public key cryptography

2.2.1 Symmetric Encryption

An encryption technique in which only one key is required for encryption as well as decryption is called *symmetric encryption*. It is also called conventional encryption technique. As the name indicates, symmetric encryption algorithms use same key for encryption as well as for decryption.

For example, two friends A and B want to communicate with each other. They agreed on a symmetric encryption algorithm and a secret key. Friend A first encrypt the message by using the encryption algorithm and a secret key. Then he sends this encrypted message to B. The recipient B uses the same key and algorithm to decrypt the message. The detail graphical representation of this procedure is shown in Figure 2.2.

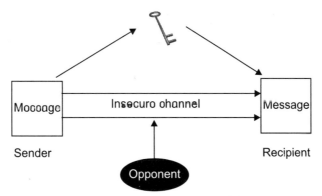

Figure 2.2 Symmetric encryption and decryption.

Most of the people use locks to keep the home secure. Similarly, symmetric encryption technique is used to provide the security to our message. To provide the security to our home we use a lock of some company to close the door. The same key is required to open and lock the door. If we use another key of the same company to open or close the door, it cannot work for that lock. Similarly, in symmetric key encryption, the same key is required for encryption as well as decryption of the message. A few well-examined encryption algorithms that everyone could use just like the model of the lock may be the same, but the keys are different. The security of the home depends upon the quality of the lock, in the same way the security of our encryption algorithm depends upon the key.

Symmetric encryption and decryption techniques have various components as shown in Figure 2.3. The components of symmetric encryptions are:

1. **Plaintext:** The original message written or created by the sender is called plaintext. It is used as input for the encryption algorithm.
2. **Encryption algorithm:** There are various algorithms available for encryption. Using one of the algorithms we can encrypt the message, i.e., convert the plaintext to ciphertext.

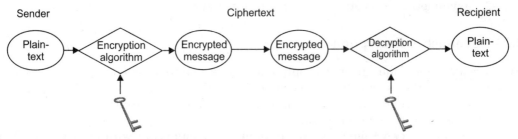

Figure 2.3 Components of symmetric encryption and decryption.

3. **Key:** Key is nothing but the pattern of alphabets/numbers used to convert the plaintext into ciphertext. In symmetric encryption, the same key is used for encryption and decryption. The security of any encryption algorithm depends upon the key. To provide more security, use new key for every new message.
4. **Ciphertext:** The encryption algorithm converts the plaintext into unreadable form using the key. This output is called *ciphertext*. The same key always produces the same cipher for the same plaintext. Whereas different keys will produce different ciphertexts for the same plaintext.
5. **Decryption algorithm:** The algorithm used to convert the ciphertext into plaintext is called the *decryption algorithm*. It uses the same key for symmetric encryption. Same encryption algorithm can be used for decryption but in reverse order.

2.2.2 Asymmetric Encryption

In asymmetric encryption, two different keys are used, one key for encryption and other key for decryption. These keys are mathematically related to each other. Sometime in asymmetric encryption, each user uses two keys called public key and private key. Public key is publically available so that not only sender and recipient but any body may know the key. Another key is private key which is a secrete key and known to the originator (owner) of the key. Asymmetric cryptography is also known as public key cryptography. Asymmetric encryption algorithms cannot be decrypy easily. For asymmetric encryption algorithms key distribution is not required as each user have their own keys. Therefore, public key cryptography provides more security as compared to symmetric encryption. We will see more detail about this in section 7.2.

2.3 CRYPTOGRAPHY

Cryptography is the practise of mathematical scrambling of word. Different encryption techniques are used for this purpose.

Parameters used by cryptographic systems are:

- *Operations used:* Encryption algorithms use various operations to convert plaintext into ciphertext. These include substitution, transpositions, etc. In substitution operation, one element in the plaintext is replaced by another element. In transposition operation, the order of rearrangement of the element is done. Most of the encryption algorithms use substitutions and transpositions.
- *Key:* Symmetric encryption technique use only one (same key) key for encryption and decryption. Whereas asymmetric encryption, two keys are required. Asymmetric encryption is also called *public key encryption*.
- *Types of processing:* Encryption techniques are classified into two types, stream cipher and block cipher, depending on processing. In *block cipher* the input plaintext is divided into a number of blocks. Each block having fixed number of elements. Then at a time one block is processed and the ciphertext is generated as a block having the same number of elements. In *stream cipher*, plaintext is processed one bit at a time. One bit of plaintext is converted into one bit of ciphertext at a time.

2.4 SUBSTITUTION CIPHERS

Classical encryption techniques are divided into two basic types: substitution ciphers and transposition ciphers.

In the substitution ciphers, one element of plaintext is substituted by other element. These ciphers are also called *monoalphabetic ciphers*. Example of this cipher is Caesar cipher. In some ciphers, the group of bits are replaced by another group of bits. These ciphers are also called *polygraphic substitution ciphers*. Examples of this cipher are Hill cipher and Playfair cipher.

In the following section, we discuss different monoalphabetic and polygraphic substitution ciphers.

2.4.1 The Caesar Cipher

The Caesar cipher is the oldest and the simplest substitution cipher. In this cipher, the ciphertext is generated by shifting each letter from the plaintext by same distance. It was first proposed by Julius Caesar so known as *Caesar cipher*. He used this cipher for his private communication. He used to replace each element in the plaintext by a shift of 3, so the plaintext letter PT_i is enciphered as ciphertext letter CT_i such as:

$$CT_i = E(PT_i) = (PT_i + 3) \bmod 26$$

In this cipher, each alphabet is numbered such as a = 0; b = 1 ----------z = 25. As there are total 26 letters mod 28 is used to convert the last three letters such as x, y and z into a, b and c respectively.

The conversion of each element of plaintext into ciphertext using Caesar cipher is given below.

Plaintext	a	b	c	d	e	f	g	h	i	j	k	l	m
Ciphertext	D	E	F	G	H	I	J	K	L	M	N	O	P
Plaintext	n	o	p	q	r	s	t	u	v	w	x	y	z
Ciphertext	Q	R	S	T	U	V	W	X	Y	Z	A	B	C

Using this encryption, the message **work patiently** would be encoded as:

Plaintext	w	o	r	k	p	a	t	i	e	n	t	l	y
Ciphertext	Z	R	U	N	S	D	W	L	H	Q	W	O	B

Advantages

- This cipher (encryption algorithm) is easy to implement.
- This cipher is very simple.

Disadvantages

- Brute force attack is easily possible.
- Its observable pattern helps the attacker to find out plaintext easily.
- Maximum number of keyspace (total number of keys) are 25 which can easily find out.

2.4.2 Monoalphabetic Ciphers

The monoalphabetic cipher is also known as a *cryptogram*. The KEY for this cipher is generated by doing the rearrangement of the alphabets. These different alphabets are then substituted for the alphabets in the plaintext. The result is a ciphertext. The same KEY is used to generate the plaintext from the ciphertext. The monoalphabetic cipher can be a permutation of the 26 alphabetic characters. So there are only 26! or greater than 4×10^{26} possible keys. This large number of keys help to eliminate the brute force attack. Suppose for each alphabet we assign the key as shown below:

Plaintext	a	b	c	d	e	f	g	h	i	j	k	l	m
Key	P	H	V	E	S	J	B	Y	O	T	G	N	X
Plaintext	n	o	p	q	r	s	t	u	v	w	x	y	z
Key	C	R	I	Z	L	W	M	A	F	K	Q	D	U

Now, suppose the plaintext is "we are the best" then, the ciphertext is as below:

Plaintext	w	e	a	r	e	t	h	e	b	e	s	t
Ciphertext	K	S	P	L	S	M	Y	S	H	S	W	M

Here the ciphertext is "KSPLSMYSHSWM". It is meaningless and also very difficult to the attacker to break as compared to Caesar cipher.

Cryptanalysis of Monoalphabetic Ciphers

The cryptanalysis of the monoalphabetic ciphers is easy as the ciphertext reflects the frequency count of the original message. In the above example, letter "S" is occurring 4 times as compared to other letters. If we study the frequency analysis of the English letters we observe that some letters such as "e, a, I" occurs more than letters like "j, z, x". This frequency analysis of the English language is used to perform the cryptanalysis. So monoalphabetic cipher is not more secure.

2.4.3 Playfair Cipher

Playfair cipher is the well-known encryption algorithm. It divided the plaintext into a group of two letters each. Each group is treated as a single unit. Using the key, groups of plaintext corresponding ciphertext groups are generated. The key generation procedure is discussed below. As the Playfair cipher uses groups of two letters to generate the ciphertext, it is a block cipher of block size two. The total encryption process is divided into three parts:

1. Preparing the Plaintext
2. Preparing the Key
3. Encryption

Preparing the Plaintext

The message is first converted into lower case, remove the punctuations and then split it into a group of two letters each. If any group has the same letters, then split that group by adding extra letters like x between these two letters. For example, if some group having the letters ll, then we can split it like lx and second letter l is paired with the first letter of the next pair and then all the letters are shifted by one position to the right. If j is present all **j**'s are replaced with **i**'s. This particular example contains no **j**'s. We will illustrate this in more detail from the following example.

Message: We live in a world full of beauty.

Step 1 Convert this message into lowercase letters and remove punctuations.

   weliveinaworldfullofbeauty

Step 2 Split the text into a pair of two.

   we li ve in aw or ld fu **ll** of be au ty

If the last group is having only one letter, then append any one letter in that group to make a pair. If both the letters in a pair are same, then split this pair by adding any letter in between the letters and rearrange the groups. In this example, one of the pairs having same letters "ll" (shown in bold). Add letter "x" in between the letters, so the group is "lxl". But the group should be of two letters, so shift the last letters of this group to the right by one position and rewrite the groups again.

   we li ve in aw or ld fu lx lo fb ea ut y

Here the last group is having only one letter, so append one more letter to complete the pair. Here we append "z" with the last letter "y" as shown below:

   we li ve in aw or ld fu lx lo fb ea ut yz

Step 3 Now, write the groups such that in one row 5 pairs are there as shown below:

we	li	ve	in	aw
or	ld	fu	lx	lo
fb	ea	ut	yz	

Now, the plaintext is ready to encrypt.

Preparing the Key

Read the key having any number of letters. Remove the duplicate letters from the key if any. Convert all the letters of the key into uppercase letters. To prepare the key, 5 × 5 matrix is constructed. We illustrate the key preparing procedure as shown below:
Suppose the key is "another"

Step 1 Convert the key into uppercase letters, the key becomes

ANOTHER

Step 2 Write the letters in the 5 × 5 matrix form, i.e., 5 letters in one row as shown below:

| A | N | O | T | H |
| E | R | R | | |

Step 3 The remaining letters of the alphabet which are not present in the key are filled in the alphabetical order as shown below:

A	N	O	T	H
E	R	B	C	D
F	G	I/J	K	L
M	P	Q	S	U
V	W	X	Y	Z

As we have to form 5 × 5 matrix and there are total 26 alphabets, we have to omit one alphabet. Generally we select such alphabet which occur less in the language, i.e., the frequency of that letter is less. Here we omit j. Still if j occurs in the plaintext, i is the replacement for j in this particular example. If the key length is long, the message is more secure. But cryptanalysis of the Playfair is easy as compared to modern ciphers.

Encryption

The next step is encryption where the two letters (a pair) of the plaintext is encrypted at a time. Take any pair of letters from the plaintext. The letters in the pair compare with the 5 × 5 key matrix. The letters in a pair may be in the same row, in the same column, or in different rows and columns of the key matrix. The encryption procedure is illustrated using the following steps:

Step 1 Read a pair of letters from the prepared plaintext. If both the letters of pair are on the same row, then each letter of a pair is replaced by the letter to the right of that letter. If the letter in a pair is the last letter (rightmost) on the row, then replace it with the first letter of the same row.

Suppose the plaintext pair is "nt", then corresponding ciphertext is "OH". Here n and t are on the same row, so we select the right side letters from the key matrix. The right side letter of n is O and the t is H. Therefore "OH" is the ciphertext for "nt". Similarly if the plaintext is "yw", then y becomes Z and w becomes X, so "ZX" is the ciphertext for "yw". If the plaintext pair is "rd", then r is replaced by B and d is replaced by E (as there is no letter to the right of d, the first letter from the same row, i.e., E, is selected. The ciphertext for "rd" is "BE".

Step 2 If both the letters of pair are in the same column, then each letter is replaced by the next letter (i.e., letter below the plaintext letter) in the same column. If the letter in a pair is the last letter in the column, then replace it with the first letter of the same column.

Suppose the plaintext pair is "em", then corresponding ciphertext is "FV". Here e and m are in the same column, so we select the next letter in the same column from the key matrix. The next letter of e is F and the m is V. Therefore "FV" is the ciphertext for "em". If the plaintext pair is "cy", then c is replaced by K and y is replaced by T (as there is no letter below y in the same column, the first letter from the same row, i.e., T, is selected. The ciphertext for "cy" is "KT".

Step 3 If both the letters of pair are neither in the same row nor in the same column, then the substitution for plaintext pair is based upon their intersection in the key matrix. Take the first letter from the plaintext pair. Locate its position in the key matrix. Then move across the row, i.e., left or right until it is lined up with the second letter in a pair. Then start with the second letter and move up and down the column until it is lined up with the first letter. The letters at the intersections are the ciphertext for the said pair.

Suppose the plaintext pair is "gs", then corresponding ciphertext is "KP". We have to apply above steps on all the pairs of the plaintext. The ciphertext for the above plaintext is:

VRFKAFGONVNBULLMIZIHIEFESHZY

In this cipher, there are $26 \times 26 = 676$ diagrams. The identification of individual diagrams is more difficult, and also the frequencies of individual letters have greater ranges which provide more security to this cipher.

Decryption

For decryption, the reverse process we have to follow.

Step 1 Break the ciphertext into pairs of letters:

VR	FK	AF	GO	NV
NB	UL	LM	IZ	IH
IE	FE	SH	ZY	

Step 2 Same as encryption, write down the alphabet square with the key "ANOTHER":

A	N	O	T	H
E	R	B	C	D
F	G	I/J	K	L
M	P	Q	S	U
V	W	X	Y	Z

Step 3 Read a pair of letters from the prepared ciphertext. If both the letters of pair are on the same row, then each letter of a pair is replaced by the letter to the left of that letter. If the letter in a pair is the first letter (leftmost) on the row, then replace it with the last letter of the same row.

Step 4 If both the letters of pair are in the same column, then each letter is replaced by the previous letter (i.e., letter above the plaintext letter) in the same column. If the letter in a pair is the first letter in the column, then replace it with the last letter of the same column.

Step 5 If both the letters of pair are neither in the same row nor in the same column, then the substitution for plaintext pair is based upon their intersection in the key matrix. Take the first letter from the plaintext pair. Locate its position in the key matrix. Then move across the row, i.e., right or left until it is lined up with the second letter in a pair. Then start with the second letter and move down and up the column until it is lined up with the first letter. The letters at the intersections are the ciphertext for the said pair.

Transform the pairs of letters in the opposite direction from that used for encryption:

WE	LI	VE	IN	AW
OR	LD	FU	LX	LO
FB	EA	UT	YZ	

This message is now readable, although removing the extra spaces and substitutions for double letters makes it more readable:

We live in a world full of beauty.

Cryptanalysis of the Playfair cipher is easy, as for the same pair of letters always converted into a same pair of ciphertext.

2.4.4 The Hill Cipher

The next classical cipher for encryption is the Hill cipher. It is a polygraphic substitution cipher. The Hill cipher is based on linear algebra. Lester S. Hill was invented this cipher in 1929. It was the first cipher in which more than three symbols operate at a time.

Working

The Hill cipher uses the basic matrix multiplication. So, the alphabets are converted into numbers. Each letter from A to Z is assigned a digit from 0 to 25 such as A = 0, B = 1, C = 2, ------- and Z = 25. As there are total 26 letters, the base is used as 26.

Data Encryption Techniques

The total encryption process is divided into three parts:
1. Preparing the Plaintext
2. Preparing the Key
3. Encryption

Preparing the Plaintext: First each letter in the message is converted into numbers such as a = 0, b = 1 and so on. Then the numbers should be written in columnar form. The number of letters in each column depends on the key matrix size. Suppose the key matrix is 2 × 2, then each column of plaintext having two elements only. For 3 × 3 size, then each column having 3 numbers. If the last column contains less elements then append necessary numbers to complete the last column. For example, for a key size of 3 × 3, the total number of elements in the plaintext should be multiple of 3, otherwise append necessary elements to make it multiple of 3. Suppose there are 19 elements in the plaintext, then in each column there are 3 elements but in the last column there is only one element. So append 2 more elements in the last column.

Consider the message 'COE'. Since 'C' is 2, 'O' is 14 and 'E' is 4, the plaintext is:

$$P = \begin{bmatrix} 2 \\ 14 \\ 4 \end{bmatrix}$$

Preparing the Key: Every letter in the key is also assigning the number like message. Then the numbers should be written in row wise. The number of letters in each row depends on the key matrix size. Suppose, the key matrix is 2 × 2, then each row having two elements only. The key matrix is always square matrix.

Consider the key "ANOTHERBZ": which is converted into numbers as: 0 13 14 19 6 4 17 1 25. Then write these numbers in matrix form as:

$$K = \begin{bmatrix} 0 & 13 & 14 \\ 19 & 6 & 4 \\ 17 & 1 & 25 \end{bmatrix}$$

Encryption: The encryption is the multiplication of key matrix and plaintext matrix. The number used for the letters are base 26. So mod 26 is used to generate the ciphertext.

$$\text{Ciphertext} = \text{Key} \times \text{Plaintext} \bmod 26$$
$$C = KP \bmod 26$$

Thus, the encryption is:

$$C = \begin{bmatrix} 0 & 13 & 14 \\ 19 & 6 & 4 \\ 17 & 1 & 25 \end{bmatrix} \begin{bmatrix} 2 \\ 14 \\ 4 \end{bmatrix} = \begin{bmatrix} 238 \\ 138 \\ 148 \end{bmatrix} \bmod 26$$

$$C = \begin{bmatrix} 4 \\ 8 \\ 18 \end{bmatrix}$$

Here the numbers are reconvert into the letters, so, 4 = E, 8 = I, 18 = S. So the ciphertext is 'EIS'.

Decryption

To convert the ciphertext into plaintext again we have to perform matrix multiplication. The inverse of key matrix is multiplied by the ciphertext matrix to generate the plaintext matrix. To calculate the inverse of the key matrix, we use standard methods with extended Euclidean algorithm. The extended Euclidean will be discussed in Chapter 6. The decryption is shown below:

$$P = K^{-1} \times C \text{ MOD } 26$$

$$K^{-1} = \frac{1}{6453} \begin{bmatrix} -146 & 311 & 32 \\ 407 & 238 & -266 \\ 83 & -211 & 247 \end{bmatrix} \text{mod } 26$$

$$K^{-1} = \frac{1}{6453} \begin{bmatrix} -16 & 25 & 6 \\ 17 & 4 & -6 \\ 5 & -3 & 13 \end{bmatrix} \text{mod } 26$$

Here first compute 6453 mod 26 = 5, then find the multiplicative inverse of 5 such that $5\,d$ mod 26 = 1, where d is the multiplicative inverse of 5.

$$K^{-1} = \frac{1}{5} \begin{bmatrix} -16 & 25 & 6 \\ 17 & 4 & -6 \\ 5 & -3 & 13 \end{bmatrix} \text{mod } 26$$

26 = 5(5) + 1	1 = 26 − 5 × (5) = 26 + (−5)(5)

Therefore, the multiplicative inverse of 5 is −5 or 21.

Now,

$$K^{-1} = 21 \begin{bmatrix} -16 & 25 & 6 \\ 17 & 4 & -6 \\ 5 & -3 & 13 \end{bmatrix} \text{mod } 26$$

$$K^{-1} = \begin{bmatrix} -24 & 5 & 22 \\ 19 & 6 & -22 \\ 1 & -11 & 13 \end{bmatrix} \text{mod } 26$$

$$K^{-1} = \begin{bmatrix} 2 & 5 & 22 \\ 19 & 6 & 4 \\ 1 & 15 & 13 \end{bmatrix} \text{mod } 26$$

Now, our ciphertext "EIS" is multiplied by this new key, we get:

$$P = \begin{bmatrix} 2 & 5 & 22 \\ 19 & 6 & 4 \\ 1 & 15 & 13 \end{bmatrix} \begin{bmatrix} 4 \\ 8 \\ 18 \end{bmatrix} \mod 26 = \begin{bmatrix} 2 \\ 14 \\ 4 \end{bmatrix}$$

The plaintext we get back is 'COE'.

One should take precaution while the selection of the key as every matrix does not have an inverse. We can find out this directly. If the determinant of the matrix is 0 then the inverse of that matrix is not exit. If the matrix has common factors with the modulus then the inverse of that matrix is not exit. Here we use 26 as modulus so the matrix having common factors of 2 and 13 cannot be used. So discard such matrix and select new key.

Security

The Hill cipher use matrix multiplication, therefore the ciphertext letter generated for a letter in plaintext is not dependent upon only a single plaintext letter but it is a combination of many letters. This helps to avoid the letter frequency problem. It is therefore difficult for cryptanalysis and provides more security. But this cipher uses linear algebra, which makes easy for a known plaintext attack.

Cryptanalysis of the Hill Cipher: We know that the Hill cipher is vulnerable to chosen plaintext attack. We will see how the key can be determined by considering Example 2.1.

EXAMPLE 2.1 Suppose the plaintext is P, ciphertext C, therefore $P = C = Z(2/4)$ is given. The plaintext be "ATTACK", and the message is encrypted using a = 0, t = 1, c = 2, and k = 3. The ciphertext is "CATKAC". Determine the key used to encrypt the plaintext "ATTACK".

Solution We know that $P = C = Z_4^2$. It indicates that there are two rows in the matrices and the base is 4. So, the letters in the message are numbered from 0 to 3.

Assume that the key may be $\begin{bmatrix} a & b \\ c & d \end{bmatrix}$ and

the plaintext matrix may be $\begin{bmatrix} 0 & 1 & 2 \\ 1 & 0 & 3 \end{bmatrix}$ and

the ciphertext matrix may be $\begin{bmatrix} 2 & 1 & 0 \\ 0 & 3 & 2 \end{bmatrix}$

For Hill cipher, $C = K \times P \mod (base)$,
Here using the above matrices we get:

$$\begin{bmatrix} 2 & 1 & 0 \\ 0 & 3 & 2 \end{bmatrix} = \begin{bmatrix} a & b \\ c & d \end{bmatrix} \begin{bmatrix} 0 & 1 & 2 \\ 1 & 0 & 3 \end{bmatrix}$$

Let us consider the first two letters of the message, i.e., "AT". The first column of plaintext matrix $\begin{bmatrix} 0 \\ 1 \end{bmatrix}$ represents these two letters. The second pair of letters is

"TA" = $\begin{bmatrix} 1 \\ 0 \end{bmatrix}$ and the third pair is $\begin{bmatrix} 2 \\ 3 \end{bmatrix}$. Thus we try to find out the key by solving for one pair of letters at a time. We solve this for the above data:

$$K \times P = C$$

$$\begin{bmatrix} a & b \\ c & d \end{bmatrix} \begin{bmatrix} 0 \\ 1 \end{bmatrix} = \begin{bmatrix} b \\ d \end{bmatrix} = \begin{bmatrix} 2 \\ 0 \end{bmatrix}$$

Therefore, b = 2 and d = 2

Similarly, $\begin{bmatrix} a & b \\ c & d \end{bmatrix} \begin{bmatrix} 1 \\ 0 \end{bmatrix} = \begin{bmatrix} a \\ c \end{bmatrix} = \begin{bmatrix} 1 \\ 3 \end{bmatrix}$

Therefore, a = 1 and c = 3.

From the above, key matrix is $\begin{bmatrix} a & b \\ c & d \end{bmatrix} = \begin{bmatrix} 1 & 2 \\ 3 & 0 \end{bmatrix}$

2.4.5 Polyalphabetic Ciphers

Above ciphers are simple substitution ciphers. They are not secure as the cryptanalysis of these ciphers are easy due to frequency analysis. If the ciphertext is sufficiently large, cryptanalysis can be made. Given a sufficiently large ciphertext, it can easily be broken. For large ciphertext, it is possible to find out the letter frequencies easily. Therefore, to provide more security and solve the problem of frequency analysis, there is a need to design a new cipher. Polyalphabetic cipher solves this problem. In the polyalphabetic cipher, a single letter of plaintext can be converted to several different letters of the ciphertext instead of just one letter.

The well-known polyalphabetic substitution cipher is Vigenere cipher. In this cipher, a set of related monoalphabetic substitution rules consists of the 26 Caesar ciphers. The Caesar cipher uses the shift of 3 places whereas Vigenere cipher uses shifts of 0 to 25. The key is the permutations of the alphabet called a Vigenere square. In this cipher, there are 25 rows and 25 columns. 25 rows of this square can be used as keys, where the row number gives the amount it is shifted.

There are two different methods to form a polyalphabetic cipher from Vigenere ciphers. In the first method during encryption, select all the 25 rows of the Vigenere square one by one. Therefore, every 25th letter is encrypted with the same key. In the second method, a key is created which gives the order of the rows is to be selected. This means only selected rows are used instead of all 25 rows of the Vigenere square. For example, the key is created could be $K = (5, 2, 16)$ and then repetition of these three rows is done. It means every third letter is encrypted with the same key. In this cipher each single letter of plaintext is encrypted using only one key. Therefore, it works like monoalphabetic ciphers.

The Vigenere cipher, proposed by Blaise de Vigenere in the 16th century, is a polyalphabetic substitution cipher based on Table 2.1.

Data Encryption Techniques

Table 2.1 The Vigenere table

	a	b	c	d	e	f	g	h	i	j	k	l	m	n	o	p	q	r	s	t	u	v	w	x	y	z
a	A	B	C	D	E	F	G	H	I	J	K	L	M	N	O	P	Q	R	S	T	U	V	W	X	Y	Z
b	B	C	D	E	F	G	H	I	J	K	L	M	N	O	P	Q	R	S	T	U	V	W	X	Y	Z	A
c	C	D	E	F	G	H	I	J	K	L	M	N	O	P	Q	R	S	T	U	V	W	X	Y	Z	A	B
d	D	E	F	G	H	I	J	K	L	M	N	O	P	Q	R	S	T	U	V	W	X	Y	Z	A	B	C
e	E	F	G	H	I	J	K	L	M	N	O	P	Q	R	S	T	U	V	W	X	Y	Z	A	B	C	D
f	F	G	H	I	J	K	L	M	N	O	P	Q	R	S	T	U	V	W	X	Y	Z	A	B	C	D	E
g	G	H	I	J	K	L	M	N	O	P	Q	R	S	T	U	V	W	X	Y	Z	A	B	C	D	E	F
h	H	I	J	K	L	M	N	O	P	Q	R	S	T	U	V	W	X	Y	Z	A	B	C	D	E	F	G
i	I	J	K	L	M	N	O	P	Q	R	S	T	U	V	W	X	Y	Z	A	B	C	D	E	F	G	H
j	J	K	L	M	N	O	P	Q	R	S	T	U	V	W	X	Y	Z	A	B	C	D	E	F	G	H	I
k	K	L	M	N	O	P	Q	R	S	T	U	V	W	X	Y	Z	A	B	C	D	E	F	G	H	I	J
l	L	M	N	O	P	Q	R	S	T	U	V	W	X	Y	Z	A	B	C	D	E	F	G	H	I	J	K
m	M	N	O	P	Q	R	S	T	U	V	W	X	Y	Z	A	B	C	D	E	F	G	H	I	J	K	L
n	N	O	P	Q	R	S	T	U	V	W	X	Y	Z	A	B	C	D	E	F	G	H	I	J	K	L	M
o	O	P	Q	R	S	T	U	V	W	X	Y	Z	A	B	C	D	E	F	G	H	I	J	K	L	M	N
p	P	Q	R	S	T	U	V	W	X	Y	Z	A	B	C	D	E	F	G	H	I	J	K	L	M	N	O
q	Q	R	S	T	U	V	W	X	Y	Z	A	B	C	D	E	F	G	H	I	J	K	L	M	N	O	P
r	R	S	T	U	V	W	X	Y	Z	A	B	C	D	E	F	G	H	I	J	K	L	M	N	O	P	Q
s	S	T	U	V	W	X	Y	Z	A	B	C	D	E	F	G	H	I	J	K	L	M	N	O	P	Q	R
t	T	U	V	W	X	Y	Z	A	B	C	D	E	F	G	H	I	J	K	L	M	N	O	P	Q	R	S
u	U	V	W	X	Y	Z	A	B	C	D	E	F	G	H	I	J	K	L	M	N	O	P	Q	R	S	T
v	V	W	X	Y	Z	A	B	C	D	E	F	G	H	I	J	K	L	M	N	O	P	Q	R	S	T	U
w	W	X	Y	Z	A	B	C	D	E	F	G	H	I	J	K	L	M	N	O	P	Q	R	S	T	U	V
x	X	Y	Z	A	B	C	D	E	F	G	H	I	J	K	L	M	N	O	P	Q	R	S	T	U	V	W
y	Y	Z	A	B	C	D	E	F	G	H	I	J	K	L	M	N	O	P	Q	R	S	T	U	V	W	X
z	Z	A	B	C	D	E	F	G	H	I	J	K	L	M	N	O	P	Q	R	S	T	U	V	W	X	Y

There are 25 rows and 25 columns in the Vigenere square. Each row of the table corresponds to a Caesar cipher. There is a shift of 0 positions in the first row, a shift of 1 position in the second row, a shift of n^{-1} position in the nth row.
For example, the message is:

She is very happy and beautiful girl.

And the key is 'another'.
To encrypt this message, first write the key. The letters of the key is repeated as many times as the length of the plaintext. Write the plaintext below the key so that one letter of the plaintext is below the one letter of the plaintext.

Keyword: anoth   erano   thera   nothe   ranot   heran
Plaintext: sheis   veryh   appya   ndbea   utifu   lgirl

The ciphertext is generated using the Vigenere square. Key letters indicate the row and plaintext letters indicate the column. First find the intersection of the row and column using each letter of the key with corresponding letter in the plaintext. Note down all the intersections. This gives you the ciphertext.

The ciphertext generated using Vigenere cipher is shown below:

Keyword:	anoth	erano	thera	nothe	ranot	heran
Plaintext:	sheis	veryh	appya	ndbea	utifu	lgirl
Ciphertext:	SUSBZ	ZVRLV	TWTPA	ARULE	LTVTN	SKZRY

The decryption also followed the same procedure. First write the letters of the key in the same way as we write for encryption. Then write the ciphertext below the letters of key as shown below:

Keyword:	anoth	erano	thera	nothe	ranot	heran
Ciphertext:	SUSBZ	ZVRLV	TWTPA	ARULE	LTVTN	SKZRY

For decryption, the key letters indicate the column and ciphertext letter indicate row. Select the column for a key letter and then select the row correspond to the plaintext letter. The intersection is the plaintext for the corresponding ciphertext letter. The plaintext generated is shown below:

Keyword:	anoth	erano	thera	nothe	ranot	heran
Ciphertext:	SUSBZ	ZVRLV	TWTPA	ARULE	LTVTN	SKZRY
Plaintext:	SHEIS	VERYH	APPYA	NDBEA	UTIFU	LGIRL

In Vigenere cipher, for the same plaintext there are multiple ciphertext. This helps to avoid the frequency analysis of the cipher and makes the cipher secure. For example, in the above plaintext there are 3 e's that they have been encrypted by 'S,' 'V,' 'L', respectively. This helps to hide the count of occurrence of e in the plaintext. So, it makes frequency analysis of the letters in the plaintext difficult. The implementation of this cipher is easy.

Cryptanalysis of the Vigenere Cipher

The Vigenere cipher is secure from the attack using frequency analysis. But it is not completely secure cipher. If the attacker is able to find out the length of the key, then frequency analysis is possible. The chosen-plaintext attack is possible against this cipher.

2.4.6 One-time Pad or Vernam Cipher

In 1918, Gilbert Verman developed a cipher called as *one-time pad*. It is the most secure cryptographic algorithm. In this cipher, the key is a set of random numbers generated by pseudo-random number generator. This generator is used only once to encrypt a message. One-time pad and key is used for decryption. Mauborgne developed a method of one-time pad. A one-time pad is a very simple *symmetric* cipher. The key is selected randomly so that every time new key is used for encryption. Therefore, for the same message next time different ciphertext is generated. So, it is difficult to break this cipher. For decryption, same key is used, so secure key transmission is the problem.

Properties of One-time Pad

1. The number of possible keys is equal to the number of possible plaintexts.
2. The key is selected at random.
3. Key should be used only once.

Working of the Cipher

The key or one-time pad is a string of characters or numbers. User should note that no part of the key be reused again. Length of the one-time pad is equal to the length of the message. Then perform XOR operation between the plaintext (message) and one-time pad (key). The result is ciphertext.

Encryption: $C_i = P_i \oplus K_i \quad i = 1,2,3,...$
Decryption: $P_i = C_i \oplus K_i \quad i = 1,2,3,...$

where

P_i: plaintext bits
K_i: key (key-stream) bits
C_i: ciphertext bits

EXAMPLE 2.2 Encrypt the following message using one-time pad and then decrypt the encrypted massage.

Message: WE LIVE IN A WORLD FULL OF BEAUTY

The key is given as:

Key: ABCDEFGHIJKLMNOPQRSTUVWXYZ

Solution:

PLAINTEXT	W	E	L	I	V	E	I	N	A	W	O	R	L	D	F	U	L	L	O	F	B	E	A	U	T	Y
	22	04	11	8	21	4	8	13	0	22	14	17	11	3	5	20	11	11	14	5	1	4	0	20	19	24
OTP KEY	A	B	C	D	E	F	G	H	I	J	K	L	M	N	O	P	Q	R	S	T	U	V	W	X	Y	Z
	0	1	2	3	4	5	6	7	8	9	10	11	12	13	14	15	16	17	18	19	20	21	22	23	24	25
RESULT	22	5	13	11	25	9	14	20	8	31	24	28	23	16	19	35	27	28	32	24	21	25	22	43	43	49
MOD 26	22	5	13	11	25	9	14	20	8	5	24	2	23	16	19	9	1	2	6	24	21	25	22	17	17	23
CIPHERTEXT	W	F	N	L	Z	J	O	U	I	F	Y	C	X	Q	T	J	B	C	G	Y	V	Z	W	R	R	X

The ciphertext is "WFNLZJOUIFYCXQTJBCGYVZWRRX"

Decryption of the above is derived as shown below:

CIPHERTEXT	W	F	N	L	Z	J	O	U	I	F	Y	C	X	Q	T	J	B	C	G	Y	V	Z	W	R	R	X
	22	5	13	11	25	9	14	20	8	5	24	2	23	16	19	9	1	2	6	24	21	25	22	17	17	23
OTP KEY	A	B	C	D	E	F	G	H	I	J	K	L	M	N	O	P	Q	R	S	T	U	V	W	X	Y	Z
	0	1	2	3	4	5	6	7	8	9	10	11	12	13	14	15	16	17	18	19	20	21	22	23	24	25
RESULT	22	4	11	8	21	4	8	13	0	−4	14	−9	11	3	5	−6	−15	−15	−12	5	1	4	0	−6	−6	−2
MOD 26	22	4	11	8	21	4	8	13	0	22	14	17	11	3	5	20	11	11	14	5	1	4	0	20	20	24
PLAINTEXT	W	E	L	I	V	E	I	N	A	W	O	R	L	D	F	U	L	L	O	F	B	E	A	U	T	Y

Number of bits in the one-time pad and the plaintext are same. Therefore, the length of the key is large. This is the drawback of this cipher because it is difficult to remember or make the transmission of key securely. But it also makes this cipher more secure.

2.5 TRANSPOSITION CIPHERS

One more classical encryption cipher is transposition ciphers. In transposition cipher, the letters are written in a row under the key and then arrange the column as per alphabetical order. There are two types of transposition ciphers: single columnar and double columnar transposition ciphers.

2.5.1 Single Columnar Transposition

Single columnar transposition cipher is the simple cipher. Read the key, and numbered each letter of the key as per their appearance in the alphabet. The total encryption process is divided into three parts:
1. Preparing the Key
2. Preparing the Plaintext
3. Encryption

Preparing the Key: Suppose the key is 'another'. We can assign the number to each letter in this key as shown below:

a	n	o	t	h	e	r
1	4	5	7	3	2	6

That is, the first letter 'a' is numbered 1. There are no B's or C's, so the next letter to be numbered is the 'e'. So e is numbered 2, followed by h, and so on. In the key if the same letter has occurred more than one time, it should be numbered 1, 2, 3, etc. from left to write. For example, the key is "heaven". Here 'e' is occurred two times. So first 'e' from left hand side is numbered as 2, whereas second 'e' is numbered as 3.

h	e	a	v	e	n
4	2	1	6	3	5

Preparing the Plaintext: The letters from the message is written in rows under the numbered letters of the key. One letter from message is to be written under each letter of the key. Let us say that the message is "we are the best". We can write it as shown below:

h	e	a	v	e	n
4	2	1	6	3	5
W	E	A	R	E	T
H	E	B	E	S	T

Encryption: Now, arrange the above message written in rows under the numbered letters of the key as per ascending order of the numbers at the top of the plaintext letters.

a	e	e	h	n	v
1	2	3	4	5	6
A	E	E	W	T	R
B	E	S	H	T	E

Then the letters are copied down column wise from top to bottom. The result is ciphertext, i.e.,

ABEEESWHTTRE

For decryption, first calculate the number of letters present in the ciphertext. Using the number of letters in the key, we can calculate the number of letters present in the last row. As it can be seen above, all the columns contain only two letters and this is important. In the above example, there are 12 letters and the key having 6 letters, so there are two rows and the last row have 6 letters. This gives us the idea about number of rows and number of letters in each column. Here there are two rows and each row having two ciphertext letters. For decryption, the key is prepared as for encryption. Then write the first two letters below the column number '1'.

```
h   e   a   v   e   n
4   2   1   6   3   5
        A
        B
```

Next two letters below column number two.

```
h   e   a   v   e   n
4   2   1   6   3   5
    E   A
    E   B
```

Next two letters below column number 3 and so on. In this way write all the letters from ciphertext. It will look like this:

```
h   e   a   v   e   n
4   2   1   6   3   5
W   E   A   R   E   T
H   E   B   E   S   T
```

Now, write down the letters in row wise, the result is the plaintext as below:

WEARETHEBEST

Separate the words by spaces, we will get the message, i.e.,

WE ARE THE BEST

2.5.2 Double Columnar Transposition

The single columnar transposition cipher is not much secure. To provide stronger transposition cipher, double columnar transposition is used. The working of double columnar cipher is similar to the single columnar transposition, but the process is repeated twice. Here we can use either the same key both times or two different keys. Suppose the plaintext is "we are the best", and the keys are "heaven" and "another".

```
h   e   a   v   e   n
4   2   1   6   3   5
W   E   A   R   E   T
H   E   B   E   S   T
```

This first encryption gives: ABEEESWHTTRE. These letters are written under the second key, thus we get:

a	n	o	t	h	e	r
1	4	5	7	3	2	6
A	B	E	E	E	S	W
H	T	T		R		E

If the last row like the above example, having less letters than the first row, then we can add some more letters to complete the row. But this reduces the security of the cipher. So, one can encrypt the plaintext by not adding any dummy letters in the last row. The ciphertext is as below:

AHSEEBTETWER

The double columnar transposition cipher uses two keys so it is stronger than the single columnar transposition. The cryptanalysis of double columnar is difficult as compared to that of single columnar cipher.

2.6 CRYPTANALYSIS

The study of methods of breaking the ciphers is called *cryptanalysis*. In cryptanalysis, the cryptanalyst tries to search for flaws or loopholes in the design of the ciphers. The cryptanalyst guesses the key and a very large number of guesses for the key were incorrect, we can ensure that the cipher is stronger and not easily breakable. If the message length is long and the key size is small, cryptanalysis is easy.

In the transposition cipher, the order of letters in the plaintext is shuffled around. However, if the key length is short, then it is possible to break the ciphers. In a columnar transposition cipher, the message is written row wise. The number of letters in a row is fixed and equal to the length of a key. The ciphertext is generated by noting down the letters column wise form a block of letters in each column. Then permutation is performed on the letters in each block. This gives the key and helps to break the cipher.

2.6.1 Enumerate All Short Keywords

The cryptanalysis is started by trying all possible short keys. For a key of length up to 9 characters/letters we can do this very fast. For permutation of every key we find out same text. Select the most meaningful text as our plaintext. The possible number of rearrangements for a key of length N is $N!$ (N factorial). If the key length increases then the number of rearrangements increases very fast. For various key lengths the possible keys and its numbers are shown in Table 2.2.

Up to key length 6, it is easy to test all possible combinations of the keys. If the key having length more than 6 letters, it is difficult to try all possible combinations to find out the key. So for better security, the key length should be large enough.

Table 2.2 Number of possible keys for various length keywords

Key length	Possible keys	No. of permutations
2	AB, BA	2
3	ABC, BAC, CBA, ...	6
4	ABCD, ABDC, ACBD, ...	24
5	ABCDE, ABCED, ...	120
6	ABCDEF, ABDCFE, ...	720
7	ABCDEFG, ABDCGEF, ...	5,040
8	ABCDEFGH, ...	40,320
9	ABCDEFGHI, ...	362,880
10	ABCDEFGHIJ, ...	3,628,800
11	ABCDEFGHIJK, ...	39,916,800
12	ABCDEFGHIJKL, ...	479,001,600

2.6.2 Dictionary Attacks

If the above cryptanalysis method failed, we now try for another method. Generally the columnar transposition cipher uses a key with a word or a phrase. So instead of checking all possible keys, we may only go to check only common words. For this a dictionary should be prepared. It must consist of a large list of words such as place names, famous people names, mythological names, historical names, etc. From this dictionary we generate a text file of possible keys. Select the words having length greater than 6 letters as a key, as the keys having length up to 6 is checked by above method. Now use these words to decrypt the ciphertext. Note down the key with meaningful plaintext. This method can work if the key was one of the words that are present in the dictionary, but it fails to work if the key is something like 'THECOLDINOCTOMBER'. It is not possible to include all the places or phrases in the dictionary.

Ciphertext attack is not that simple for transposition cipher. Suppose we obtain the ciphertext as:

Ciphertext: GSMOEVMTEFMTPYPEIRSPIOEVIEEOMP

We assume that this is encrypted by columnar transposition using a key. Cryptanalyst tries to find out the key and the plaintext by following the steps given below:

Step 1 Count the number of letters in the ciphertext. There are 30 letters in the ciphertext.

Step 2 Assuming the possible dimension of an array. The array could have any of the following dimensions: 6 × 5 or 5 × 6 or 10 × **3** or **3** × 10. Suppose that we first try a 6 × 5 array. This helps us to guess the key length. For this array, the key length is 6. Then the ciphertext array is as shown in Table 2.3.

Step 3 Now, observe the top row of the array in Table 2.3 and try to find the meaningful word. As per this word, identify the columns and permute these columns as shown in Table 2.4. After permutation, we observe the word

GIVE in the first row of Table 2.4. Also there are words or partial words in the other rows of Table 2.4. If this gives meaning statement then the key is almost recovered.

In this example, the encryption key is 152634 and the plaintext is **GIVE ME SOME TIME TO PROVE MYSELF.**

Table 2.3 Ciphertext array

1	2	3	4	5	6
G	V	M	E	I	E
S	M	T	I	O	E
M	T	P	R	E	O
O	E	Y	S	V	M
E	F	P	P	I	P

Table 2.4 Permutated ciphertext array

1	5	2	6	3	4
G	I	V	E	M	E
S	O	M	E	T	I
M	E	T	O	P	R
O	V	E	M	Y	S
E	L	F	P	P	P

Therefore, the plaintext is "GIVEMESOMETIMETOPROVEMYSELFPPP". Here last three characters are "PPP" with no meaning. So we remove "PPP" and the plaintext is "**GIVE ME SOME TIME TO PROVE MYSELF**".

2.7 STEGANOGRAPHY

The art and science of hiding information by embedding message within another message is called *steganography*. Steganography helps to keep the message secret. In this technique, the useless or unused bits are replaced with bits of the information which we want to hide. This can be done on the text/graphics files, encrypted messages or images. Steganography can be used to hide text or images. It is used to support the encryption.

2.7.1 Applications

Steganography can be used for legitimate as well as illegitimate purposes.

Legitimate Purposes

1. For copyright protection, one can insert watermark into the original image.
2. To tag notes to online images.
3. To maintain the confidentiality of valuable information.
4. To protect the data from unauthorised access.

Data Encryption Techniques

Illegitimate purposes
1. For stealing the data.
2. Militants use this technique to send their message.

2.7.2 Limitations

Steganography also have certain drawbacks:
1. A lot of overhead is required to hide a relatively few bits of information.
2. Once the attacker knows the system, it becomes virtually worthless.

SOLVED PROBLEMS

2.1 Find the key for decryption using Hill cipher if the key for encryption is "DIMENSION".
Solution:
Step 1 First convert the letters in the key in number form such as a = 0, b = 1, and so on.

Write the key in 3 × 3 matrix form in row wise.

$$K = \begin{bmatrix} d & i & m \\ e & n & s \\ i & o & n \end{bmatrix} = \begin{bmatrix} 3 & 8 & 12 \\ 4 & 13 & 18 \\ 8 & 14 & 13 \end{bmatrix}$$

Step 2 Calculate the determinant of K.

Det (K) = 3(13 × 13 − 14 × 18) − 8(4 × 13 − 8 × 18) + 12(4 × 14 − 8 × 13)
= 3(169 − 252) − 8(52 − 144) + 12(56 − 104)
= 3(−83) + 8(92) + 12(−48)
= −249 + 736 − 576
= −89

Step 3 Calculate the adjoint of K.

$$\text{Adj }(K) = \begin{bmatrix} -83 & 64 & -12 \\ 92 & -57 & -6 \\ -48 & 22 & 7 \end{bmatrix}$$

Step 4 Find out the multiplicative inverse of 89 mod 26.

To find the multiplicative inverse, we use two methods:
1. ab mod 26 = 1 where a = −89 and we have to find out the possible value of b by putting one by one value. GCD (a, b) = 1. We know that −89 mod 26 = 11 mod 26. Therefore, a = 11 and possible value of b = 19.

Modular multiplicative inverse of −89 mod 26 = 19

2. Extended Euclidean algorithm for multiplicative inverse (refer Chapter 6 for more detail).

Step 5 Find the mod of adjoint matrix.

$$K^{-1} = \begin{bmatrix} -83 & 64 & -12 \\ 92 & -57 & -6 \\ -48 & 22 & 7 \end{bmatrix} \mod 26$$

Step 6 Find the inverse of the matrix.

$$K^{-1} = \frac{1}{\det(K)} adj(K)$$

$$K^{-1} = \left(\frac{1}{-89}\right) \begin{bmatrix} -83 & 64 & -12 \\ 92 & -57 & -6 \\ -48 & 22 & 7 \end{bmatrix} \mod 26$$

$$K^{-1} = \left(\frac{1}{89}\right) \begin{bmatrix} 83 & -64 & 12 \\ -92 & 57 & 6 \\ 48 & -22 & -7 \end{bmatrix} \mod 26$$

$$K^{-1} = 19 \begin{bmatrix} 83 & -64 & 12 \\ -92 & 57 & 6 \\ 48 & -22 & -7 \end{bmatrix} \mod 26$$

$$K^{-1} = (19) \begin{bmatrix} 5 & 14 & 12 \\ 12 & 5 & 6 \\ 22 & 4 & 19 \end{bmatrix} \mod 26$$

$$K^{-1} = \begin{bmatrix} 95 & 266 & 228 \\ 228 & 95 & 114 \\ 418 & 76 & 361 \end{bmatrix} \mod 26$$

Therefore, the key for decryption is,

$$K^{-1} = \begin{bmatrix} 17 & 6 & 20 \\ 20 & 17 & 10 \\ 2 & 24 & 23 \end{bmatrix}$$

2.2 Use Hill cipher to encrypt and decrypt the message, "I CANT DO IT". The key for encryption is "DIMENSION".

Solution:

Encryption: First convert the letters in the key and the plaintext in number form such as a = 0, b = 1, and so on.

$$K = \begin{bmatrix} d & i & m \\ e & n & s \\ i & o & n \end{bmatrix} = \begin{bmatrix} 3 & 8 & 12 \\ 4 & 13 & 18 \\ 8 & 14 & 13 \end{bmatrix}$$

$$\text{Plaintext } P = \begin{bmatrix} 8 & 13 & 14 \\ 2 & 19 & 8 \\ 0 & 3 & 19 \end{bmatrix}$$

C (Ciphertext) $= K$ (Key) $\times P$ (Plaintext)

$$C = \begin{bmatrix} 3 & 8 & 12 \\ 4 & 13 & 18 \\ 8 & 14 & 13 \end{bmatrix} \begin{bmatrix} 8 & 13 & 14 \\ 2 & 19 & 8 \\ 0 & 3 & 19 \end{bmatrix}$$

$$C = \begin{bmatrix} 40 & 227 & 334 \\ 58 & 353 & 502 \\ 92 & 409 & 471 \end{bmatrix} \bmod 26$$

$$C = \begin{bmatrix} 14 & 19 & 22 \\ 6 & 15 & 8 \\ 14 & 19 & 3 \end{bmatrix}$$

Convert the numbers into alphabets.

$$= \begin{bmatrix} O & T & W \\ G & P & I \\ O & T & D \end{bmatrix}$$

Read the characters from the matrix in column wise vertically downward direction. The ciphertext is: OGOTPTWID

Decryption: The key for encryption is DIMENSION. So the key for decryption is as below: (For detail refer Problem 2.1)

$$P = K^{-1} \times C$$

$$P = \begin{bmatrix} 17 & 6 & 20 \\ 20 & 17 & 10 \\ 2 & 24 & 23 \end{bmatrix} \begin{bmatrix} 14 & 19 & 22 \\ 6 & 15 & 8 \\ 14 & 19 & 3 \end{bmatrix}$$

$$P = \begin{bmatrix} 554 & 793 & 482 \\ 522 & 825 & 606 \\ 494 & 835 & 305 \end{bmatrix} \bmod 26$$

$$P = \begin{bmatrix} 8 & 13 & 14 \\ 2 & 19 & 8 \\ 0 & 3 & 19 \end{bmatrix}$$

$$P = \begin{bmatrix} I & N & O \\ C & T & I \\ A & D & T \end{bmatrix}$$

Read the matrix column wise, the plaintext is: "ICANTDOIT"

2.3 Use Hill cipher to encrypt and decrypt the message "ESSENTIAL". The key for encryption is "ANOTHERBZ".

Solution: First convert the letters in the key and the plaintext in number form such as a = 0, b = 1, and so on.

The key matrix is,
$$K = \begin{bmatrix} 0 & 13 & 14 \\ 19 & 6 & 4 \\ 17 & 1 & 25 \end{bmatrix}$$

The plaintext matrix is,
$$P = \begin{bmatrix} 4 & 4 & 8 \\ 18 & 13 & 0 \\ 18 & 19 & 11 \end{bmatrix}$$

Encryption:
Ciphertext matrix is, $C = K \times P \mod 26$

$$C = \begin{bmatrix} 0 & 13 & 14 \\ 19 & 6 & 4 \\ 17 & 1 & 25 \end{bmatrix} \begin{bmatrix} 4 & 4 & 8 \\ 18 & 13 & 0 \\ 18 & 19 & 11 \end{bmatrix} \mod 26$$

$$C = \begin{bmatrix} 486 & 435 & 154 \\ 256 & 230 & 196 \\ 536 & 556 & 411 \end{bmatrix} \mod 26$$

$$C = \begin{bmatrix} 18 & 19 & 24 \\ 22 & 22 & 14 \\ 16 & 10 & 21 \end{bmatrix} \mod 26$$

$$C = \begin{bmatrix} S & T & Y \\ W & W & O \\ Q & K & V \end{bmatrix} \mod 26$$

Read the characters from the matrix in column wise vertically downward direction. The ciphertext is: "SWQTWKYOV"

Decryption:
Plaintext matrix is, $P = K^{-1} \times C \mod 26$
First we find out the key for decryption which is K^{-1}.

$$K^{-1} = \frac{1}{6453} \begin{bmatrix} -146 & 311 & 32 \\ 407 & 238 & -266 \\ 83 & -211 & 247 \end{bmatrix} \mod 26$$

$$K^{-1} = \begin{bmatrix} 2 & 5 & 22 \\ 19 & 6 & 4 \\ 1 & 13 & 13 \end{bmatrix}$$

$$= \begin{bmatrix} 2 & 5 & 22 \\ 19 & 6 & 4 \\ 1 & 13 & 13 \end{bmatrix} \begin{bmatrix} 18 & 19 & 24 \\ 22 & 22 & 14 \\ 16 & 10 & 21 \end{bmatrix} \bmod 26$$

$$= \begin{bmatrix} 498 & 368 & 580 \\ 538 & 533 & 624 \\ 512 & 435 & 479 \end{bmatrix} \bmod 26$$

$$= \begin{bmatrix} 4 & 4 & 8 \\ 18 & 13 & 0 \\ 18 & 19 & 11 \end{bmatrix}$$

$$= \begin{bmatrix} E & E & I \\ S & N & A \\ S & T & L \end{bmatrix}$$

Read the characters from the matrix in column wise vertically downward direction. The plaintext is "ESSENTIAL"

2.4 The chosen plaintext attack is on Hill Cipher with $P = C = Z(2/7)$. Suppose the plaintext be "ESSENTIALA" and the message is encoded using: E = 0, S = 1, N = 2, T = 3, I = 4, A = 5 and L = 6. The ciphertext is "TNSLIIALEI". Find the key used in this cipher.

Solution: Assume the key be $\begin{bmatrix} a & b \\ c & d \end{bmatrix}$ and

the plaintext matrix is $\begin{bmatrix} 0 & 1 & 2 & 4 & 6 \\ 1 & 0 & 3 & 5 & 5 \end{bmatrix}$ and

the ciphertext matrix is $\begin{bmatrix} 3 & 1 & 4 & 5 & 0 \\ 2 & 6 & 4 & 6 & 4 \end{bmatrix}$

We know that $C = K \times P$

$$\begin{bmatrix} 3 & 1 & 4 & 5 & 0 \\ 2 & 6 & 4 & 6 & 4 \end{bmatrix} = \begin{bmatrix} a & b \\ c & d \end{bmatrix} \begin{bmatrix} 0 & 1 & 2 & 4 & 6 \\ 1 & 0 & 3 & 5 & 5 \end{bmatrix}$$

Let's consider the first two letters of the message, i.e., "ES". The first column of plaintext matrix $\begin{bmatrix} 0 \\ 1 \end{bmatrix}$ represents these two letters. The second pair of letters is "SE" = $\begin{bmatrix} 1 \\ 0 \end{bmatrix}$, the third pair of letters is "NT" = $\begin{bmatrix} 4 \\ 4 \end{bmatrix}$, the fourth pair of letters is "IA" = $\begin{bmatrix} 4 \\ 5 \end{bmatrix}$, and the last pair of letters is "LA" = $\begin{bmatrix} 6 \\ 5 \end{bmatrix}$, Thus, we try to find out the key by solving for one pair of letters at a time. We solve this for above data:

$$K \times P = C$$
$$\begin{bmatrix} a & b \\ c & d \end{bmatrix} \begin{bmatrix} 0 \\ 1 \end{bmatrix} = \begin{bmatrix} b \\ d \end{bmatrix} = \begin{bmatrix} 3 \\ 2 \end{bmatrix}$$

Solving this we get, b = 3 and a = 1

Similarly $\begin{bmatrix} a & b \\ c & d \end{bmatrix} \begin{bmatrix} 1 \\ 0 \end{bmatrix} = \begin{bmatrix} a \\ c \end{bmatrix} = \begin{bmatrix} 1 \\ 6 \end{bmatrix}$

Therefore d = 2 and c = 6.
From above the key matrix is $\begin{bmatrix} a & b \\ c & d \end{bmatrix} = \begin{bmatrix} 1 & 3 \\ 6 & 2 \end{bmatrix}$

2.5 Use transposition cipher to encrypt and decrypt the message "MEET ME AT BOAT CLUB CANTEEN" using the key "EXAMPLE".
Solution:

E	X	A	M	P	L	E
M	E	E	T	M	E	A
T	B	O	A	T	C	L
U	B	C	A	N	T	E
E	N					

Here the last row is not fully filled, so we add any letter (but same letter in all columns) in the unfilled columns of the last row. Suppose we use letter "X" for this purpose. The matrix is now as below:

E	X	A	M	P	L	E
M	E	E	T	M	E	A
T	B	O	A	T	C	L
U	B	C	A	N	T	E
E	N	X	X	X	X	X

Give the numbering to the columns as per their alphabetical order.

E	X	A	M	P	L	E
2	7	1	5	6	4	3
M	E	E	T	M	E	A
T	B	O	A	T	C	L
U	B	C	A	N	T	E
E	N	X	X	X	X	X

Next arrange the table as per ascending order of the numbers given to each column.

Data Encryption Techniques

A	E	E	L	M	P	X
1	2	3	4	5	6	7
E	M	A	E	T	M	E
O	T	L	C	A	T	B
C	U	E	T	A	N	B
X	E	X	X	X	X	N

Now note down the letters column wise. This is the ciphertext as below:

EOCXMTUEALEXECTXTAAXMTNXEBBN

For decryption, first calculate the number of letters present in the ciphertext. Using the number of letters in the key, we can calculate the number of letters present in the last row. As can be seen above, all the columns contain only four letters and this is important. In the above example there are 28 letters and the key having 7 letters, so there are four rows and each row has 7 letters. For decryption, the key is prepared as for encryption. Then write the first four letters below the column number '1'.

E	X	A	M	P	L	E
		1				
		E				
		O				
		C				
		X				

In the same way, fill all the columns one by one.

E	X	A	M	P	L	E
2		1				
M		E				
T		O				
U		C				
E		X				

and we get the output is as below:

E	X	A	M	P	L	E
2	7	1	5	6	4	3
M	E	E	T	M	E	A
T	B	O	A	T	C	L
U	B	C	A	N	T	E
E	N	X	X	X	X	X

Note down the letters row wise, we get the plaintext as:

MEETMEATBOATCLUBCANTEENXXX

From above text, the last three characters are XXX. This indicates that these characters are added just for padding and not the part of message. So remove these letters and insert the spaces in between the meaningful words. We get the final plaintext is as below:

MEET ME AT BOAT CLUB CANTEEN

2.6 Apply cryptanalysis on the following ciphertext which was encrypted using single columnar transposition.

Ciphertext: EOCXMTUEALEXECTXTAAXMTNXEBBN

Solution: We assume that this is encrypted by columnar transposition using a key. Cryptanalyst tries to find out the key and the plaintext by following the steps given below:

Step 1 Count the number of letters in the ciphertext. There are 28 letters in the ciphertext.

Step 2 Assuming the possible dimension of an array. The array could have any of the following dimensions: 7 × 4 or 4 × 7 or 14 × 2 or 2 × 14. Suppose that we first try a 7 × 4 array. This helps us to guess the key length. For this array, the key length is 7. Then the ciphertext array is as shown in table given below:

1	2	3	4	5	6	7
E	M	A	E	T	M	E
O	T	L	C	A	T	B
C	U	E	T	A	N	B
X	E	X	X	X	X	N

2	1	4	5	6	7	3
M	E	E	T	M	E	A
T	O	C	A	T	B	L
U	C	T	A	N	B	E
E	X	X	X	X	N	X

Step 3 Now, observe the top row of the array in the above table and try to find the meaningful word. As per this word, identify the columns and permute these columns as shown in table given below.

2	7	1	5	6	4	3
M	E	E	T	M	E	A
T	B	O	A	T	C	L
U	B	C	A	N	T	E
E	N	X	X	X	X	X

After permutation, we observe the word MEET in the first row of the table. Also there are words or partial words in the other rows of the table. If this gives meaning statement then, the key is almost recovered.

We start our cryptanalysis from column 2 using word MEET in the first row. But using this sequence we cannot get the meaningful message. So, again some rearrangement of the columns is needed. Therefore, we rearrange the sequence as per word "BOAT" from second row as shown in table given below:

Now we get the meaningful words and the encryption key 2715643. The plaintext is MEETMEATBOATCLUBXXX. Last three letters are XXX and have no meaning so delete those letters and the final plaintext is:

MEET ME AT BOAT CLUB.

2.7 The ciphertext given below was encrypted with substitution cipher:

AIIXGILHCHA

The rule for encryption is given as:

$$C = (P + K) \bmod 26$$

where C is the ciphertext, P is the plaintext and K is the key. Assume that the plaintext is in English. If the first plaintext letter is G, find the key and the plaintext.

Solution: We know that mod 26 is used means the alphabets are numbered as a = 0, b = 1, c = 2, d = 3, e = 4, f = 5, g = 6, h = 7, i = 8, j = 9, k = 10, l = 11, m = 12, n = 13, o = 14, p = 15, q = 16, r = 17, s = 18, t = 19, u = 20, v = 21, w = 22, x = 23, y = 24, z = 25.

Therefore, the ciphertext is: A = 0, S = 18, S = 18, X = 23, G = 6, S = 18, L = 11, H = 7, C = 2, H = 7, A = 0.

The plaintext $P = (C - K) \bmod 26$

The first plaintext letter is G = 6 is given and the first ciphertext letter is A = 0. Using formula given, we get:

$$6 = (0 - K) \bmod 26$$

Therefore, $K = -6$

Therefore, plaintext is:
    0 − (−6) mod 26 = 6 = G
    8 − (−6) mod 26 = 14 = O
    8 − (−6) mod 26 = 14 = O
    23 − (−6) mod 26 = 3 = D
    6 − (−6) mod 26 = 12 = M
    8 − (−6) mod 26 = 14 = O
    11 − (−6) mod 26 = 17 = R
    7 − (−6) mod 26 = 13 = N
    2 − (−6) mod 26 = 8 = I
    7 − (−6) mod 26 = 13 = N
    0 − (−6) mod 26 = 6 = G

The plaintext is GOODMORNING.

SUMMARY

In this chapter, we discussed about classical encryption techniques. Encryption is the process of converting the original information which is in meaningful and readable form into unreadable form.

While encoding, the meaning of the message is not obvious. Decryption is the reverse process of encryption. There are two types of encryption methods: symmetric encryption and asymmetric encryption. In symmetric key encryption, the same key is used for encryption as well as decryption. While in asymmetric encryption, one key is used for encryption and another key for decryption.

The area of study in which one can study various techniques of encryption is known as *cryptography*. There are various techniques available to derive the plaintext or decrypt the ciphertext without much knowledge about the key and plaintext. This process is called *cryptanalysis*. Substitution ciphers and transposition ciphers are the two building blocks of all encryption techniques. In the monoalphabetic cipher, a KEY is the rearrangement of the letters of the alphabet. Hill cipher is a polygraphic substitution cipher which uses simple linear equations. Playfair cipher is the well-known encryption algorithm. It divided the plaintext into a group of two letters each. The cryptanalysis of the monoalphabetic ciphers is easy as the ciphertext reflects the frequency count of the original message. To overcome this problem, polyalphabetic cipher emerged in which a single letter can be encrypted to several different letters instead of just one letter. A one-time pad is a block of random data used to encrypt a block of equal length plaintext data. It is the most secure cryptographic algorithm. In this cipher, the key is a set of random numbers generated by pseudo-random number generator. Transposition ciphers encrypt plaintext by rearranging the elements of the plaintext without any change in the identity of the elements. The goal of steganography is to hide the data from a third party. Steganography is significantly more sophisticated, allowing a user to hide large amounts of information within image and audio files.

EXERCISES

2.1 What is encryption? What are the different types of encryption techniques?

2.2 Explain symmetric and asymmetric encryption techniques. Explain the various components of symmetric and asymmetric encryption.

2.3 What are cryptanalysis and cryptography?

2.4 Why there is no need to keep the symmetric encryption algorithms secret?

2.5 What are the different types of substitution ciphers?

2.6 Using the Caesar cipher encrypt and decrypt the following message:
"I want to see your college".

2.7 What are the advantages and disadvantages of Caesar cipher?

2.8 Using monoalphabetic cipher, encrypt and decrypt the following message.
"That was just what Samiksha had been waiting for". And the key is "heaven".

2.9 Explain the Playfair cipher with example.

2.10 Using the Hill cipher, encrypt and decrypt the message "PIET". Assume any key.

2.11 What is the drawback of substitution ciphers?

2.12 Explain one-time pad.

2.13 Explain the transposition cipher with its merits and demerits.

2.14 What is steganography?

2.15 Use one-time pad and find the ciphertext for the following plaintext.

Key: X V H E U W N O P G D Z X V H E U W N O P G D Z X V
Plaintext: WE LIVE IN A WORLD FULL OF BEAUTY

Prove (mathematically) that one-time pad is secure.

2.16 Assume that you are to cryptanalyse a ciphertext that you know was encrypted with a columnar transposition cipher using a full rectangular array. For each of the following message lengths, determine what row × column dimensions for the array are possible.
(a) 36
(b) 33
(c) 24

2.17 What is the difference between a substitution cipher and a transposition cipher?

2.18 For columnar transposition, would it be easier to break a ciphertext of 85 letters if a 5 × 17 or a 17 × 5 rectangle was used for encrypting? Explain.

2.19 If we tried to cryptanalyse a message that had been encrypted with columnar transposition with a rectangular array that was not "full", i.e., the message did not completely fill the rectangle. What problems would we encounter?

2.20 Cryptanalyse the following message that was encrypted using columnar transposition.

ABEEESWHTTRE

MULTIPLE CHOICE QUESTIONS

2.1 The method of hiding the secret is called _____
(a) Cryptanalysis   (b) Watermarking
(c) Steganography   (d) Cryptography

2.2 _____ is the art of breaking the code.
(a) Cryptanalysis   (b) Steganography
(c) Cryptography   (d) Cryptosystem

2.3 One-time pad is also called as
(a) Perfect hiding   (b) Perfect secrecy
(c) Perfect writing   (d) Perfect encryption

2.4 An encryption scheme means _____
(a) A private key
(b) A plaintext message
(c) A method of encoding information
(c) A ciphertext message

2.5 The field which deals with _____ called cryptography.
  (a) Encryption schemes and secure systems
  (b) Firewalls, operating systems, and routers
  (c) Keys
  (d) Complex systems

Answers

    2.1 (d)   **2.2** (a)   **2.3** (b)   **2.4** (c)   **2.5** (a)

CHAPTER 3

Data Encryption Standards

3.1 INDRODUCTION

Encryption techniques are useful to provide the confidentiality to the data. Encryption techniques are classified into two types: block encryption techniques and stream encryption techniques. This classification is based on the number of bits processed at a time. In block cipher, a block of fixed number of bits is processed at a time whereas in stream cipher, one bit is processed at a time. Block ciphers are faster than stream cipher. In this chapter, we will discuss a block cipher called data enecryption standard (DES).

3.2 BLOCK CIPHERS

In the last chapter we have learnt about different classical encryption techniques. Encryption can be performed on a single bit/letter or a group of bits/letters. Therefore, there are two types of encryptions ciphers: a stream cipher and a block cipher.

When encryption algorithms process a block of data at a time and generate a block of data as a ciphertext, then it is called *block cipher*. Symmetric encryption ciphers/ algorithms use a block of bits for processing. The size of block is fixed for a particular algorithm. For example, data encryption standards (DES) uses a plaintext block of size of 64 bits, whereas advanced encryption standard (AES) uses a plaintext block of size of 128, 192 or 256 bits. For symmetric encryption, only one key is required for encryption. The same key is used for decryption.

When an encryption algorithm processes a single bit of data at a time and generates a single bit of data as a ciphertext, then it is called *stream cipher*. RC4 is a stream cipher.

In block cipher, the size of plaintext block and ciphertext block is same. When the number of bits in the plaintext/message are not multiple of the block size, then the technique is called modes of operation. There are various modes of operations such as electronic code book (ECB) mode, cipher block chaining (CBC) mode, feedback modes, and counter mode. Symmetric encryption algorithms use any one of these modes. These modes of operation provide some advantages to the basic encryption algorithms.

Advantages of Modes of Operation

- For any symmetric encryption algorithm, the block size is fixed. But it is not necessary that the number of bits in the plaintext or message should always multiples of the block size. In such case these symmetric encryption algorithms with modes of operation can encrypt and decrypt the message.
- Modes of operation help to provide additional level of security to the encryption algorithm.
- Replay attack of packets can be avoided using modes of operation.

Section 3.3 discuss these modes of operation in detail.

3.3 BLOCK CIPHER MODES OF OPERATION

There are different modes of operation which help the encryption algorithms to process the encryption more easily. Some modes of operations are as below:

1. Electronic code book (ECB) mode
2. Cipher block chaining (CBC) mode
3. Feedback modes
4. Counter mode

3.3.1 Electronic Code Book (ECB) Mode

One of the simple mode of operation is the electronic code book mode. The input for this mode of operation is a plaintext block of 64 bits. The ciphertext block generated using ECB is also of 64 bits. In electronic code book mode, each plaintext blocks are processed independently of other plaintext blocks. The working of electronic code book mode for encryption is shown in Figure 3.1.

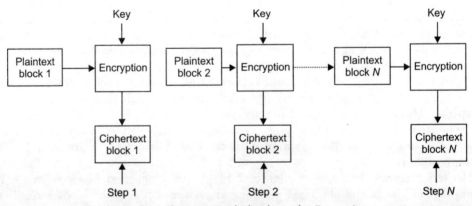

Figure 3.1 Electronic code book mode: Encryption.

The plaintext/message is first divided into blocks of size 64 bits. If the last block of plaintext/message is not having sufficient number of bits, i.e., 64, then the necessary number of bits is appended to the plaintext to complete the block size. Then process each block independently using the key. Same key is used for encryption of all the blocks. The ciphertext is generated which is unique for each plaintext block. But if two plaintext blocks are identical, then the ciphertext block generated are also same. This helps the cryptanalysis of the encryption easy. Here encryption algorithm may be DES, AES or any block cipher. Here we assume data encryption standard (DES). The security of this mode of operation is same as the encryption algorithm used.

Decryption using ECB is the reverse process of encryption using the same key. During decryption, two identical ciphertext blocks also produce the same plaintext blocks. The working of electronic code book mode for decryption is shown in Figure 3.2.

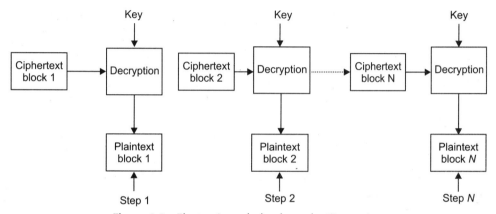

Figure 3.2 Electronic code book mode: Decryption.

Advantages

1. As we can process each block of plaintext independently of each other, we can process multiple blocks simultaneously.
2. If any plaintext or ciphertext blocks lost, it does not affect on the output of other blocks.
3. Parallel processing during encryption as well as decryption helps to increase the speed and the performance of the algorithm.

Disadvantages

If two plaintext blocks are identical, then the ciphertext block generated are also same. Therefore, known plaintext attack is possible.

3.3.2 Cipher Block Chaining (CBC) Mode

Electronic code book mode suffers by known plaintext attack. Cipher block chaining (CBC) overcomes this drawback of electronic code book mode. In CBC, like ECB, plaintext/message is first divided into blocks of size 64 bits. If the last block of plaintext/message is not having sufficient number of bits, i.e., 64, then the necessary number of bits is appended to the plaintext to complete the block size. An initialisation vector is selected. It is nothing but the random number which helps to increase the security. A key is used for encryption of all the blocks. Then perform XOR operation between the first plaintext block and the initialisation vector. The output is 64-bit block, which is encrypted using the secret key. Now, the output is 64-bit ciphertext.

The next block of plaintext is now XOR with the 64-bit ciphertext of the previous step. That is, for N^{th} plaintext, $(N\text{-}1)^{th}$ ciphertext block is used. Therefore, for the identical blocks of plaintext, different ciphertext blocks are generated. The encryption process is shown in Figure 3.3.

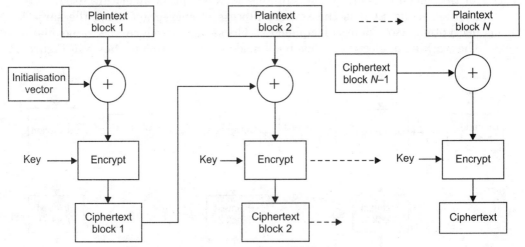

Figure 3.3 Cipher block chaining mode: Encryption.

Decryption is the reverse process of encryption. For decryption, the same key is used as encryption. First block of ciphertext is decrypted using the key. Then XOR operation is performed with the initialisation vector. The output is a plaintext. Same operation is repeated for each ciphertext blocks. Only difference is that instead of initialisation vector, plaintext block of previous step is used. The complete decryption process is as shown in Figure 3.4.

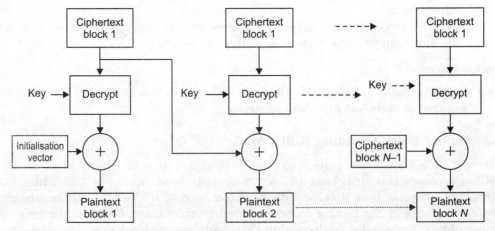

Figure 3.4 Cipher block chaining mode: Decryption.

Cipher block chaining can be used to generate the hash value. The last ciphertext block is used as hash value for the given message. Because the last ciphertext block is dependent on all the plaintext blocks. This hash value helps to check if any one of the ciphertext blocks lost or modified. CBC cannot use parallelisation, as the ciphertext of the first plaintext block is used for the processing of the next plaintext block.

Advantages
1. For identical blocks of plaintext, different ciphertext blocks are generated. So, CBC is more secure as compared to ECB mode.
2. Hash value, i.e., last ciphertext block, helps to identify if the message is original or modified.

Disadvantages
1. Parallel operation cannot be performed. So, it is slower as compared to ECB.
2. Lost/missing of any block of ciphertext stops the decryption process of the remaining blocks.

3.3.3 Feedback Mode

In the above two modes of operation, if the last block does not have sufficient number of bits, padding some bits is required. For feedback mode, this is not required. In this mode, the ciphertext of the previous step is given as input to the next step just like feedback. There are two types of feedback mode: cipher feedback mode and output feedback mode.

Cipher Feedback Mode

If the block size is smaller than the required block size, then the cipher feedback mode can be used to encrypt plaintext. The block size may be a bit or bytes, so there is no need of padding. The encryption process using cipher feedback mode is shown in Figure 3.5.

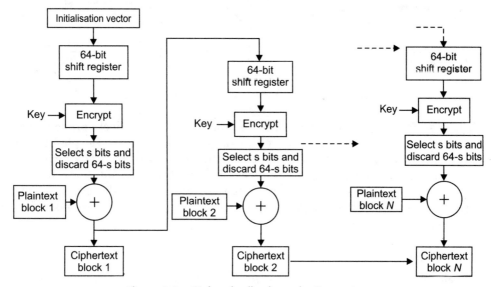

Figure 3.5 Cipher feedback mode: Encryption.

In this mode, 64-bit shift register is used. In the first step, shift register is filled by initialisation vector, i.e., random number. The output of the shift register is encrypted using a key of size 64 bits. Then select leftmost "s" bits from the 64 bits and discard remaining bits. "s" is equal to the number of bits in the plaintext block. Then XOR operation is performed between the plaintext and the "s" bits. The output is ciphertext of block size "s". The ciphertext is also sent as input to the next step as input to the shift register. This process continues on all the blocks of plaintext to generate the ciphertext.

In decryption, initially the shift register is filled with initialisation vector. The initialisation vector is same as used for encryption. Then encrypt the bits in the shift register using the key and then select "j" bits from the 64 bits and XOR with the ciphertext. The output is plaintext. Figure 3.6 shows the decryption using cipher feedback mode.

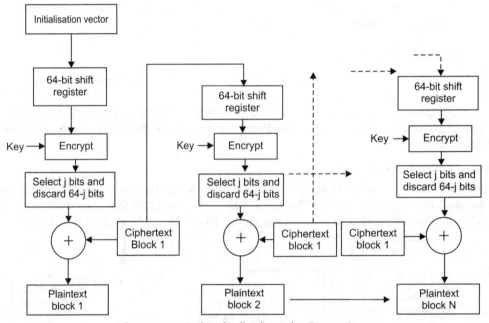

Figure 3.6 Cipher feedback mode: Decryption.

CFB is suffered from bit errors. If in the incoming cipher block, any one bit error is there, then it causes the bit error at the same bit position in the plaintext block. The same ciphertext block is used as input to the shift register of the next step and causes bit errors in the next plaintext block. In this way, the bit error in the shift error remains till the bit remains in the shift register. Suppose there is a bit error at 4th bit position of the 8-bit CFB, then subsequent 8 bytes will be garbled. After that the correct plaintext will be generated.

Output Feedback Mode

Another feedback mode is an output feedback mode. This mode can also process the plaintext block of any size less than or equal to 64 bits. In this mode instead of the ciphertext, the encrypted output of the shift register is given as input to the shift register of the next step. The complete process of output feedback mode is shown in Figure 3.7.

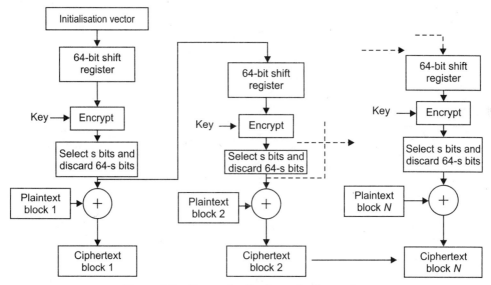

Figure 3.7 Output feedback mode: Encryption.

First step is to select 64-bit random value, called initialisation vector. This value is given as input to the 64-bit shift register. The encryption algorithm is used to encrypt the output of shift register with the key. Then select "s" (value of "s" is equal to the size of plaintext block) bits from the encrypted output and discard 64-s bits. Next step is performed XOR operation between the selected "s" bit and the plaintext block. The output is ciphertext. The selected "s" bits are used as input for the shift register on the next step. In this way, the processing of each block of plaintext is done.

Bit error is occurring in CBC and CFB due to an error in any one bit of the ciphertext. In output feedback, the encrypted output of the shift register instead of ciphertext block is used as input to the shift register of the next step. Here, ciphertext is not used for the processing of the next plaintext block. Therefore, output feedback mode is not suffered by bit error. But cryptanalysis of output feedback mode is easy as only a ciphertext block and encrypted "s" bits are sufficient to get the plaintext block. Here information about the key is not required, which help the cryptanalyst to break the cipher easily. Therefore, this mode is less secure than cipher feedback mode.

The decryption process of output feedback mode is similar to encryption. The only difference is that instead of plaintext block, corresponding ciphertext block is used for XOR operation. The detail decryption using output feedback mode is shown in Figure 3.8.

Modern stream ciphers are faster than block ciphers, this trim down the importance of the feedback modes.

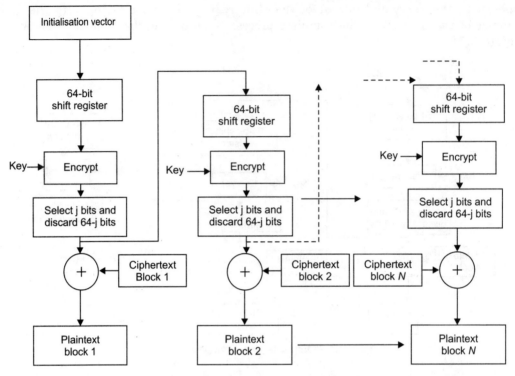

Figure 3.8 Output feedback mode: Decryption.

Advantage

- Free from bit error rate.

Disadvantage

- Vulnerable to a stream modification attack.

3.3.4 Counter Mode

The counter mode (CTR) is the most important mode of operation. In the counter mode, a block cipher is worked like a stream cipher. The counter is used whose value is changed in each round. Initially, the user has to set some value to the counter. The encryption algorithm (DES algorithm) processes the counter value and the key. This encrypted value is XOR with the block of plaintext. The result is a block of ciphertext. For the two identical blocks of plaintext, two different blocks of ciphertext are generated. Encryption process using the counter mode is shown in Figure 3.9.

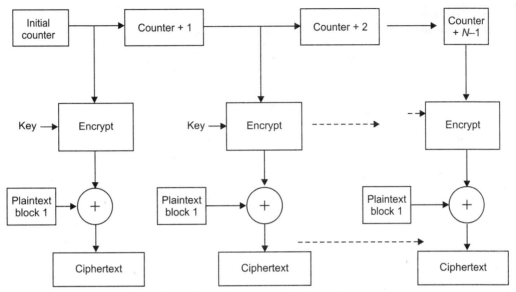

Figure 3.9 Counter mode: Encryption.

Decryption process is similar to encryption except ciphertext blocks are used instead of plaintext blocks. Key and the value of counter are same as encryption. Decryption process is shown in Figure 3.10.

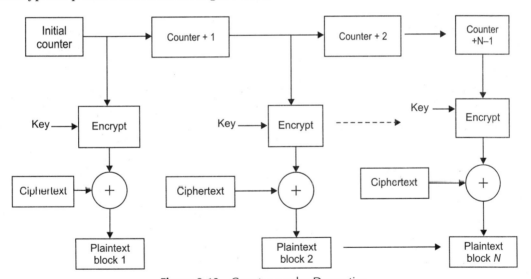

Figure 3.10 Counter mode: Decryption.

Advantages

1. The counter mode may be faster than of cipher block chaining mode.
2. Encryption can be done in parallel.

3. Padding is not required.
4. Processing of plaintext blocks can be done randomly.
5. Only encryption algorithm is required.
6. It is as secure as the other modes.

Disadvantages

1. Integrity of the message is not maintained.
2. Reuse of counter value, compromise the security.

3.4 FEISTEL CIPHERS

Feistel ciphers are a block cipher. In this, cipher iterations are carried on the blocks. In this cipher, the single plaintext block undergoes through different rounds repeatedly. Each round has a number of transformations. After going through a number of rounds, the ciphertext is generated. Feistel structure is the building block for many block ciphers. The design of data encryption standard (DES) algorithm is based on Feistel structures. Initially, the plaintext is split into the blocks of equal size. Then each block is split into two equal parts: left part and right part. The Feistel structure has many rounds and each round has different subkeys. These subkeys are generated from the key entered by the user. Different mathematical operations are performed on the right part of the plaintext with one of the subkeys. These mathematical operations include the hash or round function. The XOR operation is performed between the output of function and the left part of the plaintext.

Then the right and left parts are interchanged. This completes the round one of the Feistel cipher. For the next round, output of the previous round is used as input for the next round, i.e., left part of previous round is used as right part for the next round and right part is used as left part. This process is repeated for all the rounds. In the last round, there is no interchange of left and right part. Combine both the parts to get the ciphertext.

By reversing the order of subkeys(i.e., the last subkey of encryption is used for the first round of decryption), the same Feistel structure can be used for encryption and decryption. The complete operation of Feistel is shown in Figure 3.11.

The security of Feistel cipher depends on the key size and hash function. The design of Feistel cipher depends on following parameters:

1. *Block size:* Block size indicates the total number of bits in a block as DES algorithm uses the design of Feistel cipher. DES uses a block of 64 bits.
2. *Key length:* It is the length of key. DES uses 64-bit key.
3. *Number of rounds:* The security of any block ciphers depend on the number of rounds in the cipher. DES has 16 rounds, so every plaintext block undergoes 16 iterations.
4. *Subkeys:* Each round uses different keys called subkeys. These subkeys are derived from an original key.
5. *Round function:* The mathematical operation performs on each plaintext block in each round called round function.

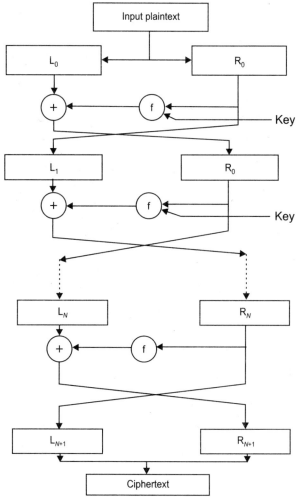

Figure 3.11 Feistel cipher.

3.5 DATA ENCRYPTION STANDARD

Data encryption standard (DES) is a block cipher. The design of DES depends on Feistel-structure. DES was published in 1977. DES uses 64 bits plaintext block and 64 bits key (actually DES uses 56 bits out of 64 bits).To add more security, it was modified time to time. Hardware version of DES is faster than software version. Using brute force attack, DES is broken in 1998. In 1998 a modified DES version was published known as Triple DES or 3DES. It is more secure than simple DES but it consumes more time for encryption. DES is broken and there was a need for new cipher. In 1999, a new block cipher known as advanced encryption standard (AES) was superseded the DES cipher. In this chapter we will discuss the detail working of DES, 3DES and the cryptanalysis of DES algorithm. Chapter 4 covered the detail working of AES.

Design of DES is based on Feistel structure. Various permutations and S-boxes (substitution boxes) are used to provide confusion and diffusion. Diffusion means the wide range of ciphertext is generated from plaintext. The purpose of diffusion is to make the relationship between the plaintext and ciphertext as complex as possible. That means there is no linear mathematical relation between the plaintext and the ciphertext. Each bit of plaintext affects the value of many bits of ciphertext. Confusion means the relationship between the key and the ciphertext as complex as possible. Confusion and diffusion are the attributes for defining the strong encryption algorithm.

The message is divided into a plaintext block of 64 bits. Each plaintext block undergoes various permutations and substitution operations. There are total 16 rounds in DES. The plaintext block used is of size 64 bits. The key size for DES is 64 bits of which 56 bits are actually used as a key. From this key 16 subkeys are generated, one subkey for each round. Same encryption algorithm is used as decryption except the subkeys are used in reverse order. The detail working of DES is discussed below.

3.5.1 Working of DES

DES algorithm is designed for encryption and decryption of blocks of plaintext. The size of plaintext block is of 64 bits which is encrypted into a ciphertext block of 64 bits. Each bit may be either 1 or 0. Initially a block of plaintext undergoes permutation called initial permutation. This allows 2^{64} possible arrangements of the 64 bits in a plaintext block. The architecture of DES is shown in Figure 3.12.

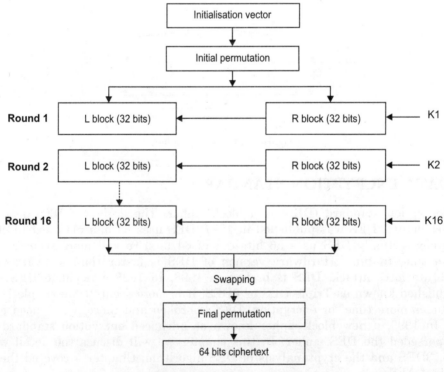

Figure 3.12 Steps in DES.

The working of DES algorithm is divided into following four parts.

1. Subkey generation
2. Initial permutation
3. 1 to 16 rounds
4. Final permutation

Now we will discuss each key generation first and then each step for first round in detail:

Subkey Generation

DES uses the key of size of 64 bits. The first step is to apply initial permutation on 64-bit key using initial permutation (64 bits) table. Then remove the parity bits from the 64-bit key and reduced to 56-bit key. We can do this by not selecting the parity bits (i.e., bits position 8, 16, 24, 32, 40, 48, 56 and 64). Apply expansion permutation on this 56-bit key using expansion permutation (56 bits) table. Next, divide this 56 bit key into two halves, viz. left and right. Each half has 28 bits. Each halve undergoes circular left shift. The shift of bits by 1 or 2 positions is round dependent as shown in Table 3.1.

Table 3.1

Round	1	2	3	4	5	6	7	8	9	10	11	12	13	14	15	16
Bits shifted left	1	1	2	2	2	2	2	2	1	2	2	2	2	2	2	1

To generate 16 subkeys, the above procedure is carried out on each subkey. After shifting each halve, concatenate two halves to get 56 bits key. Then apply the compression permutation (48 bits) on 56 bit keys. The result is 48-bit subkey. Figure 3.13 shows the subkey generation in details.

The 64-bit key is permutated using following permutation tables (Table 3.2(a-c)).

Table 3.2 Permutation tables

(a) Initial permutation (64 bits)	(b) Expansion permutation (56 bits)	(c) Compression permutation (56 bits)
$\begin{bmatrix} 58 & 50 & 42 & 34 & 26 & 18 & 10 & 2 \\ 60 & 52 & 44 & 36 & 28 & 20 & 12 & 4 \\ 62 & 54 & 46 & 38 & 30 & 22 & 14 & 6 \\ 64 & 56 & 48 & 40 & 32 & 24 & 16 & 8 \\ 57 & 49 & 41 & 33 & 25 & 17 & 9 & 1 \\ 59 & 51 & 43 & 35 & 27 & 19 & 11 & 3 \\ 61 & 53 & 45 & 37 & 29 & 21 & 13 & 5 \\ 63 & 55 & 47 & 39 & 31 & 23 & 15 & 7 \end{bmatrix}$	$\begin{bmatrix} 57 & 49 & 41 & 33 & 25 & 17 & 9 \\ 1 & 58 & 50 & 42 & 34 & 26 & 18 \\ 10 & 2 & 59 & 51 & 43 & 35 & 27 \\ 19 & 11 & 3 & 60 & 52 & 44 & 36 \\ 63 & 55 & 47 & 39 & 31 & 23 & 15 \\ 7 & 62 & 54 & 46 & 38 & 30 & 22 \\ 14 & 6 & 61 & 53 & 45 & 37 & 29 \\ 21 & 13 & 5 & 28 & 20 & 12 & 4 \end{bmatrix}$	$\begin{bmatrix} 14 & 17 & 11 & 24 & 1 & 5 \\ 3 & 28 & 15 & 6 & 21 & 10 \\ 23 & 19 & 12 & 4 & 26 & 8 \\ 16 & 7 & 27 & 20 & 13 & 2 \\ 41 & 52 & 31 & 37 & 47 & 55 \\ 30 & 40 & 51 & 45 & 33 & 48 \\ 44 & 49 & 39 & 56 & 34 & 53 \\ 46 & 42 & 50 & 36 & 29 & 32 \end{bmatrix}$

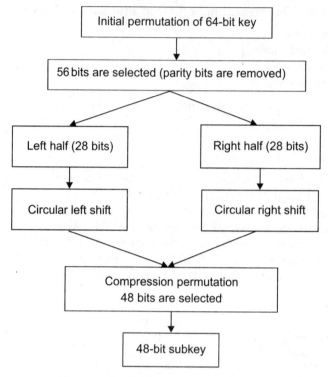

Figure 3.13 Subkey generation for DES.

Subkey generation steps are summarised as below:
1. Apply initial permutation on 64-bit key using expansion table.
2. Remove the parity bits from 64 bits to reduce the key to 56 bits.
3. Apply permutation on the 56-bit key.
4. Split the 56-bit key into two halves 28 bits each.
5. Apply circular left shift on each halve.
6. Concatenate the two halves.
7. Apply compression permutation to reduce the key to 48 bits.

Initial Permutation

The message is converted into binary form. Then each bit allocates its position starting from right (0th position) to left (64th position). Initial permutation is applied on 64-bit block of plaintext using Table 3.3. The first bit is the 58th bit from the plaintext block; second bit is the 50th bit and so on. This table performs the permutations of the plaintext bits.

Data Encryption Standards

Table 3.3 Initial permutation

$$\begin{bmatrix} 58 & 50 & 42 & 34 & 26 & 18 & 10 & 2 \\ 60 & 52 & 44 & 36 & 28 & 20 & 12 & 4 \\ 62 & 54 & 46 & 38 & 30 & 22 & 14 & 6 \\ 64 & 56 & 48 & 40 & 32 & 24 & 16 & 8 \\ 57 & 49 & 41 & 33 & 25 & 17 & 9 & 1 \\ 59 & 51 & 43 & 35 & 27 & 19 & 11 & 3 \\ 61 & 53 & 45 & 37 & 29 & 21 & 13 & 5 \\ 63 & 55 & 47 & 39 & 31 & 23 & 15 & 7 \end{bmatrix}$$

Then this 64-bit plaintext block undergoes different operation from round 1 to 10.

Rounds 1 to 16

There are 16 rounds in DES. All the 16 rounds have similar operations of the plaintext blocks. Single round of DES is explained diagrammatically in Figure 3.14. The 64 bits plaintext block is split into two parts of 32 bits each called right and left parts. Each round of DES has following steps:

(a) Expansion permutation
(b) XOR operation
(c) S-box substitution
(d) P-box permutation
(e) XOR operation
(f) Swapping

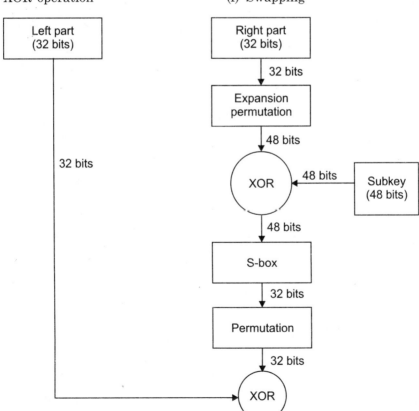

Figure 3.14 Details of single round of DES.

Expansion permutation: The right part having 32 bits undergoes expansion permutation using Table 3.4. This step expands the right half part to 48 bits. Therefore, some of the bits are repeated. The new bit position is as per the table, i.e., first bit is the 32nd bit, and second bit is the 1st bit and so on.

Table 3.4   Expansion permutation

$$\begin{bmatrix} 32 & 1 & 2 & 3 & 4 & 5 \\ 4 & 5 & 6 & 7 & 8 & 9 \\ 8 & 9 & 10 & 11 & 12 & 13 \\ 12 & 13 & 14 & 15 & 16 & 17 \\ 16 & 17 & 18 & 19 & 20 & 21 \\ 20 & 21 & 22 & 23 & 24 & 25 \\ 24 & 25 & 26 & 27 & 28 & 29 \\ 28 & 29 & 30 & 31 & 32 & 1 \end{bmatrix}$$

XOR operation: In this step XOR operation is performed between the 48 bits of right half and the subkey. This creates key dependency.

S-box substitution: The 48 bits of right half are divided into 8 groups. Each group has 6 bits. There are eight S-boxes, one for each group. The selection of S-boxes is very important as proper selection of S-boxes make the cryptanalysis of DES difficult. The S-box structure is shown in Table 3.5.

Table 3.5   S-box structure

R\C	0	1	2	3	4	5	6	7	8	9	10	11	12	13	14	15
0	12	9	15	8	3	6	10	14	0	4	13	7	1	11	2	5
1	3	7	1	6	11	4	0	15	2	8	5	12	10	14	13	9
2	15	4	5	14	12	0	3	11	7	1	10	6	13	9	2	8
3	8	11	9	13	0	5	10	7	12	6	3	2	15	14	4	1

The input to the S-box is a group of 6 bits and the output of S-box is 4 bits. There are total eight S-boxes in each round which convert 48 bits (6 bits per group × 8 groups) input to 32 bits (4 bits per group × 8 groups) output. S-box can be used as follow:

1. 48 bit plaintext is split into eight groups of 6 bits each.
2. Then select MSB and LSB, i.e., the first and the last bit of a group. These two bits form a 2-bit binary number. The decimal equivalent of this number is a row number from the S-box. For example, suppose a group is 100000, then MSB is 1 and LSB is 0. The pair is 10 (binary). The decimal equivalent of $(10)_2$ is $(02)_{10}$. So row 2 is selected.
3. Then select the middle four bits of the same group. These four bits form a 4-bit binary number. The equivalent decimal number is a column number from the S-box. For example, suppose a group is 100000, then middle four bits are

0000. Then the binary number is 0000 (binary). The decimal equivalent of $(0000)_2$ is $(00)_{10}$. So column 0 is selected.

4. The intersection of the selected row and column is the output in decimal. For the above example, row 2 and column 0 is selected. The intersection from S-box is $(15)_{10}$.

5. The binary equivalent of this decimal number is the 4-bit output from the S-box. In this example, the output is $(1111)_2$.

Using the above procedure, for all 8 groups and 8 different S-boxes, 8 groups of 4 bits each is generated. S-boxes are used to provide the confusion to the algorithm. Figure 3.15 shows the use of S-boxes.

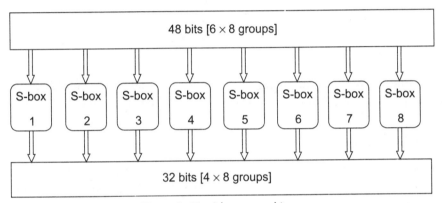

Figure 3.15 S-boxes working.

P-box permutation: The output of S-boxes (32 bits) is sent as input for permutation to P-box. Here every bit is used once. The output of P-box is of 32 bits. Table 3.6 is used for permutation. Permutation is used to provide the diffusion to the algorithm.

Table 3.6 Permutation table

$$\begin{bmatrix} 16 & 7 & 20 & 21 \\ 29 & 12 & 28 & 17 \\ 1 & 15 & 23 & 26 \\ 5 & 18 & 31 & 10 \\ 2 & 8 & 24 & 14 \\ 32 & 27 & 3 & 9 \\ 19 & 13 & 30 & 6 \\ 22 & 11 & 4 & 25 \end{bmatrix}$$

XOR operation: The XOR operation is carried out between the output of the P-box and the left half part. The result is 32-bit output.

Swapping: The result of XOR is used as a new right half for the next round and the old right half part is used as a new left half for the next round.

Final Permutation

This procedure continues for total 16 rounds with each round using a different subkey. Then the invert permutation is applied on the output of last round. This gives 64-bit ciphertext block of 64 bits for a plaintext block of 64 bits.

Same process is repeated for all plaintext which gives the ciphertext for a given message. DES uses same encryption algorithm for decryption. But the order of subkeys is reversed, i.e., first round uses 16th subkey, second round uses 15th subkey, in the same way the last round uses 1st subkey.

3.5.2 Cracking DES

Diffie and Hellma proved that DES can break by brute force attack. As the key size for DES is 56 bits, maximum number of possible keys using 56 bits is 2^{56}. To break DES by brute force attack, maximum number of keys required is 2^{56}. So, they raise some objections about the use of data encryption standard. Next attack on DES was made by John Gilmore and his team. They proved that DES can break within 4.5 days. Using high performance, they announced that DES had broken in 22 hours.

3.6 TRIPLE DES

From above attempts, it was known that DES is not secure. So, the alternative algorithm or improvement in DES was expected. From time to time various versions of DES were proposed. One of the versions of DES is double DES. The working of double DES is same as that of simple DES. Only difference is the data encryption is done two times. Two keys are required for double DES. It is more secure than simple DES because key size is 112 bits (two keys of 56 bits each). To break double DES by brute force attack, maximum number of keys required is 2^{112}. Therefore, it makes brute force attack more difficult as compared to simple DES. But double DES suffers by meeting in the middle attack. The next version of DES is triple DES also known as 3 DES. Triple DES uses three keys and encrypted the data three times. So triple DES takes more time as compared to DES algorithm. As three keys are used, brute force attack is difficult against triple DES. It is more secure algorithm than DES algorithm.

3.6.1 Working of Triple DES

The working of triple DES is same as DES. But the complete encryption process is repeated three times. Three keys of 64 bits each are used for triple DES. Therefore, the overall key length is 192 bits. In triple DES, the data is encrypted thrice using these three keys. The first step is encrypting the data using first key. The second step is to decrypt the ciphertext (output of the first step) using second key. The output of the second step is encrypted using third key (Figure 3.16). So, DES algorithm has to run three times. Mathematically, triple DES encryption can be represented as:

$$C = E_{K1}(D_{K2}(E_{K1}(P)))$$

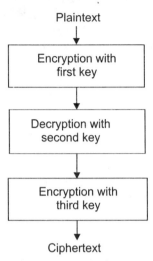

Figure 3.16 Triple DES.

The first step is simple execution of DES algorithm. The second step is decryption in which DES is executed in reverse order of encryption. If any two keys such as first and second or second and third keys are same then the encryption in triple DES is same as simple DES. So for more security three different keys should be selected. There are no current known practical attacks of triple DES.

3.6.2 Modes of Operation

Triple Electronic Code Book (3ECB)

The triple electronic code book works like the ECB mode of simple DES.

Triple CBC (Cipher Block Chaining)

Cipher block chaining (CBC) mode of operation for triple DES is similar to that of simple DES. The first 64-bit key used as the initialisation vector. Triple CBC is then executed for a single 64-bit block of plaintext. Then XOR operation is performed between the ciphertext and the next block of plaintext. CBC provides more security to triple DES.

3.7 DES DESIGN CRITERIA

3.7.1 Design of S-box

For more secure DES, S-box plays the major role. We know that S-box provides confusion property to the DES. Large S-box provides more resistance to cryptanalysis. In DES, other than S-box, other operations are linear which are helpful for cryptanalysis of the algorithm. So, one should take more care for the design of S-box. Large S-box provides more confusion but it is difficult to design larger S-box. There for more time and effort have to spend for the design of S-box. Strong S-box is designed using the non-linear Boolean function. The NIST set the design criteria for S-1. If we select the values of S-box randomly, then the S-box may be weak and cryptanalysis of such S-box is easy. So, the values in the S-box are selected using the non-linear Boolean function, such as Bent functions, which provide strong S-boxes. Due to a change in one bit of input, each bit in the output will change. This is called *Avalanche effect*. The S-box should achieve Avalanche effect.

Design criteria for a good S-box are:

- For the design of $n \times n$ S-box, mapping from input to output should be one-to-one and onto.
- Use a function such that for a change in one bit in the input, at least 50% of the bits in the output should change. This helps to achieve Avalanche effect.
- Output bits act independently from each other.
- There should not be a linear relationship between the input and the output of the S-box.
- The number of 0's and 1's in the S-box should be equal.

3.8 OTHER BLOCK CIPHERS

Apart from DES and triple DES, there are other block ciphers which have been developed from time to time. Some of the known block ciphers are advanced encryption standard (AES), CAST-128, IDEA, and Blowfish. AES is a block cipher having a variable number of rounds (10, 12 or 14 rounds), 128-bit block of plaintext and 128-bit/192-bit/256-bit key for encryption. CAST is a block cipher having 16 rounds, 64-bit plaintext block, and 128-bit key. Another block cipher is the international data encryption algorithm (IDEA). Another block cipher is Blow fish. It is unpatented algorithm. Its architecture is based on Feistel structure. Like AES, it also uses a key of variable length. We learn in detail about these algorithms in the next chapters.

3.9 DIFFERENTIAL CRYPTANALYSIS

Biham and Shamir introduced a cryptanalysis technique known as *differential cryptanalysis*. This technique helps for the study and attack of the cryptographic algorithms. This cryptanalysis technique is a chosen-plaintext or chosen-ciphertext attack. In this technique, the difference in plaintext blocks is compared with the difference in ciphertext blocks to know the key. To get the correct key, large number of plaintext blocks and ciphertext blocks comparison should be done. Cryptanalyst first chooses pairs of plaintext with some particular difference among them. The corresponding ciphertext with these pairs is taken. Then study the difference between the ciphertext pairs and plaintext pairs. Using this information, cryptanalyst tries to find out the key. This technique is generally used for the cryptanalysis of the block ciphers. It is also used for the cryptanalysis of stream ciphers. The basic architecture of DES is based on substitution and diffusion.

3.10 LINEAR CRYPTANALYSIS

Another form of cryptanalysis technique is linear cryptanalysis which is based on linear approximations. This cryptanalysis technique can be used against both the stream and block ciphers. The loopholes in the cipher can be found out using linear cryptanalysis. This helps to improve the performance of the cipher. In this technique, both plaintext and ciphertext are used for cryptanalysis. The key is found out by using the plaintext through a simplified cipher in the complete ciphertext. XOR operation is used to get the key. Some bits of the plaintext are XOR, also some bits of the ciphertext are XOR. The result is XOR together. This result is same as the XOR of some bits of the key. This helps to get the complete key.

3.11 WEAK KEYS IN DES ALGORITHMS

The performance of any encryption algorithm is based on the keys used. But all the keys may not be strong. Some ciphertexts are relatively easy for cryptanalysis. The keys used for generation of such ciphertexts are called *weak keys*. The keys having high degree of similarity are called *simple weak key*.

For example, if any key is composed of:

- all bits are zeros,
- all bits are ones,
- alternating bits are ones and zeroes, and
- alternating bits are zeroes and ones, weak keys have one of the above combinations. For DES, there are total 2^{56} keys of which sixteen keys are considered as weak keys. With the above combinations, following 16 weak keys are produced:

Table 3.7 Weak keys

	L_0	L_0	L_0	L_0
R_0	0,0..	1,0..	0,1..	1,1..
R_0	0,0..	0,0..	0,0..	0,0..
R_0	1,0..	1,0..	1,0..	1,0..
R_0	0,1..	0,1..	0,1..	0,1..
R_0	**1,1..**	**1,1..**	**1,1..**	**1,1..**

From Table 3.7, two keys which have all the bits of L_0 and R_0 as zeroes or ones. These keys are weak because they have their own inverses. Permutation and shifting does not change the key. Therefore, subkeys of these two keys are the same keys. Therefore, all the rounds have the same key. Other than these two subkeys, there are two other keys having each half all ones or zeroes. That means left 28 bits are zeroes and right 28 bits are ones and vice-versa. These four keys are very weak keys and recommended for not to use. Other twelve keys are the combinations of zeroes and ones, such as alternate bits in the key are ones and zeroes as per the table. These twelve keys are called *semi-weak keys*. For good encryption it is recommended not to select such keys.

EXAMPLE 3.1 Let the message be M = COMPITDT and the key be K = COEPPUNE. USE DES algorithm to encrypt and decrypt the message.

Convert M to ASCII and rewrite it in binary format, we get the 64-bit block of plaintext:

M = 01100011 01101111 01101101 01110000 01101001 01110100 01100100 01110100
L = 01100011 01101111 01101101 01110000
R = 01101001 01110100 01100100 01110100

We first write the message in 8 X 8 matrix form as below:

    01100011
    01101111
    01101101
    01110000
    01101001
    01110100
    01100100
    01110100

The first bit of M is "0". The last bit is "0". We read from left to right.
Convert K to ASCII and rewrite it in binary format, we get the 64-bit key as:

K = 01100011 01101111 01100101 01110000 01110000 01110101 01101110 01100101

Write the key in 8 X 8 matrix form as below:

    01100011
    01101111
    01100101
    01110000
    01110000
    01110101
    01101110
    01100101

Solution The DES algorithm uses the following steps.

Step 1 *Generate 16* subkeys (48-bit length)

    Round=1   key=111000001011111011101110110100000100000010011110
    Round=2   key=111000001011011011110110100010001101011011000100
    Round=3   key=111101001101111001110110001010000010011010010001
    Round=4   key=111001101111001101110010011110110110000000000111
    Round=5   key=101011101101011101110110010011001000001100001010
    Round=6   key=111011110101001101011011100001000011000101000111
    Round=7   key=001011111010011111100111100110100001011100000
    Round=8   key=100111101011001110110110101000010001111101001011

Round=9   key=0001111101001011110110110110010010010101000110 0
Round=10 key=0011111101111001100111011000100000010100111011 10
Round=11 key=0001111100101101110011010100110011011010101000 01
Round=12 key=0101101101101100101111010001001001001100011110 01
Round=13 key=1101110110101101101011001000101110011001000100 00
Round=14 key=1101001010101110101011110000010110011100110000
Round=15 key=1111100110111110001001100111001000010100000010 0
Round=16 key=1110001101111100010111000010010100000100111010 0

Plaintext after rounds

10100010
00001111
11100011
01010000
01011100
11101111
01010011
00001110

Printing Ciphertext in int form

60   126   178   178   137   100   173   100

Ciphertext generated:

< ~ ² ² ‰ d d

---------DECRPTION------------

After initial permutation

1 0 1 0 0 0 1 0
0 0 0 0 1 1 1 1
1 1 1 0 0 0 1 1
0 1 0 1 0 0 0 0
0 1 0 1 1 1 0 0
1 1 1 0 1 1 1 1
0 1 0 1 0 0 1 1
0 0 0 0 1 1 1 0

Plaintext matrix after Decryption

0 1 1 0 0 0 1 1
0 1 1 0 1 1 1 1
0 1 1 0 1 1 0 1
0 1 1 1 0 0 0 0
0 1 1 0 1 0 0 1
0 1 1 1 0 1 0 0
0 1 1 0 0 1 0 0
0 1 1 1 0 1 0 0

After Decryption
compitdt

SUMMARY

This chapter discussed about different modes of operation which support the basic encryption algorithms. Depending upon the number of bits encrypted at a time, the encrypted algorithms can be categorised into two types—a stream cipher and a block cipher. When encryption algorithms process a block of data at a time and generate a block of data as a ciphertext, then it is called block cipher. Symmetric encryption ciphers/algorithms use a block of bits for processing. When an encryption algorithm processes a single bit of data at a time and generates a single bit of data as a ciphertext, then it is called stream cipher. RC4 is a stream cipher.

Feistel ciphers are block ciphers. In this cipher, the single plaintext block undergoes through different rounds repeatedly. Each round has number of transformations. After going through a number of rounds, the ciphertext is generated. Feistel structure is the building block for many block ciphers. The design of data encryption standard (DES) algorithm is based on Feistel structures. Data encryption standard (DES) is a block cipher. The key size for DES is 64 bits of which 56 bits are actually used as a key. The plaintext block used is of size 64 bits. There are total 16 rounds in DES. To break DES by brute force attack, maximum number of keys required is 2^{56} and DES had broken in 22 hours.

One of the versions of DES is double DES. The working of double DES is same as that of simple DES. Double DES suffers by meeting in the middle attack. The next version of DES is triple DES also known as 3DES. Triple DES uses three keys and encrypted the data three times. Brute force attack is difficult against triple DES. It is more secure algorithm than DES algorithm. We know that S-box provides confusion property to the DES. Large S-box provides more resistance to cryptanalysis. Due to a change in one bit of input, each bit in the output will change. This is called Avalanche effect. The S-box should achieve Avalanche effect.

Some ciphertexts are relatively easy for cryptanalysis. The keys used for generation of such ciphertexts are called weak keys. There are 16 keys which are recommended as weak key for DES algorithm.

EXERCISES

3.1 What is a block cipher? Explain various modes of the operation of block cipher.
3.2 What are the advantages of CTR mode?
3.3 What are the design parameters of Feistel cipher?
3.4 Explain the working of DES in detail.
3.5 Explain the key transformation in DES.
3.6 Discuss triple DES.
3.7 Explain the modes of operation in triple DES.
3.8 Discuss the design criteria for DES.
3.9 Explain differential cryptanalysis.
3.10 What is linear cryptanalysis?
3.11 Compare the modes of operation in triple DES and DES.
3.12 During the transmission of $C4$ (the fourth cipher block) an error in the 3rd bit occurred. How many plaintext blocks will be affected, if we are using:16-bit CFB mode for DES? Explain why?

3.13 Explain the detail functioning of the first round of DES algorithm for encryption with block diagram for the first round.

3.14 What type of security is provided by the CBC mode of operation in DES?

MULTIPLE CHOICE QUESTIONS

3.1 If one uses electronic code book (ECB) mode for the transition of data, which of the following is true?
   (a) A single bit error occurs in the fourth block will corrupt the decryption of that block only.
   (b) A single bit error occurs in the fourth block will corrupt the decryption of the fourth and fifth block.
   (c) A single bit error in the fourth block will corrupt the decryption of the fourth block and the next two blocks.
   (d) A single bit error in the fourth block will corrupt decryption of all blocks of the transmission.

3.2 In symmetric cryptography, which of the following MUST be true?
   (a) For encryption and decryption, same amount of time is required.
   (b) For encryption and decryption, different algorithms are used.
   (c) Cryptographic operations are one-way, and not reversible.
   (d) For encryption and decryption, the same key is used.

3.3 In asymmetric cryptography, which of the following MUST be true?
   (a) For encryption and decryption, different keys are used.
   (b) For encryption and decryption, different algorithms are used.
   (c) Cryptographic operations are one-way, and not reversible.
   (d) Time taken for encryption is much longer than decryption.

3.4 Ram and Sita share a secret key that is known by nobody else except Ram and Sita. Ram encrypts a message using secret key and send it to Sita. When Sita receives and decrypts the message, which of the following does she NOT know?
   (a) The message could have been created and send only by Ram
   (b) Nobody except herself and Ram can read the message
   (c) Both of the above
   (d) None of the above

3.5 Which type of ciphers ECB and CBC are?
   (a) Stream   (b) Block   (c) Field   (d) None of the above

3.6 Which of the following encryption algorithm uses 56-bit round key?
   (a) RSA   (b) AES   (c) IDEA   (d) DES

Answers

3.1 (d),   3.2 (a)   3.3 (c)   3.4 (b)   3.5 (b)   3.6 (b)

CHAPTER 4

Advanced Encryption Standard

4.1 INTRODUCTION

Data encryption suffers by brute force attack. Triple DES is the successor of DES and hard to break using brute force attack, but it is very slow. So, there is a need of algorithm which can provide strong resistance to cryptanalysis and it must be more efficient. Advanced encryption standard (AES) is also called Rijndael algorithm, emerges as the alternative option to triple DES. As triple DES takes more time, AES is the best alternative to it.

The National Institute of Standards and Technology (NIST) conducted a competition for a good encryption algorithm. NIST had selected the Rijndael algorithm developed by Joan Daemen and Vincent Rijmen from this competition. This algorithm is also known as AES. But AES is not exactly the Rijndael algorithm. Rijndael algorithm supports for a flexible plaintext block and key sizes. Key and block sizes for Rijndael are from 128 bits to 256 bits. This size is selected in multiple of 32 bits. AES is a symmetric block cipher like DES. AES supports for a variety of key sizes. It can use key lengths up to 256 bits, but generally uses the keys of length 128 bits, 192 bits or 256 bits. The number of rounds in AES is also variable depending upon the key size. AES is computationally more efficient as compared to triple DES. It is relatively easy to implement. So, AES is one of the strongest and efficient encryption algorithm. More security can be provided by selecting the key size of 256 bits. This makes cryptanalysis of AES more difficult. AES has a lot of flexibility for implementation due to its parallel and symmetric architecture. Government and private organisations use AES as encryption algorithm.

4.2 ADVANCED ENCRYPTION STANDARD (AES)

Any encryption can be selected using different criteria as:
- Resistant against all known attacks
- Time complexity and space complexity on different platforms
- Design simplicity

Before selecting AES as the encryption algorithm, it is compared with DES and triple DES. The analysis of its advantages and limitations are investigated with respect to DES and triple DES. For example, DES has 16 weak keys whereas AES resolved this problem of weak keys. The subkey generation in DES is linear operation whereas in AES it is non-linear operation. The key size for DES is 64 bits whereas in AES it is variable such as 128 bits, 192 bits or 256 bits. As compared to triple DES, AES is faster. This supports the claim of AES as a strong symmetric encryption algorithm over DES and triple DES.

4.3 OVERVIEW OF RIJNDAEL

NIST selected the Rijndael algorithm from the competition and was adopted in October 2000 as the advanced encryption system (AES). As DES is breakable by brute force attack, AES emerges as a strong encryption algorithm. Rijndael uses a variable number of rounds. The number of rounds depends on the key and block size as given in Table 4.1.

Table 4.1 AES key size

Key size/block size	Number of rounds
128 bits	10
192 bits	12
256 bits	14

AES algorithm design does not base on Feistel structure. It is based on linear transformation. Different transformations AES use are substitution which is a single byte at a time, permutation which is row wise, the mix column provides mixing of bytes column wise and round key addition. This transformation forms a state. A state defines the current condition of the block during encryption. A state is nothing but the block of 4 × 4 matrix of bytes which is currently being processed on. As each round is executed, a state change. Key is an array having 4 rows. The number of columns is dependent upon the key size.

Working of AES

The overall structure of AES shows that the input to AES is 128-bit block of plaintext. The key size is variable and it may be 128, 192 or 256 bits. The output generated is 128-bit ciphertext block. Both for encryption and decryption at a time, only one plaintext block is processed. The overall structure of AES is shown in Figure 4.1.

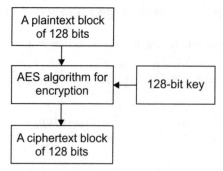

Figure 4.1 Overall block diagram of AES.

For a key size of 128 bits, there are 10 rounds in the AES. The internal structures of all the rounds are identical except last round. The working of AES begins with pre-round transformation step called *add round key* or *add subkey round*. Add subkey or add round key step followed by 10 rounds of which 9 rounds are identical in working than the tenth round. The first nine rounds have four steps each whereas last tenth round has only three steps. Mix column step is absent in the last round. Encryption and decryption process for AES is same except each step in decryption is the inverse of its corresponding step in the encryption. Working of AES is broadly shown in Figure 4.2.

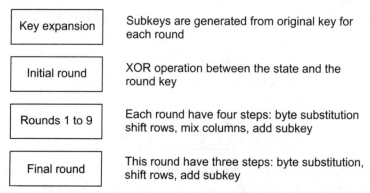

Figure 4.2 Structure of AES.

4.4 KEY GENERATION

The encryption of AES is initiated by XOR operation between the plaintext block and a key. AES has total 10 rounds for a 128-bit key. Therefore, total 11 subkeys are required for total encryption, one for initial round and ten for 10 rounds. These 11 subkeys are generated from the original key. One key have 128 bits or 16 bytes or 4 word length (a word = 32 bits = 4 bytes). These subkeys never be reused. The logic of subkey generation is designed in such a way that changes in one bit of a key, affects the subkeys of the several rounds. This provides confusion in the AES algorithm. The subkeys generation process has following steps:

Step 1 The key for AES is 128 bits or 16 bytes, i.e., 4-word key. This 16 bytes are arranged in the form of 4 × 4 matrix. The key matrix is an array of 4 × 4 bytes. That means every element of a matrix is a byte and not a bit. So, the first column of a matrix is filled by first 4 bytes or a word. The second column is filled by second 4 bytes, the third column filled by third 4 bytes and the last column is filled by last 4 bytes of a key. Let the key have bytes b_0 to b_{15}. The matrix looks as given below:

$$\begin{bmatrix} b_0 & b_4 & b_8 & b_{12} \\ b_1 & b_5 & b_9 & b_{13} \\ b_2 & b_6 & b_{10} & b_{14} \\ b_3 & b_7 & b_{11} & b_{15} \end{bmatrix}$$

$$\begin{bmatrix} w_0 & w_1 & w_2 & w_3 \end{bmatrix}$$

Each column stands as one word of key "w". Such as:

$w_0 = (b_0; \quad b_1; \quad b_2; \quad b_3)$
$w_1 = (b_4; \quad b_5; \quad b_6; \quad b_7)$
$w_2 = (b_8; \quad b_9; \quad b_{10}; \quad b_{11})$
$w_3 = (b_{12}; \quad b_{13}; \quad b_{14}; \quad b_{15})$

This is the key used for initial round. Subkey for the next round is generated from this key.

Step 2 Calculate $g[w_3]$ using following steps.
(a) Perform circular left shift of the bytes of w_3 (fourth word of a key).
(b) Perform substitution of the bytes using S-box.
(b) Add round constant (round constant depends on the particular round. It is explained later on in this section).

Step 3 Generation of round key for first round.
Perform XOR ($\oplus$) between w_0 and $g[w_3]$. The result is w_4.

$w_4 = w_0 \oplus g[w_3]$
$w_5 = w_1 \oplus w_4$
$w_6 = w_2 \oplus w_5$
$w_7 = w_3 \oplus w_6$

Therefore, the round key for first round is $[w_4, w_5, w_6, w_7]$. Repeat steps 1 to 3 above to generate the key for all the keys.

Pseudocode for the generation of subkeys for AES:

```
Subkeygeneration(byte b[16], skey w[44])
{
skey temp
for (i=0; i< 4; i++)
w[i] = (b[4*i], b[4*i + 1], b[4*i + 2], b[4*i + 3]);   // The first
four words is    filled by the original key
for (i=4; i< 44; i++)
```

```
{
    temp = w[i-1];                    //generation of remaining keys
    if (i % 4 = 0)
temp = substitutebyte(rotateword(temp)) XOR roundconstant[i/4];
w[i] = w[i-4] XOR temp;
}
}
```

4.4.1 Round Constant

To calculate $g(w)$, round constant is used. For each round, the fixed value is used so called round constant. Round constant is a word. The three rightmost bytes of the round constant are always zero. For each round, constant is different. It is defined as:

$$\text{Rcon}[i] = (\text{Rcon}[i], \quad 0, \quad 0, \quad 0)$$

Where $\text{Rcon}[1] = 1$, $\text{Rcon}[i] = 2 * \text{Rcon}[i-1]$

Multiplication is defined over Galois field multiplication. It can be implemented in lookup table as in Table 4.2.

Table 4.2 Lookup table

Round	Constant (hexadecimal)
1	01 00 00 00
2	02 00 00 00
3	04 00 00 00
4	08 00 00 00
5	10 00 00 00
6	20 00 00 00
7	40 00 00 00
8	80 00 00 00
9	1B 00 00 00
10	36 00 00 00

The detail structure of AES for encryption and decryption is shown in Figure 4.3. There are total 44 keys for one initial round and 10 rounds.

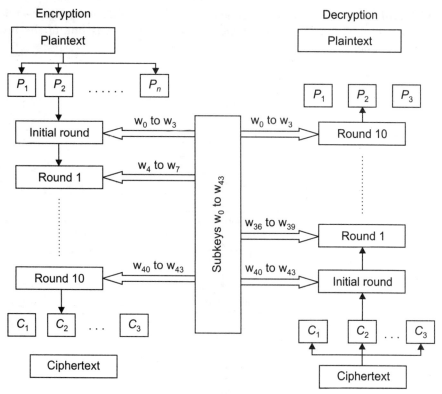

Figure 4.3 AES structure for 128-bit key.

4.5 ENCRYPTION

AES encrypt a block of 128 bits plaintext at a time. After the initial round, a plaintext block processes through ten rounds (assume key size of 128 bits). Each round has following four steps:

- *Byte substitution:* It is also called SubBytes step. In this step, substitution is done for original bytes. It is a single one byte-based substitution. This is a non-linear operation. Like DES, AES also uses S-box for substitution where each byte of a 128-bit block is substituted by a byte from the S-box.
- *Shift rows:* It is a simple transposition step which uses permutation of the bytes. In this step, rows are shifted left circularly based on row number. For plaintext block of sizes 128 and 192 bit, row n is shifted left circular $(n - 1)$ bytes where n is the row number. While for plaintext block of size 256 bits, row 2 is shifted left circular by 1 byte and rows 3 and 4 are shifted 2 bytes and 3 bytes, respectively. The first row remains unchanged.
- *Mix columns:* The four bytes of every column are mixed in a linear fashion. In this step, shift left and XOR operations are used with the round result. In this step, mixing of bytes is done. Matrix multiplication is performed using Galois field of multiplications. These provide both confusion and diffusion.

- *Add subkey:* A subkey for a particular round is XOR with the result of mix column step. This operation provides confusion which is one of the properties of strong encryption algorithm.

Figure 4.4 shows the details working of one single round of AES.

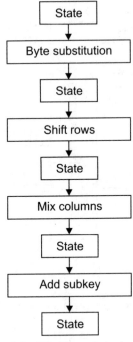

Figure 4.4 Working of single round.

An iteration of the above four steps is called a round. The input is firstly split into the blocks of size 128 bits each. Then pre-round transformation step called add round key or add subkey round is performed on this block. The XOR operation is performed between the subkey and the plaintext block. After this preprocessing the plaintext undergoes through different rounds. There are variable number of rounds depending on the key size as mentioned earlier. The working of all the rounds is similar except the last round. In the last round all other operations are performed except mix columns. This helps to make the algorithm reversible during decryption. The structure of Rijndael shows a high degree of modular design. Figure 4.4 shows the encryption process of AES for 10 rounds for a 128-bit key. From this figure, it is clear that there is no mix columns step on the last round.

Now, we discuss these steps in detail.

4.5.1 Initial Round

It is also called round 0. In this round, each byte of a block of plaintext and the each byte of original key is XOR. The output is called *state matrix*.

$$\begin{bmatrix} p_0 & p_4 & p_8 & p_{12} \\ p_1 & p_5 & p_9 & p_{13} \\ p_2 & p_6 & p_{10} & p_{14} \\ p_3 & p_7 & p_{11} & p_{15} \end{bmatrix} \oplus \begin{bmatrix} b_0 & b_4 & b_8 & b_{12} \\ b_1 & b_5 & b_9 & b_{13} \\ b_2 & b_6 & b_{10} & b_{14} \\ b_3 & b_7 & b_{11} & b_{15} \end{bmatrix} = \begin{bmatrix} s_0 & s_4 & s_8 & s_{12} \\ s_1 & s_5 & s_9 & s_{13} \\ s_2 & s_6 & s_{10} & s_{14} \\ s_3 & s_7 & s_{11} & s_{15} \end{bmatrix}$$

A block of plaintext   Key matrix   State matrix

Such that

$s_0 = p_0 \oplus b_0$
$s_1 = p_1 \oplus b_1$
$s_2 = p_2 \oplus b_2$
$s_3 = p_3 \oplus b_3$

and so on.

4.5.2 Round 1

Each round has following four steps:

(a) Byte substitution   (b) Shift rows
(c) Mix columns   (d) Add subkey

The operation of each round is shown in Figure 4.5.

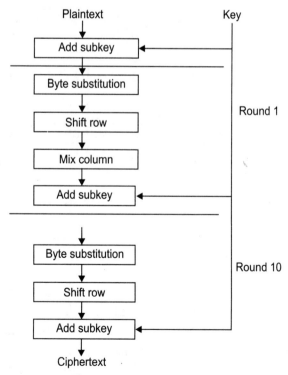

Figure 4.5 AES encryption.

Byte Substitution

The input to byte substitution state is the state matrix, i.e., the output of the previous state. For the first round, the output of initial round is the input for this step. In this step, each byte in the state matrix is replaced by the corresponding byte in S-box which is a 16 × 16 matrix. The unit place digit of a byte in the state matrix indicates column number and the tenth place digit indicates the row number. The intersection of row-column of S-box is the replacement digit to the digits in the state matrix. The numbers in S-box are hexadecimal. Suppose from the state matrix DB is the number, the unit place digit (B) indicates the column of the S-box and the digit at the tenth place (D) indicates the row of the S-box. So replace DB by the corresponding digit, i.e., B9 from the S-box. Following example shows the byte substitution for state matrix using the S-box shown in Table 4.3.

$$\begin{bmatrix} 24 & 02 & 54 & 48 \\ 65 & DB & 3C & 51 \\ 12 & 37 & 29 & A2 \\ 4E & 00 & 19 & 76 \end{bmatrix} = \begin{bmatrix} 36 & 77 & 20 & 52 \\ 4D & B9 & EB & D1 \\ C9 & 9A & A5 & 3A \\ 2F & 63 & D9 & 38 \end{bmatrix}$$

State matrix　　　　　　　Output

Table 4.3 S-box

		0	1	2	3	4	5	6	7	8	9	A	B	C	D	E	F
	0	63	7C	77	7B	F2	6B	6F	C5	30	01	67	2B	FE	D7	AB	76
	1	CA	82	C9	7D	FA	59	47	F0	AD	D4	A2	AF	9C	A4	72	C0
	2	B7	FD	93	26	36	3F	F7	CC	34	A5	E5	F1	71	D8	31	15
	3	04	C7	23	C3	18	96	05	9A	07	12	80	E2	EB	27	B2	75
	4	09	83	2C	1A	1B	6E	5A	A0	52	3B	D6	B3	29	E3	2F	84
	5	53	D1	00	ED	20	FC	B1	5B	6A	CB	BE	39	4A	4C	58	CF
	6	D0	EF	AA	FB	43	4D	33	85	45	F9	02	7F	50	3C	9F	A8
x	7	51	A3	40	8F	92	9D	38	F5	BC	B6	DA	21	10	FF	F3	D2
	8	CD	0C	13	EC	5F	97	44	17	C4	A7	7E	3D	64	5D	19	73
	9	60	81	4F	DC	22	2A	90	88	46	EE	B8	14	DE	5E	0B	DB
	A	E0	32	3A	0A	49	06	24	5C	C2	D3	AC	62	91	95	E4	79
	B	E7	C8	37	6D	8D	D5	4E	A9	6C	56	F4	EA	65	7A	AE	08
	C	BA	78	25	2E	1C	A6	B4	C6	E8	DD	74	1F	4B	BD	8B	8A
	D	70	3E	B5	66	48	03	F6	0E	61	35	57	B9	86	C1	1D	9E
	E	E1	F8	98	11	69	D9	8E	94	9B	1E	87	E9	CE	55	28	DF
	F	8C	A1	89	0D	BF	E6	42	68	41	99	2D	0F	B0	54	BB	16

In this step, each byte of the state is modified. This output is the state matrix for the next step. This provides the non-linearity in the algorithm which makes cryptanalysis difficult. For better security, S-box design is very important.

Shift Rows

In this step, the circular left shift is applied to the bytes of the output of byte substitution step. This step provides the scrambling of bytes in the state matrix. The first row of the state matrix is not shifted, it remains as it is. The second row is cyclically shifted left by one byte. The third row is cyclically shifted left by 2 bytes and the fourth row is cyclically shifted left by 3 bytes. In general n^{th} row is circular shifted left by $(n - 1)$ byte. Following example shows the shift row process in detail.

$$\begin{bmatrix} 36 & 77 & 20 & 52 \\ 4D & B9 & EB & D1 \\ C9 & 9A & A5 & 3A \\ 2F & 63 & D9 & 38 \end{bmatrix} = \begin{bmatrix} 36 & 77 & 20 & 52 \\ B9 & EB & D1 & 4D \\ A5 & 3A & C9 & 9A \\ 38 & 2F & 63 & D9 \end{bmatrix}$$

State matrix Output

Mix Columns

The output of the shift row step is used as a state matrix for this step. Here each column of the state matrix is processed separately. For this, one matrix having its elements 1 to 3 is selected for multiplication. Then the matrix multiplication is carried out between this selected matrix and the state matrix. Each byte of the output matrix is dependent on all the bytes of a column of the state matrix. The matrix multiplication uses GF of multiplication. Suppose the matrix selected for multiplication is as below:

$$\begin{bmatrix} 1 & 2 & 3 & 3 \\ 2 & 1 & 2 & 3 \\ 2 & 2 & 1 & 2 \\ 3 & 2 & 2 & 1 \end{bmatrix} \qquad \begin{bmatrix} s_0 & s_4 & s_8 & s_{12} \\ s_1 & s_5 & s_9 & s_{13} \\ s_2 & s_6 & s_{10} & s_{14} \\ s_3 & s_7 & s_{11} & s_{15} \end{bmatrix}$$

Selected matrix State matrix

The matrix multiplication is carried out as first row of selected matrix to the first column of the state matrix.

$$s_0 = (1 * s_0) \oplus (1 * s_1) \oplus (3 * s_2) \oplus (3 * s_3)$$
$$s_1 = (2 * s_0) \oplus (1 * s_1) \oplus (2 * s_2) \oplus (3 * s_3)$$
$$s_2 = (2 * s_0) \oplus (2 * s_1) \oplus (1 * s_2) \oplus (2 * s_3)$$
$$s_3 = (3 * s_0) \oplus (2 * s_1) \oplus (2 * s_2) \oplus (1 * s_3)$$

where s_0, s_1, s_2 and s_3 represent the first column of the output matrix. The multiplication is done using Galois field of multiplication. So, first take a look on Galois field of multiplication.

There are three numbers 1, 2 and 3 in the selected matrix. Following cases are arrived.

(i) If the multiplication of the elements in the state matrix is by 1, then the result is the same element. Suppose $1 * s_0$ then the result is s_0. For example, the binary number is 01111011, then $1 * 01111011 = 01111011$.

(ii) If the multiplication of the elements in the state matrix is by 2, convert the number into binary. For example, the number is $b_7b_6b_5b_4b_3b_2b_1b_0$. Then one of the following two cases are arising.

- If MSB of the binary number is 0 (i.e., bit b_7 is 0), then apply left shift to all the bits of that number by 1 position and LSB of the number is 0 (i.e., bit b_0 is 0). For example, the binary number is 01111011, then 2 * 01111011 = 11110110.
- If MSB of the binary number is 1 (i.e., bit b_7 is 1), then apply left shift to all the bits of that number by 1 position and LSB of the number is 0 (i.e., bit b_0 is 0). (Repeat *Step 1*) and perform XOR with 1B (i.e., 0001 1011).

For example: 02 * 85
02 * 85 = 1000 0101 [85]
Here B7 bit is 1
So shift left by 1 bit position and B0 = 0
0000 1010
Now, XOR this with 1B (0001 1011)

$$\begin{array}{r} 0000\ 1010 \\ 0001\ 1011 \\ \hline 0001\ 0001\ [11] \end{array}$$

(iii) If the multiplication of the elements in the state matrix is by 3 then convert the number into binary first. For example, the number is n, $(b_7b_6b_5b_4b_3b_2b_1b_0)$. The multiplication can be performed as below:

$$03 * n = n \text{ XOR } 02 * n$$

Also it can be shown as:

$$03 * (b_7b_6b_5b_4b_3b_2b_1b_0) = (b_7b_6b_5b_4b_3b_2b_1b_0) \text{ XOR } 02 * (b_7b_6b_5b_4b_3b_2b_1b_0)$$

03 · 7B can be written as:
7B ⊕ {02 * 7B}

$$7B = 0111\quad 1011$$
$$\{02 * 7B\} = 0111\quad 1011$$

Here b_7 bit is 0; apply left shift by 1 position and $b_0 = 0$

$$\{02 * 7B\} = 1111\quad 0110$$

7B ⊕ {02 * 7B} = (01111011) ⊕ (11110110)

$$\begin{array}{r} 0\,1\,1\,1\,1\,0\,1\,1 \\ \oplus\ 1\,1\,1\,1\,0\,1\,1\,0 \\ \hline 1\,0\,0\,0\,1\,1\,0\,1 \end{array}$$

03 · 7B = 8D

Suppose, the selected matrix and current state matrices are:

$$\begin{bmatrix} 1 & 2 & 3 & 3 \\ 2 & 1 & 2 & 3 \\ 2 & 2 & 1 & 2 \\ 3 & 2 & 2 & 1 \end{bmatrix} \qquad \begin{bmatrix} 36 & 77 & 20 & 52 \\ B9 & EB & D1 & 4D \\ A5 & 3A & C9 & 9A \\ 38 & 2F & 63 & D9 \end{bmatrix}$$

Selected matrix   State matrix

$(1 * 36) \oplus (2 * B9) \oplus (3 * A5) \oplus (3 * 38)$

$1 * 36 = 36 =$ **0011 0110**   (i)

$2 * B9 = 1011\ 1001$
          0111 0010   (shift left and LSB = 0)
      $\oplus$ 0001 1011   (As MSB is 1 (of B9) XOR 1B)
         0110 1001   (ii)

$3 * A5 = A5 \oplus (2 * A5)$

$2 * A5 = 1010\ 0101$
          0100 1010   (shift left and LSB = 0)
      $\oplus$ 0001 1011   (As MSB is 1 (of A5) XOR 1B)
         0101 0001

$A5 \oplus (2 * A5) = 1010\ 0101$
               $\oplus$ 0101 0001
                1111 0100   (iii)

$3 * 38 = 38 \oplus (2 * 38)$
$2 * 38 = 0011\ 1000$
        0111 0000   (shift left and LSB = 0; As MSB is 0, no need to XOR with 1B)

$38 \oplus (2 * 38) = 0011\ 1000$
            $\oplus$ 0111 0000
               0100 1000   (iv)

Now, perform XOR($\oplus$) of equation (i), (ii), (iii) and (iv).

    0011 0110
    0110 1001
    1111 0100
    0100 1000
    1110 0011   (D3)

$(1 * 36) \oplus (2 * B9) \oplus (3 * A5) \oplus (3 * 38) = D3$.
Therefore, the first element of the state matrix is D3.

(d) *Add subkey:* After mix column step, the result is XOR with the subkey generated. This step is similar to initial round. This completes the round 1. The result is the ciphertext after round 1. Repeat the same process for next 8 rounds (round 2 to 9). The last round (i.e., 10th round) does not have mix column step. Other steps are similar to the first round. The result of 10th round is the 128-bit ciphertext.

4.6 DECRYPTION

Decryption process of AES is similar to encryption. Unlike DES, the decryption algorithm of AES is different than the encryption algorithm. Only the inverse operations are used. The decryption process is started from inverse initial round.

4.6.1 Initial Round

It is similar to round 0 of encryption. In this round, the each byte of a block of plaintext is XOR with last four subkeys, i.e., w_{40}, w_{41}, w_{42} and w_{44}. The output is called state matrix.

$$\begin{bmatrix} c_0 & c_4 & c_8 & c_{12} \\ c_1 & c_5 & c_9 & c_{13} \\ c_2 & c_6 & c_{10} & c_{14} \\ c_3 & c_7 & c_{11} & c_{15} \end{bmatrix} \oplus \begin{bmatrix} b_0 & b_4 & b_8 & b_{12} \\ b_1 & b_5 & b_9 & b_{13} \\ b_2 & b_6 & b_{10} & b_{14} \\ b_3 & b_7 & b_{11} & b_{15} \end{bmatrix} = \begin{bmatrix} s_0 & s_4 & s_8 & s_{12} \\ s_1 & s_5 & s_9 & s_{13} \\ s_2 & s_6 & s_{10} & s_{14} \\ s_3 & s_7 & s_{11} & s_{15} \end{bmatrix}$$

A block of plaint   Key matrix   State matrix

Such that

$$s_0 = c_0 \oplus b_0$$
$$s_1 = c_1 \oplus b_1$$
$$s_2 = c_2 \oplus b_2$$
$$s_3 = c_3 \oplus b_3$$

and so on.

4.6.2 Round 1

The next step is the execution of rounds. The order of execution of the four steps is different from encryption. The nine rounds of the decryption algorithm consist of following 4 steps:

(a) Inverse shift rows
(b) Inverse byte substitution
(c) Add subkey
(d) Inverse mix columns

In the last round (tenth round) consists of first three steps. Inverse mix columns step is not carried out in the last round. The decryption process is explained step by step as given below:

Inverse Shift Rows

This is similar to shift row step of encryption but the only difference is that the byte are shifted towards right. In this step, the circular right shift is applied to the bytes of the state matrix. This step provides the scrambling of bytes in the state matrix as in encryption. The first row of the state matrix is not shifted, it remains as it is. The second row is cyclically shifted right by one byte. The third row is cyclically shifted right by 2 bytes and the fourth row is cyclically shifted right by 3 bytes. In general n^{th} row is circular shifted right by $(n - 1)$ byte. Following example shows the shift row process in detail.

$$\begin{bmatrix} 36 & 77 & 20 & 52 \\ 4D & B9 & EB & D1 \\ C9 & 9A & A5 & 3A \\ 2F & 63 & D9 & 38 \end{bmatrix} = \begin{bmatrix} 36 & 77 & 20 & 52 \\ B9 & EB & D1 & 4D \\ A5 & 3A & C9 & 9A \\ 38 & 2F & 63 & D9 \end{bmatrix}$$

State matrix   Output

Inverse Byte Substitution

This round is similar to byte substitution step for encryption. Only difference is that this step uses inverse S-box as in Table 4.4. The numbers in S-box are in hexadecimal. Here the column is determined by unit place digit, i.e., LHB (the least significant bit), and the row is determined by the tenth place digit, i.e., MSB (most significant bit) of the state matrix. For example, the value 5A is converted into 46 as given in inverse S-box. The inverse S-box is simply the S-box run in reverse. The following table represents Rijndael's inverse S-box.

Table 4.4 Inverse S-box

		0	1	2	3	4	5	6	7	8	9	A	B	C	D	E	F
	0	52	09	6A	D5	30	36	A5	38	BF	40	A3	9E	81	F3	D7	FB
	1	7C	E3	39	82	9B	2F	FF	87	34	8E	43	44	C4	DE	E9	CB
	2	54	7B	94	32	A6	C2	23	3D	EE	4C	95	0B	42	FA	C3	4E
	3	08	2E	A1	66	28	D9	24	B2	76	5B	A2	49	6D	8B	D1	25
	4	72	F8	F6	64	86	68	98	16	D4	A4	5C	CC	5D	65	B6	92
	5	6C	70	48	50	FD	ED	B9	DA	5E	15	46	57	A7	8D	9D	84
	6	90	D8	AB	00	8C	BC	D3	0A	F7	E4	58	05	B8	B3	45	06
x	7	D0	2C	1E	8F	CA	3F	0F	02	C1	AF	BD	03	01	13	8A	6B
	8	3A	91	11	41	4F	67	DC	EA	97	F2	CF	CE	F0	B4	E6	73
	9	96	AC	74	22	E7	AD	35	85	E2	F9	37	E8	1C	75	DF	6E
	A	47	F1	1A	71	1D	29	C5	89	6F	B7	62	0E	AA	18	BE	1B
	B	FC	56	3E	4B	C6	D2	79	20	9A	DB	C0	FE	78	CD	5A	F4
	C	1F	DD	A8	33	88	07	C7	31	B1	12	10	59	27	80	EC	5F
	D	60	51	7F	A9	19	B5	4A	0D	2D	E5	7A	9F	93	C9	9C	EF
	E	A0	E0	3B	4D	AE	2A	F5	B0	C8	EB	BB	3C	83	53	99	61
	F	17	2B	04	7E	BA	77	D6	26	E1	69	14	63	55	21	0C	7D

Add Subkey

After inverse S-box step, the result is XOR with the particular subkey of the round. This step is similar to initial round.

Inverse Mix Columns

Similar to encryption, same operation is to be performed.

4.7 GALOIS FIELD OF MULTIPLICATION

Multiplication of a value by 02 can be implemented as below:

If bit b_7 (MSB) is 0, then shift all the bits to the left by 1 position and bit b_0 (LSB) is 0. If bit b_7 is 1, then shift all the bits to the left by 1 position and write bit b_0 is 0 (step 1) and then the result performs XOR operation with 1B. Multiplication of a value by 03 to N can be implemented as N (XOR) $02 \cdot N$.

For example,

Multiplication of any value by 02

1. 02 * 53

$$53 = 0101\ 0011$$

Here b_7 bit is 0
Therefore, shift all the bits to the left by 1 position and write bit b_0 is 0, i.e.,

$$101\ 00110$$

Therefore, 02 * 53 = 1010 0110 = A6

2. 02 * 95

$$95 = 1001\ 0101$$

Here, b_7 bit is 1
Therefore, shift all the bits to the left by 1 position and write bit b_0 is 0, i.e.,

$$0010\ 1010$$

Now, XOR this with 1B (0001 1011)

```
         0 0 1 0 1 0 1 0
XOR      0 0 0 1 1 0 1 1
         ―――――――――――――――
         0 0 0 1 1 0 1 1
```

Multiplication of any value by 03 to $N = N$ (XOR) $02 \cdot N$

03·A4 can be written as:
A4 (XOR) {02 * A4}
A4 = 1010 0100
{02 * A4}
A4 = 1010 0100

Here, b_7 bit is 1

Advanced Encryption Standard

So, shift left by 1 bit position and B0 = 010 0 1000

$$\begin{array}{r} 0\,1\,0\,0\,1\,0\,0\,0 \\ \text{XOR}\ \underline{0\,0\,0\,1\,1\,0\,1\,1} \\ 0\,1\,0\,1\,0\,0\,1\,1 \end{array}$$

Therefore, {02 * A4} = 01010011 = 53

$$\begin{array}{r} 1\,0\,1\,0\,0\,1\,0\,0 \\ \text{XOR}\ \underline{0\,1\,0\,1\,0\,0\,1\,1} \\ 1\,1\,1\,1\,0\,1\,1\,1 \end{array}$$

03 · A4 = A4 (XOR) {02 * A4} = 11110111 = F7

Now, using GF multiplication we can solve the multiplication of state matrix and the output of shift row step.

2	3	1	1		95	90	89	F3
1	2	3	1		65	BF	67	C9
1	1	2	3		FD	B1	A6	6E
3	1	1	2		C3	92	70	FF

Here, multiplication is as shown below using GF multiplication.
Steps to solve 2 * 95 ⊕ 3 * 65 ⊕ 1 * FD ⊕ 1 * C3 = A0 are shown below:

2 * 95	3 * 65	1 * FD	1 * C3
95 = 10010101 b_7 = 1 therefore shift left by one position and place 0 at b_0 position we get 00101010 Now, 00101010 ⊕ with 1B	65 ⊕ (02 * 65) 65 = 0110 0101 b_7 = 0 therefore shift left by one position and place 0 at b_0 position we get 02 * 65 = 1100 1010	1 * FD = FD = 1111 1101	1 * C3 = C3 = 1100 0011
00101010 ⊕ 00011011	65 ⊕ (02 * 65) 0110 0101 ⊕ 1100 1010		
0011 0001	10101111	1111 1101	1100 0011
0011 0001 ⊕ 1010 1111 ⊕ 1111 1101 ⊕ 1100 0011			
1010 0000 = (A0)$_{16}$			

Steps to solve 2 * 90 ⊕ 3 * BF ⊕ 1 * B1 ⊕ 1 * 92 are shown below.

2 * 90	3 * BF = BF ⊕ (2 * BF)	1 * B1	1 * 92	

1001 0000
0010 0000
⊕ 0001 1011
	1011 1111
	0111 1110
	⊕ 0001 1011
		1011 0001	1011 0001	0011 1011
				⊕ 1101 1010
				   1011 0001
				   1011 0001

0011 1011	0110 0101 ⊕ 1011 1111			1100 0010
	1101 1010			C2

Steps to solve 2 * 89 ⊕ 3 * 67 ⊕ 1 * A6 ⊕ 1 * 70 are shown below.

2 * 89	3 * 67 = 67 ⊕ (2 * 67)	1 * A6	1 * 70	

1000 1001
0001 0010
⊕ 0001 1011
	0110 0111
	1100 1110
	⊕ 0110 0111
		1010 0110	0111 0000	0000 1001
				⊕ 1010 1001
				   1010 0110
				   0111 0000

0000 1001	1010 1001			0111 0110
				76

Steps to solve 2 * F3 ⊕ 3 * C9 ⊕ 1 * 6E ⊕ 1 * FF are shown below.

2 * F3	3 * C9 = C9 ⊕ (2 * C9)	1 * 6E	1 * FF	

1111 0011
1110 0110
⊕ 0001 1011
	1100 1001
	1001 0010
	⊕ 0001 1011
		0110 1110	1111 1111	1111 1101
				⊕ 1000 1001
				   0110 1110
				   1111 1111

1111 1101	1000 1001			1110 0101
				E5

Similarly, solve the other elements of the matrix, we get following state matrix.

A0	C2	76	E5
80	AF	C6	37
4F	FB	29	FC
A1	9A	A1	4C

4.8 ADVANTAGES OF AES

(i) Design of AES algorithm is simple.
(ii) AES supports for key of variable length.
(iii) AES supports for variable number of rounds.
(iv) Code for AES is small, so small amount of RAM is required.
(v) Parallel processing can be applied.

4.9 COMPARISON OF AES WITH OTHER CIPHERS

Comparison with DES

We know that the cryptanalysis of DES is easy and now it is not secure algorithm. DES having a plaintext block of 64 bits whereas AES uses 128-bit block of plaintext. The key size of DES is fixed and it is 64 bits but for AES key size is flexible and one can use 128 bits or 192 bits or 256 bits. The number of rounds of DES is fixed and it is 16 rounds whereas for AES, number of rounds may be 10 or 12 or 14. This number of rounds depends upon the key size. DES uses Feistel structure whereas AES does not use Feistel structure. AES uses substitution and mixing of bytes. Comparison of AES with DES is shown in Table 4.5.

Table 4.5 Comparison of AES and DES

	AES	DES
Block size (in bits)	128	64
Key size (in bits)	128, 192, 256	64 (actually 56 bits are used)
Rounds	10, 12, 14	16
Speed	High	Low
Encryption primitives	Substitution, shift, bit mixing	Substitution, permutation
Cryptographic primitives	Diffusion, confusion	Diffusion, confusion diffusion

Comparison with triple DES

Both triple DES and AES are symmetric block ciphers but triple DES uses Feistel cipher whereas AES uses substitution and mixing of bytes. The key size of triple DES is 192 bits as compared to 128 bits of AES. AES may use the key of size 128, 192 or 256 bits but the mostly use version of AES have a key length of 128 bits. Cryptanalysis of DES is easy as compared to AES. AES is faster than DES. So, AES is more secure as compared to triple DES. Comparison of AES with triple DES is shown in Table 4.6.

Table 4.6 Comparison of AES and triple DES

	AES	Triple DES
Type of algorithm	Symmetric block cipher	Symmetric Feistel structure
Key Length (in bits)	128, 192, 256	192
Rounds	10/12/14	48 (16 × 3)
Resource consumption	Low	Medium

SOLVED PROBLEMS

4.1 Generate the subkey for the first round of the AES algorithm. The key in hexadecimal is:
64 46 5A 65 82 AB 7C 73 4E 5B 47 8D 9A 12 35 57
w[0] = (64 46 5A 65);
w[1] = (82 AB 7C 73);

w[2] = (4E 5B 47 8D);
w[3] = (9A 12 35 57)

Find out g(w[3]):

w[3] = (9A 12 35 57)

Solution Circular byte left shift of w[3]: (12 35 57, 9A)
Byte substitution (S-box): (C9, 96, 5B, B8)
Adding round constant (01; 00; 00; 00)
gives: g(w[3]) = (C8, 96, 5B, B8)

w[0]	0110 0100	0100 0110	0101 1010	0110 0101
⊕ g(w[3])	1100 1000	1001 0110	0101 1011	1011 1000
w[4]	1010 1100 (AC)	1101 0000 (D0)	0000 0001 (01)	1101 1101 (DD)

w[4] = w[0] ⊕ g(w[3]) = (AC D0 01 DD)
w[5] = w[4] ⊕ w[1] = (2E 7B 7D AE)
w[6] = w[5] ⊕ w[2] = (60 20 3A 23)
w[7] = w[6] ⊕ w[3] = (FA 32 0F 74)

First round key:

AC D0 01 DD 2E 7B 7D AE 60 20 3A 23 FA 32 0F 74

4.2 The key in hexadecimal:

41 50 47 41 41 4d 4b 53 4b 50 53 53 50 41 42 58

The plaintext in hexadecimal:

47 48 41 54 45 4d 55 4c 49 4b 44 53 52 42 48 55

Solution Round keys for all rounds are shown below.

Round	Key				Round	Key			
Round 0	C3	7C	2D	12	Round 3	90	FF	E	F1
	82	31	66	41		8F	50	B1	F9
	C9	61	35	12		AD	26	A6	A7
	99	20	77	4A		2B	A9	6E	1C
Round 1	76	89	FB	FC	Round 4	53	60	92	0
	F4	B8	9D	BD		DC	30	23	F9
	3D	D9	A8	AF		71	16	85	A7
	A4	F9	DF	ES		5A	BF	EB	BB
Round 2	EB	17	22	B5	Round 5	7B	89	78	BE
	1F	AF	BF	8		A7	B9	5B	47
	22	76	17	A7		D6	AF	DE	E0
	86	8F	C8	42		8C	10	35	5B

Advanced Encryption Standard

Round 6	F1	1F	41	DA	Round 9	69	DF	D7	55
	56	A6	1A	9D		14	97	55	1A
	80	9	C4	7D		1A	CE	BF	91
	C	19	F1	26		6B	9F	CC	F8
Round 7	A5	BE	B6	24	Round 10	6	18	6	15
	F3	18	AC	B9		4	0	1E	1F
	73	11	68	C4		2	1B	17	0
	7F	8	99	E2		2	3	A	D
Round 8	8E	50	2E	F6					
	7D	48	82	4F					
	E	59	EA	8B					
	71	51	73	69					

The plaintext matrix

$$\begin{bmatrix} 47 & 45 & 49 & 52 \\ 48 & 4D & 4B & 42 \\ 41 & 55 & 44 & 48 \\ 54 & 4C & 53 & 55 \end{bmatrix}$$

Round 1
$$\begin{bmatrix} 6F & F2 & 77 & 77 \\ AD & 63 & AF & 7B \\ 6F & 72 & F0 & 67 \\ 59 & C0 & 63 & D7 \end{bmatrix} \begin{bmatrix} 6F & F2 & 77 & 77 \\ 63 & AF & 7B & AD \\ F0 & 67 & 6F & 72 \\ D7 & 59 & C0 & 63 \end{bmatrix} \begin{bmatrix} 5C & 2B & CC & 13 \\ 75 & 47 & F0 & C3 \\ 95 & 78 & 89 & 9B \\ 97 & 77 & 16 & 80 \end{bmatrix} \begin{bmatrix} 9F & 9 & B8 & 85 \\ A9 & 76 & 1E & 36 \\ 5 & 91 & BC & 4 \\ 8A & E3 & EC & CA \end{bmatrix}$$

Round 2
$$\begin{bmatrix} DB & D3 & 6B & 7E \\ 1 & 38 & 81 & 11 \\ 6C & 72 & 65 & CE \\ 97 & 5 & F2 & 74 \end{bmatrix} \begin{bmatrix} DB & D3 & 6B & 7E \\ 38 & 81 & 11 & 1 \\ 65 & CE & 6C & 72 \\ 74 & 97 & 5 & F2 \end{bmatrix} \begin{bmatrix} F4 & 7C & 8C & 7F \\ 70 & 14 & F8 & 18 \\ B5 & 77 & AD & 96 \\ C3 & 14 & CA & E \end{bmatrix} \begin{bmatrix} 82 & F9 & 4E & 3F \\ 88 & AC & EA & A9 \\ B1 & 21 & 5 & 65 \\ DB & E1 & 49 & EB \end{bmatrix}$$

Round 3
$$\begin{bmatrix} 13 & C4 & C8 & B9 \\ 99 & 91 & FD & F8 \\ 2F & 87 & 6B & 3B \\ 75 & D3 & 4D & E9 \end{bmatrix} \begin{bmatrix} 13 & C4 & C8 & B9 \\ 91 & FD & F8 & 99 \\ 6B & 3B & 2F & 87 \\ E9 & 75 & D3 & 4D \end{bmatrix} \begin{bmatrix} C & C1 & 64 & 13 \\ 7E & 1D & 81 & 4F \\ 74 & D0 & 15 & E2 \\ 6 & 7B & 29 & 54 \end{bmatrix} \begin{bmatrix} E7 & 69 & 56 & B3 \\ DE & B2 & 6F & 73 \\ 46 & F7 & 17 & 8E \\ 95 & C0 & 2A & 16 \end{bmatrix}$$

Round 4
$$\begin{bmatrix} 94 & 1D & 5A & 2A \\ F9 & 37 & 68 & BA \\ B1 & A8 & F0 & E5 \\ 6D & 8F & 19 & 47 \end{bmatrix} \begin{bmatrix} 94 & 1D & 5A & 2A \\ 37 & 68 & BA & F9 \\ F0 & E5 & B1 & A8 \\ 47 & 6D & 8F & 19 \end{bmatrix} \begin{bmatrix} DD & A & 5F & F5 \\ B6 & 94 & 72 & 39 \\ 91 & 13 & 13 & B3 \\ EE & 70 & E0 & 1D \end{bmatrix} \begin{bmatrix} 4D & 49 & 9F & 1F \\ 85 & C4 & A2 & 89 \\ F2 & 54 & B5 & BE \\ DE & 90 & DD & 1 \end{bmatrix}$$

Round 5	$\begin{bmatrix} E3 & 97 & 89 & 1D \\ 3B & 1C & 20 & 60 \\ DB & 3A & D5 & C1 \\ C0 & A7 & AE & 7C \end{bmatrix}$	$\begin{bmatrix} E3 & 97 & 89 & 1D \\ 1C & 20 & 60 & 3B \\ D5 & C1 & DB & 3A \\ 7C & C0 & A7 & AE \end{bmatrix}$	$\begin{bmatrix} 50 & 54 & D5 & E3 \\ C3 & 4F & 98 & 8B \\ CA & 75 & B6 & BB \\ F & D8 & 6E & 61 \end{bmatrix}$	$\begin{bmatrix} 3 & A3 & 58 & F \\ 88 & 7F & 56 & 21 \\ A4 & 8E & 33 & C9 \\ B8 & 34 & 50 & DA \end{bmatrix}$
Round 6	$\begin{bmatrix} 7B & C4 & 49 & 56 \\ A & D2 & 19 & 18 \\ 6A & B1 & C3 & 53 \\ 76 & FD & DD & 57 \end{bmatrix}$	$\begin{bmatrix} 7B & C4 & 49 & 56 \\ D2 & 19 & 18 & A \\ C3 & 53 & 6A & B1 \\ 57 & 76 & FD & DD \end{bmatrix}$	$\begin{bmatrix} F & 9D & 2D & DE \\ CD & 75 & 3A & 57 \\ CD & E1 & 99 & 59 \\ 32 & F1 & 48 & e0 \end{bmatrix}$	$\begin{bmatrix} 74 & 44 & B5 & 8C \\ 3A & CC & BA & B6 \\ FB & 95 & 47 & A8 \\ 52 & 47 & 6C & BB \end{bmatrix}$
Round 7	$\begin{bmatrix} 92 & 80 & F & 64 \\ 1B & 4B & 2A & A0 \\ D5 & F4 & A0 & 50 \\ 64 & 4E & C2 & EA \end{bmatrix}$	$\begin{bmatrix} 92 & 80 & F & 64 \\ 4B & 2A & A0 & 1B \\ A0 & 50 & D5 & F4 \\ EA & 64 & 4E & C2 \end{bmatrix}$	$\begin{bmatrix} A8 & 51 & 7E & 1B \\ 15 & 40 & 7E & F3 \\ A7 & A6 & CC & B5 \\ 89 & 29 & F8 & 70 \end{bmatrix}$	$\begin{bmatrix} 59 & A & E6 & 53 \\ 7 & E6 & BC & B4 \\ FE & 77 & 8 & 85 \\ 17 & EA & 44 & 56 \end{bmatrix}$
Round 8	$\begin{bmatrix} CB & C5 & BB & F0 \\ 67 & 8E & F5 & 87 \\ 8E & 65 & 30 & 1B \\ ED & 8D & 97 & B1 \end{bmatrix}$	$\begin{bmatrix} CB & C5 & BB & F0 \\ 8E & F5 & 87 & 67 \\ 30 & 1B & 8E & 65 \\ B1 & ED & 8D & 97 \end{bmatrix}$	$\begin{bmatrix} 85 & 63 & FC & A0 \\ 2D & F4 & AA & 6 \\ ED & 2A & B7 & FF \\ 81 & 7B & DE & 3C \end{bmatrix}$	$\begin{bmatrix} 20 & 93 & 5B & A5 \\ 90 & EC & 86 & C2 \\ 8F & BB & DF & 1A \\ DF & E & 66 & DE \end{bmatrix}$
Round 9	$\begin{bmatrix} B7 & 60 & 73 & 9E \\ DC & CE & EA & AB \\ 39 & 44 & 9E & 33 \\ 6 & 25 & A2 & 1 \end{bmatrix}$	$\begin{bmatrix} B7 & 60 & 73 & 9E \\ CE & EA & AB & DC \\ 9E & 33 & 39 & 44 \\ 1D & 6 & 25 & A2 \end{bmatrix}$	$\begin{bmatrix} BF & D0 & 1C & BE \\ 94 & FC & 50 & 53 \\ 79 & E6 & C5 & 37 \\ A8 & 75 & 4D & 7E \end{bmatrix}$	$\begin{bmatrix} 31 & C4 & 57 & 5E \\ AD & B4 & 64 & 3A \\ 12 & 9 & 2F & C6 \\ CF & 2 & 44 & 17 \end{bmatrix}$
Round 10	$\begin{bmatrix} C7 & 95 & C9 & 8A \\ 1C & 8D & 1 & 77 \\ 5B & 43 & 15 & 1B \\ 58 & 80 & B4 & F0 \end{bmatrix}$	$\begin{bmatrix} C7 & 95 & C9 & 8A \\ 8D & 1 & 77 & 1C \\ 15 & 1B & 5B & 43 \\ F0 & 58 & 80 & B4 \end{bmatrix}$		$\begin{bmatrix} AE & 52 & C2 & A5 \\ 81 & 96 & 4E & 42 \\ D3 & B9 & E4 & 11 \\ E1 & 83 & 8F & 4C \end{bmatrix}$

Cipher text generated

AE 52 C2 A5 81 96 4E 42 D3 B9 E4 11 E1 83 8F 4C

4.3 The key in hexadecimal:

54 48 41 41 47 52 42 41 43 43 48 41 50 41 4E 44

The plaintext in hexadecimal:

41 4D 49 53 48 49 4A 41 59 4E 49 4B 4E 41 56 4E

Solution Round keys for all rounds:

Advanced Encryption Standard

Round	Key				Round	Key			
Round 0	54	48	41	41	Round 6	72	49	BA	F3
	47	52	42	41		3D	3E	BE	BA
	43	43	48	41		6E	F3	BD	80
	50	41	4E	44		D9	FC	C8	BF
Round 1	D6	67	5A	12	Round 7	82	A1	82	C6
	91	35	18	53		BF	9F	3C	7C
	D2	76	50	12		D1	6C	81	FC
	82	37	1E	56		8	90	49	43
Round 2	4E	15	EB	1	Round 8	62	9A	98	F6
	DF	20	F3	52		DD	5	A4	8A
	D	56	A3	40		C	69	25	76
	8F	61	BD	16		4	F9	6C	35
Round 3	A5	6F	AC	72	Round 9	E0	CA	E	4
	7A	4F	5F	20		3D	CF	AA	8E
	77	19	FC	60		31	A6	8F	F8
	F8	78	41	76		35	5F	E3	CD
Round 4	11	EC	94	33	Round 10	19	DB	B3	92
	6B	A3	CB	13		24	14	19	1C
	1C	BA	37	73		15	B2	96	E4
	E4	C2	76	5		20	ED	75	29
Round 5	24	D4	FF	5A					
	4F	77	34	49					
	53	CD	3	3A					
	B7	F	75	3F					

The plaintext matrix

$$\begin{bmatrix} 41 & 48 & 59 & 4E \\ 4D & 49 & 4E & 41 \\ 49 & 4A & 49 & 56 \\ 53 & 41 & 4B & 4E \end{bmatrix}$$

Add subkey

$$\begin{bmatrix} 15 & F & 1A & 1E \\ 5 & 1B & D & 0 \\ 8 & 8 & 1 & 18 \\ 12 & 0 & A & A \end{bmatrix}$$

Round	Byte substitution	Shift rows	Mix columns	Add subkey
Round 1	59 76 A2 72 6B AF D7 63 30 30 7V D C9 63 67 67	59 76 A2 72 AF D7 63 6B 7C AD 30 30 67 C9 63 67	43 EA A9 E FF E6 57 93 A7 A0 4 D0 F6 69 68 3	95 7B 7B 8C 98 D3 21 A4 FD B8 54 CE E4 3A 7A 55
Round 2	2A 21 21 64 46 66 FD 49 54 6C 20 8B 69 80 DA FC	2A 21 21 64 66 FD 49 46 20 8B 54 6C FC 69 80 DA	22 BC 4D B4 7A 2F CF 86 13 6A 5B 8F DB C7 65 29	6C 63 40 3B 6F F 99 E7 F8 99 F8 32 DA 95 25 3F
Round 3	50 FB 9 E2 A8 76 EE 94 41 EE 41 23 57 2A 3F 75	50 FB 9 E2 76 EE 94 A8 41 23 41 EE 75 57 2A 3F	E B0 DE ED A E D3 BF 3B AA 61 CC 2D 75 9A 5	AB CA A9 15 65 41 CA C7 97 F5 9D 8D 5F 55 FA 73
Round 4	62 74 D3 59 4D 83 74 C6 88 E6 5E 5D CF FC 2D 8F	62 74 D3 59 83 74 C6 4D 5E 5D 88 E6 8F CF FC 2D	8B E6 98 AE 12 B4 3B DF D7 F0 1 B4 7E 30 C3 1A	9A 8D 84 4A FE 17 81 1D 43 3B 36 C2 4D 23 B0 1F
Round 5	B8 5D 5F D6 BB F0 C A4 1A E2 5 25 E3 26 E7 C0	B8 5D 5F D6 F0 C A4 BB 5 25 1A E2 C0 E3 26 E7	A5 68 75 64 8C C9 4 61 19 25 A5 80 BD 13 13 ED	81 27 26 D3 58 BE C9 6E E6 11 A6 F5 E7 5A 29 D2
Round 6	C CC F7 66 6A AE DD 9F 8E 82 24 E6 94 BE A5 B5	C CC F7 66 AE DD 9F 6A 24 E6 8E 82 B5 94 BE A5	60 8D 7F 55 92 C8 E5 8A 2E 61 B6 E7 EF 47 74 13	12 B0 11 8C DB F6 16 76 A4 DF B 2F 1C FD F4 AC
Round 7	C9 E7 82 64 B9 42 47 38 49 9E 2B 15 9C 54 BF 91	C9 E7 82 64 42 47 38 B9 2B 15 49 9E 91 9C 54 BF	F5 95 4A 39 A1 CA 7D B 75 35 D4 20 10 43 44 EE	77 2A 9B 31 0 55 11 9B F7 9 55 69 D6 3F B8 AD
Round 8	F5 E5 14 C7 63 FC 82 14 68 1 FC F9 F6 75 6C 95	F5 E5 14 C7 FC 82 14 63 FC F9 68 1 95 F6 75 6C	87 43 9 5D 9C 1C F1 6E 4E 8F 4F 12 35 B8 AA E8	E5 9E 5 59 6 19 98 97 D6 2B 6A 7E C3 32 DC DD
Round 9	D9 B 6B CB 6F D4 46 88 F6 F1 2 F3 2E 23 86 C1	D9 B 6B CB D4 46 88 6F 2 F3 F6 F1 C1 2E 23 86	D 1 80 4B AD A7 42 9B 51 C2 71 CC 3F F4 85 CF	ED 3C B1 7E 67 68 E4 C4 5F 68 FE 2F 3B 7A 7D 2
Round 10	55 EB C8 F3 85 45 69 1C CF 45 BB 15 E2 DA FF 77	55 EB C8 F3 45 69 1C 85 BB 15 CF 45 77 E2 DA FF		4C CF DD D3 9E 7D AE 68 8 C 59 30 E5 FE 3E D6

Cipher text generated

4C CF DD D3 9E 7D AE 68 8 C 59 30 E5 FE 3E D6

SUMMARY

Advanced encryption standard (AES) is a symmetric block cipher. The key length for AES is variable such as 128, 192 or 256 bits. For the AES, weak or semi-weak keys have not been identified. AES algorithm design is based on linear transformation. There are variable number of rounds. For a key size of 128 bits, there are ten rounds in the AES. AES encrypts a block of 128 bits plaintext at a time. After the initial round, a plaintext block process through ten rounds (assume key size of 128 bits). Each round has four steps: byte substitution, shift rows, mix columns, and add subkey. The last round does not have mix column step. Decryption process of AES is similar to encryption. Unlike DES, the decryption algorithm of AES is different than the encryption algorithm. Only the inverse operations are used. The decryption process is started from inverse initial round. The nine rounds of the decryption algorithm consist of 4 steps: inverse shift rows, inverse byte substitution, add subkey and inverse mix columns. AES code is small in size so can be used for smartcard applications. Parallel implementation of round is possible so faster than triple DES. It is more secure than triple DES.

EXERCISES

4.1 Which were the criteria used for the analysis of AES?

4.2 What is the key size used by Rijndael if the number of rounds is 10?

4.3 Which are the four stages in each round of AES?

4.4 Describe the Rijndael S-box.

4.5 Discuss the advantages and limitations of Rijndael.

4.6 Compare AES with DES.

4.7 Compare AES with triple DES.

4.8 Is AES more secure to attack than DES? Justify your answer.

4.9 Using mix columns, solve the following multiplication.

4.10 Shift the following matrix using the shift rows step in AES.

4.11 Compute the 0th and the first 4×4 round key matrices w[0,3] and w[4,7] produced by the key expansion procedure in an AES algorithm when all the bits of 128-bit key is ones.

4.12 How is diffusion across S-boxes provided in the AES encryption function? Briefly explain the diffusion-related operations and their roles.

4.13 What are the four basic operations in the AES round function? Which are responsible for confusion? Which are responsible for diffusion?

MULTIPLE CHOICE QUESTIONS

4.1 If the key size is 24 bytes in AES, what would be the number of rounds?
    (a) 10
    (b) 12
    (c) 15
    (d) 14

4.2 If the key size is 32 bytes in AES, what would be the number of rounds?
    (a) 10
    (b) 12
    (c) 15
    (d) 14

4.3 In the last round of AES, which of the following step is absent?
    (a) Shift row
    (b) Mix columns
    (c) Byte substitution
    (d) Add subkey

Answers

    4.1 (b)   **4.2** (d)   **4.3** (b)

CHAPTER 5

Symmetric Ciphers

5.1 INTRODUCTION

In the last two chapters, we learn two symmetric encryption ciphers: DES and AES. There are many other symmetric encryption ciphers. In this chapter, we are going to discuss symmetric encryption ciphers such as Blowfish, RC4, RC5, RC6 and IDEA. RC4 is a stream cipher whereas Blowfish, RC5, RC6 and IDEA are block ciphers.

5.2 BLOWFISH ENCRYPTION ALGORITHM

Another encryption algorithm is Blowfish algorithm. It is a symmetric encryption block cipher. It is based on Feistel structure. Bruce Schneier designed it in 1993 as an alternative to DES and IDEA algorithm. Blowfish uses the plaintext block of 64 bits length and variable key length from 32 bits to 448 bits. It is unpatented algorithm.

Characteristics of Blowfish algorithm:

- A symmetric block cipher with 64-bit plaintext block.
- Key length is variable and it is from 32 bits to 448 bits.
- Stronger and faster than contemporary ciphers such as DES and IDEA.
- Less memory is required and easy for implementation.
- It is unpatented and so freely available.

The working of Blowfish algorithm is divided into following two parts:

1. Key expansion
2. Encryption

The important feature of Blowfish is its key scheduling. The eighteen subkeys are generated from the original key. Even shortkeys can be used for Blowfish.

The cryptanalysis of the keys for this algorithm is difficult. The beauty of Blowfish algorithm architecture is the use of round keys, the S-boxes, and number of iterations. This makes Blowfish stronger and faster than contemporary ciphers such as DES and IDEA.

5.2.1 Key Expansion

Blowfish needs eighteen subkeys for encryption. Same subkeys are used for decryption. These keys are generated by processing the original key having maximum length 448 bits. During encryption, the original key is converted into eighteen subkeys having total 4168 bytes. There are two arrays: key-array and S-boxes as shown in Figure 5.1. The key-array consists of eighteen subkeys of length 32 bits each. The subkeys are K_1, K_2, ..., K_{18}. All the boxes are initialised with a fixed string.

1. The key-array consists of 18 subkeys of 32 bits each such as: K_1, K_2, ..., K_{18}.
2. There are four S-boxes such as S_1, S_2, S_3 and S_4. The size of each S-box is 32 bits. In each S-box there are total 256 entries as from 0 to 255.

$$S_{1,0}, S_{1,1}, ..., S_{1,255}$$
$$S_{2,0}, S_{2,1}, ..., S_{2,255}$$
$$S_{3,0}, S_{3,1}, ..., S_{3,255}$$
$$S_{4,0}, S_{4,1}, ..., S_{4,255}$$

The key generation process for the Blowfish algorithm is as follows:

Step 1 Initialise the key-array first and then the four S-boxes, with the fixed hexadecimal digits.
$$K_1 = 0 \times 243f6a88$$
$$K_2 = 0 \times 85a308d3$$
$$K_3 = 0 \times 13198a2e$$
$$K_4 = 0 \times 03707344$$

Step 2 The first 32 bits of the original key are XOR with the first 32 bits of the key-array, i.e., K_1. The second 32 bits of the original key are XOR with the second 32 bits of the key-array, i.e., K_2. Repeat this for all the entries of the key-array is XOR with the original key. There is at least one equivalent longkey for every shortkey. For example, suppose the shortkey is X, there may be equivalent longkeys as XX, XXX, XXXX, etc.

Step 3 Use the above subkeys to encrypt (using Blowfish algorithm) all-zero string.

Step 4 Replace K_1 and K_2 with the output of Step 3.

Step 5 Use these modified subkeys to encrypt (using Blowfish algorithm) the output of Step 3.

Step 6 Replace K_3 and K_4 with the output of Step 5.

Step 7 Continue the above process. Replace all entries of the K-array, and then all S-boxes with the changing output of the algorithm.

Total 521 iterations are required for the generation of eighteen subkeys. Generation of subkeys needs large memory. The same subkey can be used for next time so it is important to store these subkeys. This required memory for storage. Due to this requirement, Blowfish is not suitable for applications where frequently changes in keys are required.

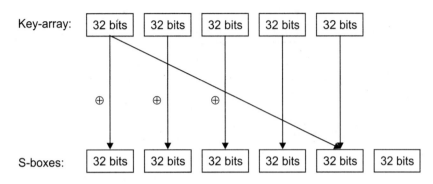

Figure 5.1 Subkeys generation.

5.2.2 Encryption

The Blowfish algorithm has sixteen rounds. First divide the plaintext into a block of 64 bits. Then each block of plaintext is divided into two halves: left part and right part. The left part undergoes the "f" function. This is opposite to DES, where the "f" function is applied to the right half of the block. The result is XOR with the right half of the block. The working of each round has following steps:

Step 1 Left half of the plaintext block is XOR with the subkey for that particular round.

Step 2 Apply the f-function to the output of first step.

Step 3 The result of second step XOR with the right half of the plaintext block.

Step 4 The result of Step 3 is shifted as left half for the next step and the output of the first step is shifted as right half for the next step.

Repeat above steps for all sixteen rounds. At the end of sixteenth round the 17th subkeyis XOR with the right half and the 18th subkey is XOR with the left half. Then interchange the right and left halves. Concatenate the left and right half to get the ciphertext. Each round uses one subkey for XOR operation with the left half. The "f" function uses S-boxes which are dependent on the key. The use of addition and bitwise XOR operations make the cryptanalysis of Blowfish more difficult.

The architecture of Blowfish for encryption is shown in Figure 5.2.

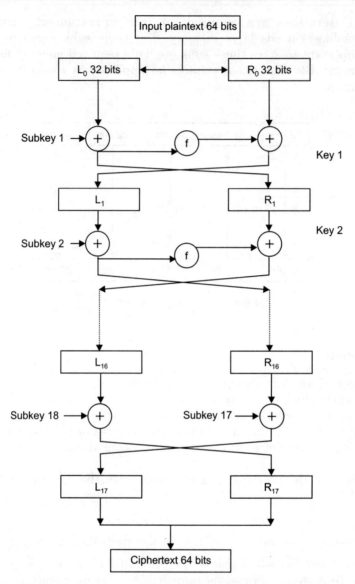

Figure 5.2 Architecture of Blowfish algorithm for encryption.

Decryption follows the same procedure as encryption. The subkeys are used in the reverse order of encryption. First round uses 18th subkey and the first and second subkeys are used after the last round. The function "f" and S-boxes are same as encryption. The architecture of Blowfish for decryption process is shown in Figure 5.3.

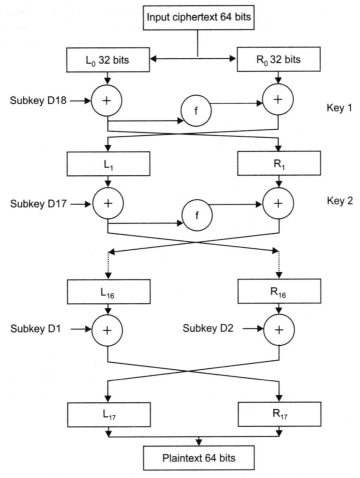

Figure 5.3 Architecture of Blowfish for decryption.

5.2.3 Blowfish Architecture

The architecture of Blowfish algorithm depends on the Feistel structure. Like DES, Blowfish also have 16 rounds with 18 subkeys. There are one subkey for each round and two subkeys are used after the last round. Here the subkeys are used to perform XOR with the left part of the plaintext in each round whereas the output of the last round, each part is XOR separately with the last two subkeys respectively. Blowfish uses four S-boxes. The S-boxes are used to convert the 8-bit input into 32-bit output. The output of the last round is XOR in such a way that left part is XOR with the 17th subkey and right part is XOR with the 18th subkey. The output of these XOR is concatenating to get the ciphertext.

Figure 5.4 shows the architecture of Blowfish's f-function. The left 32-bit plaintext block after XOR with key is the input for S-boxes. This 32-bit input is split into four groups. Each group have 8 bits each. There are four S-boxes, one for each group. For each S-box, the output is 32 bit. Then addition modulo 2^{32} is carried out for all the four outputs of the S-boxes and then XOR operation is performed which produce the 32-bit output.

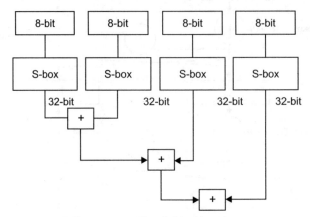

Figure 5.4 Blowfish's f-function.

5.2.4 Cryptanalysis of Blowfish

Blowfish algorithm is more secure against the cryptanalysis. There is no known cryptanalysis attack against Blowfish algorithm. Vaudenay found a known plaintext attack in 1996 against Blowfish. This requires 2^{8n+1} known plaintexts to break this algorithm, where n is the number of rounds. But for $n = 16$ rounds, this attack is not successful. He also claims about some weakkeys for Blowfish. Blowfish is suitable for applications having small plaintext but for large plaintext it may not be suitable algorithm.

5.3 RC5

One more block cipher algorithm is RC5. It is a symmetric encryption algorithm. It is designed by Prof. Ronald Rivest of MIT in 1994. RC5 architecture is based on the Feistal structure. It is a parameterised algorithm such as *w/r/b* parameters. Where *w* is word size in bits, *r* is number of rounds and *b* is number of bytes in the secret key K. It is a very fast algorithm. RC5 uses rotation of bits which is data dependent and mixture of different operations. This makes linear and differential cryptanalysis of RC5 more difficult.

RC5 has the variable number of rounds. Also it uses the plaintext block and the key of variable length. The number of rounds used by RC5 may be from 1 to 255. The plaintext block may be of size: 32 bits, 64 bits or 128 bits. RC5 uses the key of size from 0 to 2048 bits. If the plaintext block is of size of 64 bits then the key of size of 28 bits is recommended. The variability in number of rounds, block size and the key length provide flexibility in the working of RC5 algorithm. This helps to provide suitable security to RC5. User can select the number of rounds, size of plaintext block and the key length as per his/her requirements depending on the applications.

RC5 encryption is shown in Figure 5.5.

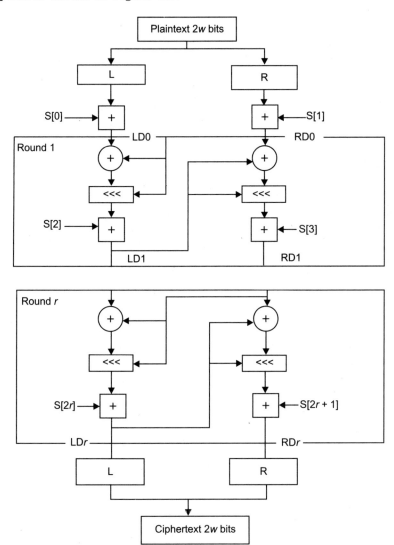

Figure 5.5 RC5 encryption.

5.3.1 Characteristics of RC5

- Uses number of parameters and variables
- Variable number of rounds (from 1 to 255)
- Variable plaintext block size (32 bits, 64 bits or 128 bits)
- Variable key length (0 to 2048 bits)
- Rotation of bits is data dependent
- Uses mixture of different operations like, 2's complement, addition words modulo 2^w, bitwise XOR of words
- Fast and simple software and hardware implementation.

5.3.2 Parameters

RC5 has number of parameters and variables as below:
RC5 uses three parameters such as w, r and b.

- 'w': word size in bits, RC5 encrypts plaintext blocks of 2 words at a time. Allowable values are: 16, 32, 64 bits.
- 'r': number of rounds. Allowable values are: 0, 1, 2, - - - -, 255.
- 'b': number of bytes in the secret K (1 byte = 8 bits). Allowable values are: 0, 1, 2, - - - -, 255.
- The working of RC5 algorithm is divided into following three parts.

1. *Key expansion:* The key expansion algorithm consists of 4 steps. In this, original key is used to fill the expanded key table. The size of the key table depends on the number of rounds.
   - Definition of the constant
   - Converting the key from bytes to words
   - Initialising the S-array
   - Mixing the key

   Two constants are used for key expansion step. These constants are of size 2-word binary number. For $w = 32$, the constants are: B7E1 (1011 0111 1110 0001) and 9E37 (1001 1110 0011 0111). The key is stored in an array A[0, 1, ------, $n-1$]. Where A-array consists of $n = (r-1)$ w-bit words. Copy this key from array A to another array B[0, 1, 2, ------, $m-1$] where $m = n/p$, where $p = w/8$ is the number of bytes per word. Unfilled positions of B are filled with zeroes. Then initialise the S-array such as

   S[0] = first-constant.
   S[i] = S[i −1] + second constant.

   Then mix the original key in three passes over B-array and S-array. The size of B and S-arrays are different. So, the array having large size should process three times and other array process more than three times.

   The above key expansion process is one way and it is difficult to find out the key from the S-array.

2. *Encryption:* The encryption part consists of three operations: add words modulo 2^w, bitwise XOR of words and left hand rotation. The encryption using RC5 is shown in Figure 5.4. The plaintext is divided into a block of two words of size w bits each. Suppose the two plaintext words are P and Q. The encryption algorithm can work as:
   ```
   P = P + S[0];
   Q = Q + S[1];
   for i = 1; i< r; i++
   {
       P = ((P Xor Q) <<< Q) + S[ 2 * i ]
       Q = ((Q Xor P) <<< P) + S[ 2 * i + 1]
   }
   ```
   The result is ciphertext of length $2w$.

3. *Decryption:* It is the reverse of the encryption process. Last round of encryption is processed first. The last but one round is processed second and the first round processed last. It uses subtraction words modulo 2^w, bitwise XOR of words and right hand rotation. The encryption algorithm can work as:

```
for i = r; i > 1; i--
{
    Q = ((Q - S[ 2 * i + 1]>>> P) XOR P);
    P = ((P - S[ 2 * i ]>>> Q) XOR Q);
}
P = P - S[0];
Q = Q - S[1];
```

5.3.3 Cipher Modes in RC5

RC5 have four different cipher modes of operation:

1. *The raw block cipher mode:* Fixed size block of plaintext is converted into a fixed size block of ciphertext.
2. *Cipher block chaining (CBC):* It helps RC5 to process the messages of variable length. Like DES, for RC5 it generates different ciphertext for the similar plaintext blocks.
3. *CBC pad mode:* Generally, the plaintext is not always multiples of block size. So, the last block has less than necessary number of bytes. So, extra bytes are appended to get the required number of bytes in the last block. This makes the processing of the last block possible. All the padding bytes should have same pattern. For example, if there are 2 bytes of padding, each byte has the pattern 1110 0010.
4. *CTS cipher mode:* It is the ciphertext stealing mode. This mode handles plaintext block of any size. The ciphertext blocks generated are of the same size as that of plaintext blocks.

The cryptanalysis of RC5 is difficult due to its flexible number of rounds, key length and plaintext block selection. RC5 can use rounds from 1 to 255 but RC5 with 12 rounds provide sufficient security against differential and linear cryptanalysis. RC5 with more number of rounds provides more security but this also increases the processing time. For maximum number of rounds, the performance of RC5 decreases. Brute force attack is difficult for 128 bits key length. This provides sufficient security to RC5. Increasing the key size provide more security but the key expansion takes more time as compared to small key. However, the total time required for encryption depends only on the number of rounds and not on the key size. The strength of RC5 is its data dependent rotation. Shift operation depends on mod w. If w is a power of 2, lower bits of $\log_2 w$ determine the number of shift positions. XOR operation in RC5 provides an Avalanche effect.

5.4 RC4

In 1987, a cipher designed by Prof. Ron Rivest is RC4 cipher. It is also known as Ron's code 4. It is publicly available in 1994. It is a stream cipher. RC4 uses keys of variable length. RC4 processing is based on byte-oriented operations. The cryptanalysis of RC4 is difficult. RC4 used in different applications such as secure socket layer (SSL), IEEE 802.11 wireless networking security standard, wireless WER and email encryption products.

5.4.1 Design

RC4 is a binary additive stream cipher. It uses variable length key ranges from 8 to 2048 bits in multiples of 8. The key generation function in RC4 generates the keys which are XOR with the plaintext bits. The reuse of these keys makes the cryptanalysis of RC4 easier. This algorithm works in two parts: key generation and encryption.

5.4.2 Characteristics

- Variable key length (8 to 2048 bits)
- Use random permutation
- Encryption is faster than decryption
- Design is simple and effective

5.4.3 Algorithms

A random key is generated first. This key is XOR with the plaintext. Decryption uses the same process as encryption. To generate the key, the RC4 uses following steps:

Step 1 Uses 256 bytes array A, contains the permutation of the values from 0 to 255 byte.

Step 2 The RC4 cipher uses two algorithms: the key-scheduling algorithm, and the pseudo-random generating algorithm.

The key-scheduling algorithm is given as:

```
Initialisation

Input: p,
    key length (in bytes) = n;
    for i = 0 to 2^p - 1
        {
            A[i] := i;
        }
    j=0;

Scrambling of bits
```

```
For i=0 to 2^P - 1
   j=j+A[i]+B[i mod n]
   swap(A[i], A[j])
```

The pseudo-random generating algorithm is given as:

```
Initialisation
i = 0;
j = 0;

Generation loop
Loop
    i:=i+1
    j:=j+A[i]
    swap(A[i],A[j])
    output A[A[i]+A[j]]
end Loop
```

RC4 has a weak key problem. Out of every 256 keys, one key is a weak key. Cryptanalyst can find out this key and able to find one or more generator bytes.

5.5 RC6

RC6 is a symmetric block cipher designed by Ronald Rivest, Matt Robshaw, Ray Sidney, and Yiqun Lisa Yin at RSA Laboratories. It is one of the algorithms selected by others for the final round to become the new federal advanced encryption standard (AES). It is an improvement over RC5. Like RC5, it is a parameterised algorithm. RC6 consists of three parts: a key expansion, an encryption, and a decryption. RC6 uses the variable size plaintext block, variable length key and variable number of rounds. RC6 uses four w-bit registers, integer multiplications, quadratic equations and shifting by fixed bits.

RC6 uses 44 subkeys, S_0 to S_{43} Each sub key is of 32 bits sizes RC6 uses 128-bit plaintext block. For each round of RC6, two subkeys are required. It usesfour registers: A, B, C and D each of 32 bits to store the plaintext. Least significant byte of register A is used to store the first byte of plaintext or ciphertext. Most significant byte of register D is used to store the last byte of plaintext or ciphertext. Two subkeys are used at the initial step before the start of the first round. RC6 begins with an initial step: register B is XOR with subkey S_0, and register D is XOR with subkey S_1. Each round of RC6 uses two subkeys. The first round uses subkeys S_2 and S_3, and next rounds use consecutive subkeys. The block diagram of RC6 is shown in Figure 5.6.

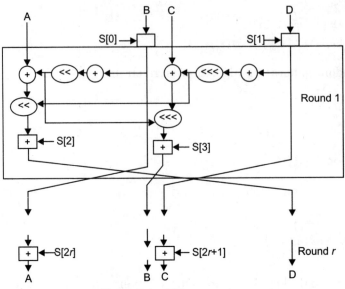

Figure 5.6 RC6 encryption.

5.5.1 Parameters of RC6

RC6-$w/r/b$ parameters:

    Word size: w(32 bits)
    Number of rounds: r(20)
    Size of key: b(16, 24, or 32 bytes)

Key expansion:

    Key-array S[0 ... 2r + 3] of w-bit round keys.
    Encryption and decryption: 4 input/output registers

5.5.2 Basic Operations

RC6 operates on units of four w-bit words using the following six basic operations.

- Integer addition modulo 2^w: ($a + b$)
- Integer subtraction modulo 2^w: ($a - b$)
- Bitwise XOR of w-bit words ($a \oplus b$)
- Integer multiplication modulo 2^w ($a \times b$)
- Shift left the w-bit word a by the amount given by the LSB (least significant bit) $\log_2(w)$ bits of b(a<<<b)
- Shift right the w-bit word a by the amount given by LSB $\log_2 w$ bits of b (a>>>b)

5.5.3 Working of RC6

The encryption of RC6 consists of following three stages:
- pre-whitening stage
- an inner loop of rounds, and
- post-whitening stage

First and last stage help to remove the possibility of the plaintext informative part of the input to the first round of encryption and the ciphertext informative part of the input to the last round of encryption. The encryption process in RC6 can work as:

- The registers B and D undergo pre-whitening.
- The registers B and D are put through the quadratic equation which is defined as $f(x) = x(2x + 1)$ and applied circular left shift by $\log_2 w$ bits.
- The XOR is performed between the value of register B and the value of register A. Also XOR is performed between the value of register D and the value of register C.
- Apply circular left shift on the value of t by u bits. The result is added to round key S[2i].
- Apply circular left shift on the resulting value of register D and C by t bits and added to round key S[2i + 1].
- Then permutation is applied on A, B, C, D registers. This is done by using parallel assignment to mix the AB computation with the CD computation. This makes difficulty for cryptanalysis (Rivest et al., 1998a).
- Registers A and C undergo post-whitening.

In decryption, the first step, i.e., pre-whitening step is started from registers C and A instead of B and D. The loop runs in reverse for the number of r rounds.

The decryption process in RC6 can work as:

- Registers C and A undergo pre-whitening.
- The registers D and B are put through the quadratic equation which is defined as $f(x) = x(2x + 1)$ and apply circular right shift by $\log_2 w$ bits.
- Apply circular left shift on the resulting value for u and t respectively by $\log_2 w$ bits.
- The subkey S[2i + 1] for that particular round is subtracted from register C. The result is circular right shifted by t bits.
- Subkey S[2i] is subtracted from register A, the result of which is right-shifted by u bits.
- The values of register C and u undergo XOR operation. The values of register A is XOR with the value of t.
- Registers D and B undergo a post-whitening.

5.6 COMPARISON BETWEEN RC6 AND RC5

RC6 added two new features which are not present in RC5. These features are: (i) Integer multiplication modulo 2^w, and (ii) four w-bit word registers A, B, C and

D. RC5 uses two registers of 2-bit. Use of integer multiplication in RC6, increases the diffusion achieved per round. Due to this, the cipher is faster and less number of rounds are required to provide the necessary security.

5.7 IDEA

The international data encryption algorithm (IDEA) is a symmetric encryption block cipher. It is designed by Xuejia Lai and James Massey of ETH Zurich. It was first published in 1991. The main intention of this algorithm is to find out the alternate solution to the data encryption standard (DES).

IDEA algorithm uses the plaintext block of size 64 bits and the key of size 128 bits. There are total nine rounds of which working of the first eight rounds are identical. The last round is a half round which uses only first four steps (operations) of the other rounds. Decryption uses the same steps as encryption. But the subkeys for decryption are different from encryption. Different groups of operations are performed in the round of IDEA. This provides the security and makes cryptanalysis difficult. The different operations include modular addition, modular multiplication and bitwise XOR. These operators are:

- Bitwise XOR
- Addition modulo 2^{16}
- Multiplication modulo $2^{16} + 1$, where the all-zero word (0×0000) is interpreted as 2^{16}.

The architecture of the IDEA is as shown in Figure 5.6 which explains the working of IDEA.

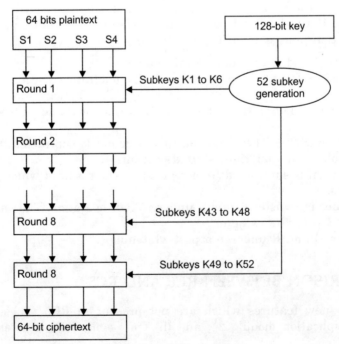

Figure 5.7 IDEA structure.

5.7.1 Working of IDEA

The working of IDEA is divided into two parts:
1. Key generation
2. Encryption

Key Generation

IDEA algorithm has total nine rounds. First eight rounds use six subkeys whereas last round uses only four keys. Therefore, total 52 subkeys of 16 bits are required for encryption. Same number of keys are required for decryption. For decryption, the key generation process is different from key generation process of encryption. The first step of the algorithm is to generate 52 subkeys, K_1 to K_{52}. The original key for IDEA is 128-bit key. This key is used to generate the subkeys. The subkey generation process is as follows.

(a) Initially, split the 128-bit key into 8 parts of 16 bits each. These are the first eight subkeys K_1 to K_8. This process is shown in Table 5.1.

Table 5.1 Original key (128-bit)

Bit position	1 to 16	17 to 32	33 to 48	49 to 64	65 to 80	81 to 96	97 to 112	113 to 128
Subkey	K_1	K_2	K_3	K_4	K_5	K_6	K_7	K_8

(b) Then apply circular left shift by 25 bits position on the 128-bit key and split the key again into eight parts of 16 bits each. As shown in Table 5.2, this gives next 8 subkeys, i.e., K_9 to K_{16}. Subkey K_9 is started from bit 26 to 41 of the original key. Subkey K_{15} having bits 122 to 128 and bits 1 to 9 of the original key. The process is as shown in the Table 5.2.

Table 5.2 128-bit key

Bit position	26 to 41	42 to 57	58 to 73	74 to 89	90 to 105	106 to 121	122 to 9	10 to 25
Subkey	K_9	K_{10}	K_{11}	K_{12}	K_{13}	K_{14}	K_{15}	K_{16}

(c) Repeat step (b) until all 52 subkeys are generated. Subkeys K_{17} to K_{24} are generated by starting from bit number 51 of the original key. Subkeys K_{25} to K_{32} are generated by starting from bit number 76 of the original key. Subkeys K_{33} to K_{40} are generated by starting from bit number 101 of the original key. Subkeys K_{41} to K_{48} are generated by starting from bit number 125 of the original key. Subkeys K_{49} to K_{52} are generated by starting from bit number 22 of the original key.

The repetitions in the subkeys are avoided due to circular left shift of 25 bits.

Encryption

In IDEA algorithm there are total nine rounds, eight complete and one half rounds. The encryption is done using 52 subkeys such that the first eight rounds use 6 subkeys each and the last round uses 4 subkeys. So, the first round uses subkeys K_1 to K_6. The transformation operations use field $F(2^{16}+1)$, i.e., the output will be calculated using modulo $(2^{16}+1)$. A round looks like this:

The message is split into plaintext blocks of 64 bits each. Then a plaintext block is split into four sub-blocks of 16 bits each. Suppose the sub-blocks are P_1, P_2, P_3, and P_4. K_1 to K_6 are the subkeys and S_1 to S_{14} are the result of respective step.

$$P_1 \times K_1 \to S_1$$
$$P_2 + K_2 \to S_2$$
$$P_3 + K_3 \to S_3$$
$$P_4 \times K_4 \to S_4$$
$$S_1 \oplus S_3 \to S_5$$
$$S_2 \oplus S_4 \to S_6$$
$$S_5 \times K_5 \to S_7$$
$$S_6 + S_7 \to S_8$$
$$S_8 \times K_6 \to S_9$$
$$S_7 + S_9 \to S_{10}$$
$$S_1 \oplus S_9 \to S_{11}$$
$$S_3 \oplus S_9 \to S_{12}$$
$$S_2 \oplus S_{10} \to S_{13}$$
$$S_4 \oplus S_{10} \to S_{14}$$

Here multiplication modulo $2^{16}+1$ is used which is shown by symbol ($\times$). Addition modulo 2^{16} is shown by symbol ($+$) and XOR is shown by symbol ($\oplus$). The output of last four steps is used as sub-blocks of plaintext for the next round. So, we set $P_1 = S_{11}$, $P_2 = S_{13}$, $P_3 = S_{12}$, $P_4 = S_{14}$. The subkeys K_7 to K_{12} are used for the second round. Continue this process for eight rounds. In the last round there are only first four steps. The last four subkeys, i.e., $K_{49},...,K_{52}$ are used for this round. The output is 4 sub-blocks of ciphertext C_1, C_2, C_3 and C_4 which after concatenate gives 64-bit ciphertext. The steps in the last round are shown as:

$$P_1 \times K_{49} \to C_1$$
$$P_2 + K_{50} \to C_2$$
$$P_3 + K_{51} \to C_3$$
$$P_4 \times K_{52} \to C_4$$

IDEA algorithm for single round is as follows:

ALGORITHM

1. Multiplication modulo $2^{16}+1$ between P_1 and the first subkey K_1. The result is S_1.
2. Addition modulo 2^{16} between P_2 and the second subkey K_2. The result is S_2.
3. Addition modulo 2^{16} between P_3 and the third subkey K_3. The result is S_3.
4. Multiplication modulo $2^{16}+1$ between P_4 and the fourth subkey K_4. The result is S_4.
5. Apply XOR between S_1 and S_3. The result is S_5.

6. Apply XOR between S_2 and S_4. The result is S_6.
7. Multiplication modulo $2^{16}+1$ between S_5 and the fifth subkey K_5. The result is S_7.
8. Addition modulo 2^{16} between S_6 and S_7. The result is S_8.
9. Multiplication modulo $2^{16}+1$ between S_8 and the sixth subkey K_6. The result is S_9.
10. Addition modulo 2^{16} between S_7 and S_9. The result is S_{10}.
11. Apply XOR between S_1 and S_9. The result is S_{11}.
12. Apply XOR between S_3 and S_9. The result is S_{12}.
13. Apply XOR between S_2 and S_{10}. The result is S_{13}.
14. Apply XOR between S_4 and S_{10}. The result is S_{14}.

The working of the single round of IDEA is shown in Figure 5.8.

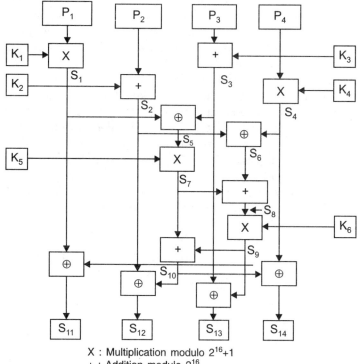

X : Multiplication modulo $2^{16}+1$
+ : Addition modulo 2^{16}
⊕ : XOR operation

Figure 5.8 Working of single round of IDEA.

The last round (9th round) of IDEA has only first four steps. It uses only four subkeys K_{49} to K_{52}. The output of this round is C_1, C_2, C_3 and C_4. After concatenating C_1, C_2, C_3 and C_4, the ciphertext is generated for one plaintext block. Repeat the same procedure for all the plaintext blocks, the complete ciphertext is generated. The working of last round of IDEA is shown in Figure 5.9.

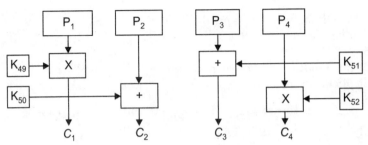

Figure 5.9 Working of last round of IDEA.

5.7.2 Decryption

In IDEA algorithm, the decryption process is exactly the same as the encryption process, except the use of subkeys. The subkeys for decryption are generated from the subkeys used for encryption. This makes it difficult for cryptanalysis. For generation of subkeys, reverse order subkeys are used, i.e., encryption subkeys K_{49} to K_{52} are used to generate decryption subkeys K_1 to K_4. For generation of these subkeys, multiplicative inverse and additive inverse are used.

Suppose the key for encryption is denoted by K and the key for decryption is denoted by Z. Then, K_j^i denotes the jth subkey for ith round of the encryption and Z_j^i denotes the jth subkey for ith round of the decryption. For the first round of decryption $i = 1$, and for first subkey $j = 1$. The decryption subkey is calculated from the 9th round (last round) and first subkey. Therefore, $Z_1^1 = (K_1^9)^{-1}$ where $(K_1^9)^{-1}$ denotes the multiplicative inverse of the first encryption key of encryption round 9. Second subkey can be calculated using, $Z_2^1 = - (K_2^9)$ where $- (K_2^9)$ denotes the additive inverse of the second encryption key of encryption round 9 modulo 16; $Z_3^1 = - (K_3^9)$, $Z_4^1 = - (K_4^9)^{-1}$. The last two subkeys for the first round of decryption is the last two keys of 8th round such as $Z_5^1 = (K_4^8)$, $Z_6^1 = (K_4^8)$. Similarly, the subkeys for all the eight rounds of decryption are generated. The subkeys for the last 9th round of the decryption are: $Z_1^9 = (K_1^1)^{-1}$, $Z_2^9 = -(K_2^1)$, $Z_3^9 = -(K_3^1)$, $Z_4^9 = (K_4^1)^{-1}$. The subkeys for the first round of decryption are illustrated from the following examples.

The decryption subkey Z_1 is the multiplicative inverse of K_{49}. This is illustrated by following example. Suppose, the subkey K_{49} is 0111 (decimal number is 7_{10}). The multiplicative inverse of 7 mod 17 is 5 (i.e., 7 * 5 mod 17 = 1). So, the decryption subkey equivalent to 0111 (7_{10}) is 0101 (5_{10}) which is the first subkey Z_1 for decryption.

The decryption subkeys Z_2 and Z_3 are the additive inverse of K_{50} and K_{51}. This is illustrated by following example. Suppose, the subkey K_{50} is 1001 (decimal number is 9_{10}). The additive inverse of 9 mod 16 is 7 (i.e., 9 + 7 mod 16 = 0). So, the decryption subkey equivalent to 1001 (9_{10}) is 0111 (7_{10}) which is the second subkey Z_2 for decryption. This can be done by subtracting the decimal value of subkey from 16. Here, 16 – 9 = 7. So, the subkey Z_2 is 7.

Suppose the subkey K_{51} is 1101 (decimal number is 13_{10}). The additive inverse of 13 mod 16 is 3 (i.e., 13 + 3 mod 16 = 0). So, the decryption subkey equivalent to 1101 (13_{10}) is 0011 (3_{10}) which is the third subkey Z_3 for decryption. This can be done by subtracting the decimal value of subkey from 16. Here, 16 – 13 = 3. So, the decryption subkey Z_3 is 3.

Symmetric Ciphers 115

The decryption subkey Z_4 is the multiplicative inverse of K_{52}. This is illustrated by following example. Suppose the subkey K_{52} is 1010 (decimal number is 10_{10}). The multiplicative inverse of 10 mod 17 is 12 (i.e., $10 * 12 \mod 17 = 1$). So, the decryption subkey equivalent to 1010 (10_{10}) is 1100 (12_{10}) which is the fourth subkey Z_4 for decryption.

The decryption subkey Z_5 and Z_6 are the last two subkeys of 8th round. $Z_5 = K_{47}$ and $Z_6 = K_{48}$. Suppose, the subkeys K_{47} is 1100 and K_{48} is 0110, then Z_5 is 1100 and Z_6 is 0110. In this way the subkeys for all the rounds of decryption are generated.

5.7.3 Security

Cryptanalysis is possible against IDEA algorithm but this is for 5 rounds. Brute force attack is possible but it takes large time due to 128-bit key. There are weak keys in IDEA. So, key selection for IDEA should be done carefully. Against IDEA algorithm, linear cryptanalysis attack is not reported where differential cryptanalysis attack is possible.

SOLVED PROBLEMS

5.1 Encrypt the following message using IDEA algorithm
Message: 1111 1011 1101 1010
Key: 10101001110111110110010111000011

Solution:

Plaintext: 1111 1011 1101 1010
Key: 1010 1001 1101 1111 0110 0101 1100 0011
             0111 0111 1101 1001 0111 0000 1110 1010
             1111 0110 0101 1100 0011 1010 1001 1101
             1001 0111 0000 1110 1010 0111 0111 1101

Generation of encryption keys:

	Round–1	Round–2	Round–3	Round–4	Round–5
Key–1	1010	1100	0111	0101	1001
Key–2	1001	0011 *	0000	1100	0111
Key–3	1101	0111	1110	0011	0000
Key–4	1111	0111	1010 *	1010	1110
Key–5	0110	1101	1111	1001	
Key–6	0101	1001	0110	1101*	

Inverses of nibbles for addition modulo 16:

Number in binary	Number in decimal	Inverse in binary	Inverse in decimal
0000	0	0000	0
0001	1	1111	15

Number in binary	Number in decimal	Inverse in binary	Inverse in decimal
0010	2	1110	14
0011	3	1101	13
0100	4	1100	12
0101	5	1011	11
0110	6	1010	10
0111	7	1001	9
1000	8	1000	8
1001	9	0111	7
1010	10	0110	6
1011	11	0101	5
1100	12	0100	4
1101	13	0011	3
1110	14	0010	2
1111	15	0001	1

Inverses of nibbles for multiplication modulo 17:

Number in binary	Number in decimal	Inverse in binary	Inverse in decimal
0001	1	0001	1
0010	2	1001	9
0011	3	0110	6
0100	4	1101	13
0101	5	0111	7
0110	6	0011	3
0111	7	0101	5
1000	8	1111	15
1001	9	0010	2
1010	10	1100	12
1011	11	1110	14
1100	12	1010	10
1101	13	0100	4
1110	14	1011	11
1111	15	1000	8
0000	16 = −1	0000	16 = −1

Round–1

$S_1 = P_1 \times K_1$	$S_2 = P_2 + K_2$	$S_3 = P_3 + K_3$	$S_4 = P_4 \times K_4$
1111	1011	1101	1010
1010	1001	1101	1111
1110	0100	1010	1110
$S_5 = S_1 \oplus S_3$			$S_6 = S_2 \oplus S_4$
1110			0100
1010			1110
0100			1010
$S_7 = S_5 \times K_5$			$S_8 = S_6 + S_7$
0100			1010
0110			0111
0111			0001
$S_{10} = S_7 + S_9$			$S_9 = S_8 \times K_6$
0111			0001
0101			0101
1100			0101
$S_{11} = S_9 \oplus S_1$	$S_{12} = S_9 \oplus S_3$	$S_{13} = S_{10} \oplus S_2$	$S_{14} = S_{10} \oplus S_4$
0101	0101	1100	1100
1110	1010	0100	1110
1011	1111	1000	0010
$P_1 = S_{11}$	$P_2 = S_{13}$	$P_3 = S_{12}$	$P_4 = S_{14}$
1011	1000	1111	0010

Round–2

$S_1 = P_1 \times K_1$	$S_2 = P_2 + K_2$	$S_3 = P_3 + K_3$	$S_4 = P_4 \times K_4$
1011	1000	1111	0010
1100	0011	0111	0111
1101	1011	0110	1110
$S_5 = S_1 \oplus S_3$			$S_6 = S_2 \oplus S_4$
1101			1011
0110			1110
1011			0101

$S_7 = S_5 \times K_5$
1011
1101
0111

$S_8 = S_6 + S_7$
0101
0111
1100

$S_{10} = S_7 + S_9$
0111
0110
1101

$S_9 = S_8 \times K_6$
1100
1001
0110

$S_{11} = S_9 \oplus S_1$
0110
1101
1011

$S_{12} = S_9 \oplus S_3$
0110
0110
0000

$S_{13} = S_{10} \oplus S_2$
1101
1011
0110

$S_{14} = S_{10} \oplus S_4$
1101
1110
0011

$P_1 = S_{11}$
1011

$P_2 = S_{13}$
0110

$P_3 = S_{12}$
0000

$P_4 = S_{14}$
0011

Round–3

$S_1 = P_1 \times K_1$
1011
0111
1001

$S_2 = P_2 + K_2$
0110
0000
0110

$S_3 = P_3 + K_3$
0000
1110
1110

$S_4 = P_4 \times K_4$
0011
1010
1101

$S_5 = S_1 \oplus S_3$
1001
1110
0111

$S_6 = S_2 \oplus S_4$
0110
1101
1011

$S_7 = S_5 \times K_5$
0111
1111
0011

$S_8 = S_6 + S_7$
1011
0011
1110

$S_{10} = S_7 + S_9$
0011
0000
0011

$S_9 = S_8 \times K_6$
1110
0110
0000

$S_{11} = S_9 \oplus S_1$	$S_{12} = S_9 \oplus S_3$	$S_{13} = S_{10} \oplus S_2$	$S_{14} = S_{10} \oplus S_4$
0000	0000	0011	0011
1001	1110	0110	1101
1001	1110	0101	1110

$P_1 = S_{11}$	$P_2 = S_{13}$	$P_3 = S_{12}$	$P_4 = S_{14}$
1001	0101	1110	1110

Round–4

$S_1 = P_1 \times K_1$	$S_2 = P_2 + K_2$	$S_3 = P_3 + K_3$	$S_4 = P_4 \times K_4$
1001	0101	1110	1110
0101	1100	0011	1010
1011	0001	0001	0100

$S_5 = S_1 \oplus S_3$			$S_6 = S_2 \oplus S_4$
1011			0001
0001			0100
1010			0101

$S_7 = S_5 \times K_5$			$S_8 = S_6 + S_7$
1010			0101
1001			0101
0101			1010

$S_{10} = S_7 + S_9$			$S_9 = S_8 \times K_6$
0101			1010
1011			1101
0000			1011

$S_{11} = S_9 \oplus S_1$	$S_{12} = S_9 \oplus S_3$	$S_{13} = S_{10} \oplus S_2$	$S_{14} = S_{10} \oplus S_4$
1011	1011	0000	0000
1011	0001	0001	0100
0000	1010	0001	0100

$P_1 = S_{11}$	$P_2 = S_{13}$	$P_3 = S_{12}$	$P_4 = S_{14}$
0000	0001	1010	0100

Round–5

$S_1 = P_1 \times K_1$ $S_2 = P_2 + K_2$ $S_3 = P_3 + K_3$ $S_4 = P_4 \times K_4$

0000   0001   1010   0100

1001   0111   0000   1110

0000   1000   1010   0101

The ciphertext is: 0000 1000 1010 0101

5.2 Generate the key for decryption from the following encryption key.

Key: 1010100111011111011001011100011

Solution:

	(K_j^i)	Integer	Inverse in integer	Z_j^i	Key for 1st round
(K_1^5)	1001	9	2 (multiplicative modulo 17)	0010	Z_1^1
(K_2^5)	0111	7	6 (addition modulo 16)	1001	Z_2^1
(K_3^5)	0000	0	(Addition modulo 16)	0000	Z_3^1
(K_4^5)	1110	14	11 (Multiplicative modulo 17)	1011	Z_4^1
(K_5^4)	1001	9	9	1001	Z_5^1
(K_6^4)	1101	13	13	1101	Z_6^1

We can generate the keys as above for all 5 rounds as shown below:

Generation of decryption keys:

	Round–1	Round–2	Round–3	Round–4	Round–5
Key–1	0010	0111	0101	1010	1100
Key–2	1001	0100	0000	1101	0111
Key–3	0000	1101	0010	1001	0011
Key–4	1011	1100	1100	0101	1000
Key–5	1001	1111	1101	0110	
Key–6	1101	0110	1001	0101	

5.3 Use IDEA algorithm for encryption and decryption of the following message:

Message: 1110 1111 1001 0101
Key: 1100 0110 0011 0101 1111 0111 0101 1010

Solution:
Plaintext: 1110 1111 1001 0101
Key: 1100 0110 0011 0101 1111 0111 0101 1010

Generation of encryption keys:

	Round–1	Round–2	Round–3	Round–4	Round–5
Key–1	1100	0101	1101	0111	1101
Key–2	0110	1010	0110	0101	1101
Key–3	0011	1000	1011	1010	0110
Key–4	0101	1101	0001	1100	1011
Key–5	1111	0111	0101	0110	
Key–6	0111	1101	1111	0011	

Round–1

$S_1 = P_1 \times K_1$ $S_2 = P_2 + K_2$ $S_3 = P_3 + K_3$ $S_4 = P_4 \times K_4$
1110   1111   1001   0101
1100   0110   0011   0101
1111   0101   1100   1000

$S_5 = S_1 \oplus S_3$ $S_6 = S_2 \oplus S_4$
1111   0101
1100   1000
0011   1101

$S_7 = S_5 \times K_5$ $S_8 = S_6 + S_7$
0011   1101
1111   1011
1011   1000

$S_{10} = S_7 + S_9$ $S_9 = S_8 \times K_6$
1011   1000
0101   0111
0000   0101

$S_{11} = S_9 \oplus S_1$ $S_{12} = S_9 \oplus S_3$ $S_{13} = S_{10} \oplus S_2$ $S_{14} = S_{10} \oplus S_4$
0101   0101   0000   0000
1111   1100   0101   1000
1010   1001   0101   1000

$P_1 = S_{11}$ $P_2 = S_{13}$ $P_3 = S_{12}$ $P_4 = S_{14}$
1010   0101   1001   1000

Input to Round–2: 1010 0101 1001 1000

Round–2

$S_1 = P_1 \times K_1$	$S_2 = P_2 + K_2$	$S_3 = P_3 + K_3$	$S_4 = P_4 \times K_4$
1010	0101	1001	1000
0101	1010	1000	1101
0000	1111	0001	0010

$S_5 = S_1 \oplus S_3$			$S_6 = S_2 \oplus S_4$
0000			1111
0001			0010
0001			1101

$S_7 = S_5 \times K_5$			$S_8 = S_6 + S_7$
0001			1101
0111			0111
0111			0100

$S_{10} = S_7 + S_9$			$S_9 = S_8 \times K_6$
0111			0100
0001			1101
1000			0001

$S_{11} = S_9 \oplus S_1$	$S_{12} = S_9 \oplus S_3$	$S_{13} = S_{10} \oplus S_2$	$S_{14} = S_{10} \oplus S_4$
0001	0001	1000	1000
0000	0001	1111	0010
0001	0000	0111	1010

$P_1 = S_{11}$	$P_2 = S_{13}$	$P_3 = S_{12}$	$P_4 = S_{14}$
0001	0111	0000	1010

Input to Round–3: 0001 0111 0000 1010

Round–3

$S_1 = P_1 \times K_1$	$S_2 = P_2 + K_2$	$S_3 = P_3 + K_3$	$S_4 = P_4 \times K_4$
0001	0111	0000	1010
1101	0110	1011	0001
1101	1101	1011	1010

$S_5 = S_1 \oplus S_3$			$S_6 = S_2 \oplus S_4$
1101			1101
1011			1010
0110			0111

$S_7 = S_5 \times K_5$

0110

0101

1101

$S_8 = S_6 + S_7$

0111

1101

0100

$S_{10} = S_7 + S_9$

1101

1001

0110

$S_9 = S_8 \times K_6$

0100

1111

1001

$S_{11} = S_9 \oplus S_1$

1001

1101

0100

$S_{12} = S_9 \oplus S_3$

1001

1011

0010

$S_{13} = S_{10} \oplus S_2$

0110

1101

1011

$S_{14} = S_{10} \oplus S_4$

0110

1010

1100

$P_1 = S_{11}$

0100

$P_2 = S_{13}$

1011

$P_3 = S_{12}$

0010

$P_4 = S_{14}$

1100

Input for Round–4:   0100 1011 0010 1100

Round–4

$S_1 = P_1 \times K_1$

0100

0111

1011

$S_2 = P_2 + K_2$

1011

0101

0000

$S_3 = P_3 + K_3$

0010

1010

1100

$S_4 = P_4 \times K_4$

1100

1100

1000

$S_5 = S_1 \oplus S_3$

1011

1100

0111

$S_6 = S_2 \oplus S_4$

0000

1000

1000

$S_7 = S_5 \times K_5$

0111

0110

1000

$S_8 = S_6 + S_7$

1000

1000

0000

$S_{10} = S_7 + S_9$

1000

1110

0110

$S_9 = S_8 \times K_6$

0000

0011

1110

$S_{11} = S_9 \oplus S_1$	$S_{12} = S_9 \oplus S_3$	$S_{13} = S_{10} \oplus S_2$	$S_{14} = S_{10} \oplus S_4$
1110	1110	0110	0110
1011	1100	0000	1000
0101	0010	0110	1110

$P_1 = S_{11}$	$P_2 = S_{13}$	$P_3 = S_{12}$	$P_4 = S_{14}$
0101	0110	0010	1110

Input to Round–5:   0101 0110 0010 1110

Round–5

$S_1 = P_1 \times K_1$	$S_2 = P_2 + K_2$	$S_3 = P_3 + K_3$	$S_4 = P_4 \times K_4$
0101	0110	0010	1110
1101	1101	0110	1011
1110	0011	1000	0001

The ciphertext is: 1110 0011 1100 0001

Decryption

New keys are generated

K_j^i – jth encryption key for encryption round i
Z_j^i – jth decryption key for decryption round i
$Z_1^1 = (K_1^5)^{-1}$, $Z_2^1 = -K_2^5$, $Z_3^1 = -K_3^5$, $Z_4^1 = (K_4^5)^{-1}$ $Z_5^1 = K_5^4$, $Z_6^1 = K_6^4$

For remaining rounds, decryption keys are similarly generated.

	Round–1	Round–2	Round–3	Round–4	Round–5
Key–1	0100	0101	0100	0111	1010
Key–2	0011	1011	1010	0110	1010
Key–3	1010	0110	0101	1000	1101
Key–4	1110	1010	0001	0100	0111
Key–5	0110	0101	0111	1111	
Key–6	0011	1111	1101	0111	

Round–1

$S_1 = P_1 \times Z_1$	$S_2 = P_2 + Z_2$	$S_3 = P_3 + Z_3$	$S_4 = P_4 \times Z_4$
1110	0011	1000	0001
0100	0011	1010	1110
0101	0110	0010	1110

$S_5 = S_1 \oplus S_3$ $\qquad\qquad\qquad\qquad$ $S_6 = S_2 \oplus S_4$
$\qquad$ 0101 $\qquad\qquad\qquad\qquad\qquad\qquad$ 0110
$\qquad$ 0010 $\qquad\qquad\qquad\qquad\qquad\qquad$ 1110
$\qquad$ 0111 $\qquad\qquad\qquad\qquad\qquad\qquad$ 1000

$S_7 = S_5 \times Z_5$ $\qquad\qquad\qquad\qquad$ $S_8 = S_6 + S_7$
$\qquad$ 0111 $\qquad\qquad\qquad\qquad\qquad\qquad$ 1000
$\qquad$ 0110 $\qquad\qquad\qquad\qquad\qquad\qquad$ 1000
$\qquad$ 1000 $\qquad\qquad\qquad\qquad\qquad\qquad$ 0000

$S_{10} = S_7 + S_9$ $\qquad\qquad\qquad\qquad$ $S_9 = S_8 \times Z_6$
$\qquad$ 1000 $\qquad\qquad\qquad\qquad\qquad\qquad$ 0000
$\qquad$ 1110 $\qquad\qquad\qquad\qquad\qquad\qquad$ 0011
$\qquad$ 0110 $\qquad\qquad\qquad\qquad\qquad\qquad$ 1110

$S_{11} = S_9 \oplus S_1$ $\quad$ $S_{12} = S_9 \oplus S_3$ $\quad$ $S_{13} = S_{10} \oplus S_2$ $\quad$ $S_{14} = S_{10} \oplus S_4$
$\qquad$ 1110 $\qquad\qquad$ 1110 $\qquad\qquad$ 0110 $\qquad\qquad$ 0110
$\qquad$ 0101 $\qquad\qquad$ 0010 $\qquad\qquad$ 0110 $\qquad\qquad$ 1110
$\qquad$ 1011 $\qquad\qquad$ 1100 $\qquad\qquad$ 0000 $\qquad\qquad$ 1000

$\qquad$ $P_1 = S_{11}$ $\qquad\quad$ $P_2 = S_{13}$ $\qquad\quad$ $P_3 = S_{12}$ $\qquad\quad$ $P_4 = S_{14}$
$\qquad\qquad$ 1011 $\qquad\qquad\quad$ 0000 $\qquad\qquad\quad$ 1100 $\qquad\qquad\quad$ 1000

Input to Round–2: 1011 0000 1100 1000

Round–2

$\qquad$ $S_1 = P_1 \times Z_1$ $\quad$ $S_2 = P_2 + Z_2$ $\quad$ $S_3 = P_3 + Z_3$ $\quad$ $S_4 = P_4 \times Z_4$
$\qquad\qquad$ 1011 $\qquad\qquad\quad$ 0000 $\qquad\qquad\quad$ 1100 $\qquad\qquad\quad$ 1000
$\qquad\qquad$ 0101 $\qquad\qquad\quad$ 1011 $\qquad\qquad\quad$ 0110 $\qquad\qquad\quad$ 1010
$\qquad\qquad$ 0100 $\qquad\qquad\quad$ 1011 $\qquad\qquad\quad$ 0010 $\qquad\qquad\quad$ 1100

$\qquad\qquad$ $S_5 = S_1 \oplus S_3$ $\qquad\qquad\qquad\qquad$ $S_6 = S_2 \oplus S_4$
$\qquad\qquad\qquad$ 0100 $\qquad\qquad\qquad\qquad\qquad\qquad$ 1011
$\qquad\qquad\qquad$ 0010 $\qquad\qquad\qquad\qquad\qquad\qquad$ 1100
$\qquad\qquad\qquad$ 0110 $\qquad\qquad\qquad\qquad\qquad\qquad$ 0111

$\qquad\qquad$ $S_7 = S_5 \times Z_5$ $\qquad\qquad\qquad\qquad$ $S_8 = S_6 + S_7$
$\qquad\qquad\qquad$ 0110 $\qquad\qquad\qquad\qquad\qquad\qquad$ 0111
$\qquad\qquad\qquad$ 0101 $\qquad\qquad\qquad\qquad\qquad\qquad$ 1101
$\qquad\qquad\qquad$ 1101 $\qquad\qquad\qquad\qquad\qquad\qquad$ 0100

$$S_{10} = S_7 + S_9$$
1101
1001
0110

$$S_9 = S_8 \times Z_6$$
0100
1111
1001

$$S_{11} = S_9 \oplus S_1$$
1001
0100
1101

$$S_{12} = S_9 \oplus S_3$$
1001
0010
1011

$$S_{13} = S_{10} \oplus S_2$$
0110
1011
1101

$$S_{14} = S_{10} \oplus S_4$$
0110
1100
1010

$$P_1 = S_{11}$$
1101

$$P_2 = S_{13}$$
1101

$$P_3 = S_{12}$$
1011

$$P_4 = S_{14}$$
1010

Input to Round–3: 1101 1101 1011 1010

Round–3

$$S_1 = P_1 \times Z_1$$
1101
0100
0001

$$S_2 = P_2 + Z_2$$
1101
1010
0111

$$S_3 = P_3 + Z_3$$
1011
0101
0000

$$S_4 = P_4 \times Z_4$$
1010
0001
1010

$$S_5 = S_1 \oplus S_3$$
0001
0000
0001

$$S_6 = S_2 \oplus S_4$$
0111
1010
1101

$$S_7 = S_5 \times Z_5$$
0001
0111
0111

$$S_8 = S_6 + S_7$$
1101
0111
0100

$$S_{10} = S_7 + S_9$$
0111
0001
1000

$$S_9 = S_8 \times Z_6$$
0100
1101
0001

$$S_{11} = S_9 \oplus S_1$$
0001
0001
0000

$$S_{12} = S_9 \oplus S_3$$
0001
0000
0001

$$S_{13} = S_{10} \oplus S_2$$
1000
0111
1111

$$S_{14} = S_{10} \oplus S_4$$
1000
1010
0010

$$P_1 = S_{11}$$
0000

$$P_2 = S_{13}$$
1111

$$P_3 = S_{12}$$
0001

$$P_4 = S_{14}$$
0010

Input to Round–4: 0000 1111 0001 0010

Round–4

$S_1 = P_1 \times Z_1$	$S_2 = P_2 + Z_2$	$S_3 = P_3 + Z_3$	$S_4 = P_4 \times Z_4$
0000	1111	0001	0010
0111	0110	1000	0100
1010	0101	1001	1000

$S_5 = S_1 \oplus S_3$			$S_6 = S_2 \oplus S_4$
1010			0101
1001			1000
0011			1101

$S_7 = S_5 \times Z_5$			$S_8 = S_6 + S_7$
0011			1101
1111			1011
1011			1000

$S_{10} = S_7 + S_9$			$S_9 = S_8 \times Z_6$
1011			1000
0101			0111
0000			0101

$S_{11} = S_9 \oplus S_1$	$S_{12} = S_9 \oplus S_3$	$S_{13} = S_{10} \oplus S_2$	$S_{14} = S_{10} \oplus S_4$
0101	0101	0000	0000
1010	1001	0101	0000
1111	1100	0101	1000

$P_1 = S_{11}$	$P_2 = S_{13}$	$P_3 = S_{12}$	$P_4 = S_{14}$
1111	0101	1100	1000

Input to Round–5: 1111 0101 1100 1000

Round–5

$S_1 = P_1 \times Z_1$	$S_2 = P_2 + Z_2$	$S_3 = P_3 + Z_3$	$S_4 = P_4 \times Z_4$
1111	0101	1100	1000
1010	1010	1101	0111
1110	1111	1001	0101

The plaintext is: 1110 1111 1001 0101

SUMMARY

Blowfish algorithm is a symmetric encryption block cipher which is based on Feistel structure. The Blowfish algorithm has sixteen rounds. Blowfish uses the plaintext block of 64-bit length and variable key length from 32 bits to 448 bits. There is no known cryptanalysis attack against Blowfish algorithm. Blowfish is suitable for applications having small plaintext but for large plaintext it may not be suitable algorithm. RC5 is a symmetric encryption block cipher. RC5 architecture is based on the Feistal structure. It is a parameterised algorithm such as $w/r/b$ parameters. It is a very fast algorithm. RC5 has the variable number of rounds. Also it uses the plaintext block and the key of variable length. RC4 is a stream cipher. It uses keys of variable length. RC4 is processing is based on byte-oriented operations. The cryptanalysis of RC4 is difficult. RC4 used in different applications such as secure socket layer (SSL), IEEE 802.11 wireless networking security standard, wireless WER and email encryption products. RC6 is a symmetric encryption block cipher. RC6 uses the variable size plaintext block, variable length key, and variable number of rounds. RC6 uses four w-bit registers, integer multiplications, quadratic equations and shifting by fixed bits. The international data encryption algorithm (IDEA is a symmetric encryption block cipher. It uses the plaintext block of size of 64 bits and the key of size of 12 bits. There are total nine rounds of which working of the first eight rounds are identical. The last round is a half round which uses only first four steps (operations) of the other rounds. Cryptanalysis is possible against IDEA algorithm but this is for 5 rounds. Brute force attack is possible and there are weak keys in IDEA.

EXERCISES

5.1 State the characteristics of Blowfish.
5.2 Explain the methodology of generating the subkeys in Blowfish.
5.3 Explain the working of Blowfish algorithm.
5.4 What is RC5?
5.5 Compare RC5 with RC6.
5.6 State the characteristics of RC5.
5.7 What are the parameters used in RC5?
5.8 Explain the key expansion, encryption and decryption routines in RC5.
5.9 Discuss the cipher modes in RC5.
5.10 Explain the working of RC4.
5.11 Explain the working of one round of IDEA in detail.
5.12 How the subkeys are generated for IDEA?
5.13 Explain the subkey generation for decryption for the IDEA algorithm.
5.14 Explain the strength and weaknesses of the IDEA.
5.15 Discuss the weaknesses of RC4.
5.16 Explain the working of RC6.
5.17 Explain the working of IDEA.

5.18 Write a note on security in IDEA.

5.19 Generate the ciphertext using IDEA algorithm for the message "1100 0110 1110 1001". The key for encryption is 0110 1111 1001 1101 1111 1101 1001 1100.

5.20 Generate the sub keys for encryption and decryption using IDEA algorithm for the following key.

Key: 1101 0111 1110 1001 1100 0110 1110 1101

MULTIPLE CHOICE QUESTIONS

5.1 Total number of subkeys uses in each round of IDEA is
 (a) 2 (b) 4
 (c) 6 (d) 8

5.2 IDEA algorithm uses total _____ subkeys.
 (a) 16 (b) 28
 (c) 48 (d) 52

5.3 IDEA algorithm has total _____ rounds.
 (a) 5 (b) 8
 (c) 9 (d) 10

5.4 What does IDEA stand for?
 (a) International Data Encryption Algorithm
 (b) Integrity of Data Emergency Algorithms
 (c) Individualised Date Encryption Algorithm
 (d) Independent Data Encryption Algorithms

5.5 Total number of subkeys uses in each round of Blowfish is
 (a) 1 (b) 2
 (c) 6 (d) 8

5.6 Blowfish algorithm uses total _____ subkeys.
 (a) 16 (b) 18
 (c) 20 (d) 24

5.7 Blowfish algorithm has total _____ rounds.
 (a) 5 (b) 10
 (c) 12 (d) 16

Answers

 5.1 (c)   5.2 (d)   5.3 (c)   5.4 (a)   5.5 (a)   5.6 (b)   5.7 (d)

CHAPTER 6

Number Theory

6.1 INTRODUCTION

Since ancient times, the study of number systems especially prime numbers has fascinated mathematicians. On the other hand due to increase of internet for communication there is a need for security in the transmission of information. In the last twenty five years, there are number of discoveries of new mathematical methods. This helps to increase the computation speed. Number system is the base of cryptographic algorithms. It is difficult to find out the largest prime number as there is no simple and efficient algorithms are available to find out such prime number. The strength of any encryption algorithm depends on the selection of various parameters, i.e., numbers. The most secure methods for transmission of information depends on properties of prime number. This chapter provides the basic of number theory which is useful for different cryptographic algorithms. In this chapter, we are going to discuss about prime numbers, modular arithmetic, Fermat's theorem, Euler's theorem, Euclidean algorithm, different methods for primality test, Chinese remainder theorem, discrete logarithms.

6.2 PRIME NUMBERS

We learn about various classical and symmetric encryption techniques. Every one of us knows about prime number. To design a strong encryption algorithm, prime number plays a very important role. So in cryptography, prime number has its own important role. A positive integer number which is greater than 1 and has no factors other than 1 and that number itself is called a *prime number*. In other word, the number which is divisible only by itself and 1 called prime number. Prime numbers are always positive integers. For example, 2, 3, 5, 7, 11, 13. These numbers have the factors as 1 and itself only. If we consider the number 14, the factors are 1, 2, 7 and 14. So, 14 is not a prime number. Positive integer numbers greater than 2, which are not prime numbers, are called *composite numbers*. The smallest prime numbers less than 50 are 2, 3, 5, 7, 11, 13, 17, 19, 23, 29, 31, 37, 41, 43 and 47. The integer number 1 is neither prime nor composite. There are infinite numbers of prime numbers.

6.2.1 Relative Prime Numbers

Two numbers are called relatively prime if the greatest common divisor (GCD) of those numbers is 1. The numbers 8 and 15 are relatively prime number, in respect to each other. The factors of 8 are 1, 2, 4, 8 and the factors of 15 are 1, 3, 5 15. Examples of relatively prime numbers are: (10, 21), (14, 15), (45, 91), ...

The greatest common divisor (GCD) of two numbers can be determined by comparing their prime factors and selecting the least powers of the factor. For example, the two numbers are 81 and 99.

The factors of these numbers are:

$$81 = 1 * 9 * 9 = 1 * 3 * 3 * 3 * 3 = 1 * 3^4$$
$$99 = 1 * 3 * 33 = 1 * 3 * 3 * 11 = 1 * 3^2 * 11$$

The GCD is the least power of a number in the factors,

So, $\qquad$ GCD(81, 99) = $1 * 3^2 * 11^0 = 9$

If the GCD of two numbers is 1, then those numbers are relatively prime. Therefore, 81 and 89 are not relatively prime numbers.
For example, two relative prime numbers are 45 and 91.

The factors of these numbers are:

$$45 = 1 * 3 * 3 * 5 = 1 * 3^2 * 5$$

And $\qquad$ $91 = 1 * 7 * 13$

So, $\qquad$ GCD(45, 91) = 1

Therefore, 45 and 91 are relatively prime numbers. It is not necessary that both the numbers should be prime number. A prime number is also relatively prime number to any other number other than itself and 1. Large prime number provides more security in cryptography.

6.3 MODULAR ARITHMETIC

We are familiar to find out the mod of any number with some base. Suppose we have to find out the mod of a number m with base n as:

$$m \bmod n$$

The mod with respect to n is (0, 1, 2, ... $n - 1$).
Suppose $m = 23$ and $n = 9$, then

$$23 \bmod 9 = 5$$

For any value of m, the value of m mod 9 is from (0, 1, 2, ... 8).

If m is negative, suppose $m = -15$, then

$$-15 \bmod 9 = -6 \bmod 9$$
$$= (9 - 6) \bmod 9$$
$$= 3 \bmod 9$$

Table 6.1 shows the value of $m \bmod 9$ for different values of m.

Table 6.1 Values of $m \bmod 9$

18	19	20	21	22	23	24	25	26
9	10	11	12	13	14	15	16	17
0	1	2	3	4	5	6	7	8
9	−8	−7	−6	−5	−4	−3	−2	−1
−18	−17	−16	−15	−14	−13	−12	−11	−10
−27	−26	−25	−24	−23	−22	−21	−20	−19

6.3.1 Properties

1. *Addition of modular number*
   The addition of two numbers p and q with same modular base n is:

   $$(p \bmod n + q \bmod n) \bmod n = (p + q) \bmod n$$

   For example:

   $$15 \bmod 9 + 17 \bmod 9 = (15 \bmod 9 + 17 \bmod 9) \bmod 9$$
   $$= (6 + 8) \bmod 9$$
   $$= 14 \bmod 9 = 5$$

   OR

   $$15 \bmod 9 + 17 \bmod 9 = (15 + 17) \bmod 9$$
   $$= (32) \bmod 9 = 5$$

2. *Subtraction of modular number*
   The subtraction of two numbers p and q with same modular base n is:

   $$(p \bmod n - q \bmod n) \bmod n = (p - q) \bmod n$$

   For example:

   $$17 \bmod 9 - 15 \bmod 9 = (17 \bmod 9 - 15 \bmod 9) \bmod 9$$
   $$= (8 - 6) \bmod 9$$
   $$= 2 \bmod 9 = 12$$

   OR

   $$17 \bmod 9 - 15 \bmod 9 = (17 - 15) \bmod 9$$
   $$= 2 \bmod 9 = 2$$

Number Theory

3. *Multiplication of modular number*
   The multiplication of two numbers p and q with same modular base n is:

   $$(p \bmod n * q \bmod n) \bmod n = (p * q) \bmod n$$

   For example:

   $$17 \bmod 9 * 15 \bmod 9 = (17 \bmod 9 * 15 \bmod 9) \bmod 9$$
   $$= (8 * 6) \bmod 9$$
   $$= 48 \bmod 9 = 3$$

   OR

   $$17 \bmod 9 * 15 \bmod 9 = (17 * 15) \bmod 9$$
   $$= (255) \bmod 9 = 3$$

   Note: $m^a \bmod n = m^{pq} \bmod n$ where $a = p * q$
   $$= (m^p \bmod n)^q \bmod n$$

EXAMPLE 6.1 Find the value of $7^7 \bmod 9$.

Solution $7^7 \bmod 9 = (7^2)^3 * 7 \bmod 9$
$$= (7^2 \bmod 9)^3 \bmod 9 * 7 \bmod 9$$
$7^2 \bmod 9 = 49 \bmod 9 = 4$
$7^6 \bmod 9 = (7^2)^3 \bmod 9 = 4^3 \bmod 9 = 64 \bmod 9 = 1$
$7^7 = 7^6 * 7 \bmod 9 = 1 * 7 \bmod 9 = 7$

EXAMPLE 6.2 Find $3^{110} \bmod 13$

Solution $3^1 \bmod 13 = 3$
$3^2 \bmod 13 = 9 \bmod 13 = 9$
$3^3 \bmod 13 = 27 \bmod 13 = 1$

Now, 3^{110} may be split into: $3^{108} * 3^2$ (since 108 is divisible by 3)

$3^{108} \bmod 13 = (3^3)^{36} \bmod 13 = 1^{36} \bmod 13 = 1$ (since $3^3 \bmod 13 = 1$)

Therefore, $3^{110} = 3^{108} * 3^2 \bmod 13$
$$= 1 * 9 \bmod 13$$
$$= 9 \bmod 13 = 9$$

EXAMPLE 6.3 Find the value of unit place digit of 51^{51}.

Solution We know that unit place digit can be found by taking mod 10 of the given number.

Here, $51 \bmod 10 = 1$

Therefore, $51^{51} \bmod 10 = 1^{51} \bmod 10 = 1$

Therefore, the unit place digit of 51^{51} is 1.

EXAMPLE 6.4 Find the value of final digit (LSB) of $(((((((((7^7)^7)^7)^7)^7)^7)^7)^7$?

Solution To find out the LSB we have to take mod 10 for the given value. We first find out

$$7^2 \bmod 10 = 49 \bmod 10$$
$$= 9 \bmod 10$$
$$= (-1) \bmod 10 \quad \text{(since } 9 \bmod 10 = -1 \bmod 10\text{)}$$

We know that
$$7^7 = (7^2)^3 * 7$$
$$7^7 \bmod 10 = (7^2)^3 * 7 \bmod 10$$
$$= (-1)^3 * 7 \bmod 10 \quad \text{(since } 7^2 \bmod 10 = -1\text{)}$$
$$= -7 \bmod 10$$

Now, $(7^7)^7 \bmod 10 = (-7)^7 \bmod 10$
$$= (-1)^7 (7)^7 \bmod 10$$
$$= -1 * (-7) \bmod 10 \quad \text{(since } 7^7 \bmod 10 = -7\text{)}$$
$$= 7 \bmod 10$$

Now, $((7^7)^7)^7 \bmod 10 = (7)^7 \bmod 10 \quad \text{(since } (7^7)^7 \bmod 10 = 7\text{)}$
$$= -7 \bmod 10 \quad \text{(since } 7^7 \bmod 10 = -7\text{)}$$

Now, $(((7^7)^7)^7)^7 \bmod 10 = (-7)^7 \bmod 10 \quad \text{(since } ((7^7)^7)^7 \bmod 10 = -7\text{)}$
$$= (-1)^7 (7)^7 \bmod 10$$
$$= - (-7) \bmod 10 \quad \text{(since } 7^7 \bmod 10 = -7\text{)}$$
$$= 7 \bmod 10$$

As 7 to the power 7 for odd number of times answer is $-7 \bmod 10$ and even number of times answer is $7 \bmod 10$

Therefore, $(((((((((7^7)^7)^7)^7)^7)^7)^7)^7 = -7 \bmod 10$
$$= 3 \bmod 10$$
$$= 3$$

6.4 FERMAT'S THEOREM

Fermat's theorem is one of the most important theorems in cryptography. It is also known as Fermat's Little theorem. It is useful in public key encryption techniques and primality testing.

Fermat's theorem states that if p is a prime number and n is a positive integer number which is not divisible by p, then

$$n^p = n \bmod p$$

Therefore, $\quad n^{p-1} = 1 \bmod p$

$$n^{p-1} \bmod p = 1 \qquad (6.1)$$

where p is prime and GCD $(n, p) = 1$

$$\boxed{\text{Fermat's theorem} \quad n^{p-1} = 1 \bmod p}$$

Number Theory

EXAMPLE 6.5 Suppose, the prime number $p = 7$ and a positive integer number $n = 3$ then prove Fermat's Little theorem.

Solution Using Fermat's Little theorem (Equation 6.1), we have:
$$3^{7-1} \mod 7 = 3^6 \mod 7$$
$$= 729 \mod 7$$
$$= 1$$

Therefore, $3^{7-1} \mod 7 = 1$
Hence, the theorem is proved.

EXAMPLE 6.6 Suppose $n = 7$ and $p = 19$ then prove Fermat's Little theorem.

Solution Using Equation (6.1), we have:
$$7^{19} \mod 19 = 1$$
$$7^2 = 49 \mod 19 = 11 \;(\mod 19)$$
$$7^4 = (7^2)^2 = (11)^2 = 121 = 7 \;(\mod 19)$$
$$7^8 = (7^4)^2 = (7)^2 = 49 \mod 19 = 11 \;(\mod 19)$$
$$7^{16} = (7^8)^2 = (11)^2 = 121 \mod 19 = 7 \;(\mod 19)$$
$$n^{p-1} = 7^{18} = 7^{16} \times 7^2 = \mathbf{7 \times 11 = 77}$$
$$n^{p-1} \;(\mod p) = 77 \;(\mod 19) = 1$$

Hence proved.

EXAMPLE 6.7 Find the smallest positive residue y in the following congruence.
$$7^{69} = y \mod 23$$

Solution Here $n = 7$ and $p = 23$ as p is prime number and we can apply Fermat's Little theorem to solve this problem.

Fermat's Little theorem is
$$n^{p-1} = 1 \mod p$$

By substituting the values of n and p and rewrite the equation:
$$7^{(23-1)} = 1 \mod 23$$
$$7^{(22)} = 1 \mod 23$$

We can write 7^{69} as $(7^{22})^3 * 7^3$
Therefore,
$$7^{69} = y \mod 23$$

And can be written as:
$$7^{69} = 7^{66} * 7^3$$
$$7^{69} = (7^{22})^3 * 7^3 \mod 23$$
$$7^{69} = (1)^3 * 7^3 \mod 23$$
$$7^{69} = 343 \mod 23$$

Therefore, the smallest positive residue $y = 343$.

EXAMPLE 6.8 Find the smallest positive residue y in the following congruence.

$$3^{101} = y \bmod 13$$

Solution Here $n = 3$ and $p = 13$ as p is prime number and we can apply Fermat's Little theorem to solve this problem.

Fermat's Little theorem is

$$n^{p-1} = 1 \bmod p$$

By substituting the values of n and p and rewrite the equation:

$$3^{(13-1)} = 1 \bmod 13$$
$$3^{(12)} = 1 \bmod 13$$

We can write 3^{101} as $(3^{12})^8 * 3^5$

Therefore,
$$3^{101} = y \bmod 13$$

And can be written as:

$$3^{101} = 3^{96} * 3^5$$
$$3^{101} = (3^{12})^8 * 3^5 \bmod 13$$
$$3^{101} = (1)^8 * 3^5 \bmod 13$$
$$3^{101} = 243 \bmod 13$$
$$3^{101} = 9 \bmod 13$$

Therefore, the smallest positive residue $y = 9$.

6.4.1 An Application of Fermat's Little Theorem and Congruence

Suppose a positive integer be p and two integers x and y are congruent mod p. This is shown as:

$$x \equiv y \bmod p \quad \text{if } p \mid (x - y)$$

For example:

    (i) $5 \equiv 2 \bmod 3$
    (ii) $12 \equiv \bmod 19$
    (iii) $23 \equiv -1 \bmod 12$
    (iv) $-8 \equiv 0 \bmod 4$

Properties

Suppose p is a positive integer number and w, x, y, z are the integers then it follows following properties:

1. $x \equiv x \bmod p$.
2. If $x \equiv y \bmod p$, then $y \equiv x \bmod p$.
3. If $x \equiv y \bmod p$ and $y \equiv z \bmod p$, then $x \equiv z \bmod p$.

Number Theory

4. (a) If $x \equiv Ap + B \bmod p$, then $x \equiv B \bmod p$.
   (b) Every integer x is congruent with mod p to exactly one of 0, 1, 2, ..., $p - 1$.
5. If $x \equiv y \bmod p$ and $z \equiv w \bmod p$, then
   $x \pm z \equiv y \pm w \bmod p$ and $xz \equiv yw \bmod p$.
6. If $(z, p) = 1$ and $xz \equiv yz \bmod p$, then $x \equiv y \bmod p$.

To find all the solutions of the congruence $zx \equiv y \bmod p$, following steps should be followed.

Step 1 Calculate the GCD of z and p. If the GCD is not equal to 1, then there is no solutions for the said congruence.

Step 2 If GCD is 1, find the multiplicative inverse of $z \bmod p$.

Step 3 Write the equation as $x = y * w \bmod p$, where w is the multiplicative inverse of $z \bmod p$.

After solving Step 3, we get the solution of the congruence in terms of $x = \bmod p$.

EXAMPLE 6.9 Find all solutions of the following congruence.

$$4x \equiv 8 \bmod 11$$

Solution
1. Calculate the GCD of 4 and 11.

$$GCD(4, 11) = 1$$

2. As GCD is 1, find the multiplicative inverse.
   The multiplicative inverse of $1 = 4 \bmod 11$ is 3. (As $4 * 3 = 12 \bmod 11 = 1$)
3. $x = 8 * 3 \bmod 11$
   $x = 2 \bmod 11$

All the solutions of the given congruence is $x = 2 \bmod 11$.

EXAMPLE 6.10 Find all solutions of the following congruence.

$$2x \equiv 7 \bmod 10$$

Solution
1. Calculate the GCD of 2 and 10.

$$GCD(2, 10) = 2$$

2. As GCD is 2, the theorem cannot be apply directly.
   $2x = 7 \bmod 10$ is equivalent to $2x - 10y = 7$. This is not possible as LHS is divisible by 2 whereas RHS is not divisible by 2.

So, there is no solution for the given congruence $2x = 7 \bmod 10$.

EXAMPLE 6.11 Find the last digit (unit place digit) of $(7654321)^{23456789}$.

Solution: We know that the unit place digit can be calculated by taking mod 10 of the given number.

Therefore, 7654321 = 1 mod 10

Therefore, $(7654321)^{23456789} = (1)^{23456789} = 1$ mod 10

Therefore, the last digit (unit place digit) of $(7654321)^{23456789}$ is 1.

EXAMPLE 6.12 Compute the value of $12345^{23456789}$ mod 101.

Solution By Fermat's Little theorem $n^{p-1} = 1$ mod p where $n = 12345$ and $p = 101$.

$$12345^{(101-1)} \bmod 101 = 1$$

$$12345^{100} \bmod 101 = 1$$

Therefore, $12345^{23456789}$ mod 101 = $(12345^{100})^{234567} * 12345^{89}$ mod 101

$$= 1 * 12345^{89} \bmod 101$$

$$= 12345^{89} \bmod 101$$

But $\qquad 12345 \bmod 101 = 23$

Therefore, 23^{89} mod 101

$$23 \bmod 101 = 23$$
$$23^2 \bmod 101 = 24$$
$$23^3 \bmod 101 = 47$$
$$23^4 \bmod 101 = 71$$
$$23^5 \bmod 101 = 17$$
$$23^7 \bmod 101 = 4$$
$$23^{89} \bmod 101 = (23^7)^{12}\, 23^5 \bmod 101$$
$$= 4^{12} * 17 \bmod 101$$
$$= 5 * 17 \bmod 101$$
$$= 85$$

Therefore, the value of $12345^{23456789}$ mod 101 = 85.

6.5 EULER'S THEOREM

Before discussing Euler's theorem, we first take a look on Euler totient function. In cryptography, Euler's totient function plays an important role. The totient of a positive integer n is the total number of the positive integer numbers which are less than n and are relatively prime to n. It is shown as $\Phi(n)$, where $\Phi(n)$ is the number of positive integers less than n and relative prime to n.

If $n = 8$, the positive integers less than 8 are 1, 2, 3, 4, 5, 6, 7. Out of these numbers, only 1, 3, 5 and 7 are relatively prime to 8. These numbers do not have any factors common with 8. There are total four such numbers which are relatively prime to 8, therefore $\Phi(8) = 4$.

Take another number $n = 7$, where 7 is the prime number. The positive integers less than 7 are 1, 2, 3, 4, 5, 6, 7. As 7 is a prime number, all the positive integers from 1 to 7 are relatively prime to 7. Thus, $\Phi(7) = 6$. For any prime number n, $\phi(n) = n - 1$.

We can see the totient function for some more numbers as:

$\Phi(3) = 2$ (numbers relatively prime to 3 are 1, 2)

$\Phi(4) = 2$ (numbers relatively prime to 4 are 1, 3)

$\Phi(5) = 4$ (numbers relatively prime to 5 are 1, 2, 3, 4)

$\Phi(6) = 2$ (numbers relatively prime to 6 are 1, 5)

$\Phi(9) = 4$ (numbers relatively prime to 9 are 1, 2, 4, 5)

$\Phi(10) = 4$ (numbers relatively prime to 10 are 1, 3, 7, 9)

$\Phi(11) = 10$ (numbers relatively prime to 11 are 1, 2, 3, 4, 5, 6, 7, 8, 9, 10)

$\Phi(n)$ = Total numbers between 1 and $n–1$ which are relatively prime to n.

As you can see from the above examples that if n is a prime number $\Phi(n) = n - 1$. This helps to calculate the totient function when the factors of n are two different prime numbers. For example, suppose n has two factors A and B, where A and B are primes, then

$$\Phi(n) = \Phi(A * B)$$
$$= \Phi(A) * \Phi(B)$$
$$= (A - 1)*(B - 1)$$

EXAMPLE 6.13 To find the totient function of $n = 91$.

Solution
$$\Phi(91) = \Phi(13 * 7)$$
$$= \Phi(13) * \Phi(7)$$
$$= (13 - 1)*(7 - 1)$$
$$= 12 * 6$$
$$= 72$$

Thus, using above properties it is easy to find out the totient function of a large number whose factors are two prime numbers.

$$\Phi(n) = \Phi(A * B) = \Phi(A) * \Phi(B) = (A - 1) * (B - 1)$$

If A and B are prime numbers

6.5.1 The General Formula to Compute $\Phi(n)$

For a prime number A, the totient function is $\Phi(A) = A - 1$ (because all the numbers less than A are relatively prime to A).

If $B = A^p$, then the numbers which have a common factor with B are the multiples of A. These factors are: $A, AA, AAA, \ldots (A^{p-1})A$. There is total A^{p-1} multiples of A. Therefore, total number of factors relatively prime to A^p is

$$\Phi(A^p) = A^p - A^{p-1}$$
$$= A^{p-1}(A-1)$$
$$= A * A^{p-1}\left(1 - \frac{1}{A}\right)$$
$$= A^p\left(1 - \frac{1}{A}\right)$$

Consider a general form, B is divisible by A. Let $\Phi_A(B)$ be the positive integer number $\leq B$ but not divisible by A and have common factors as: $A, 2A, \ldots (B/A)B$.

$$\Phi_A(B) = B - \frac{B}{A}$$
$$= B\left(1 - \frac{1}{A}\right)$$

Now, C is the prime number which is dividing B. The integer numbers which are divisible by C are $C, 2C, \ldots (B/C)C$. But this duplicate $AC, 2AC, \ldots (B/(AC))AC$. So, the total number of terms that must be subtracted from Φ_A to obtain Φ_{AC} is

$$\Delta\Phi_C(B) = \frac{B}{C} - \frac{B}{AC}$$
$$= \frac{B}{C}\left(1 - \frac{1}{A}\right) \text{ and}$$

$$\Phi_{AC}(B) = \Phi_A(B) - \Delta\Phi_C(B)$$
$$= B\left(1 - \frac{1}{A}\right) - \frac{B}{C}\left(1 - \frac{1}{A}\right)$$
$$= B\left(1 - \frac{1}{A}\right)\left(1 - \frac{1}{C}\right)$$

By induction, the general case is then

$$\Phi(n) = n\prod_{A|n}\left(1 - \frac{1}{A}\right)$$

The generalise formula to calculate $\Phi(n)$ of a number n is:

$$\Phi(n) = A_1^{m_1} * A_2^{m_2} * A_3^{m_n} * \ldots * A_n^{m_n}$$
$$= n * \left(1 - \frac{1}{A_1}\right) * \left(1 - \frac{1}{A_2}\right) * \left(1 - \frac{1}{A_3}\right) * \ldots \left(1 - \frac{1}{A_n}\right)$$

$\Phi(n^m) = n^{m-1}\Phi(n)$ [identity relating to $\Phi(n^m)$ to $\Phi(n)$]

Number Theory

For example, $\Phi(43) = 43 - 1 = 42$

$$\Phi(21) = \Phi(3 \times 7) = \Phi(3) \times \Phi(7) = (3-1) \times (7-1) = 2 \times 6 = 12$$

$$4 = 2^2, \Phi(4) = 4 * \left(1 - \frac{1}{2}\right) = 2$$

$$15 = 3 * 5, \Phi(15) = 15 * \left(1 - \frac{1}{3}\right) * \left(1 - \frac{1}{5}\right) = 15 * \left(\frac{2}{3}\right) * \left(\frac{4}{5}\right) = 8$$

EXAMPLE 6.14 If $n = 9$, find $\Phi(n)$.

Solution $9 = 3^2$, here $A = 3$

$$\Phi(9) = 9 * \left(1 - \frac{1}{3}\right)$$
$$= 9 * \left(\frac{2}{3}\right)$$
$$= 6$$

EXAMPLE 6.15 If $n = 75$, find $\Phi(n)$.

Solution $75 = 5 * 15$
$$= 5 * 5 * 3$$
$$= 5^2 * 3; \text{ here } A_1 = 5 \text{ and } A_2 = 3$$

$$\Phi(75) = 75 * (1 - 1/5) * \left(1 - \frac{1}{3}\right)$$
$$= 75 * \left(\frac{4}{5}\right) * \left(\frac{2}{3}\right)$$
$$= 40$$

Therefore, $\Phi(75) = 40$.

EXAMPLE 6.16 If $n = 5488$, find $\Phi(n)$.

Solution $5488 = 16 * 343$
$$= 2^4 * 7^3; \text{ here } A_1 = 2 \text{ and } A_2 = 7$$
$$= 5488 * \left(1 - \frac{1}{2}\right) * \left(1 - \frac{1}{7}\right)$$
$$= 5488 * \left(\frac{1}{2}\right) * \left(\frac{6}{7}\right)$$
$$= 2352$$

$$\Phi(n) = A_1^{m_1} * A_2^{m_2} * A_3^{m_n} * \ldots * A_n^{m_n}$$
$$= n * \left(1 - \frac{1}{A_1}\right) * \left(1 - \frac{1}{A_2}\right) * 1 - \frac{1}{A_3} * \ldots \left(1 - \frac{1}{A_n}\right)$$

Thus, when we calculate arithmetic modulo n, we get a complete set of residues as $(0, 1, 2, ..., n - 1)$. From this set of residues, the numbers which are relatively prime to n forms a set called the *reduced set of residues*.

For example, if $n = 15$, the complete set of residues is $r_1 = \{0, 1, 2, 3, 4, 5, 6, 7, 8, 9, 10, 11, 12, 13, 14\}$ and the reduced set of residues is $r_2 = \{1, 2, 4, 7, 8, 11, 13, 14\}$. All the numbers from set r_2 are relatively prime to 15. The total count of number in r_2 is called the *Euler totient function* $\Phi(n)$.

Based on the above explanations, the Euler's theorem state that for every a and n that are relatively prime:

$$a^{\Phi(n)} = 1 \bmod(n)$$

$$a = 3; \; n = 8$$

$$\Phi(8) = 4$$

$$3^4 = 81 = 1 \bmod 8$$

where $\Phi(n)$ equals Euler's totient function.

Euler's totient theorem generalises Fermat's theorem. This theorem is an important key to the RSA algorithm. If $GCD(a, n) = 1$, and $a < n$, then $a^{\Phi(n)} = 1 (\bmod n)$. In other words, if a and n are relatively prime, with a being the smaller integer, and when we multiply a with itself $\Phi(n)$ times and divide the result by n, the remainder will be 1.

For any number n, let the reduced set of residues be $\{r_1, r_2, r_3, ... , r_p\}$ then totient function $= \Phi(n) = p$. Multiply each remainder by a and divide by n.

$$r_p a = q_p n + r_p \Phi(n)$$

where r_p is a positive integer less than n.

Then r'_i is relatively prime to n because any common factor of $q_i n$ and r'_i would be a factor of ria.

$$ria = r'_i \bmod (n)$$

Two different remainders r_i and r_j cannot have the same congruence. Therefore, r_i and r'_i run through the same set of remainders.

EXAMPLE 6.17 Let $n = 9$, $a = 5$. Show that $a^{\Phi(n)} \bmod(n) = 1$.

Solution The totient value of 9 is $\Phi(9) = 6$. Therefore, the residues of 9 which are relatively prime to 9 are: 1, 2, 4, 5, 7, 8. Multiply all remainders by $a = 5$ and congruence $\bmod(n = 9)$.

$$1a = 5 \bmod 9 = 5$$
$$2a = 10 \bmod 9 = 1$$
$$4a = 20 \bmod 9 = 2$$
$$5a = 25 \bmod 9 = 7$$
$$7a = 35 \bmod 9 = 8$$
$$8a = 40 \bmod 9 = 4$$

Multiplying all congruence together:

$$5^6 (1)(2)(4)(5)(7)(8) \bmod(9) = (5)(1)(2)(7)(8)\,(4) \bmod(9)$$

$5^6 \mod(9) = 1 \mod(10)$

$5^{\Phi(9)} \mod(9) = 1 \mod(10)$ (since $6 = \Phi(9)$)

This prove the Fermat's little theorem.

EXAMPLE 6.18 Let $n = 15$, $a = 8$. Show that $a^{\Phi(n)} \mod(n) = 1$.

Solution The totient value of $\Phi(15) = 8$. Therefore, the residues of 15 which are relatively prime to 15 are 1, 2, 4, 7, 8, 11, 13, 14. Multiply all remainders by $a = 8$ and congruence $\mod(n = 15)$.

$$1a = 8 \mod 15 = 8$$
$$2a = 16 \mod 15 = 1$$
$$4a = 32 \mod 15 = 2$$
$$7a = 56 \mod 15 = 11$$
$$8a = 64 \mod 15 = 4$$
$$11a = 88 \mod 15 = 13$$
$$13a = 104 \mod 15 = 14$$
$$14a = 112 \mod 15 = 7$$

Multiplying all congruence together:

$$8^8(1)(2)(4)(7)(8)(11)(13)(14) \mod(15) = (1)(2)(4)(7)(8)(11)(13)(14) \mod(15)$$
$$8^8 \mod(15) = 1 \mod(15)$$
$$8^{\Phi(15)} \mod(15) = 1 \mod(15) \text{ (since } 8 = \Phi(15))$$

This prove the Fermat's little theorem.

6.6 EUCLIDEAN ALGORITHM

GCD is a common problem in number theory. Suppose p and q are two numbers. GCD (p, q) is the largest number that divides evenly both p and q. Euclidean algorithm is used to compute the greatest common divisor (GCD) of two integer numbers. This algorithm is also known called as *Euclid's algorithm*. It is named after the Greek mathematician Euclid. This algorithm has many theoretical and practical applications. In modern number theory, this theorem uses as a basic tool for proving theorems.

Euclid theorem: $GCD(p, q) = GCD(q, p \mod q)$

Euclid's algorithm to compute $GCD(p, q)$:

```
n = p, m = q
while m > 0
r = n mod m
n = m, m = r
return n
```

Program to find the GCD of two given numbers.

```
void main()
{
   clrscr();
    int p, q,n,m,r;
    cout<<"Please enter two numbers";
    cin>>p>>q;
    if(p>q)
    {
    n=p;
    m=q;
    }
    else
    {
    n=q;
    m=p;
    }
Loop: r=n%m;
   if(r==0) goto exit;
   else
       n=m;
       m=r;
       goto Loop;
    exit: cout<<"GCD of two numbers is"<<m;
    getch();
}
```

Let p and q be integers, and both are not zero. We know that GCD (p, q) is the greatest common divisor of p and q. Above algorithm gives us the GCD of p and q. We illustrate this theorem using some examples below:

EXAMPLE 6.19 Compute GCD(831, 366) using Euclid's algorithm

Solution

$$831 = 2 * 366 + 265$$
$$366 = 1 * 265 + 101$$
$$265 = 2 * 101 + 63$$
$$101 = 1 * 63 + 38$$
$$63 = 1 * 38 + 25$$
$$38 = 1 * 25 + 13$$
$$25 = 1 * 13 + 12$$
$$13 = 1 * 12 + 1$$
$$12 = 12 * 1 + 0$$

GCD (831, 366) = 1

Number Theory

EXAMPLE 6.20 Compute GCD(2071, 206) using Euclid's algorithm.

Solution

$$2071 = 10 * 206 + 11$$
$$206 = 18 * 11 + 8$$
$$11 = 1 * 8 + 3$$
$$8 = 2 * 3 + 2$$
$$3 = 1 * 2 + 1$$
$$2 = 2 * 1 + 0$$

The GCD(2071, 206) = 1

EXAMPLE 6.21 Compute GCD(2222, 1234) using Euclid's algorithm.

Solution

$$2222 = 1 * 1234 + 988$$
$$1234 = 1 * 988 + 246$$
$$988 = 4 * 246 + 4$$
$$246 = 61 * 4 + 2$$
$$4 = 2 * 2 + 0$$

GCD(2222, 1234) = 2

Example 6.22 Compute GCD(12345, 2345678) using Euclid's algorithm.

Solution

$$2345678 = 190 * 12345 + 128$$
$$12345 = 96 * 128 + 57$$
$$128 = 2 * 57 + 14$$
$$57 = 4 * 14 + 1$$
$$14 = 14 * 1 + 0$$

GCD(12345, 2345678) = 1

6.6.1 Extended Euclidean Algorithm

Suppose p and q are two integer numbers. There exist two integers x and y such that $xp + yq = \text{GCD}(p, q)$. p and b are expressed as trivial combinations: $x = 1x + 0y$ and $y = 0x + 1y$. Now, use extended Euclidean algorithm to find the value of x and y.

Write the two linear combinations vertically as shown below and apply Euclid's algorithm to get $g = \text{GCD}(p, q)$ and the values of x and the y to satisfy the equation $xp + yq = g$.

$$x = 1 \cdot x + 0 \cdot y$$
$$y = 0 \cdot x + 1 \cdot y$$
$$r = 1 \cdot x + (-z) \cdot y$$

Extended Euclidean Algorithm

1. Enter two positive integer numbers p and q such that $p \geq q$.
2. If $q = 0$ then $r = p$, $x_1 = 1$, $y_1 = 0$, and return(r, x_1, y_1).
3. If $q > 0$, do
   (a) $z = p/q$, $r = p \bmod q$, $x_1 = x_3 - zx_2$, $y_1 = y_3 - zy_2$.
   (b) $p = q$, $q = r$, $x_3 = x_2$, $x_2 = x_1$, $y_3 = y_2$, $y_2 = y_1$.
4. $g = p$, $x_1 = x_3$, $y_1 = y_3$, and return (g, x_1, y_1).
5. Print g, x_1 and y_1

EXAMPLE 6.23 Find integers p and q such that $2322p + 654q = 6$ and also find the GCD(2322, 654).

Solution The identity states for 2 numbers x and y with greatest common divisor g, an equation exists that says $g = xp + yq$.

i	x math*	x_i	y math	y_i	r math	r	z math	z
1	Set to 1	1	Set to 0	0		2322		
2	Set to 0	0	Set to 1	1		654	Quotient of 2322/654	3
3	$1 - (3 * 0)$ $x_1 - z_2 * x_2$	1	$0 - (3 * 1)$ $y_1 - z * y_2$	-3	Remainder of 2322/654	360	Quotient of 654/360	1
4	$0 - (1 * 1)$ $x_2 - z_3 * x_3$	-1	$1 - (1 * -3)$ $y_2 - z * y_3$	4	Remainder of 654/360	294	Quotient of 360/294	1
5	$1 - (1 * -1)$ $x_3 - z_4 * x_4$	2	$-3 - (1 * 4)$ $y_3 - z * y_4$	-7	Remainder of 360/294	66	Quotient of 294/66	4
6	$-1 - (4 * 2)$ $x_4 - z_5 * x_5$	-9	$4 - (4 * -7)$ $y_4 - z * y_5$	32	Remainder of 294/66	30	Quotient of 66/30	2
7	$2 - (2 * -9)$ $x_5 - z_6 * x_6$	20	$-7 - (2 * 32)$ $y_5 - z * y_6$	-71	Remainder of 66/30	6	Quotient of 30/6	5
					Remainder of 30/6	0		

*Math indicates the mathematical computations for the values of x, y, z and r.

By taking the last non-zero row, we get: $x = 20$ and $y = -71$ and GCD = 6.
Therefore, $20 * 2322 - 71 * 654 = 6$.
Here, 20 and 71 are relatively prime numbers. This is true for $xm + yn = GCD(x, y)$.
Note: For the above example, this is not the unique solution. But this method gives the simplest solution.

Alternative Method
$2322p + 654q = 6$

$2322 = 654(3) + 360$	$360 = 2322 - 654(3)$
$654 = 360(1) + 294$	$294 = 654 - 360(1)$
$360 = 294(1) + 66$	$66 = 360 - 294(1)$
$294 = 66(4) + 30$	$30 = 294 - 66(4)$
$66 = 30(2) + 6(GCD)$	$6 = 66 - 30(2)$
$30 = 6(5) + 0$	

Number Theory

$$6 = 66 - 30(2)$$
$$6 = 66 - [294 - 66(4)](2)$$
$$6 = 66(9) - 294(2)$$
$$6 = [360 - 294(1)](9) - 294(2)$$
$$6 = 360(9) - 294(11)$$
$$6 = 360(9) - [654 - 360(1)](11)$$
$$6 = 360(20) - 654(11)$$
$$6 = [2322 - 654(3)](20) - 654(11)$$
$$6 = 2322(20) - 654(71)$$

Therefore, the values of $p = 20$ and $q = -71$ and GCD = 6.

EXAMPLE 6.24 Find integers p and q such that $51p + 36q = 3$. Also find the GCD (51, 36).

Solution The identity states for 2 numbers x and y with greatest common divisor g, an equation exists that says $g = xp + yq$.

i	x math	x_i	y math	y_i	r math	r	z math	z
1	Set to 1	1	Set to 0	0		51		
2	Set to 0	0	Set to 1	1		36	Quotient of 51/36	1
3	$1 - (1*0)$ $x_1 - z_2 * x_2$	1	$0 - (1*1)$ $y_1 - z*y_2$	−1	Remainder of 51/36	15	Quotient of 36/15	2
4	$0 - (2*1)$ $x_2 - z_3 * x_3$	−2	$1 - (2*-1)$ $y_2 - z*y_3$	3	Remainder of 36/15	6	Quotient of 15/6	2
5	$1 - (2*-2)$ $x_3 - z_4 * x_4$	5	$-1 - (2*3)$ $y_3 - z*y_4$	−7	Remainder of 15/6	3	Quotient of 6/3	2
					Remainder of 6/3	0		

By taking the last non-zero row, we get: $x = 5$ and $y = -7$ and GCD(51, 36) = 3. Therefore, $$5 * 52 - 7 * 36 = 3.$$

Here, 5 and 7 are relatively prime numbers. This is true for $xm + yn - GCD(x, y)$.

Alternative Method

$51p + 36q = 3$

$51 = 36(1) + 15$	$15 = 51 - 36(1)$
$36 = 15(2) + 6$	$6 = 36 - 15(2)$
$15 = 6(2) + 3$ (GCD)	$3 = 15 - 6(2)$
$6 = 3(2) + 0$	

$$3 = 15 - 6(2)$$
$$3 = 15 - [36 - 15(2)](2)$$
$$3 = 15(5) - 36(2)$$

$3 = [51 - 36(1)](5) - 36(2)$

$3 = 51(5) - 36(5) - 36(2)$

$3 = 51(5) - 36(7)$

$3 = 51(5) + 36(-7)$

Therefore, the values of $p = 5$ and $q = -7$ and GCD = 3.

EXAMPLE 6.25 Find integers p and q such that $56p + 72q = 40$ and also find the GCD(56, 72).

Solution The identity states for 2 numbers x and y with greatest common divisor g, an equation exists that says $g = xp + yq$.

i	x math	x_i	y math	y_i	r math	r	z math	z
1	Set to 1	1	Set to 0	0		56		
2	Set to 0	0	Set to 1	1		72	Quotient of 56/72	0
3	$1 - (0 * 0)$ $x_1 - z_2 * x_2$	1	$0 - (0 * 1)$ $y_1 - z * y_2$	0	Remainder of 56/72	56	Quotient of 72/56	1
4	$0 - (1 * 1)$ $x_2 - z_3 * x_3$	-1	$1 - (1 * 0)$ $y_2 - z * y_3$	1	Remainder of 72/56	16	Quotient of 56/16	3
5	$1 - (3 * -1)$ $x_3 - z_4 * x_4$	4	$0 - (3 * 1)$ $y_3 - z * y_4$	-3	Remainder of 56/16	8	Quotient of 16/8	2
					Remainder of 16/8	0		

By taking the last non-zero row, we get: $x = 4$ and $y = -3$ and GCD = 8.

Therefore, $56 * 4 + 72 * (-3) = 8$.

Here, 4 and 3 are relatively prime numbers. This is true for $xm + yn = GCD(x, y)$.

Note: For the above example, this is not the unique solution. But this method gives the simplest solution.

Alternative Method

$56p + 72q = 40$

$72 = 56(1) + 16$	$16 = 72 - 56(1)$
$56 = 16(3) + 8$(GCD)	$8 = 56 - 16(3)$
$16 = 8(2) + 0$	

$8 = 56 - 16(3)$

$8 = 56 - [72 - 56(1)](3)$

$8 = 56 - 72(3) + 56(3)$

$8 = 56(4) - 72(3)$

$8 = 56(4) + 72(-3)$

We get: $x = 4$ and $y = -3$ and GCD = 8

EXAMPLE 6.26 Use the extended Euclidean algorithm to find the multiplicative inverse of 77 mod 5.

Solution Apply Euclidean algorithm to compute GCD as shown in the left column. It will verify that GCD(77, 5) = 1. Then we will solve for the remainders in the right column.

77 = 5(15) + 2 5 = 2(2) + 1 1 = 5 − 2(2) 2 = 2(1) + 0	2 = 77 − 5(15) 1 = 5 − 2(2)

Use the equations on the right side and perform reverse operation as:

$$1 = 5 - 2(2)$$
$$1 = 5 - [77 - 5(15)](2)$$
$$1 = 5(31) + 77(-2)$$

Therefore, $1 \equiv 77(-2) \mod 5$, or if we prefer a residue value for the multiplicative inverse,

$$1 \equiv 77(3) \mod 101.$$

Therefore, 3 is the multiplicative inverse of 77.

The order of the numbers is important so be careful about the same.

EXAMPLE 6.27 Find the multiplicative inverse of 35 mod 11, using the extended Euclidean algorithm.

Solution Apply Euclidean algorithm first as shown in the left column. It will verify that GCD(35, 11) = 1. Then we will solve for the remainders in the right column, before back solving.

35 = 11(3) + 2 11 = 2(5) + 1 2 = 1(2) + 0	2 = 35 − 11(3) 1 = 11 − 2(5)

Use the equations on the right and perform reverse operation as:

$$1 = 11 - 2(5)$$
$$1 = 11 - [35 - 11(3)](5)$$
$$1 = 11(16) - 35(5)$$
$$1 = 11(16) + 35(-5)$$

Therefore, $1 \equiv 35(-5) \mod 11$, and $-5 \mod 11 = 6$ (since $11 - 5 = 6$)

Therefore, −5 or 6 is the multiplicative inverse of 11.

EXAMPLE 6.28 Find the multiplicative inverse of 40 mod 197, using the extended Euclidean algorithm.

Solution Apply Euclidean algorithm first as shown in the left column. It will verify that GCD(40, 197) = 1. Then we will solve for the remainders in the right column, before back solving.

$197 = 40(4) + 37$	$37 = 197 - 40(4)$
$40 = 37(1) + 3$	$3 = 40 - 37(1)$
$37 = 3(12) + 1$	$1 = 37 - 3(12)$
$3 = 1(3) + 0$	

Use the equations on the right and perform reverse operation as:

$$1 = 37 - 3(12)$$
$$1 = 37 - [40 - 37(1)](12)$$
$$1 = [197 - 40(4)] - [40(12) - (197 - 40(4))(12)]$$
$$1 = 197 - 40(4) - 40(12) + 197(12) - 40(48)$$
$$1 = 197(13) - 40(64)$$
$$1 = 197(13) + 40(-64)$$

Therefore, $1 \equiv 40(-64) \bmod 197$, and $-64 \bmod 197 = 133$ (since $197 - 64 = 133$)

Therefore, -64 or 133 is the multiplicative inverse of 40.

EXAMPLE 6.29 Find the multiplicative inverse of $-74 \bmod 501$, using the extended Euclidean algorithm.

Solution $-74 \bmod 501 = (501 - 74) \bmod 501 = 427 \bmod 501$. Apply Euclidean algorithm first as shown in the left column. It will verify that $\gcd(427, 501) = 1$. Then we will solve for the remainders in the right column, before back solving.

$501 = 74(6) + 57$	$57 = 501 - 74(6)$
$74 = 57(1) + 17$	$17 = 74 - 57(1)$
$57 = 17(3) + 6$	$6 = 57 - 17(3)$
$17 = 6(2) + 5$	$5 = 17 - 6(2)$
$6 = 5(1) + 1$	$1 = 6 - 5(1)$
$5 = 1(5) + 0$	

Use the equations on the right and perform reverse operation as:

$$1 = 6 - 5(1)$$
$$1 = 6 - [17 - 6(2)](1)$$
$$1 = 6(3) - 17(1)$$
$$1 = [57 - 17(3)](3) - 17(1)$$
$$1 = 57(3) - 17(10)$$
$$1 = [57(3) - (74 - 57(1))(10)]$$
$$1 = 57(3) - 74(10) + 57(10)$$
$$1 = [501 - 74(6)](13) - 74(10)$$
$$1 = 501(13) - 74(88)$$

Therefore, $1 \equiv -74(88) \bmod 501$.

Therefore, 88 is the multiplicative inverse of $-74 \bmod 501$.

6.7 PRIMALITY TEST

There is no simple and efficient mechanism to find out the prime number. To know whether a given number is prime or not, a test is conducted. That test is called as *primality test*. It is an algorithm which checks whether a given number is prime or not. Primality testing and integer factorisation is different. Factorisation is a computationally hard as compared to primality testing. We know that the frequency of prime number for different equal intervals is not same. There are around 4 * 1097 prime numbers in an integer number of 200 digits. Primality tests are of two types: deterministic test and probabilistic test. The first test, deterministic test always correctly determines the prime number. Its accuracy is 100%. But it is slower as compared to probabilistic test. The second test, probabilistic test is less accurate. Its accuracy is not 100% as sometime it may falsely determine a composite number as a prime. But it is faster than deterministic test.

6.7.1 Naïve Methods

The simplest primality test follows the following steps.

Step 1 Enter the positive integer number n.
Step 2 Set the value of $m = 2$.
Step 3 Divide n by m. Find the remainder, if the remainder is zero, then n is divisible by m and go to step 7.
Step 4 Increase the value of m by 1.
Step 5 Repeat steps 3 and 4 until $m < n/2$.
Step 6 Number n is a prime number and exit.
Step 7 Number n is a composite number and exit.

Program to print prime numbers

```
void main()
{
   clrscr();
   cout<<"\n\n Program to Print Prime number upto given number\n\n ";
   int i,n,r,a,k;
   cout<<" Please enter the number.\n\n ";
   cin>>k;
   cout<<"The Prime Numbers are:\n\n ";
   for(n=3; n<=k; n++)
   {
   for(i=2; i<n; i++)
      {
      r=n%i;
      if(r==0)
      {
```

```
        goto Loop;
        }
    }
        cout<<"\n "<<n;
Loop:
}
    getch();
}
```

If the number is not divisible by 2 then it is not divisible by any even number. So, there is no need to check the divisibility by other even numbers. Therefore, value of m should be 2 and all odd numbers and less than $n/2$. This improves the efficiency of the method. A Naïve algorithm is as follows:

1. Enter any positive integer greater than 2, suppose the number be n.
2. Divide the number (n) by all odd positive integer numbers from 3 to square root of number (n).
3. If the number (n) is divisible by any one of these numbers, then the number (n) is composite.
4. Otherwise it is prime number.

6.7.2 Probabilistic Tests

The probabilistic test checks whether a number is prime or not. The accuracy of this method is not 100%. Sometime the composite number is also identifying as prime number. This test is very fast.

1. Enter any positive integer greater than 2, suppose the number be n.
2. Select one integer number (p) randomly such that $p \in Z(n)$.
3. If $p \in W(n)$, then n is a composite number otherwise it is a prime number

6.7.3 Fermat Primality Test

Fermat's theorem is one of the most important theorems in cryptography. It is also known as *Fermat's Little* theorem. It is useful in public key encryption techniques and primality testing. It is a statement about powers in modular arithmetic in the special case where the modular base is a prime number. Fermat primality test is the simple test for identifying whether a given number is a prime number or not.

Fermat's theorem states that if p is a prime number and n is an integer number which is relatively prime to p, then

$$np - 1 = \mod p$$

But this equation fails for some cases, when p is composite. The Fermat's test for finding the primality of an integer number p is:

1. Enter any positive integer greater than 2, suppose the number be p.
2. Select an integer number n such that $n \in \{2, \dots p - 1\}$.
3. Find the GCD(n, p). If GCD is greater than 1, then p is composite number.

4. Find n^{p-1} mod p, if it is not 1, then stop. The result is p which is a composite number.
5. If $n^{p-1} = 1$ mod p, then p is probably prime.

This test is simple and efficient. But its accuracy is not 100% because composite numbers will always pass Step 3 from above algorithm

6.7.4 Miller–Rabin Primality Test

The faster algorithm for primality testing is Miller–Rabin primality test and Solovay–Strassen primality test. These tests detect all composite numbers.

Step 1 Select an odd integer number p, such that $p > 1$ and $p - 1 = 2^k q$ where q is odd number. Select another random integer number n such that $1 < n < p - 1$.

Step 2 Calculate $b_0 = n^q$ mod p.
   (a) If $b_0 = -1$ mod p, then go to Step 3.
   (b) Otherwise calculate $b_1 = b_0^2$ mod p. If $b_1 = 1$ mod p, then go to step 4.
   (c) If $b_1 = -1$ mod p then go to Step 3.
   (d) Otherwise, calculate $b_2 = b_1^2$ mod p. If $b_2 = 1$ mod p then go to step 4.
   (e) If $b_2 = -1$ mod p, then go to step 3.
   Continue the process until b_{k-1}.

Step 3 p is probably prime and stop.

Step 4 p is composite and stop.

Miller–Rabin test is correct under extended Riemann hypothesis. The time complexity of this test is $O(\log n)$.

6.7.5 Agrawal, Kayal and Saxena Primality Test (AKS Test)

In 2002, the three Indian scientists, Mahindra Agrawal, Neeraj Kayal and Nitin Saxena constructed a primality test, called *AKS test*. AKS test is based on the generalisation of Fermat's Little theorem.

The AKS theorem is as follows:

Enter any positive integer $n > 1$ and select another positive integer r for which n has order $> (\log n)^2$ mod r. Then n is prime if and only if:
   (a) n is not a perfect square
   (b) It does not have any prime factor $\leq r$
   (c) $((X + a)^n \neq X^n + a \pmod{X^r - 1, n})$ for each integer a such that $1 \leq a \leq$ sqrt $(r) \log n$

Enter any positive integer $n > 1$
1. If $(n = a^b$ for $a \in N$ and $b > 1)$, then the number is composite.
2. Find the smallest r such that $O_r(n) > \log^2 n$.
3. If $1 < (a, n) < n$ for some $a \leq r$, then the number is composite.

4. If $n \leq r$, then the number is prime.
5. For $a = 1$ to $\lfloor \text{sqrt}(\Phi(r)) \log(n) \rfloor$ do
   if $((X + a)^n \neq X^n + a \pmod{X^r - 1, n})$, then the number is composite.
6. The number is prime.

6.8 CHINESE REMAINDER THEOREM

According to D. Wells, the problem posed by Sun Tsu (4th century AD) there are certain things whose numbers are not known. Suppose there is some number p which is divided by 2, the remainder is 1, if p is divided by 3, the remainder is 1 and if p is divided by 4, 5 and 6, the remainder is 1. But if it is divided by 7, the remainder is zero. Then what is the smallest value of p. Chinese remainder theorem is used to get the solution of such problem. Using this theorem we get the value of p.

Chinese remainder theorem: There are two relatively prime numbers m and n, which are modulo m and n, the congruence

$$p \equiv a \bmod m$$
$$p \equiv b \bmod n$$

have a unique solution: $\quad p \bmod mn$

Theorem Suppose $n_1, n_2, ..., n_r$ are the relatively prime integer numbers and $b_1, b_2, ..., b_r$ are the remainders for $n_1, n_2, ..., n_r$ respectively. Then the system of congruence, $p \equiv b_i \pmod{n_i}$ for $1 \leq i \leq r$, has a unique solution.

$$N = n_1 * n_2 * \cdots * n_r,$$

which is given by:

$$p \equiv b_1 N_1 y_1 + b_2 N_2 y_2 + \cdots + b_r N_r y_r \pmod{N},$$

where $N_i = N/n_i$ and

$$y_i \equiv (N_i)^{-1} \pmod{n_i} \text{ for } 1 \leq i \leq r,$$

where y_i is the multiplicative inverse of $(N_i) \pmod{n_i}$. (Use extended Euclidean algorithm to calculate multiplicative inverse)

Observe that $\text{GCD}(N_i, n_i) = 1$ for $1 \leq i \leq r$. Therefore, all y_i exist. Now, notice that since $N_i y_i \equiv 1 \pmod{n_i}$,

we have $b_i N_i y_i \equiv b_i \pmod{n_i}$ for $1 \leq i \leq r$.

On the other hand, $b_i N_i y_i \equiv 0 \pmod{n_j}$ if $j \neq i$ (since $n_j \mid N_i$ in this case).

Thus, we see that $p \equiv b_i \pmod{n_i}$ for $1 \leq i \leq r$.

If p_0 and p_1 are the solutions, then we would have

$p_0 - p_1 \equiv 0 \pmod{n_i}$ for all i, so $p_0 - p_1 \equiv 0 \pmod{N}$, i.e., they are the same modulo N.

Number Theory

> **Chinese Remainder Theorem**
> 1. Firstly expressed the problem as a system of congruence,
> $$p \equiv b_i(\text{mod } n_i)$$
> where, n_i are relatively prime numbers: n_1, n_2, n_3 and so on
> b_i is the respective remainder for modulo n_i such that b_1 for n_1, b_2 for n_2 and so on.
> p is the value of solution.
> 2. Calculate the value of N
> $$N = n_1 * n_2 * \cdots * n_i$$
> 3. Calculate the value of $N_i = N/n_i$ such that $N_1 = N/n_1$, $N_2 = N/n_2$ and so on.
> 4. Calculate the multiplicative inverse for $y_i \equiv (N_i)^{-1} \pmod{n_i}$
> where y_i is the multiplicative inverse of N_i mod n_i.
> 5. The value of p is calculated as:
> $$p \equiv (b_1 N_1 y_1 + b_2 N_2 y_2 + \ldots + b_r N_r y_r) \text{ mod } N$$
> where, p is the solution of the problem.

EXAMPLE 6.30 Find the smallest multiple of 10 which has remainder 1 when divided by 3, remainder 6 when divided by 7 and remainder 6 when divided by 11.

Solution The factors of 10 are: 2 and 5.
Problem is now expressed as a system of congruence as:
$$p \equiv b_i(\text{mod } n_i)$$
where $n = 2, 3, 5, 7$ and 11 which are relatively prime and $b = 0, 1, 0, 6$ and 6 are the remainders for respective value of n.

$p = 0 \text{ mod } 2$
$p = 1 \text{ mod } 3$
$p = 0 \text{ mod } 5$
$p = 6 \text{ mod } 7$
$p = 6 \text{ mod } 11$

To solve for p we first calculate the value of N as:
$N = n_1 * n_2 * \ldots * n_r$
$N = 2 * 3 * 5 * 7 * 11 = 2310$
and find the value of $N_i = N/n_i$ as:
$N_2 = 2310/2 = 1155$
$N_3 = 2310/3 = 770$
$N_5 = 2310/5 = 462$
$N_7 = 2310/7 = 330$
$N_{11} = 2310/11 = 210$

Now, find out the multiplicative inverse as:

$$y_i \equiv (N_i)^{-1} (\bmod\ n_i)$$
$$y_2 = (1155)^{-1}(\bmod\ 2) = 1$$
$$y_3 = (770)^{-1}(\bmod\ 3) = 2$$
$$y_5 = (462)^{-1}(\bmod\ 5) = 3$$
$$y_7 = (330)^{-1}(\bmod\ 7) = 1$$
$$y_{11} = (210)^{-1}(\bmod\ 11) = 1$$

The solution for the above problem is:

$$p \equiv b_1 N_1 y_1 + b_2 N_2 y_2 + \cdots + b_r N_r y_r\ (\bmod\ N),$$
$$p = 0(N_2 * y_2) + 2(N_3 * y_3) + 0(N_5 * y_5) + 6(N_7 * y_7) + 6(N_{11} * y_{11})$$
$$p = 0(1155)(1) + 1(770)(2) + 0(462)(3) + 6(330)(1) + 6(210)(1)$$
$$p = 0 + 1540 + 0 + 1980 + 1260$$
$$p = 4780\ \bmod\ 2310 = 160.$$

EXAMPLE 6.31 An old woman purchases a basket of some eggs from the market. While walking on the road she stops for a while and keep her basket of eggs down on the road. A horse running on the road accidentally steps on the basket and crushing all the eggs in the basket. The rider offers to pay the old woman for the damaged eggs. So, he asks her about the total number of eggs she had brought. The old woman does not remember the exact number of eggs in the basket. So she told the rider that when she had taken out two eggs at a time from the basket, there was one egg left. When she had taken out three eggs at a time from the basket, there were two eggs left. When she had taken out five eggs at a time from the basket, there were four eggs left. Find out, the smallest number of eggs an old woman could have had in her basket?

(Above puzzle is mentioned by Oystein Ore taken from Brahma-Sphuta-Siddhanta by Brahmagupta (born 598 AD)):

Solution Problem is now expressed as a system of congruence as:

$$p \equiv b_i\ (\bmod\ n_i)$$

where $n = 2, 3, 5$ and $b = 1, 2, 4$.

$$p = 1\ \bmod\ 2$$
$$p = 2\ \bmod\ 3$$
$$p = 4\ \bmod\ 5$$

To solve for p we first calculate the value of N as

$$N = n_1 * n_2 * \ldots * n_r$$
$$N = 2 * 3 * 5 = 30$$

and find the value of $N_i = N/n_i$ as:

$$N_2 = 30/2 = 15$$
$$N_3 = 30/3 = 10$$
$$N_5 = 30/5 = 6$$

Now, find out the multiplicative inverse as:
$$y_i \equiv (N_i)^{-1}(\bmod\ n_i)$$
$$y_2 = (15)^{-1}(\bmod\ 2) = 1$$
$$y_3 = (10)^{-1}(\bmod\ 3) = 2$$
$$y_5 = (6)^{-1}(\bmod\ 5) = 3$$

The solution for the above problem is:
$$p \equiv b_1 N_1 y_1 + b_2 N_2 y_2 + \ldots + b_r N_r y_r (\bmod\ N)$$
$$p = b_2(N_2 * y_2) + b_3(N_3 * y_3) + b_5(N_5 * y_5)$$
$$p = 1(15)(1) + 2(10)(1) + 4(6)(1)$$
$$p = 15 + 20 + 24$$
$$p = 59\ \bmod\ 30 = 29.$$

There are total 29 eggs in the basket.

EXAMPLE 6.32 Monica breeds some pets. She does not know the exact number of pets she has. So she told that when she takes rounds, she observed some things. In the morning there are five pets in each group except one group which has only two pets. In the afternoon there are seven pets in each group except one group which has six pets. In the evening, there are eleven pets in each group. Monica is sure that there are fewer than 150 pets. Find out, the smallest number of pets does she have.

Solution Problem is now expressed as a system of congruence as:
$$p \equiv b_i(\bmod\ n_i)$$
where n = 5, 7, 11 and b = 2, 6, 0
$$p = 2\ \bmod\ 5$$
$$p = 6\ \bmod\ 7$$
$$p = 0\ \bmod\ 11$$

To solve for p we first calculate the value of N as:
$$N = n_1 * n_2 * \ldots * n_r$$
$$N = 5 * 7 * 11 = 385$$
and find the value of $N_i - N/n_i$ as:
$$N_5 = 385/5 = 77$$
$$N_7 = 385/7 = 55$$
$$N_{11} = 385/11 = 35$$

Now, find out the multiplicative inverse as:
$$y_i \equiv (N_i)^{-1}(\bmod\ n_i)$$
$$y_5 = (77)^{-1}(\bmod\ 5) = 3$$
$$y_7 = (55)^{-1}(\bmod\ 7) = 6$$
$$y_{11} = (35)^{-1}(\bmod\ 11) = 6$$

The solution for the above problem is:
$$p \equiv b_1 N_1 y_1 + b_2 N_2 y_2 + \ldots + b_r N_r y_r \pmod{N},$$
$$p = b_2(N_2 * y_2) + b_3(N_3 * y_3) + b_5(N_5 * y_5)$$
$$p = 2(77)(3) + 6(55)(6) + 0(35)(6)$$
$$p = 462 + 1980 + 0$$
$$p = 2442 \bmod 385$$
$$p = 132$$

There are total 132 pets.

6.9 DISCRETE LOGARITHMS

Discrete logarithms have an important role in Diffie–Hellman and the digital signature algorithms.

From Euler's theorem, for every p and n which are relatively prime we have,
$$p^{\Phi(n)} = 1 \bmod(n)$$
where $\Phi(n)$ is the number of positive integers less than n and relative prime to n.

So in general it is:
$$p^n = 1 \bmod n$$

If p and n are relatively prime, then there is at least one integer n that satisfies above equation.

Suppose $p = 3$ and $n = 13$ are the numbers which are relatively prime. Let us see the power of 3, modulo 13:
$$3^1 = 3 = 3 \bmod 13$$
$$3^2 = 9 = 9 \bmod 13$$
$$3^3 = 27 = 13 * 2 + 1 = 1 \bmod 13$$
$$3^4 = 81 = 13 * 6 + 3 = 3 \bmod 13$$
$$3^5 = 243 = 13 * 18 + 9 = 9 \bmod 13$$

This can prove that $3^3 = 1 \bmod 13$ and therefore $3^{3+i} = 3^3 \, 3^i = 3^i \bmod 13$ and hence any two powers of 3 whose exponents differ by 3 are congruent to each other (mod 13).

In general, let F be a finite cyclic group with n elements. We assume that the group is written multiplicatively. Let p be a generator of F; then every element f of F can be written in the form $f = p^k$ for some integer k. Furthermore, any two such integers representing f will be congruent modulo n. We can thus define a function
$$\log_b : F = Z_n$$

(where Z_n denotes the ring of integers modulo n) by assigning to f the congruence class of k modulo n. This function is a group isomorphism, called the *discrete logarithm* to base p.

The familiar base change formula for ordinary logarithms remains valid: If y is another generator of F, then we have
$$\log_y(f) = \log_y(p) \cdot \log_p(f)$$

6.9.1 Index Calculus Algorithm

The index calculus algorithm is used for computing discrete logarithms. The discrete logarithms used to find p using $g^p = h$ mod n, where g, h and n are given.

The discrete logarithms algorithm applies to the group where p is a prime using a factor base.

Factor base is a set of small primes. For example, factor base having n elements are $= \{p_1, p_2, p_3, \ldots p_n\}$. For $n = 5$, the factor base $= \{2, 3, 5, 7, 11\}$ i.e., five prime numbers. If the factor base is small, the efficiency of the algorithm increases. But if the group is large the factor base must be relatively large.

Smooth Integer

If the biggest prime factor of q is less than or equal number r then the number q is called r-smooth.

For example, if our $r = 11$, then the number $q = 100$ is r-smooth because it factorises to $2 * 2 * 5 * 5 = 2^2 * 5^2$ and the biggest prime factor is 5 which is less than 11 ($5 \leq 11$). If we take the number 248, it is NOT r-smooth because it factorises to $2 * 2 * 2 * 31 = 2^3 * 31$ and the biggest prime factor is 31 which is greater than 11 ($31 \leq 11$).

The algorithm is divided in two parts.

1. Gathering a number of linear relations between the factor base and powers of the generator g and solving the logarithms using linear algebra.
2. Computation of the discrete logarithm of a desired element.

Now, find out x using algebraic manipulation.

Given p, g, $x = g^a$(mod p), determine a.

Choose bound B and factor base.

Suppose $p_0, p_1, \ldots, p_{n-1}$ are primes in factor base.

Pre-compute discrete logs:

$\log_g p_i$ for each i

Randomly select $k \in \{0, 1, 2, \ldots, p-2\}$ and

compute $y = x \cdot g^k$ (mod p) until find y that factors completely over factor base.

Then,

$y = x \cdot g^k = p_0^{d_0} \cdot p_1^{d_1} \ldots p_{n-1}^{d_{n-1}}$ (mod p)

Take $\log_g$ of y we get,

$a = \log_g x = (d_0 \log_g p_0 + d_0 \log_g p_0 + \ldots + d_0 \log_g p_0 - k)$ (mod $(p-1)$)

This gives us a value of 'a'.

Note: $p - 1$ follows from Fermat's Little theorem.

SUMMARY

Prime number theory is very important in cryptography. There is no simple and efficient algorithms available to find out the largest prime number. Primality test is used to check whether the number is prime or not. Two numbers are relatively prime if their GCD is 1. Fermat's theorem is useful in public key encryption techniques and primality testing. The totient of a positive integer n is the total number of positive integer numbers which are less than n and are relatively prime to n. It is shown as $\Phi(n)$. Suppose there are two relatively prime numbers m and n, which are modulo m and n, Chinese remainder theorem provides the solution of the congruence. The index calculus algorithm is used for computing discrete logarithms. The discrete logarithms used to find p using $g^p = h \bmod n$, where g, h and n are given. Factor base is a set of small primes. If the biggest prime factor of q is less than or equal number r then the number q is called r-smooth. Euclid's algorithm is used to calculate the GCD of two numbers, whereas extended algorithm is used to find the multiplicative inverse of a number.

EXERCISES

6.1 Define prime number. What are the different tests to check whether a number is prime or not?

6.2 Explain Euler's totient function. Find the totient value for 25.

6.3 What is the primitive root of a number? How many primitive roots the number 15 has? Calculate all possible primitive roots for 15.

6.4 Explain index calculus algorithm.

6.5 Compare an index calculus algorithm with a discrete logarithm.

6.6 Explain fast deterministic test.

6.7 What is primality test?

6.8 Explain Fermat's theorem.

6.9 m and $m + 1$ are two consecutive integers. Prove why GCD $(m, m + 1) = 1$.

6.10 How many primitive roots the number 10 has? Find all primitive roots of 10.

6.11 Using Fermat's theorem, find $3^{110} \bmod 13$. [Ans: 9]

6.12 Find the value of $12346^{23456789} \bmod 11$?

6.13 Find the value of final digit (LSB) of $(((((((((9^9)^9)^9)^9)^9)^9)^9)^9)^9$?

6.14 Find the value of $\Phi(243)$. [Ans: 162]

6.15 Find the multiplicative inverse of 55 mod 101, using the Euclidean algorithm. [Ans: 90]

6.16 Compute GCD (1276, 244). [Ans: 4]

6.17 Find the GCD of 2740 and 1760 using Euclidean algorithm. [Ans: 20]

6.18 Compute GCD (12345, 120). [Ans: 15]

Number Theory

6.19 Find the multiplicative inverse of 121 mod 1245, using the Euclidean algorithm.

[Ans: 391]

6.20 Find the multiplicative inverse of 1761 mod 2740, using the Euclidean algorithm.

[Ans: 2281]

6.21 Find the value of $\Phi(144)$. [Ans: 48]

6.22 Find integers p and q for the equation $1124p + 84q$ and also find the GCD.

[**Ans:** $p = 8$, $y = -107$]

6.23 Find integers p and q such that $52p + 56q = 36$ and also find the GCD.

[Ans: There is no positive solution for the equation]

6.24 Find integers p and q such that $7920p + 4536q = 72$. [Ans: $p = -4$, $q = 7$]

6.25 Find all solutions of the following congruence
(a) $7x = 9 \bmod 15$
(b) $6x = 23 \bmod 31$
(c) $11x = 2 \bmod 45$
(d) $2x = 7 \bmod 11$

6.26 Use Chinese theorem and solve the following puzzle.

Five robbers and a monkey are stucked on an island. The robbers have collected a pile of bananas. They decided to divide the bananas equally among themselves in the next morning. The robbers are not having trust on one another. One robber wakes up during the night and divides the bananas into five equal parts with one left over, which he gives to the monkey. The robber then hides his portion of the pile. During the night, each of the other robbers does exactly the same thing by dividing the pile he finds into five equal parts leaving one banana for the monkey and hiding his portion. In the morning, the robbers gather and split the remaining pile of bananas into five equal parts and again one is left over for the monkey. What is the smallest number of bananas the robbers could have collected for their original pile?

MULTIPLE CHOICE QUESTIONS

6.1 The extended Euclidean algorithm is of interest to cryptographers because
(a) Large composites number can be factorised easily using this algorithm
(b) A multiplicative inverse can be calculated using this algorithm easily
(c) Primality of large primes can be checked using this algorithm
(d) None of of the above

6.2 If $n = 143 = 11 * 13$, calculate $15^{241} \bmod n$
(a) 18
(b) 9
(c) 1
(d) 15

6.3 If $n = 77$, then calculate $\Phi(n)$
(a) 5
(b) 14
(c) 30
(d) 60

6.4 Calculate $(36^{106} \bmod 107) \bmod 37$
(a) 1
(b) 3
(c) 107
(d) 7

Answers

6.1 (b)   **6.2** (d)   **6.3** (d)   **6.4** (a)

CHAPTER 7

Public Key Cryptosystems

7.1 INTRODUCTION

Encryption techniques are of two types, symmetric encryption and asymmetric encryption. In symmetric encryption same key is used by both the users for encryption as well as decryption. But the encryption is done by the sender and decryption is done by the recipient. So, both the users should know the key. As the sender and recipient are located at different physical locations, so the key should be transmitted securely from sender to recipient. This needs that the transmission channel should be secure so that the key transmitted securely between two users. But if the transmission channel is secure, then not only key, the message also transmitted securely. So, in this case encryption is not required. That means, this channel is not 100% secure. So, some mechanism is required for transmission of key. This secure transmission of key is called *key distribution*.

In asymmetric encryption, two different keys are used, one for encryption and another for decryption. These keys are mathematically related to each other. Sometime, in asymmetric encryption, two keys are used by each user, i.e., public key and private key. Public key is publicaly available so that not only sender and recipient but anybody may know the key. Another key is private key which is a secret key known to the originator (owner) of the key. In all these techniques, some mechanism called key distribution technique is used.

For symmetric encryption, initially both the users should agree on the key. This key may be transmitted through e-mail, phone, postal system or some other medium. The security of the message is dependent on the security of the key. The key should be known to the sender and the recipient. If someone other than the sender and the recipient knows the key, then he/she can misuse it and decrypt the message. This key distribution is the most important part of the symmetric encryption system. To maintain the security of the key, only the secrecy of the key in transmission is not sufficient but one should take care of secrecy of key from the creation of the key to

distribution and storage of it. The different steps used for secrecy of key between the sender and the recipient are called *key management*. Key management includes:
1. Authentication of the users of the key
2. Generation of key
3. Distribution of key
4. Storage of key

In cryptography, there are different algorithms which support for key management. RSA algorithm, the well known key generation algorithm, provides the mechanism for securely generation of key. We will learn more detail of RSA in Section 7.3. Diffie-Hellman algorithm solves the problem of key distribution. In this algorithm, using the public key of the users, the session key is generated without transmitting the private key of the users. We will learn more detail about Diffie-Hellman algorithm in Chapter 8.

Asymmetric cryptography is also known as public key cryptography. We know that asymmetric key encryption algorithms are of two types:
 (i) There are two keys, one for each user;
 (ii) There are four keys, each user have a pair of keys; the public key–private key.

There is no need to keep the public key secret. For type 1 algorithms, both the keys must be kept secret. Symmetric encryption algorithms have some drawbacks. Cryptanalysis is easy. Week key problem with some symmetric encryption blocks ciphers. Key distribution is the major issue with symmetric encryption. Authentication of the users cannot be done in symmetric encryption. Public key cryptography provides the solution for these issues. Asymmetric encryption algorithms cannot be decrypted easily. Key distribution is not required as each user have own keys. Therefore, public key cryptography provides more security as compared to symmetric encryption.

7.2 PUBLIC KEY CRYPTOGRAPHY

Asymmetric encryption system is also known as *public key cryptography*. It is different from symmetric encryption system. In asymmetric encryption system, a pair of keys is used to call public key and private key. A key which is freely available to all users is called *public key*. Whereas private is a secret key and it is never transmitted from the owner to any other users. Mathematically, it is not possible to determine the private key from the public key. From a pair of keys, either key is used for encryption and other key for decryption.

The components of asymmetric encryptions are:
- Plaintext
- Encryption algorithm
- Public key and private key
- Ciphertext
- Decryption algorithm

The working of public key cryptography is shown in Figure 7.1.

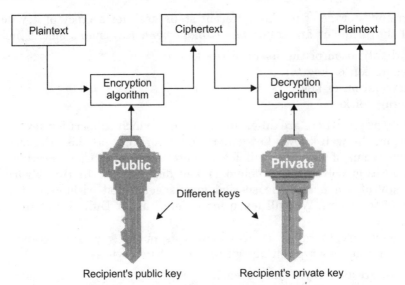

Figure 7.1 Public key cryptography—secrecy.

The scheme showed in Figure 7.1 shows that the user can broadcast his key without keeping it secret. Using the public key of recipient, the sender encrypts the message and sends the ciphertext to the recipient. When the message received, the recipient uses his private key and decrypts the ciphertext. As the private key is known to the recipient only, anybody else cannot decrypt the ciphertext. In this way the secrecy of the message is provided. As the public key of the recipient is publicaly available to anybody, any person has the key and can encrypt the message and send it to the recipient. There is no way to check, whether the message is sent by the expected sender or somebody else. So, in this scheme authentication of the sender cannot be taken place.

Asymmetric encryption technique takes more computation time as compared to symmetric encryption technique. Therefore, asymmetric encryption technique is not suitable for large message. But as it is more secure, it is useful to send the key for symmetric encryption. This helps to solve the problem of key distribution in symmetric encryption. The same approach is used in secure socket layer (SSL) protocol.

Alternatively, the sender may use his own private key for encryption. Then the ciphertext is sent to the recipient. The recipient decrypts the ciphertext by using sender's public key. In this scheme, the recipient knows that the ciphertext (message) is sent by the expected sender. So sender's authentication takes place. But at the same time, the ciphertext can be decrypted by any person who knows sender's public key. That means, confidentiality of the message cannot be maintained.

We can summarise asymmetric encryption technique as:

- **Use of two keys:** *private key* and *public key*
- **Private key:** Key is known only by its owner.
- **Public key:** Key is known to everyone.
- **Relation between both keys:** One key is use for encryption and other key is use for decryption, and vice-versa

7.2.1 Authentication, Secrecy and Confidentiality

Authentication means to verify the origin and the integrity of a document. It verifies whether the message is sent by the intended recipient or not. It allows the recipient to verify about the origin of the message. Authentication can be done using different techniques. These techniques are based on secret information. This information should be known only to the users.

Authentication is provided by using a private key for encryption of the message by the sender so that the recipient knows that the message is encrypted by the sender and not anybody else because only the sender knows his own private key. In this, authentication (origin) of the sender is done. As the message is encrypted by the sender's private key and if the attacker captures the data and tries to modify it and sends it, he should know the private key of the sender. And the private key is secret and known to sender only, so the attacker cannot encrypt the message using the same key. If he uses some other key for encryption, then the message cannot be decrypted using sender's public key. Instead of it, attacker's private key is needed which is not available with recipient and the recipient knows that the message is not sent by the authenticated person. In this way authentication and origin of the message and sender can be verified. This also helps to keep the message unchanged, i.e., integrity of the message be maintained. For example, we have our email id and password for the same. This id and password are analogous to public key and the password respectively. One can send the message from his email account by using his password (analogous to private key). The recipient of the message knows that only the intended sender sends the message. So, authentication of the sender takes place. The senders can send the message to anybody using their email id (analogous to public key). The recipient opens this mail account using his password and then read the message. So only authenticate recipient read the message. This provides secrecy.

Figure 7.2 shows the authentication mechanism using private key for encryption and public key for decryption. This provides authentication and not the secrecy.

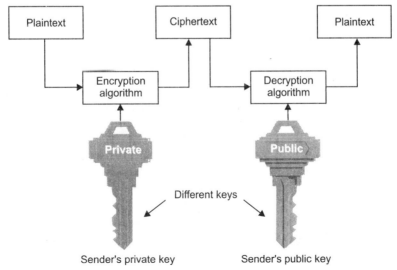

Figure 7.2 Public key encryption—authentication.

Because any third person can have a sender's public key and can decrypt the message sent by the authenticated sender. So, the message cannot be secret using this scheme. Depending on the application, i.e., whether authentication is required for secrecy, one of the above schemes is useful.

In some applications, both authentication and secrecy are required. That means the authentications of both the sender and the recipient should be done. This is called *confidentiality*. Confidentiality provides both the authentication of the users and the recipient and also the integrity (secrecy) of the data. Confidentiality can be provided using the following scheme as shown in Figure 7.3.

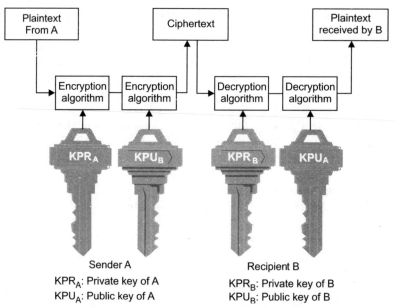

Figure 7.3 Public key encryption—secrecy and authentication.

In confidentiality, each user has two keys, i.e., public key and private key. Two algorithms are used for encryption and decryption. This is because the data or plaintext is encrypted twice before transmitting and also the ciphertext is decrypted twice. The sender first uses his private key to encrypt the message and again encrypts the ciphertext using recipient's public key. When the data is received at the receiving end the recipient's private key is required for decryption. This authenticates that only intended recipient can decrypt the message. Then public key of sender is used again to decrypt the message. This authenticates that the message is sent by the intended sender and not anybody else. In this way confidentiality is provided.

Figure 7.3, illustrated the use of private key and public key to provide authentication of the users and secrecy to the message. It is explained as:

Step 1 User A, i.e., sender, first encrypts the message by his/her own private key. As nobody knows A's private key, so nobody is able to send the encrypted message using A's private key. This provides authentication in the system.

Step 2 A uses the public key of B, i.e., receiver, to encrypt the ciphertext generated in Step 1.

Step 3 User A sends the encrypted message to user B.

Step 4 The private key of B is required to decrypt the message as his public key is used for encryption. B's private key is known to him only so, only B can decrypt the message and nobody else able to do it.

Step 5 Then decrypt the message using A's, i.e., sender's public key. Steps 3 and 4 provide secrecy to the message.

Therefore, the above scheme provides authentication and secrecy both but not confidentiality. To provide confidentiality one can use following scheme as shown in Figure 7.4.

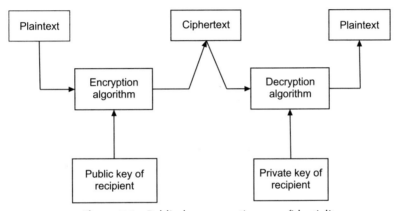

Figure 7.4 Public key encryption—confidentiality.

In this scheme, recipient's public key is used by the sender to encrypt the message. This provides the confidentiality that only recipient can decrypt the message because for decryption, recipient's private key is required. This key is known to recipient, the owner of the key. So other than recipient, nobody is able to decrypt the message and the confidentiality is achieved. At the same time, in this scheme, authentication of the sender cannot be done. So, following scheme is useful which provides authentication, confidentiality and secrecy as shown in Figure 7.5.

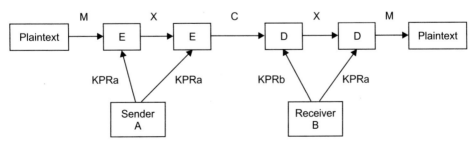

Figure 7.5 Authentications, secrecy and confidentiality.

Suppose A and B are the two users who wants to communicate with each other. They want to maintain authentication, secrecy and confidentiality in their transmission. To achieve this, they follow following steps:

Step 1 KPR_A and KPU_A are the private and public keys of A and KPR_B and KPU_B are the private and public keys of B

Step 2 User A encrypts a message M using his private key KPR_A, the encrypted ciphertext is

$$X = E[KPR_A(M)]$$

Step 3 User A again encrypts the message using B's public key KPU_B, the encrypted ciphertext is

$$C = E[KPU_B(X)]$$
$$= E\,[KPU_B\,[E[KPR_A(M)]]]$$

Step 4 User A transmits this encrypted ciphertext to user B.

Step 5 At the receiving end, user B decrypts the message. For this, first B uses his private key KPR_B. The decrypted message is

$$D[KPR_B(M)] = X$$

Step 6 Then user B again decrypts the message using A's public key. The result is original message sent by user A.

$$D[KPU_A(X)] = M$$

This scheme provides authentication, secrecy and confidentiality. The major disadvantage of both the schemes is that these schemes are slow because the in these schemes the encryption algorithms are used four times.

7.2.2 Key Length and Encryption Strength

The strength of any encryption algorithm is dependents on: the algorithm used and the length of the encryption key. Long key provides more security to the algorithm. The algorithm said to be strong if it takes more time to find out the key by the cryptanalyst. RSA algorithm uses prime number theory which makes it difficult to find out the key by reverse engineering.

7.2.3 Applications of Public Key Cryptography

In *pretty good privacy* well known as PGP, public key cryptography is very useful. PGP is used for email application. In communication with a web server, public key cryptography is used to encrypt the message. This provides security to online transaction. In this communication, the communication is encrypted using a random number which is generated by the web browser and the public key of the server. Then the session key is generated by the server and sends securely. Public key cryptography can be used to send the secret key securely in symmetric encryption techniques. Public key cryptography is also used in digital signature where the user signs a message by encrypting using his own private key.

7.2.4 Strength and Weakness of Public Key

Asymmetric encryption technique can be used for key distribution in symmetric encryption. It can be used for providing confidentiality, authentication of the two parties in communication and secrecy to the message.

Asymmetric encryption technique is very slow, so cannot be suitable for encryption of large data. Misuse of public key is possible. Known ciphertext attack is possible against this technique.

7.2.5 Comparison of Asymmetric Encryption and Symmetric Encryption

We know about asymmetric encryption and symmetric encryption techniques. The comparison between asymmetric encryption and symmetric encryption is given in Table 7.1.

Table 7.1 Comparison between asymmetric and symmetric encryption

Asymmetric encryption	Symmetric encryption
Well-known as public key encryption.	Well-known as secret key encryption.
Two keys are used: public key and private key.	One key is used.
Public key is freely available to all. It is not secret key. Private key is a secret key.	The key should be kept secret.
One key is used for encryption and another key for decryption.	Same key is used for encryption as well as for decryption.
Slower than symmetric encryption.	Usually very fast as compared to asymmetric encryption.
It is generally used for encrypting small message because its computational time is more.	It is used for encrypting small or large message.

7.3 RSA ALGORITHM

RSA algorithm is invented by Ron Rivest, Adi Shamir and Leonard Adleman in 1977. It is currently the most widely used public key encryption method in the world. It is the example of public key cryptosystem. It is an asymmetric encryption technique. This algorithm is based on the property of modular exponentiation. It is the most secure algorithm if the key is sufficiently large. In RSA algorithm, exchange of key is not required. The same algorithm can be used for encryption and decryption.

RSA uses variable key length. The more commonly used secure key of size 1024. The speed of the algorithm depends on the size of the key. Large key makes the algorithm slow but provides more security.

7.3.1 Working of RSA

The working of RSA algorithm is divided into three parts:

1. Key generation

2. Encryption
3. Decryption

Key Generation

Step 1 Generate two large prime numbers p and q randomly such that $p \neq q$.

Step 2 Calculate the modulus $n = p \cdot q$ and $m = (p-1)(q-1)$

Step 3 Select the key for encryption e such that e is relatively prime to m and $1 < e < m$.

Step 4 Calculate the key for decryption d such that
$$d = e^{-1} \bmod m \text{ or } 1 = ed \bmod m$$
where, d is the multiplicative inverse of $e \bmod m$ and $1 < d < m$.

The public key is $KP_U = (e, n)$ is used for encryption.
The private key is $KP_R = (d, n)$ is used for decryption.
For better security the values of p, q and m should be kept secret.
n is the modulus.
e is the encryption exponent.
d is the decryption exponent.

Encryption

The encryption in RSA is exponential operation. The public key $KP_U = (e, n)$ is used for encryption. Suppose the message is represented by a positive integer P. The ciphertext is computed as:
$$C = P^e \bmod n$$

Decryption

The decryption in RSA is also exponential operation. The public key $KP_R = (d, n)$ is used for decryption. The plaintext is computed as:
$$P = C^d \bmod n$$

RSA Algorithm

Step 1 Generate two large prime numbers p and q randomly
Step 2 Calculate modulus $n = p \cdot q$ and $m = (p-1)(q-1)$
Step 3 Select the key for encryption, e. This gives public key $KP_U = (e, n)$.
Step 4 Calculate the key for decryption, d. This gives private key $KP_R = (d, n)$.
Step 5 Ciphertext = (Plaintext)^e mod n.
Step 6 Plaintext = (Ciphertext)^d mod n.

Public Key Cryptosystems

EXAMPLE 7.1 Use RSA algorithm to encrypt the message M = 123 using following parameters

$$p = 11, q = 3, e = 13.$$

Solution

Key Generation

$$n = p * q = 11 * 3 = 33$$
$$m = (p - 1)(q - 1) = 10 * 2 = 20$$

The given value of $e = 13$ as the encryption key. We use extended Euclidean algorithm to find out the multiplicative inverse of e, i.e., d.

20 = 13(1) + 7	7 = 20 − 13(1)
13 = 7(1) + 6	6 = 13 − 7(1)
7 = 6(1) + 1	1 = 7 − 6(1)
6 = 1(6) + 0	

$$1 = 7 - 6(1)$$
$$1 = 7 - [13 - 7(1)] \,(1)$$
$$1 = 7 - 13(1) + 7(1)$$
$$1 = 7(2) - 13(1)$$
$$1 = [20 - 13(1)](2) - 13(1)$$
$$1 = 20(2) - 13(2) - 13(1)$$
$$1 = 20(2) - 13(3)$$
$$1 = 20(2) + 13(-3)$$

Therefore, −3 is the multiplicative inverse of 13 mod 20. So, $d = 20 − 3 = 17$.

$$\text{Public key } KP_U = (e, n) = (13, 33)$$
$$\text{Private key } KP_R = (d, n) = (17, 33)$$

Encryption

The given message M = 123, taking each number separately

$$C = M^e \bmod n = (1)^{13} \bmod 33 = 1 \bmod 33 = 1$$
$$= (2)^{13} \bmod 33 = 8 \bmod 33 = 8$$
$$= (3)^{13} \bmod 33 = 27 \bmod 33 = 27$$

Therefore, the ciphertext $C = 1 \; 8 \; 27$.

Dencryption

$$M' = C^d \bmod n = (1)^{17} \bmod 33 = 1.$$
$$= (8)^{17} \bmod 33 = 2 \bmod 33 = 2$$
$$= (27)^{17} \bmod 33 = 3 \bmod 33 = 3$$

The plaintext $P = 1 \; 2 \; 3$.

7.3.2 Key Length

The key size is the most important factor for any encryption algorithm. We know that the key sizes for various symmetric algorithms are different. For DES, it is 64-bit but actual it uses 56-bit whereas triple DES has 192-bit key. Due to long key triple DES is more secure than simple DES though the internal architecture is same for both the algorithms. AES have variable length of key such as 128, 192 and 256 bits. For IDEA algorithm, the key length is 128 bits. RSA algorithm has variable key length. If the user selects a short key, then the processing is fast and the algorithm works efficiently. But at the same time cryptanalysis is easier. If we select long key, it provides more security at the cost of reducing the performance of the algorithm. The better option is to select the key which can balance the performance as well as provides security. The key size 512-bit for RSA is no more secure. So, it is recommended that select 512-bit key. For more security, user can select 2048-bit key. As nowadays, hardware is easily available at low cost, it is easy to break even 2048 bits key.

7.3.3 Security

To provide strong algorithm and make cryptanalysis of RSA algorithm difficult, one should keep the values of p, q and m secret. This is important because if the attacker knows the values of p and q he can easily determine the value of m and if the attacker knows m and n he can compute p and q. Many attacks are possible against RSA algorithm. These include brute force attack, timing attack and mathematical attack. Selecting the large key size makes it difficult for brute force attack. The execution time of RSA depends on the key length. Different key size provides different execution time. The cryptanalyst examines the difference between the execution time for different keys. In the same way if the key size is same but the message is of different length, it also requires different execution time. This helps the cryptanalyst to know the message size. Using timing attack, the attacker tries to find out the secret information Suppose user A decrypts the ciphertext and the opponent, i.e., cryptanalyst observes the process of decryption. Using his observation he finds out the execution time required for decryption for each ciphertext. From this time, the cryptanalyst may be able to find out the value of decryption key,"d".

Protecting Timing Attack

To protect timing attack, preventive measures should be taken. Some of the preventive measures are as follows:
1. Value of e should be large
2. Value of n should be used by only one user
3. Use of padding
4. Use of delay during encryption

SOLVED PROBLEMS

7.1 Find the private key for RSA algorithm if the parameters given are:
$$p = 93, q = 47, e = 21.$$

Solution

$$n = pq = 93 * 47 = 4371$$
$$m = (p - 1)(q - 1) = 92 * 46 = 42328465$$
$$e = 21 \text{ encryption exponent}$$

Public key = (21, 4371)

We calculate decryption exponent d using Euclid's algorithm as given below

4232 = 21(201) + 11	11 = 4232 − 21(201)
21 = 11 (1) + 10	10 = 21 − 11(1)
11 = 10 (1) + 1	1 = 11 − 10(1)
10 = 1(10) + 0	

$1 = 11 - 10(1)$

$1 = 11 - [21 - 11(1)](1)$

$1 = 11(2) - 21(1)$

$1 = [4232 - 21(201)](2) - 21(1)$

$1 = 4232(2) - 21(403)$

$1 = 4232(2) + 21(-403)$

The multiplicative inverse of 21 is −403 = 3829
Therefore, decryption exponent $d = 3829$
Private key = (3829, 4371)

7.2 The parameters given are: $p = 5$, $q = 17$. Find out the possible public key and private for RSA algorithm. Also encrypt the message "4".

Solution

$$p = 5$$
$$q = 17$$

Let
$$n = p * q$$
$$n = 5 * 17$$
$$= 85$$

Let
$$m = (p - 1)(q - 1)$$
$$m = (5 - 1)(17 - 1)$$
$$= 4 * 16 = 64$$

We first find out the total number of possible values e.
As e is relatively prime to m and $e < m$.
Therefore, total number of possible values of $e = \Phi(m)$.

$$\Phi(m) = \Phi(64) = 64 * (1 - 1/2) = 64 * (1/2) = 32$$

Therefore, the total numbers of possible values of e are 32.

Key Generation

(a) Public key generation

Choose a small number, e which is relatively prime to m.
We use Euclid's algorithm to find the GCD.

$$e = 2 \Rightarrow GCD(e, 64) = 2$$
$$e = 3 \Rightarrow GCD(e, 64) = 1$$
$$e = 4 \Rightarrow GCD(e, 64) = 4$$
$$e = 5 \Rightarrow GCD(e, 64) = 1$$
$$e = 7 \Rightarrow GCD(e, 64) = 1$$

Now, we can select any one of these values whose GCD is 1. From above, suppose we select $e = 5$.

The public key is (5, 85).

(b) Private key generation

We can compute decryption exponent d, such that $d = e^{-1} \bmod m$.

We use extended Euclidean algorithm to find the value of d.

$1 = 5 \bmod 64$

$64 = 5(12) + 4$	$4 = 64 - 5(12)$
$5 = 4(1) + 1$	$1 = 5 - 4(1)$
$4 = 1(4) + 0$	
$1 = 5 - 4(1)$	
$1 = 5 - [64 - 5(12)](1)$	
$1 = 5(13) - 64(1)$	

Therefore, 13 is the multiplicative inverse of 5 mod 64.

Therefore, $d = 13$ and

Private key is (13, 85).

Encryption

The message is $P = 4$

$$C = P^e \bmod n$$
$$= 7^5 \bmod 85$$
$$= 62$$

The ciphertext is 62.

Decryption

$$P = C^d \bmod n$$
$$= 62^{13} \bmod 85$$
$$= 7$$

We can regenerate the plaintext = 7 from the ciphertext.

7.3 The parameters given are: $p = 3$, $q = 19$. Find out the possible public key and private for RSA algorithm. Also encrypt the message "6".

Solution:
$$p = 3, q = 19$$
$$n = 3 \times 19 = 57$$
$$m = \Phi(n) = 2 \times 18 = 36$$

Key Generation

(a) Public key generation

Choose a small number, e which is relatively prime to m, i.e., GCD $(e, m) = 1$

We use Euclid's algorithm to find the GCD.

$e = 2 \Rightarrow$ GCD$(e, 36) = 2$
$e = 3 \Rightarrow$ GCD$(e, 36) = 3$
$e = 4 \Rightarrow$ GCD$(e, 36) = 4$
$e = 5 \Rightarrow$ GCD$(e, 36) = 1$
$e = 7 \Rightarrow$ GCD$(e, 36) = 1$

Now, we can select any one of these values whose GCD is 1. From above, suppose we select $e = 5$ or 7, here we select $e = 7$.

The public key is (7, 57).

(b) Private key generation

We can compute decryption exponent d, such that $d = e^{-1}$ mod m.

We use extended Euclidean algorithm to find the value of d.

$1 = 7$ mod 36

$36 = 7(5) + 1$	$1 = 36 - 7(5)$
$7 = 1(7) + 0$	
$1 = 36 - 7(5)$	
$1 = 36 + 7(-5)$	

Therefore, -5 is the multiplicative inverse of 7 mod 36.

Therefore, $d = 31$ and (since $36 - 5 = 31$)

Private key is (31, 57)

Encryption

The message is $P = 6$
$$C = P^e \text{ mod } n$$
$$= 6^7 \text{ mod } 57$$
$$= 9$$

The ciphertext is 9.

Decryption

$$P = C^d \bmod n$$
$$= 9^{31} \bmod 57$$
$$= 6$$

We can regenerate the plaintext = 6 from the ciphertext.

7.4 In asymmetric encryption using RSA, the ciphertext is $C = 4$ and the public key is: $e = 89$, $p = 11$, $q = 47$.

Find

1. The key for decryption
2. The plaintext P?

Solution

$$n = p * q$$
$$n = 11 * 47 = 517$$
$$m = \text{Totient function } \phi(n) = 10 * 46 = 460$$
$$e = 67$$

Public key = (67, 517)

We have to find out the value of d in such a way that $ed \bmod m = 1$.
Therefore, $d = 103$
Private key = (d, n) = (103, 517)
Decryption
The ciphertext is 4.
Plaintext $P = C^d \bmod n$

$$P = 5^{103} \bmod 517 = 344$$

Use modulo arithmetic to compute the value of P
Message $P = 344$

SUMMARY

Encryption techniques are of two types, symmetric encryption and asymmetric encryption. In symmetric encryption same key is used by both the users for encryption as well as decryption. Asymmetric cryptography is also known as *public key cryptography*. In asymmetric encryption, two different keys are used, one for encryption and other for decryption. RSA algorithm, the well known key generation algorithm, provides the mechanism for secure generation of key. Asymmetric encryption technique takes more computation time as compared to symmetric encryption technique. Asymmetric encryption technique is not suitable for large message. But as it is more secure, it is useful to send the key for symmetric encryption. Authentication means to verify the origin and the integrity of a document. It verifies whether the message id sent by the intended recipient or not. RSA is currently the most widely used public key encryption methods in the world. It is the example of public key cryptosystem. To provide strong algorithm and make cryptanalysis of RSA algorithm difficult one should keep the values of p, q and m secret.

Public Key Cryptosystems

EXERCISES

7.1 What are the different types of encryption techniques? Explain each in brief.
7.2 What is symmetric and asymmetric encryption? Differentiate between them.
7.3 What is public key encryption? Give the characteristics of public key encryption.
7.4 What are the main elements of the public key encryption? Explain each in detail.
7.5 How secrecy and authentication is achieved in public key encryption?
7.6 What is confidentiality in public key encryption? How it can be achieved in public key encryption? Explain with some examples.
7.7 List the strength and weaknesses of the public key.
7.8 Compare symmetric and asymmetric encryption. Which of these is best? Why?
7.9 Write an algorithm for key generation in RSA.
7.10 Discuss the security aspect of RSA.
7.11 What is the timing attack on RSA? How we can prevent timing attack in RSA?
7.12 The parameters given are: $p = 61$, $q = 53$. Find out the possible public key and private key for RSA algorithm. Also encrypt the message "123 (Ans: $e = 17$, $d = 2753$, $C = 855$)
7.13 What is the counter measures taken against timing attack in RSA?
7.14 Consider the RSA algorithm where the modulus n is a large prime rather than a composite number. Would the encryption be secure? Why/why not

MULTIPLE CHOICE QUESTIONS

7.1 RSA cryptography relies on the difficulty ....
  (a) Calculating the factors of a large prime number.
  (b) Calculating the prime factors of a large composite number.
  (c) Calculating the composite factors of a large composite number.
  (d) Calculating the inverse of a large number

7.2 RSA is not suffering by ------------------.
  (a) Brute force attack
  (b) Timing attack
  (c) Meet-in-the-middle attack
  (d) Mathematical attack

7.3 Which of the following statement is not true for asymmetric encryption algorithm?
  (a) It is slower as compared to symmetric encryption algorithm
  (b) It is generally used for encrypting small message
  (c) Well-known as secret key encryption
  (d) Well-known as public key encryption

Answers

   7.1 (b)   **7.2** (c)   **7.3** (c)

Chapter 8

Key Management

8.1 INTRODUCTION

In the last chapter we learn various symmetric encryption techniques. Apart from this technique, there is asymmetric encryption technique where two different keys which are mathematically related to each other are used for encryption and decryption. In both of these techniques, i.e., symmetric encryption and asymmetric encryption, the distribution of keys is the most important issues. In this chapter, we discuss different approaches for key distribution.

8.2 KEY DISTRIBUTION

Computer is a necessary part of our day to day life. People use computers to communicate their message. This is possible due to Internet. People can send e-mail, chat their friends, and even speak on phone through internet. Now, we know that this channel of communication is not secure. Every user expects authentication, confidentiality and integrity of the message which he/she sends through computer. To provide these security services, public key infrastructure is most important. Use of these infrastructures depends upon the required degree of security which depends on the applications. Up to last chapter, we discuss various symmetric and asymmetric encryption algorithms. We know that the security strength of these algorithms depends on the security of the key. In symmetric encryption techniques, key distribution or key handling is the major issue. While transferring the key from sender to recipient, if the attackers are able to capture the key, then he can decrypt the message. So, key handling is the most important domain in public key infrastructures. In this chapter, we will focus on this problem of key management.

Asymmetric encryption or public key cryptography has two issues related to keys. We know in public key cryptography, each user has a pair of keys, i.e., public key and private key. During communication, each user should know the public key of another user. So, the first issue about key in public key infrastructure is the distribution of public keys among the users. The second issue is the private key distribution using public key encryption technique.

There are different approaches for the distribution of the public keys. The keys can be distributed using any one of the approaches given below:

- Public announcement
- Publicly available directory
- Public key authority
- Public key certificates

8.2.1 Public Announcement

In this method, the public key is broadcasted by the owner of the key. Many times users may use pretty good privacy (PGP) for broadcasting the key. The drawback of this method is that anyone can forge key and may misuse it for encryption or decryption of the data as there is no control on the accessing of the key. Figure 8.1 shows the public announcement.

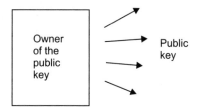

Figure 8.1 Announcement of the public key.

8.2.2 Publicly Available Directory

To avoid the drawback of the above approach, the next approach is used in which a directory of keys is maintained which is available publicaly to anybody. In a directory, the public keys of all the users are maintained. This directory is available to all legitimate users of the system. As compared to first approach, this approach provides more security.

The directory is maintained by a trusted party. This party is responsible for the control of use of this directory. The user who wants to be a part of communication system should register his public key in the directory and keep his own private key secret. The directory contains the name of the user with his public key. Figure 8.2 shows the directory structure. The access to this directory is controlled by the trusted party. The directory is protected by password. This password is shared to all the registered users of the directory. So, only registered users of the directory can access it. If the user wants to change his public key, he should inform to the trusted party about the same and store the new public key by replacing the old public one. The advantage of this scheme is that only authorised users of the directory can access the directory and able to get the public key. This scheme can work just like our telephone directory where the telephone numbers of all the users with their names are stored.

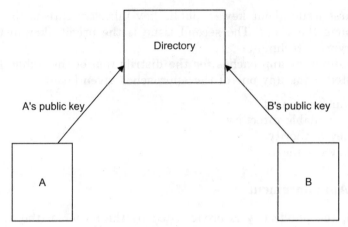

Figure 8.2 Distribution of public key using publicly available directory.

From Figure 8.2, two users A and B are the registered users of the directory. Both users A and B stored their keys in the directory. When the user A wants to communicate with user B, he accesses the directory and get B's public key. Using this key now he can encrypt the message and send it to user B.

If someone is able to get the password of this directory, then he will get the public key of any user stored in the directory and may misuse it.

8.2.3 Public Key Authority

We know that, the public key from the directory can be used if some is able to get the password of the directory. So, there is a need of new mechanism which can distribute the public keys more carefully. The public key authority approach provides the control on the distribution of the keys. The authority keeps the control on the distribution of keys by giving the password. The public key of authority is known to all the registered users. When any user makes a request for public key, the authority first verifies that whether a user is registered user or not. If he is a registered user then authority sends him the requested public key using authority's private key. The users can access the directory by using authority's password.

The communication between the authority and the users occurs as follows:

Step 1 The sender A sends the request message to the authority. The message contains the request for B's public key with time of request.

Step 2 Then the authority verifies the authentication of the user A. If user A is the authorised user then the authority responds request of A by sending the message. The message is encrypted with authority's private key. It contains the public key of B with the original request message sent by A.

Step 3 After receiving the message from the authority, user A decrypts it with the authority's public key. Then A sends a message to user B requesting for communication. This message is encrypted by user B with his public key. The message contains the network address of user A and a random number called *nounce*.

Step 4 After receiving the message from user A, user B sends the request message to the authority. The message contains the request for A's public key with time of request.

Step 5 Then the authority verifies the authentication of the user B. If user B is the authorised user then the authority responds request of B by sending the message. The message is encrypted with authority's private key. It contains the public key of A with original request message sent by B.

Step 6 Now user B sends reply message to the request of user A. The message is encrypted using A's public key. The reply message contains new random number in addition to the random number received from user A.

Step 7 User A confirms the request by replying back. This time the message contains the random number sent by user B and the message is encrypted by B's public key.

After completion of above seven steps, authentications of both the users completed and they agree for communication. This complete process is illustrated in Figure 8.3. They communicate with each other by sending the message encrypted with each other's public key. For decryption, both the users use their own private key. For better security, each user should change their public key from the directory. This helps to avoid the reuse of public key.

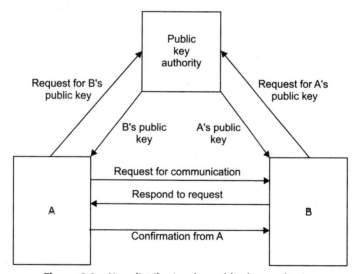

Figure 8.3 Key distribution by public key authority.

In this method, every time the users have to make a request for public key to the authority which makes the system slow.

8.2.4 Public Key Certificates

To avoid the drawback of above public key authority method, an alternative approach is used. In this approach, the certificates are used. This approach is called *public key certificates approach*. It was suggested by Kohnfelder for the first time. In this approach, the public keys are exchanged by using certificates. This avoids the need to contact the public key authority for public key. Each certificate contains some other information in addition to public key. This other information includes time of the request and network address of the user who made the request. This time in the certificate helps to differentiate one request from other. Suppose user A's private key is captured by an attacker. Therefore, user A generates a new pair of public and private keys. Then he requested for the certificate by sending his public and private key pair. Meanwhile, the attacker uses the old certificate to communicate with user B. If user B have the old public key of A and encrypt the message using this old public key, the attacker can decrypt the message and read the message.

The information in the certificate is encrypted by the authority's private key. So, only the registered users who know the authority's public key can decrypt the message. When the user A sends the request for communication to user B with his certificate, user B first verifies the certificate of user A. The communication between the two users takes place as follows:

Step 1 User A requests the certificate authority for a certificate. For this he sends his name and his public key.

Step 2 The certificate authority responds to the request by sending encrypted certificate for user A. The certificate is encrypted using authority's private key. Each certificate contains some other information in addition to public key. This other information includes time of the request and network address of the user who made the request.

Step 3 User A uses this certificate for communication with user B. Then user B decrypts the certificate using authority's public key and verifies the user A authentication. Also, user B stores the public key of A for further communication.

Step 4 User B requests the certificate authority for a certificate. For this he sends his name and his public key.

Step 5 The certificate authority sends the certificate to user B.

Step 6 User B sends the certificate to user A. User A verifies the information by decrypting the certificates by authority's public key and stores the public key of user B.

After exchanging the certificates, user A and B start communication. They use each other's public for communication. The detail process is as shown in Figure 8.4.

8.3 DIFFIE-HELLMAN KEY EXCHANGE

Whether we use symmetric encryption or public key encryption technique, transfer of key among the users is the main issue. Key exchange in public key cryptography is simple as compared to symmetric encryption. In Section 8.2 we discuss different approaches of key transfer for public key cryptography. But for symmetric encryption, the key may be handled personally using different media. Symmetric encryption techniques are faster than public key cryptography.

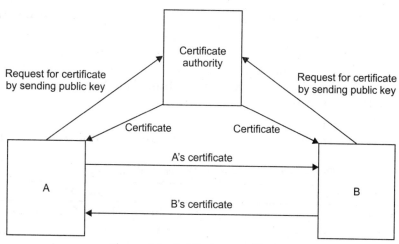

Figure 8.4 Public key certificates.

Diffie–Hellman designed an algorithm which helps for key transmission. This algorithm is known as *Diffie–Hellman key exchange algorithm*. The name is derived from the two scientists Whitefield Diffie and Martin Hellman who developed this algorithm. They developed a protocol called *key agreement protocol* in 1976. In this, the private key is exchangeable among the users using public key techniques. This algorithm can be used for key exchange and not for encryption or decryption. Using exchangeable keys, both the parties generate a key called *shared secret key* which can be used for encryption and decryption. So, actual shared secret key is never transmitted through the insecure channel. The performance of this algorithm is better than any other algorithm.

8.3.1 Description

Suppose A and B are the two users who wish to communicate with each other. They decided to use Diffie–Hellman key exchange algorithm for sharing their keys. The working of Diffie–Hellman algorithm is illustrated from the following steps.

Step 1 First, user A and user B both agree on two numbers, n and g. Where n is a large prime number and g is a primitive root of n.

Step 2 User A selects X_A as his private key randomly, such that $X_A < n$. X_A is a large positive integer number.

Step 3 Similarly, user B selects X_B as his private key randomly, such that $X_B < n$. X_B is a large positive integer number.

Step 4 User A computes his public key, Y_A, using $Y_A = (g^{X_A})$ mod n.

Step 5 Similarly, user B computes his public key, Y_B, using $Y_B = (g^{X_B})$ mod n.

Step 6 Both the users now exchange their public keys over the insecure channel.

Step 7 User A computes the key, k, called *shared secret key*, using the formula $k = (Y_B^{X_A})$ mod n.

Step 8 User B computes the key, k, called shared secret key, using the formula, $k = (Y_A^{X_B}) \bmod n$.

Step 9 Now, user A and user B communicate with each other using one of the symmetric encryption techniques. They use the shared secret key, k, as the encryption key for the selected algorithm. This key k was never transmitted over the insecure channel.

The Diffie–Hellman key exchange algorithm uses prime number n as modulo and primitive root of n. Table 8.1 illustrates the working of Diffie–Hellman algorithm.

Table 8.1 Working Of Diffice–Hallman algorithm

User A		User B	
Private key	Calculation	Private key	Calculation
X_A	n, g	X_B	n, g
	$Y_A = g^{X_A} \bmod n \rightarrow$		$\leftarrow Y_B = g^{X_B} \bmod n$
	A's public key		B's public key
	$(Y_B^{X_A}) \bmod n$		$(Y_A^{X_B}) \bmod n$
	Shared key		Shared key

User A and user B select n and g such that $n = 19$ and $g = 7$.

User A select his private key $X_A = 8$, then computes his public key $Y_A = g^{X_A} \bmod n$

$$Y_A = 7^8 \bmod 19 = 11$$

Therefore, A having private key $X_A = 8$ and public key $Y_A = 11$.

A sends his public key $Y_A = 11$ to B.

User B selects his private key $X_B = 10$, then computes his public key $Y_B = g^{X_B} \bmod n$

$$7^{10} \bmod 19 = 7$$

Therefore, B having private key $X_B = 10$ and public key $Y_B = 7$.

B sends his public key $Y_B = 7$ to A

A computes shared secret key using: $(Y_B \, X_A) \bmod n$

$$(7^8 \bmod 19) = 11$$

B computes shared secret key using: $(Y_A X_B) \bmod n$

$$11^{10} \bmod 19 = 11$$

Both users A and B have the same value of shared secret key. Note that only private keys, i.e., X_A, X_B and shared secret keys $Y_B^{X_A} = Y_A X_B$ should keep secret. All the other values, i.e., g, n, Y_A and Y_B need not be secret. The shared secret key can be used for encryption. This key is known only to A and B. Larger values of X_A, X_B, and n provide more security and make difficult for cryptanalysis. If these values are small, it is possible for the cryptanalyst to find out shared secret key easily. In the above example, we know that the values of $n = 19$, $g = 7$, $Y_A = 11$ and $Y_B = 7$ are publicaly available. Therefore, one can try $g^{X_A X_B} \bmod 19$. There are only 18 values and this equation is possible and easily determined the shared secret key. Therefore, the values of n and g should be large.

Considering above problem, Table 8.2 will illustrate how the cryptanalyst tries to find the shared secret key.

Table 8.2 Shared Secret Key

User A		User B		Cryptanalyst	
Knows	Doesn't know	Knows	Doesn't know	Knows	Doesn't know
$n = 19$	$X_B = 10$	$n = 19$	$X_A = 8$	$n = 19$	$X_A = 8$
$g = 7$		$g = 7$		$g = 7$	$X_B = 10$
$X_A = 8$		$X_B = 10$			$k_s = 11$
$7^8 \bmod 19 = 11$		$7^{10} \bmod 19 = 7$		$7^{X_A} \bmod 19 = 11$	
$7^{X_A} \bmod 19 = 7$		$7^{X_A} \bmod 19 = 11$		$7^{X_B} \bmod 19 = 7$	
$7^8 \bmod 19 = 11$		$11^{10} \bmod 19 = 11$		$k_s = 7^{X_A} \bmod 19$	
$11^{X_B} \bmod 19 = 11$		$7^{X_A} \bmod 19 = 11$		$k_s = 11^{X_B} \bmod 19$	
$7^8 \bmod 19 = 11^{X_B} \bmod 19$		$11^{10} \bmod 19 = 7^{X_A} \bmod 19$		$7^{X_A} \bmod 19 = 11^{X_B} \bmod 19$	
$K_s = 11$		$K_s = 11$			

It should not be possible for user A or user B to compute each other's private key using all available information. For this, the values of n and g should be very large. If the values of n and g are small then it is possible for A and B to find out each other's private key. In this case, it is also possible for the cryptanalyst to find out fake shared secret key by guessing his private and public keys. Then he tries for A's and B's public key.

8.3.2 Security

Diffie–Hellman algorithm is secure for large values of n and g. For small values, it is possible for the attackers to find out the X_A and X_B using discrete logarithm. So, they can derive the shared secret key once they know the private key of the users. But for large values of n and g it is very difficult to obtain the private keys of the user. To calculate a large prime n, a Sophie Germain prime number m is used. It is called a *safe prime* as in that case the factors of n is only 2 and m. g is selected as the order of m instead of n so that it is difficult to compute X_A from g^{X_A}.

After computing the secret key, there is no need of X_A and X_B. So, the private keys of the users are destroyed once the secret key is obtained. This provides forward security. But man-in-the-middle attack is possible against Diffie–Hellman algorithm. We will discuss it in the next section.

8.3.3 Man-in-the-Middle Attack

Man-in-the-middle attack is also known as *bucket brigade attack*. Suppose the two users A and B are in communication with each other. They want to exchange their public keys. Let Y_A and Y_B are their public keys. User A receives the public key Y_B indirectly. Suppose the public key of user B is computed by the attacker and send it to user A. There is no way for him to know whether Y_B sends by B or somebody else. User A calculates the shared secret key k_s from Y_B. Now, encrypt the message B uses the k_s and start communication. The attacker captures the encrypted message in between and able to decrypt it as instead of user B, the attacker's key is used by user A to compute the shared secret key.

Let us take an example. Suppose Ajay wants to communicate with Seema. Assume n and g are publicly known keys.

A writes a letter and send it through a courier as "Dear Seema, I would like to meet you in the garden tomorrow, 456, A. (Here 456 is treated as public key). Suppose there is Henry (an attacker) who works for the courier. Henry picks his own private key Z_H, and computes $Y_H = gZ_H$ mod n, slightly modifies the letter by replacing the number 456 by 1234, prints the new version of the letter, and sends it to B. Later, B replies, "I will meet you tomorrow. My magic number is 14035, B." Henry again modifies the letter replaces 14035 by his own number and sends it again to A. Now, A computes the key using 456 and uses it for communication with A, and computes the key using 14035 and uses it for communication with B.

In this example, man-in-the-middle attack is established by Henry. He uses two distinct keys, one with "Seema" and the other with "Ajay", and then tries to masquerade as "Seema" to "Ajay" and/or vice-versa, perhaps by decrypting and re-encrypting messages passed between them.

8.3.4 Authentication

Authentication of the two users has not taken place in Diffie–Hellman algorithm. So, it is suffered by man-in-the-middle attack. To avoid this attack some mechanism should be used to authenticate the users to each other. For this, any authentication algorithm can be used with Diffie–Hellman algorithm. One of the solutions is to use digital signature during transmitting the public key.

8.4 ELLIPTIC CURVE ARITHMETIC

Victor Millar first time proposed the elliptic curve cryptography (ECC) in 1985. Also Neal Koblitz proposed the Elliptic curve cryptography in the same year. ECC is standardised in 1990 and used for commercial purpose. It is more secure even for a small key. Due to small key size, the performance of Elliptic curve cryptography is better as compared to other algorithms. There is no sub-exponential algorithm due to which the cryptanalyst can break it. For selecting a small prime numbers or smaller finite fields, greater degree of security can be achieved. This saves hardware implementations for the algorithm. Elliptic curve cryptography uses discrete logarithms which provide more challenging task for finding keys of equivalent length. Today ECC is used in ad-hoc wireless networks and mobile networks.

Elliptic curve groups are formed by using elliptic curves. A group is a set of similar elements with some user-defined arithmetic operations on these elements. For elliptic curve groups, these user-defined operations are defined geometrically. The underlying fields can be created by the number of points on a curve.

8.4.1 Elliptic Curve Groups Over Real Numbers

Over a hundred people studied elliptic curves. An elliptic curve E over the real numbers is the set of points (x, y). It is a graph of an equation of the form:

$$y^2 = x^3 + ax + b$$

where x, y, a and b are real numbers. It also includes a point at infinity.

Each choice of the numbers a and b yield a different elliptic curve. For example, $a = -3$ and $b = 3$ give the elliptic curve with equation $y^2 = x^3 - 3x + 3$; the graph of this curve is shown in Figure 8.5.

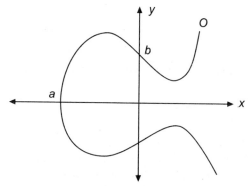

Figure 8.5 Elliptic curve.

If the given equation for elliptic curve has no repeated factors, then the given equation of elliptic curve can be used to form a group. The corresponding points on a curve form a group over real numbers with a special point O. This point O is called the *point at infinity*.

8.4.2 Elliptic Curve Addition: A Geometric Approach

The basic function of elliptic curve groups is addition, so it is additive groups. The addition of any two points on the elliptic curve can be defined geometrically.

The negative of any point $P(x_p, y_p)$ lies on the elliptic curve is $-P(x_p, -y_p \bmod P)$. If any point P lies on the elliptic curve then point $-P$ also lies on the curve.

Adding Distinct Points P and Q

Suppose $P(x_P, y_P)$ and $Q(x_Q, y_Q)$ are two distinct points on the elliptic curve such that Q is not $-P$. The point where line PQ intersects the curve is $-R$ and its reflection against x-axis is R (Figure 8.6). Then

$$P + Q = R$$

where R is the point where line PQ intersects the curve.

$$m = (y_P - y_Q)/(x_P - x_Q) \bmod P$$
$$x_R = m^2 - (x_P + x_Q) \bmod p \text{ and } y_R = -y_P + m(x_P - x_R) \bmod P$$

where m is the slope of the line PQ.

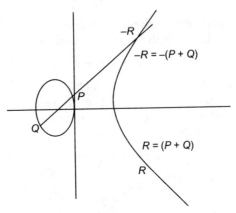

Figure 8.6 Adding distinct points P and Q.

Adding the Points R and –R

If the two points R and $-R$ join by a vertical line, it does not intersect the elliptic curve at any point other than R and $-R$. Therefore, we cannot add R and $-R$ as P and Q. Due to this, the point at infinity O is added to the elliptic curve group. O is the additive identity of the elliptic curve group. All the elliptic curves have an additive identity.

By addition property,
$$R + (-R) = O.$$

Therefore, we get
$$R + O = R \text{ is in the elliptic curve group.}$$

Figure 8.7 illustrated this property.

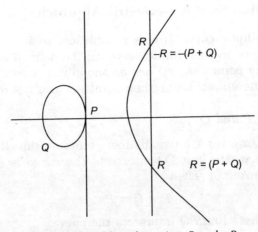

Figure 8.7 Adding the points R and $-R$.

Doubling the Point Q

Now, suppose we want to add a point Q in the group. Draw a tangent to the curve at point Q. If the y-coordinate of Q is not 0, then the tangent intersects the elliptic curve at exactly one other point. That point is $-R$. The reflection of $-R$ against x-axis is R. This is shown in Figure 8.8. This operation helps to double the point so it is called *doubling the point* Q.

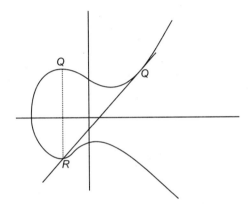

Figure 8.8 Doubling the point Q.

The law for doubling a point on an elliptic curve group is defined by:

- If y-coordinate y_Q is 0, the tangent from Q is always vertical.
- If $y_Q = 0$, then doubling the point Q.
- If $y_q = 0$, then the tangent to the elliptic curve at Q is vertical and it does not intersect the elliptic curve at any other point as shown in Figure 8.9.

By definition, $2Q = 0$ for a given point Q.

If one wanted to find $3Q$ in this situation, one can add $2Q + Q$. This becomes $Q + 0 = Q$

Thus, $\qquad 3Q = Q$.

$3Q = Q$, $4Q = 0$, $5Q = Q$, $6Q = 0$, $7Q = Q$, $8Q = 0$, $9Q = 0$, etc.

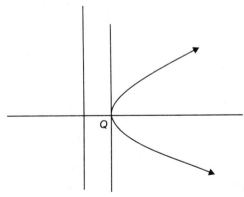

Figure 8.9 The tangent from Q is always vertical if $y_Q = 0$.

8.4.3 Elliptic Curve Addition: An Algebraic Approach

Above approach of elliptic curves provides an excellent method of illustrating elliptic curve arithmetic, but it is not a practical method for implementing arithmetic computations. So, there should be a method to construct algebraic formulae to efficiently compute the geometric arithmetic.

Adding Distinct Points P and Q

When two points on the elliptic curve, P and Q are not negative of each other, then
$$P + Q = R$$
where
$$m = (y_P - y_Q)/(x_P - x_Q)$$
$$x_R = m^2 - x_P - x_Q \text{ and } y_R = -y_P + m(x_P - x_R)$$

Note that m is the slope of line PQ.

Doubling the Point P

When y_P is not 0,
$$2P = R$$
where
$$m = (3x_P^2 + a)/(2y_P)$$
$$x_R = m^2 - 2x_P \text{ and } y_R = -y_P + m(x_P - x_R)$$

We know one of the parameters chosen with the elliptic curve is a and m is the slope of tangent on the point P.

8.4.4 Elliptic Curve Groups over F_P

Above approach use real numbers which make the execution of the algorithm very slow. At the same time rounding off the real number gives approximate results. Due to all these reasons, if we use this approach for cryptography, the performance of the cryptographic algorithms deteriorate. Cryptographic algorithms require fast and precise arithmetic. Thus, the finite fields of F_P and F_{2^m} are used in place of real number arithmetic. The field F_P uses the numbers from 0 to $P - 1$. The computations will result in an integer between 0 to $P - 1$.

For example, in F_{29} the field is composed of integers from 0 to 28, and any operation within this field will result an integer also in between 0 and 28.

An elliptic curve of F_P can be formed by selecting a and b as coefficients. The coefficients a and b are the integer numbers from 0 to $P - 1$, the field of F_P. The elliptic curve includes all points (x, y) which satisfy the elliptic curve equation modulo P (where x and y are numbers in F_P).

For example: if a and b are in F_P then $y^2 \bmod p = (x^3 + ax + b) \bmod P$ has an underlying field of F_P. The elliptic curve can be used to form a group if the term $x^3 + ax + b$ contains no repeating factors. An elliptic curve group over F_P consists of the points on the corresponding elliptic curve, together with a special point O called the point at infinity. There are finitely many points on an elliptic curve.

Example of an Elliptic Curve Group over F_P

Suppose, an elliptic curve over the field F_{13}. With $a = 1$ and $b = 0$, the elliptic curve equation is $y^2 = x^3 + x$. The point (3, 11) satisfies this equation since:

$$y^2 \bmod P = x^3 + x \bmod P$$
$$121 \bmod 13 = 27 + 3 \bmod 13$$
$$4 \bmod 13 = 30 \bmod 13$$
$$4 = 4$$

Here $P = 13$, therefore, there are 13 points which satisfy the given equation. These points are:

(0, 0), (2, 3), (2, 10), (3, 2), (3, 11), (6, 1), (6, 12), (7, 5), (7, 8), (9, 6), (9, 7), (11, 4), (11, 9)

If we observe the above points, for every value of x, there are two points. The graph is symmetric about $y = 6.5$. Over the field of F_{13}, the negative components in the y-values are taken modulo 13, resulting in a positive number as a difference from 13. Here $-P = (x_P, (-y_P \bmod 13))$.

8.4.5 Arithmetic in an Elliptic Curve Group over F_P

Elliptic curve groups over F_P and over real numbers have following difference:

1. There are finite numbers of points in elliptic curve groups over F_P. As some of the points are discrete, there is a problem of connecting these points to get a smooth curve.
2. It is difficult to apply geometric relationships. As a result, the geometry used in one group cannot be used for other groups. But, the algebraic rules of one group can be applied for other groups.
3. Due to use of real number, there is round off error in elliptic curves over real numbers. In the field of F_P there is no round-off error.

Adding Distinct Points P and Q

The negative of the point P is $-P$ where $x_P = x_P$ and $y_P = -y_P \bmod p$. If P and Q are distinct points such that P is not $-Q$, then

$$P + Q = R$$

where

$$m = (y_P - y_Q)/(x_P - x_Q) \bmod P$$
$$x_R = m^2 - x_P - x_Q \bmod p \text{ and } y_R = -y_P + m(x_P - x_R) \bmod p$$

Note that m is the slope of the line through P and Q.

Doubling the Point P

Suppose y_P is not 0,

$$2P = R$$

where

$$m = (3x_P^2 + a)/(2y_P) \bmod P$$
$$x_R = m^2 - 2x_P \bmod p \text{ and } y_R = -y_P + m(x_P - x_R) \bmod P$$

a is the parameter selected with the elliptic curve and m is the slope of the line PQ.

8.4.6 Elliptic Curve Groups over F_2n

The rules for arithmetic in F_2n can be defined by two ways:
1. Polynomial representation
2. Optimal normal basis representation.

With F_2n, an elliptic curve is formed by selecting a and b within F_2n (if $b \neq 0$). The elliptic curve equation for F_2n having a characteristic 2 is:
$$y^2 + xy = x^3 + ax^2 + b$$

Elliptic curve equation over F_2n satisfies for all points (x, y). These points together with a point at infinity form the elliptic curve. On an elliptic curve, there are finitely many points. As these points are bits, addition is controlled by using XOR operation.

An Example of an Elliptic Curve Group over F_2n

The field F_24, defined by $f(x) = x^4 + x + 1$.

The element $g = (0010)$ is a primitive root for the field.

The powers of g are:

$g^0 = (0001)$ $g^1 = (0010)$ $g^2 = (0100)$ $g^3 = (1000)$ $g^4 = (0011)$ $g^5 = (0110)$
$g^6 = (1100)$ $g^7 = (1011)$ $g^8 = (0101)$ $g^9 = (1010)$ $g^{10} = (0111)$ $g^{11} = (1110)$
$g^{12} = (1111)$ $g^{13} = (1101)$ $g^{14} = (1001)$ $g^{15} = (0001)$

The large value of n generates the more efficient table which provides more security. For adequate security, $n = 160$. The pattern allows the use of primitive root notation (g^e) rather than bit string notation, as used in the following example.
$$f(x) = x^4 + x + 1.$$
Suppose the elliptic curve $y^2 + xy = x^3 + g^4x^2 + 1$.

Here $a = g^4$ and $b = g^0 = 1$. The point (g^5, g^3) satisfies this equation over F_2n:
$$y^2 + xy = x^3 + g^4x^2 + 1$$
$$(g^3)^2 + g^5g^3 = (g^5)^3 + g^4g^{10} + 1$$
$$g^6 + g^8 = g^{15} + g^{14} + 1$$

$(1100) + (0101) = (0001) + (1001) + (0001)$

$(1001) = (1001)$

The fifteen points which satisfy this equation are:

$(1, g^{13})$ (g^3, g^{13}) (g^5, g^{11}) (g^6, g^{14}) (g^9, g^{13}) (g^{10}, g^8) (g^{12}, g^{12})
$(1, g^6)$ (g^3, g^8) (g^5, g^3) (g^6, g^8) (g^9, g^{10}) (g^{10}, g) $(g^{12}, 0)$ $(0, 1)$

8.4.7 Arithmetic in an Elliptic Curve Group over F_2m

There is finite number of points for an elliptic curve group over F_2n without round off error. Use of binary arithmetic makes the method very efficient.

The following algebraic rules are applied for arithmetic over F_2n.

Adding Distinct Points P and Q

We know that the negative of $P = -P$. If P and Q are different points then, $P \neq Q$.
Then, $$P + Q = R$$
where
$$m = (y_P - y_Q)/(x_P + x_Q)$$
$$x_R = m^2 + m + x_P + x_Q + a \text{ and } y_R = m(x_P + x_R) + x_R + y_P$$

We know that, $P + (-P) = 0$, the point at infinity and $P + 0 = P$ for all points P in the elliptic curve group.

Doubling the Point P

If $x_P = 0$, then $2P = 0$

Provided that x_P is not 0, $2P = R$
where
$$m = x_P + y_P/x_P$$
$$x_R = m^2 + m + a \text{ and } y_R = x_P^2 + (m + 1) * x_R$$

a is the parameter selected with the elliptic curve and m is the slope of the line through P and Q.

8.5 ELLIPTIC CURVE CRYPTOGRAPHY (ECC)

ECC is an alternative method for public key cryptography digital signature algorithm and RSA. ECC provides same level of security using small prime numbers than conventional encryption systems. Due to the use of small key, ECC is faster than conventional encryption system. This improves the performance of ECC and makes it efficient for public key cryptography. ECC is useful for applications which have small hardware capacity such as smart cards, cellular phones, etc. ECC is now used for implementing digital signatures and key distribution protocols.

8.5.1 Elliptic Curve Diffie–Hellman

We discuss Diffie-Hellman key exchange algorithm in Section 8.3. Elliptic Curve Diffie–Hellman (ECDH) is same as algorithm using elliptic key cryptography. Key exchange in elliptic curve can be done as: Select an elliptic curve over a finite field in the form 2^n. Select four numbers p, q, a and b. Select $g = (x_1, y_1)$.

8.5.2 Key Establishment Protocol

Suppose users A and B want to communicate with each other. Initially they agree with basic parameters. Both the users have their own private–public key pair suitable for ECC. Suppose user A has X_A and Y_A as his private key and public key respectively.

User B also has X_B, and Y_B as his private key and public key respectively. User A and user B both share each other's public keys.

User A computes the point P having coordinates $(X_k, Y_k) = d_A Q_B$. Also user B computes $(X_k, Y_k) = d_B Q_A$. The shared secret key is the x-coordinate value of point P, i.e., X_k. Here, $d_A Q_B = d_A d_B G$, $d_B Q_A = d_B d_A G$ and $d_A d_B G = d_B d_A G$, therefore, $d_A Q_B = d_B Q_A$. Therefore, the number calculated by both the users is equal. Only the public key is transferred through insecure channel. Other information is not transferred, so this algorithm is secure.

The public keys of both the user's are either static (and trusted, say via a certificate) or ephemeral. *Static key* means key is authenticated via certificate. It provides neither forward secrecy nor key compromise impersonation resilience, among other security properties. *Ephemeral keys* are not necessarily authenticated. If authentication of key is required, it should be obtained by other means.

8.6 ELLIPTIC CURVE SECURITY AND EFFICIENCY

The security of different public key cryptographic algorithm depends upon the size of key used. Most of the algorithms like Diffie–Hellman and RSA use 1024-bit key. One can select the large key size for these algorithms to provide more security as the larger key size is difficult for the cryptanalysis of the algorithm. But this deteriorates the performance of the algorithms. To increase the performance and at the same time provide the required security, one should take advantage of the research taken place in the area of public key particularly in ECC.

Selection of key size for public key cryptosystem can be determined from the strength of symmetric encryption algorithms those using public key algorithms for transfer the key. There are many symmetric encryption algorithms such as data encryption standard (DES) and advanced encryption standard (AES), international data encryption algorithm (IDEA), and Blowfish. For all these symmetric encryption algorithms, the key size is the main parameter of security. The cryptanalysis of these algorithms with key size of n-bit, it will require approximately $2n - 1$ operations.

Table 8.3 gives the key sizes recommended by the national institute of standards and technology (NIST) for symmetric encryption algorithms and other approaches which provide equivalent security.

Table 8.3 Key sizes

Symmetric encryption key size (bits)	RSA and Diffie–Hellman key size (bits)	Elliptic curve cryptography key size (bits)
80	1024	160
112	2048	224
128	3072	256
192	7680	384
256	15360	521

For the 128-bit AES, the equivalent key size for RSA or Diffie–Hellman is 3072-bit whereas for elliptic curves, it is only 256-bit. As compared to RSA and Diffie–Hellman, the key size for elliptic curve increases slowly as shown in Table 8.3. Hence, elliptic curve systems offer more security per bit increase in key size than either RSA or Diffie–Hellman algorithms.

Not only security, ECC is more attractive due to its computational efficiency than other algorithms such as RSA and Diffie–Hellman. ECC uses arithmetic which takes more computational time per bit as compared to RSA and Diffie–Hellman algorithm. But the security provided per bit by ECC is more than the extra time required for computation. Table 8.4 shows the ratio of computation of Diffie–Hellman to elliptic curve for different key sizes (in bits) listed in Table 8.3.

Table 8.4 Relative computation costs of Diffie–Hellman and elliptic curves

Security level (bits)	Ratio of DH cost: EC cost
80	3:1
112	6:1
128	10:1
192	32:1
256	64:1

If we use large key size for transferring the keys, the channel overhead is increased. So, EEC provides better solution as compared to RSA and Diffie–Hellman algorithms. There are number of elliptic curves standardised by NIST. Out of these, ten curves are for binary fields and five are for prime fields.

8.7 ZERO-KNOWLEDGE PROOF

A disadvantage of the above encryption algorithms is that when user A gives his secret key to user B, user B can thereafter impersonate user A. But, zero-knowledge (ZK) protocols allow user A to demonstrate knowledge of a secret key to user B without revealing any useful information about that secret key. Zero-knowledge proofs are probabilistic and based on interactive method. The example of zero-knowledge proof is RSA algorithm in which the user can prove that he knows the secret associated with his public key without revealing his private key. A protocol between two users in which one user is called prover and the other user is called the verifier. Prover tries to prove a certain fact to the verifier. This protocol is called *zero-knowledge protocol* or *zero-knowledge proof*. In cryptography, it is used for authentication.
Properties of zero-knowledge proof:

1. *Completeness:* If the fact is true, the honest verifier always accepts this fact and both the users follow the protocol.
2. *Soundness:* If the fact is false, the honest verifier always rejects this fact except with some small probability.
3. *Zero-knowledge:* If the fact is true, no cheating verifier learns anything other than this fact. This is Ormalised by showing that every cheating verifier has

some simulator that, given only the fact to be proven (and no access to the prover), can produce a transcript that "looks like" an interaction between the honest prover and the cheating verifier.

The first two properties are the properties of interactive systems and the third property is what makes the zero-knowledge proof.

Research in zero-knowledge proofs has been motivated due to its usefulness for authentication. In authentication, one user wants to prove his identity to a second user through some secret information. But at the same time user A does not want to learn the second user to learn anything about this secret. This is called a *zero-knowledge proof of knowledge*. However, this secret information is typically too small or insufficiently random to be used in many schemes for zero-knowledge proofs of knowledge.

Considering in mathematical sense, zero-knowledge proofs are not proofs because there is some small probability of the error called the *soundness error*. However, one can reduce this error to negligibly small values.

8.7.1 Cave Story

There is a well-known story presenting some of the ideas of zero-knowledge proofs, first published by Jean-Jacques Quisquater et al. in their paper "How to Explain Zero-Knowledge Protocols to Your Children". There are two users in a zero-knowledge proof, one is the prover of the fact and another is the verifier of the fact. Here we can call them user P and user V.

In this story, there are two users, P (she) and V (he). There is a cave which has a magic door which is open with a secret word. P claims that she knows the secret word to open a magic door of a cave. The cave is circular and there is an entrance in one side only. The other side is blocked by the magic door. User V wants the secret word and ready to pay for it. But he will pay to user P if he is sure that user P really knows the secret key. User P is also ready to tell the secret word to user V but after she will get the money. So, they plan a scheme so that P can prove that she knows the secret word without telling the secret word to V.

First, user V waits outside the cave and user P goes inside the cave. For convenience, we label the left path from the entrance as A and the right path from the entrance as B. User P randomly selects either path A or path B. Then, user V enters inside the cave and shouts the name of the path he wants user P to use to return, either A or B, chosen at random. Providing she really does know the magic word, this is easy: she opens the door, if necessary, and returns along the desired path. Note that V does not know which path P has gone down.

However, suppose P does not know the secret word. Then, she can only return by the named path if V gives the name of the same path that P entered by. Since V chooses A or B at random, P has at most a 50% chance of guessing correctly. If they repeat this trick many times, say 20 times in a row, P's chance of successfully anticipating all of V's requests becomes vanishingly small, and V should be convinced that P knows the secret word.

There is a question, why not just make P takes a known path that will force her through the door, and make V waits at the entrance. Certainly, that will prove that P knows the secret word, but it also allows the possibility of eavesdropping. By randomising the initial path that P takes and preventing V from knowing it, it reduces the chances that V can follow P and learn not just that P knows the secret word, but what the secret word actually is. This part of the exchange is important for keeping the amount of information revealed to a minimum. This is explained in Figure 8.10.

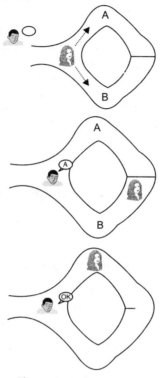

Figure 8.10 Cave story.

These ideas can be extended to a more realistic cryptography application. In this, P knows a Hamiltonian cycle for a large graph, G. She will prove that she knows this information without revealing the cycle itself. A Hamiltonian cycle in a graph is just one way to implement a zero-knowledge proof, in fact any NP-complete problem can be used. However, P does not want to simply reveal the Hamiltonian cycle or any other information to V; she wishes to keep the cycle secret.

To show that P knows this Hamiltonian cycle, she and V play several rounds of a game. At the beginning of each round, P creates H, an isomorphic graph to G. Since it is trivial to translate a Hamiltonian cycle between isomorphic graphs with known isomorphism, if P knows a Hamiltonian cycle for H, she also must know for graph G. For verification V can either ask P to show the isomorphism between H and G, or show a Hamiltonian cycle in H.

If P is asked to show that the two graphs are isomorphic, she provides the vertex translations that map G to H. V can verify that they are indeed isomorphic. If P is asked to prove that she knows a Hamiltonian cycle in H, she translates her

Hamiltonian cycle in G onto H and reveals it to V. V can then check the validity of the cycle. During each round, P does not know which question she will be asked by V until after giving H. Therefore, in order to be able to answer both, H must be isomorphic to G and P must have a Hamiltonian cycle in H. Because only someone who knows a Hamiltonian cycle in G would always be able to answer both questions, V becomes convinced that P does know this information. This takes after a sufficient number of rounds.

However, P's answers do not reveal the original Hamiltonian cycle in G. Each round, V will learn only H's isomorphism to G or a Hamiltonian cycle in H. He would need both answers for a single H to discover the cycle in G, so the information remains unknown as long as P can generate a unique H every round. Because of the nature of the isomorphic graph and Hamiltonian cycle problems, V gains no information about the Hamiltonian cycle in G from the information revealed in each round.

If P does not know the information, she can guess which question V will ask and generate either a graph isomorphic to G or a Hamiltonian cycle for an unrelated graph, but since she does not know a Hamiltonian cycle for G, she cannot do both. With this guesswork, her chance of fooling V is $n/2$ where n is the number of rounds. For all realistic purposes, it is in feasibly difficult to defeat a zero-knowledge proof with a reasonable number of rounds in this way.

Attacks

To break zero-knowledge protocol, following attacks are tried against it.

1. *Impersonation:* One entity pretends to be another entity
2. *Replay:* Capture the information from a single previous protocol and use on the same or different verifier
3. *Interleaving:* A selective combination of information from one or more previous protocol
4. *Reflection:* Sending information from an ongoing protocol execution back to the originator
5. *Forced delay:* An adversary that intercepts a message and relays it later
6. *Chosen-text:* When an adversary chooses specific challenges in an attempt to gain information about the secret

SOLVED PROBLEMS

8.1 Users A and B use the Diffie–Hellman key exchange technique. They agree with a common prime $n = 41$ and a primitive root $g = 13$.
  (a) If user A has private key $X_A = 27$, what is A's public key Y_A?
  (b) If user B has private key $X_B = 18$, what is B's public key Y_B?
  (c) What is the shared secret key?

Key Management

Solution

User A		User B	
Private key	Calculation	Private key	Calculation
$X_A = 27$	For $n = 41$ and $g = 13$	$X_B = 18$	For $n = 41$ and $g = 13$
	$Y_A = g^{X_A} \bmod n$		$Y_B = g^{X_A} \bmod n$
	$= 13^{27} \bmod 41$		$= 13^{18} \bmod 41$
	$= 15$		$= 8$
	$k_S = (Y_B)^{X_A} \bmod n$		$k_S = (Y_A)^{X_A} \bmod n$
	$= (8)^{27} \bmod 41$		$= (15)^{18} \bmod 41$
	$= 2$		$= 2$

Therefore
(a) A's public key $Y_A = 15$
(b) B's public key $Y_B = 8$
(c) The shared secret key $k_s = 2$

8.2 Users A and B use the Diffie–Hellman key exchange technique. They agree with a common prime $n = 67$ and a primitive root $g = 5$.
(a) If user A has private key $X_A = 10$, what is A's public key Y_A?
(b) If user B has private key $X_B = 24$, what is B's public key Y_B?
(c) What is the shared secret key?

Solution

User A		User B	
Private key	Calculation	Private key	Calculation
$X_A = 10$	For $n = 67$ and $g = 5$	$X_B = 24$	For $n = 67$ and $g = 5$
	$Y_A = g^{X_A} \bmod n$		$Y_B = g^{X_B} \bmod n$
	$= 40$		$= 25$
	$K = (Y_B)^{X_A} \bmod n$		$K = (Y_A)^{X_B} \bmod n$
	$= (25)^{10} \bmod 67$		$= (40)^{24} \bmod 67$
	$= 59$		$= 59$

Therefore,
(a) A's public key $Y_A = 40$
(b) B's public key $Y_B = 25$
(c) The shared secret key $= 59$

8.3 We use the Diffie–Hellman key exchange with private keys X_A and X_B and public keys $Y_A = g^{X_A} \bmod n$ and $Y_B = g^{X_B} \bmod n$. We assume $n = 71$ and $g = 7$.
(a) Give two possible pairs (X_A, X_B) such that the common key $k = 1$.
(b) An attacker knows that the product $Y_A * Y_B = 7 \bmod g$.
Give two possible pairs (X_A, X_B) that satisfy the attacker's knowledge.

Solution

(a) $k = (Y_B X_A) \mod n$

$$1 = 7^{X_B X_A} \mod 71 \quad \text{(i)}$$

Using Fermat's Little theorem $a^n = 1 \mod n$

$$a^{n-1} \mod n = 1$$

$$7^{(71-1)} \mod 71 = 1 \quad \text{(ii)}$$

From equation (i) and (ii)

$$7^{X_B X_A} \mod 71 = 7^{(71-1)} \mod 71$$

Therefore, $X_A Y_A = 70$.

Therefore, the possible values of X_A and Y_A are 10 and 7 or 14 and 5

(b) $Y_A * Y_B = 7 \mod n$

$Y_A * Y_B = g^{X_A} \mod n * g^{X_B} \mod n = 7 \mod 71$

$7^{X_A} * 7^{X_B} \mod 71 = 7 \mod 71$

$7^{(X_A + X_B)} \mod 71 = 7 \mod 71$

Using Fermat's Little theorem $a^n = a \mod n$

$$X_A + X_B = 71$$

We know that $Y_A * Y_B = 78 \mod 71 = 7 \mod 71$.

Factorise 78, we get (2, 39), (3, 26) and (6, 13) are the possible values of Y_A and Y_B.

$$6 = 7^{X_A} \mod 71 \text{ and } 13 = 7^{X_A} \mod 71$$

Solving we get $X_A = 39$ and $X_B = 32$

$$3 = 7^{X_A} \mod 71 \text{ and } 26 = 7^{X_A} \mod 71$$

We get, $X_A = 26$ and $X_B = 45$

SUMMARY

For public key cryptography, two important issues are: the distribution of public keys and the use of public key encryption for distribution of secret keys. In this chapter, we discuss different approaches for public key distribution. These include: the public announcement, publicly available directory, public key authority, and public key certificates.

Diffie–Hellman key exchange algorithm is used by two parties to generate a shared secret key. In Diffie–Hellman algorithm, there is no need of transferring the shared secret key for encryption. But it is suffered by man-in-the-middle attack. The Diffie–Hellman algorithm by itself does not provide authentication of the users. Elliptic curve cryptography is more secure even for a small key. Due to small key size, the performance of elliptic curve cryptography is better as compared to other algorithms. There is no sub-exponential algorithm due to which the cryptanalyst can break it. For selecting a small prime numbers or smaller finite fields, greater degree of security can be achieved.

A disadvantage of Diffie–Hellman or RSA algorithms is that when user A gives his secret key to user B, user B can thereafter impersonate user A. But, zero-knowledge (ZK) protocols allow user A to demonstrate knowledge of a secret key to user B without revealing any useful information about that secret key. Properties of zero-knowledge proof are completeness, soundness, zero-knowledge.

EXERCISES

8.1 What are the different approaches of key distribution? Explain each in brief.
8.2 Explain the Diffie–Hellman key exchange algorithm.
8.3 Explain security and efficiency of the elliptic curve.
8.4 Give the different uses of public key cryptography related to key distribution.
8.5 Explain the general categories of schemes for the distribution of public keys.
8.6 What is a public key certificate?
8.7 What is an elliptic curve?
8.8 What is the zero point of an elliptic curve?
8.9 Users "A" and "B" use the Diffie–Hellman key exchange technique. They agree for a common prime $n = 93$ and a primitive root $g = 11$.
(a) If user A has private key $X_A = 5$, what is A's public key Y_A?
(b) If user B has private key $X_B = 12$, what is B's public Y_B?
(c) What is the shared secret key?
8.10 What is zero knowledge proof? How it is better than public key encryption techniques? Explain with example.

MULTIPLE CHOICE QUESTIONS

8.1 Diffie–Hellman algorithm is suffered by--------------------------.
(a) Brute force attack
(b) Man-in-the-middle attack
(c) Timing attack
(d) None of the above

8.2 In cryptography the public keys can be distributed using-------------------- .
(a) Public announcement
(b) Publicly available directory
(c) Public key authority
(d) All of the above

8.3 For Diffie–Hellman algorithm, which of the following statement is true?
(a) If the values of n and g are small, it is possible for the attackers to find out the values of private keys of the users.
(b) If the values of n and g are small, it is possible for the attackers to find out the value of shared secret key.
(c) Man-in-the-middle attack is possible against Diffie–Hellman algorithm.
(d) The shared secret key is transmitted in encrypted form among the users.

Answers

8.1 (b)   **8.2** (d)   **8.3** (d)

CHAPTER 9

Authentication

9.1 INTRODUCTION

In the last chapter, we discuss about zero-knowledge proof which is useful for authentication of the users against each other. Authentication is one of the key aspects of cryptography. It can be used to guarantee that communication end-points, i.e., sender and receiver are the parties who they claim. It is the process of establishing or confirming a proof of identities, i.e., the claims made by or about the things are true. In cryptography and network security, authentication is done by verifying digital information of the sender or the recipient. Traditional method of authentication is user id and passwords. If someone knows the password, then it is assumed that the he/she is the authentic person.

For example, in some application, for the first time the user first registered by using an assigned user id and password or he can declare his own user id and password. For the subsequent use of that application, he must use that previously used user id and password. But the password is not the secure mechanism for authentication as it may be forgotten, or stolen or accidentally revealed. It is possible that while using the password, Eve may capture it. Nowadays, alternative techniques are used for password authentication. These techniques use encryption of the password, so that if it is stolen, it is difficult to decrypt and capture the password. Alternative to password authentication, new techniques are emerged which include: token-based authentication, biometric-based authentication and certificate-based authentication. Authorisation of any application needs the authentication of the user. Authorisation gives the full access to a specific application. To provide the security, the prerequisite to authorisation is authenticated. It depends on the identification of the user.

9.1.1 OBJECTIVES

The main objectives of authentication requirement are to:

- ensure that the claimants are really what they claim to be,
- avoid compromising security to an imposter.

9.1.2 Measurements

The degree of authentication which is required is dependent on the security expected for the application. The requirements of authentication are typically specified using following parameters:
- Minimum percentage of valid identities [by role, group] authenticated.
- Maximum percentage of invalid identities [by role, group] authenticated.
- Average time required for an attacker to become authenticated. It may be manually or using computer.

Authentication and authorisation are two different mechanisms. Many times people confused between them and treated both as the same. In many host-based systems, the same hardware is used for authentication as well as for authorisation. In some systems, same software is used for authentication as well as for authorisation. We can take a simple example, your computer has two login, one is admin and another is guest login. When the user wants to use your computer, he has to enter his password which is used for authentication. It is authenticated that whether he is guest user or admin user. If he is a guest user, he has limited access to the computer system. He cannot change the different setting in the system as he is not the authority to do it. But if he is admin, he can do it. Authorisation depends on the user type and not on the password.

So in authentication, the system may securely identify the users. Authentication systems provide following information about the user:
- Who is the user? i.e., identity of the user.
- Is the user really who he/she claims himself to be? i.e., authentication of the user.

An authentication system may be as simple or complicated system. Simple system includes systems which are using a plain-text password. It is the insecure authentication mechanism. Complicated system includes system like the Kerberos system where authentication process is complex. It is more secure authentication mechanism. Irrespective of type of system, i.e., whether it is a simple or complicated, authentication systems depend on some unique bit of information which is known only to the individual user who is being authenticated and the authentication system. Advanced authentication system use thumb impression, iris image or hash values derived from data related to users. For verification, the authenticating system typically challenges the user to provide his unique information. If the information provided by the user and the information stored with the authenticating system is matched, the user is considered an authenticated user of the system.

Whereas authorisation, is the mechanism through which a system determines what level of access to a particular authenticated user should have. It used to secure the resources controlled by the system. For example, in the above example, guest login allows the user to use the limited applications whereas admin user can use and change the setting of the system.

So, in authorisation of the system may control the access of the users to different applications of the system. Authorised systems provide following information about the user:

- Is user A authorised to access some particular resource in the system?
- Is user A authorised to perform some particular operation in the system?
- Is user A authorised to perform some particular operation on some particular resource?

In this way authentication and authorisation are somewhat related to each other. Authorisation depends on authentication systems for security. Figure 9.1 graphically illustrates the inter-relationship between authentication and authorised systems and a typical client/server application.

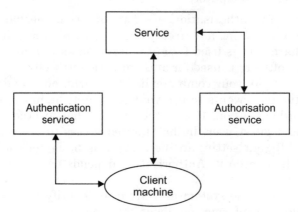

Figure 9.1 Authentication vs authorisation.

In Figure 9.1, a user working on a client system first login to the authentication system to prove his identity and request to work on the server. In turn, the server system contacts to an authorised system to know about the rights and privileges, the client's user have on the server.

9.2 AUTHENTICATION METHODS

There are different authentication methods available. But the simplest and the most common method of authentication is the traditional local authentication method.

9.2.1 Password-based Authentication Method

The password-based authentication method refers to a secret information which the user has to prove that he knows it. A password is a pattern of characters contains alphabets, numbers and special characters. It is used to verify the user who requests for accessing the computer system is actually that particular user. For a multiuser or securely protected single-user system, each user has a unique identity called *user id* which is publicaly known to all. For authentication of such users, additional identification is needed is called *password*. This password is secret and known only to that user and the computer system. When the user wants to use the computer system, he uses his user id and password. Then the authentication system verifies the user id and password with the database available with the authentication system. Once the verification is completed and the information provided by the user matches with the information available in the database, authentication system allows the user to access the necessary applications. The major problem with this method is that password may be captured by the eavesdropper.

Guidelines for good password:

- Password should be a combination of alphabets, numbers and special characters.
- It should not be a word or information related to you such as your PAN number, date of birth, name of pet, etc.
- Do not select the word that can be found in the dictionary or be a keyword.
- Do not select the password which is related to current news.
- It should not be similar to previous password.
- It should be easy to remember.
- Do not write the password on a paper or share it with anybody.

It is recommended that user should change his password periodically. Due to this, if the eavesdropper knows the password, he cannot misuse it. To provide the security, user id and password are the basic and simplest method of authentication. It is an efficient and cost-effective method. The major problem with this system is that there are number of such systems where a same user has his different user id and password. For example, nowaday many users have different passwords for online banking, e-commerce application, different e-mail account, etc. It is difficult to remember the password for all these systems.

The security of the application depends on the identification of a user. After identification only, the user can use various applications and resources of the system. Figure 9.2 provides a graphical overview of the traditional authentication method. In this system initially, the user login the client system by entering his user id and password. This password is a plaintext format. Then the client system sends user id and password to the server. Server has a database of user id and password. The user id and password sent by the client is verified by the server with this database called *password table*. If the user id and password matches, the authentication completed and the user is permitted to use different applications on the client.

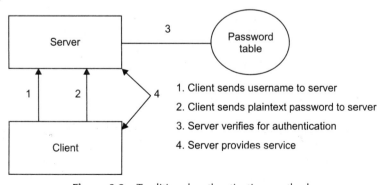

Figure 9.2 Traditional authentication method.

Weaknesses of traditional authentication method:
- In this model, the passwords are stored in plaintext form. If the attacker is able to capture the password, he can access the user id and password from the database.
- The client to server network is connected by insecure channel. Therefore, if the password is sent in plaintext form, then there is a chance that the attacker may capture it during transmission.
- Nowadays, a single user may have different accounts on different systems to use different applications. For this, single user has different id and password for different machines. To remember all this user id and password it is a difficult task for any user. So, a user may select either same id and password or less secure password which is easy to remember.
- Using different malicious software, attacker tries to capture the password. These software includes, key logger, Trojan horse, etc. which when installed on the system, it sends all the information to the attacker.

9.2.2 Two-factor Authentication Method

Traditional authentication method has different weaknesses as we discussed. So, another method called two-factor authentication is used. In this system, identification and authentication of the user take place in two different ways to establish his identity and privileges. In this method, two factors are used for identification and authentication. For example, the user wants to withdraw money from the ATM machine. For these two factors are required: the ATM card issued by the bank and the PIN number of the card. This method is called *strong authentication method*. In the above example, the ATM card is issued by the bank to the authorised account holder of the bank by taking necessary security measures. PIN for the card is initially provided by the bank which the user can change periodically. This provides necessary security. Another example is online banking where physical card is not required. Instead of that user id is required as one of the factors of authentication. The other factor is PIN which sends to the registered mobile number of the user. This PIN number is OTP (one time password). OTP is the most secure way of encryption because PIN is no longer valid to give access to the system. Its lifetime is small and for every new transaction user gets new OTP. This provides strong authentication and identification of the user. This provides more security. This system also has some drawbacks, particularly the use of new technology. Therefore, many times we read the news about hacking of bank accounts and transfer of money from victim's account. This method suffers by Trojan horse and man-in-the middle attack.

9.2.3 Biometric Authentication Method

The two-factor authentication method based on physical devices such as in the first example the ATM card and in the second example the mobile phone on which the OTP is received. The lost of ATM card or block of mobile phone by the attacker are the weakness of this method. One more method of authentication is *biometric authentication*. This method uses thumb impression, iris or voices for authentication.

You may know that in Aadhar card project of Government of India, before issuing the card, the fingerprint and the iris impression of the user is taken. This data is used for the authentication of the user. The most common and widely used authentication method is *thumb impression*. Authentication of employees in different organisation using thumb impression is the most common application of this method. Thumb impression authentication method is also used in college for taking the attendance of the students. In this method, the finger impression is used for authentication because it has distinctive and unique feature. Throughout the life span of the user his fingerprint remains invariant. In this method, the scan image of fingers is taken and stored in the database. Apply different image processing on this image which includes edge reduction feature extraction and matching algorithms. This is shown in Figure 9.3. If this step is not processed properly, there is a chance of introducing some noise in the image which creates a serious problem during authentication. The next step is similarity between two sets carried out. This can be done by performing different transformation operations on the image. These include, scaling, translation and rotations of the image. Using the score for an image is calculated which is used to take final decision. This decision is based on some threshold value of the score.

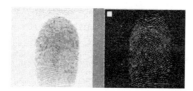

Figure 9.3 Fingerprint authentication.

If the score is below the threshold, the decision is that fingerprints are not matched; if the score is above the threshold, a correct match is declared.

There are different issues in fingerprint authentication system. First issue is performance issue. It is known as *fail to enroll rate*. This occurs as some people has no finger, or may have very faint fingerprint impression. The authentication system cannot work for such users. The second issue is a 'reject' option in the system. This issue is based on the quality of the input image. The poor quality input is not accepted by the system during authentication. And in such cases, the authentication of the user failed. This authentication is failed due to non-cooperative users, dirt on the fingers and improper usages. The performance of the authentication also depends on the quality of scanner used for this purpose.

The drawback of this method is that if there are cuts and bruises on the fingers, then match of the current finger impression and the stored finger impression in the database never match and failure in authentication of the particular user. This method also failed if noise is added during the preprocessing of the finger impression images. Due to human skin elasticity, the authentication may fail as the new finger impression cannot match with the images in the database. Apart from all these drawbacks, thumb impression is the widely used method for authentication due to its low cost and high performance.

There are two types of error in fingerprints and biometrics in authentication system. These recognition errors are the *false accept ratio* (FAR) and the *false reject ratio*

(FRR). The FAR is the probability that the wrong user is identified and authenticates by a system. FRR is the probability that a true user is treated as non-authenticate user. These ratios are exactly opposite of each other, i.e., when we try to reduce one error, other error will increase. The threshold is shown with respect to the error rates in Figure 9.4. This graph is called the ROC (receiver operating characteristic) curve. If the threshold is changed to reduce one of the error rates, other error rate would increase.

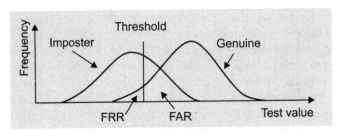

Figure 9.4 Error rates.

Biometrics-based authentication is more secure as compared to password-based authentication system. In password-based authentication, loss of physical card, forget the password, and capture the password by the attacker are the main issues. Whereas in biometric, there is no question of loss or forget at the same time it is difficult to steal or forge the biometric signals.

9.2.4 Extensible Authentication Protocol (EAP)

For more security, most of the organisations do not depend on the user id and passwords. Such organisations use new extensible authentication protocol (EAP) to support the point-to-point protocol (PPP). EAP is standard which provides an infrastructure to clients and servers for authentication.

Microsoft Windows operating system uses extensible authentication protocol to authenticate network access for point-to-point protocol (PPP) connections and for IEEE 802.1X-based network access to authenticate ethernet switches and wireless access points (APs).

With EAP, the PPP peers negotiate to perform EAP during the connection authentication phase. The peers negotiate the use of a specific EAP authentication scheme when the connection authentication phase is reached. This method is known as an *EAP method*.

Then EAP allows for an open-ended exchange of messages between the client and the authenticating server. This exchange is based on the parameters of the connection. The client first requests for the service. Once the authentication takes place, the authentication server sends the response to the client. EAP provides the flexibility to allow for secure authentication methods.

An EAP infrastructure includes:
- *Access client*: The computer that sends the request to access the network.
- *Authenticator*: It is an access point or network access server.
- *Server*: A computer system which is responsible for authentication.

The client and the authentication server exchange the messages using software and a data link layer transport protocol such as PPP or IEEE 802.1X. The EAP authenticator and the authentication server send EAP messages using RADIUS. The result is that EAP messages are exchanged between the EAP components on the client and the authentication server. Figure 9.5 shows EAP working.

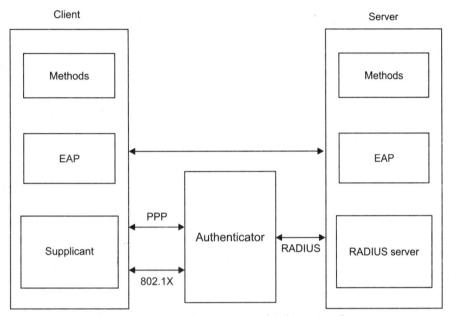

Figure 9.5 EAP infrastructure and information flow.

There is no need of the support of EAP authenticator to any specific EAP methods. User can use EAP to support authentication schemes such as Generic Token Card, One Time Password (OTP), Message Digest 5 (MD5)-Challenge, Transport Layer Security (TLS) for smart card and digital certificate-based authentication, and future authentication technologies. EAP is a critical technology component for establishing secure connections.

EAP methods, such as MD5, CHAP, are used for dial-up remote access or site to site connection, VPN. Table 9.1 lists the different types of access and the available EAP methods user can use.

Table 9.1 EAP methods for network access

Type of network access	EAP methods
Dial-up connections	MD5 CHAP, TLS
802.1X to wireless AP	PEAP-MS-CHAP v2, TLS
802.1X to an authenticating switch (wired)	TLS, MD5 CHAP, PEAP_MS-CHAP v2, PEAP-TLS
VPN	TLS, MD5 CHAP

9.3 MESSAGE DIGEST

9.3.1 MD2

Encryption techniques provide the confidentiality to the message. Authentication techniques provide the access control. But if the third party captures the message and modifies it during transmission, the integrity checking of the message is necessary. Integrity of a message is checked using the hash value or message digest calculated from the message. The hash value of the message is derived from the message which remains same if the message is unaltered. For a small change in the message, its hash value is also changed. Therefore, hash value is used to check the integrity of the message. There are various algorithms available which can generate the hash value of the message. Two of them are message digest and secure hash algorithm.

In 1989, Ronald Rivest developed a method to calculate the hash value of the message. That hash value is called *message digest* (MD) and the algorithm is called *message digest algorithm*. The initial version of message digest algorithm is MD2. It is a cryptographic hash function. This algorithm is optimised for 8-bit computers. Later on other message digest algorithms have been proposed those are MD4 and MD5. One more hashing algorithm is developed called secure hash algorithm (SHA). MD2 is used in public key infrastructures as part of certificates generated with MD2 and RSA. Each of these algorithms generate different hash value called message digest. For a message multiple of 128 bits (each block is of 128 bits), MD2 produces a message digest of 128 bits long.

The working of MD2:

1. The input is a message of an arbitrary length.
2. Pad necessary number of bits to the message to make it to a multiple of 16 octets.
3. Add a checksum of 16-byte.
4. The 128-bit message digest or hash value is generated.

Padding

Padding is always used for MD2 even if the message is of multiple of 16 octets. If the message is a multiple of 16 octets, 16 octets of padding are added. The number of padding octets is from 1 to 15 necessary to make the message a multiple of 16 octets is added. Each pad octet specifies that the total number of octets was added.

Checksum

MD2 checksum is a 16-octet. It is just like a message digest, but is not secure by itself. It is always appended to the message. For the actual calculation, a 48-byte auxiliary block and a 256-byte table generated indirectly from the digits of the fractional part of pi are used. Once all of the blocks of the modified message have been processed, the first partial block of the auxiliary block becomes the hash value of the message.

Authentication

Final Pass

It is similar to the checksum computation.

In 2004, MD2 was shown to be vulnerable to a pre-image attack with time complexity equivalent to 2^{104} applications of the compression function.

9.3.2 MD4

In 1990, Ronald Rivest developed a new version of message digest called MD4. Its operations are 32-bit word oriented. This makes it faster than MD2. Like MD2, it can also handle a message of arbitrary length.

The padding to the message is used to ensure that its length in bits plus 64 is divisible by 512. The length of the original message which is 64-bit is concatenated to the original message. The message digest generated using MD4 is a 128-bit. The message is processed in 512-bit blocks in the iterative structure. There are three distinct rounds and each block is processed in these three rounds.

MD4 is vulnerable to an attack developed by Boer, Bosselaers and others. The attack was developed on versions of MD4 with either the first or the last rounds missing. Dobbertin shows many more attacks on MD4 which prove that MD4 should now be considered broken.

9.3.3 MD5

MD4 is broken and treated as non-secure hashing algorithm. In 1991, the new version of message digest was designed by Ronald Rivest. The next and secure version of message digest is MD5 (Message–Digest algorithm 5). It is a widely used hashing function. It generates message digest with a 128-bit hash value. MD5 gains popularity by its use as an internet standard, in a wide variety of security applications, and mostly used to check the integrity of files.

In 1996, a flaw was found with MD5 design, but it is not treated as a complete weakness of MD5. But the flaws discovered in 2004, rises the questions on the use of MD5 for integrity checking of the message.

Generation of Message Digest

For MD5

    The length of input message : Arbitrary
    Block size : 512-bit: K bits
    Padding : 1 to 512 bits
    Message length : $K \bmod 2^{64}$
    The length of the output: 128-bit message digest (MD)

The message is padded with 1 to 512 bits as shown in Figure 9.6(a). Padding is always used. That means there is a minimum of 1 bit padding is used. The overall processing of a message to produce a digest is shown in Figure 9.6(b).

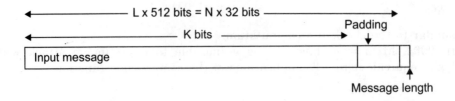

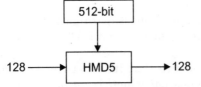

Figure 9.6(a) MD5 message with padding.

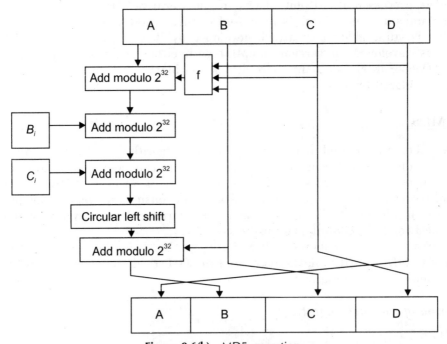

Figure 9.6(b) MD5 operation.

In MD5, there are 4 rounds. Each round has 16 operations. There are total 64 operations. Each operation uses different constants of 32 bits. Each round uses one non-linear function called f function. At a time, a block of 128 bits called state is processed in each round, which is divided into 32 bits sub-blocks each. Let the input of sub-block of the message is denoted by B_i and a 32-bit constant is denoted by C_i. Circular left shift operation is used which rotate the bits by s positions to the left. The shift s varies from round to round. Addition modulo 2^{32} operations are performed.

MD5 processes a variable-length message which is divided into 512-bit block. At a time, one block of 512 bits is processed which produces a 128-bit message digest.

The input message of arbitrary length is appended by 1 to 512 bits called padding and then the 64 bits are used to show the length of the message. This message is divided into a block of 512-bit each. The message is padded so that its length is divisible by 512. The padding works as follows: first a single bit, 1, is appended to the end of the message. This is followed by as many zeroes as are required to bring the length of the message up to 64 bits less than a multiple of 512. The remaining bits are filled up with a 64-bit integer representing the length of the original message. For example, the size of the message is 734 bits. We know that the block size for MD5 is 512 bits. Therefore, the message should be divided into two blocks of 512 bits. But 734 is not the multiples of 512 bits so, padding is required. Now, we have to decide how many bits are appended. So, 512 * 2 = 1024 bits actually required to split the message into two blocks. We know that last 64 bits are used for message length. Therefore, 960 bits (1024 – 64) should be the length of the message. But original message is 734 bits long, so we have to append 226 bits (960 – 734) to get the message of desired size. So, the padding of 226 bits gives us the message size of 1024 bits. (734 + 226 + 64). This 226 bit padding includes the first bit from LHS, i.e., MSB is 1 and other 225 bits are all zeroes, i.e., 100000......0. If the message is of size 448, with 64 bits which are reserved for length gives the message of size 512. In this case padding is also required and it is of 512 bits so that the total size is 1024 bits. If the message is of size 447 bits, then with 64 bits the size of the message is 511, so 1 more bit is used as padding to get the desired size, i.e., 512 bits. This concludes that whatever be the size of the message, the padding is always required. There is minimum 1 bit to maximum 512 bits are used for padding.

The MD5 algorithm operates on a 128-bit state which is split into four 32-bit words. It is denoted by A, B, C and D. These are initialised to certain fixed constants. Then the 512-bit message block is taken as input which modifies the state. There are four rounds in MD5 and each round has different operations such as non-linear function f, modular addition 2^{32} and shift circular left. One operation within a round is shown in Figure 9.6(b). The possible function used in each round is as shown in Table 9.2.

Table 9.2 Functions used in MD5

Round	f	$f(b, c, d)$
1	F(p, q, r)	(p AND q) OR ((NOT p) AND r)
2	G(p, q, r)	(p AND r) OR (q AND (NOT r))
3	H(p, q, r)	p XOR q XOR r
4	I(p, q, r)	q XOR (p AND (NOT r))

MD5 algorithm consists of 5 steps:

Step 1 *Padding:* Required numbers of bits append to the right hand side of the message. The original message is "padded" (extended) so that its length (in bits) is congruent to 448, modulo 512. The padding rules are:

- In MD5 padding to the original message is always used. Minimum 1 bit and maximum 512 bits are used for padding. The first bit of padding (MSB) is always '1'.
- The remaining bits of the padding are always zero.

Step 2 *Appending length:* At the end of message after padding, the 64 bits are appended which show the length of the original message in bytes. The rules of appending length are:
- The length of the original message is in bytes. Convert it binary format of 64 bits. In case of overflow, use only the low-order 64 bits.
- Divide the 64-bit length into 2 words (32-bit each).
- Appended first the low-order word and followed by the high-order word.

Step 3 *Initialising MD buffer:* MD5 algorithm has a buffer of size 128 bits. This buffer is divided into 4 words each has a specific initial value. The rules of initialising the buffer are:
- The buffer is divided into 4 words, named as A, B, C and D.
- Word A is initialised to: 0x67452301.
- Word B is initialised to: 0xEFCDAB89.
- Word C is initialised to: 0x98BADCFE.
- Word D is initialised to: 0x10325476.

Step 4 *Processing message:* The message is split in 512-bit blocks. Each block of 512-bits undergoes 4 rounds of operations. Total 16 operations are performed on each block in each round.

Step 5 *Output:* The contents in buffer words A, B, C, D are stored in sequence with low-order byte first. The 128-bit message digest is produced.

These 128 bits act as state for the next block of 512 bits. After processing of all the blocks, the contents of buffer A, B, C, D is 128-bit message digest.

Pseudocode for MD5

```
A, B, C, D: initialized buffer words

F(P, Q, R) = (P AND Q ) OR ((NOT P) AND R)
G(P, Q, R) = (P AND Z ) OR (Q AND (NOT R))
H(P, Q, R) = P XOR Q XOR R
I(P, Q, R) = Q XOR (P OR (NOT R))
const[1, 2, ..., 64]: Array of special constants (32-bit integers) as:
const[i] = int(abs(sin(i)) * 232)
M[1, 2, ..., N]: Array of blocks of message of size 512-bits

//Round 1

Round1(a, b, c, d, P, s, i)
a = b + ((a + F(b, c, d) + P + const[i]) shift left by 's' positions)

// Round 2

Round2(a, b, c, d, P, s, i)
a = b + ((a + G(b, c, d) + P + const[i]) shift left by 's' positions)

// Round 3

Round3(a, b, c, d, P, s, i)
```

```
a = b + ((a + H(b, c, d) + P + const[i]) shift left by 's' positions)

// Round 4

Round4(a, b, c, d, P, s, i)
a = b + ((a + I(b, c, d) + P + const[i]) shift left by 's' positions)

Algorithm:
for k = 1 to N do the following
AA = A
BB = B
CC = C
DD = D
(P[0], P[1], ..., P[15]) = M[k]        /* Divide M[k] into 16 words */

/* Round 1 operations. */

Round1(A,B,C,D,P[ 0], 7, 1)
Round1(D,A,B,C,P[ 1],12, 2)
Round1(C,D,A,B,P[ 2],17, 3)
Round1(B,C,D,A,P[ 3],22, 4)
Round1(A,B,C,D,P[ 4], 7, 5)
Round1(D,A,B,C,P[ 5],12, 6)
Round1(C,D,A,B,P[ 6],17, 7)
Round1(B,C,D,A,P[ 7],22, 8)
Round1(A,B,C,D,P[ 8], 7, 9)
Round1(D,A,B,C,P[ 9],12,10)
Round1(C,D,A,B,P[10],17,11)
Round1(B,C,D,A,P[11],22,12)
Round1(A,B,C,D,P[12], 7,13)
Round1(D,A,B,C,P[13],12,14)
Round1(C,D,A,B,P[14],17,15)
Round1(B,C,D,A,P[15],22,16)

/* Round 2 operations. */

Round2(A,B,C,D,P[ 1], 5,17)
Round2(D,A,B,C,P[ 6], 9,18)
Round2(C,D,A,B,P[11],14,19)
Round2(B,C,D,A,P[ 0],20,20)
Round2(A,B,C,D,P[ 5], 5,21)
Round2(D,A,B,C,P[10], 9,22)
Round2(C,D,A,B,P[15],14,23)
Round2(C,D,A,B,P[15],14,23)
Round2(A,B,C,D,P[ 9], 5,25)
Round2(D,A,B,C,P[14], 9,26)
Round2(C,D,A,B,P[ 3],14,27)
Round2(B,C,D,A,P[ 8],20,28)
Round2(A,B,C,D,P[13], 5,29)
Round2(D,A,B,C,P[ 2], 9,30)
```

```
Round2(C,D,A,B,P[ 7],14,31)
Round2(B,C,D,A,P[12],20,32)

/* Round 3 */

Round3(A,B,C,D,P[ 5], 4,33)
Round3(D,A,B,C,P[ 8],11,34)
Round3(C,D,A,B,P[11],16,35)
Round3(B,C,D,A,P[14],23,36)
Round3(A,B,C,D,P[ 1], 4,37)
Round3(D,A,B,C,P[ 4],11,38)
Round3(C,D,A,B,P[ 7],16,39)
Round3(B,C,D,A,P[10],23,40)
Round3(A,B,C,D,P[13], 4,41)
Round3(D,A,B,C,P[ 0],11,42)
Round3(C,D,A,B,P[ 3],16,43)
Round3(B,C,D,A,P[ 6],23,44)
Round3(A,B,C,D,P[ 9], 4,45)
Round3(D,A,B,C,P[12],11,46)
Round3(C,D,A,B,P[15],16,47)
Round3(B,C,D,A,P[ 2],23,48)

/* Round 4*/

Round4(A,B,C,D,P[ 0], 6,49)
Round4(D,A,B,C,P[ 7],10,50)
Round4(C,D,A,B,P[14],15,51)
Round4(B,C,D,A,P[ 5],21,52)
Round4(A,B,C,D,P[12], 6,53)
Round4(D,A,B,C,P[ 3],10,54)
Round4(C,D,A,B,P[10],15,55)
Round4(B,C,D,A,P[ 1],21,56)
Round4(A,B,C,D,P[ 8], 6,57)
Round4(D,A,B,C,P[15],10,58)
Round4(C,D,A,B,P[ 6],15,59)
Round4(B,C,D,A,P[13],21,60)
Round4(A,B,C,D,P[ 4], 6,61)
Round4(D,A,B,C,P[11],10,62)
Round4(C,D,A,B,P[ 2],15,63)
Round4(B,C,D,A,P[ 9],21,64)

A = A + AA
B = B + BB
C = C + CC
D = D + DD
End of for loop

// Output of contents A, B, C, D
128-bit Message digest
```

Applications

MD5 digests have been widely used to provide the integrity of the message receiving at the receiver's end. This can be done as follows.

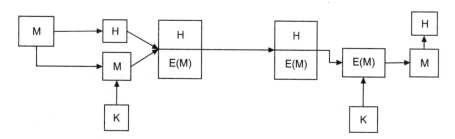

M — Plaintext message
H — Hash or message digest
K — Secret key
E(M) — Ciphertext

Figure 9.7 Verification of message using message digest.

For example, from Figure 9.7, user sends message M. First the hash value or message digest is computed by the sender. Then the message is encrypted using the secret key. Then the ciphertext with hash value is sent to the receiver. The receiver decrypts the message using the secret key and computes the hash value or message digest of the plaintext. Then compare the newly computed hash value with the hash value sent by the sender. If both hash values are same, the receiver received the same message sent by the receiver. More security is provided by encrypting the message digest with ciphertext by using public key of the receiver.

The most widely use of MD5 is to store passwords. The attack is made by decrypting the password using reverse lookup table. A number of such reverse lookup tables exist for MD5 which make it easy to decrypt password hashed with plain MD5. To prevent such attacks, we can apply the MD5 for hashing the password. Due to this, the time, for capturing the password is increased and it provides more security

Brute Force Attack

It is not possible to get back the plaintext from the message digest. There is no known way to generate plaintext from the message digest. But the cryptanalyst may be able to get back the plaintext from the message digest using brute force attack. This attack can be made by assuming some plaintext. Calculate the message digest for this assumed message. Compare the calculated message digest with the actual message digest. If both the message digest matches, the assumed message corresponding to computed message digest is the required message. MD5 message digest values are unique. There is no chance to get same message digest for two different messages using MD5. The secure hash algorithm is the replacement for MD5.

Spoofing MD5

A hash technique is repetitive. Collisions between two distinct messages have studied by a Chinese researcher, Xiaoyun Wang. He used these differences to suggest changes that would increase the chances of the two messages digest generating the same result. Another successful spoofing attack is done by Benne de Weger, a Dutch scientist against MD5. He took two colliding documents and adds non-random data. Due to this the documents collide continues. He suggests an example, suppose user A could prepare a document and he has to take a sign of his higher authority on that document. Simultaneously, he prepares one more document having the same hash value. After the signature of his higher authority on the document, he could adjust his original document with the document signed by his higher authority having the same hash value. (From *The Economist Technology Quarterly*, March 8, 2008, page 10.)

Comparison of MD5 with MD4

A comparison of MD5 with MD4 is given in Table 9.3.

Table 9.3 Comparison between MD5 and MD4

Algorithm	MD5	MD4
Number of steps	64	48
Additive constants	For each step, a different additive constant is used.	For the first round no additive constant is used. For each step of the second round same additive constant is used. Another additive constant is used for each of the steps of the third round.
Number of logical functions	4	5
Speed	Slower	Faster
Security	More secure	Less secure

9.3.4 SHA-1

The possible attacks against MD5 are possible. The more secure hash algorithm is SHA (secure hash algorithm). The hash value generated by SHA is unique for a given message. NIST proposed a secure hashing algorithm known as SHA-1. For a small change to a message will have a very high probability to get different message digests. These algorithms are called secure because, for a given algorithm, it is computationally infeasible to

- find a message which have a same message digest or
- find two different messages those have the same message digest.

There are five different variants of secure hash algorithms. The five algorithms are SHA-1, SHA-224, SHA-256, SHA-384, and SHA-512. The latter four variants are sometimes collectively referred to as SHA-2.

SHA-1 is widely used in security applications and protocols such as: PGP, TLS, IPSec, SSL, SSH, S/MIME. It has variable hash values as per its variants. No attack has been detected against SHA-2.

SHA-1 Algorithm

The message digest or hash value generated using SHA-1 is 160-bit. For a message with length $< 2^{64}$ bits, it produces a message digest of 160-bit. Like MD5, it also processes a block of 512-bit input message. The message digest or hash value generated by SHA-1 is used as input to the digital signature algorithm. This hash value is used for generation or verification of message using digital signature. This improves the performance and efficiency of the algorithm as hash value is smaller than original message. The same digital signed hash value is used to check the integrity of the message.

The hash values for two different messages are never same. It is computationally infeasible to generate the message from the hash value. This proves that SHA-1 is more secure. If there is any change happened in a message, it is possible to identify due to hash value of the message. The architecture of SHA-1 is based on MD4 architecture.

Features

SHA-1 generates a message digest of 160-bit for a message of arbitrary size. It uses padding as MD5 algorithm to make the message size is of multiples of 512-bit. But, it is not defined for the message longer than 2^{64}. Then the length of the message is added to the end of the message. The length indicates the number of bits present in the message. For empty message, the length is 0-bit. For compactness, the message is represented in hexadecimal. The working of SHA-1 is shown in Figure 9.8.

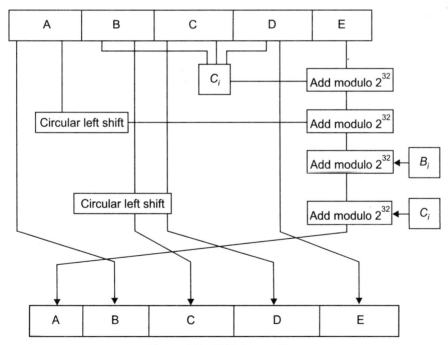

Figure 9.8 SHA-1 operation.

From Figure 9.8, there are 5 states A, B, C, D, E and each has 16 operations. So, there are 80 operations in SHA-1. The bits are rotated by circular left shift operations by s bit positions. The value of s varies for each operation. The size of each state is 32-bit. A non-linear function f is used which varies for different rounds. Addition modulo 2^{32} is used for modular additions. A constant C_i is used in each round. Each block of message of size 512-bit is indicated as B_i. The cryptanalysis of SHA-1 is more difficult than its predecessor SHA-0.

NIST has published four variants of SHA are: SHA-224, SHA-256, SHA-384, and SHA-512. The number indicates the message digest generated in bits. The SHA-256 uses 32 words; SHA-512 uses 64-bit words. They use different shift amounts and additive constants. Other operations are identical for both SHA-256 and SHA-512. The number of rounds is different for SHA-256 and SHA-512. But SHA-1 is more popular than other variants of SHA family.

SHA-1 Working

The following example illustrates the padding process in SHA-1. It is similar to MD5.

Message is appended by 1 and necessary number of "0" followed by a 64-bit integer are appended to the end of the message to produce a padded message of length 512 * n. The 64-bit integer shows the length of the original message. The padded message is then processed by the SHA-1 as 512-bit blocks at a time. Suppose a message has length $l < 2^{64}$. Before it is input to the SHA-1, the message is padded on the right as follows:

(a) "1" is appended.
For example, if the original message is "01010110", this is padded to "010101101".

(b) "0"s are appended. The number of "0"s will depend on the original length of the message. The last 64 bits of the last 512-bit block are reserved for the length of the original message.
For example, suppose the original message is:
11100101 01100110 01101011 01100100 01101101 01101101.
Since there are 48 bits in the message, total 400 bits are needed to append the original message to get 448 mod 512. First append "1" to the message, we get:
1110 0101 0110 0110 0110 1011 0110 0100 0110 1101 0110 1101 1.
Remaining 399 bits append should be "0". The result in hexadecimal is:
  E5666764 6D80000 00000000 00000000 00000000 00000000 00000000 00000000 00000000 00000000 00000000 00000000 00000000 00000000.

(c) Obtain the 2-word representation of length of the original message. If $l < 2^{32}$, then the first word is all zeroes. Append these two words to the padded message.
For example, suppose the original message is above having 48 bits length. Length should be computed before padding so it is 48 bits. The two-word representation of 48 is hex 00000000 00000030. Hence, the final message after padding and appending message in hexadecimal is:

E5666764 6D80000 00000000 00000000 00000000 00000000 00000000 00000000 00000000 00000000 00000000 00000000 00000000 00000000 00000000 00000030.

The new message is now multiples of 512. As each block is of 512 bits, there are n blocks of 512 bits in the new message. Then process each block sequentially one by one.

Functions and constants: SHA-1 uses 80 functions and operates on three 32-bit words and produces a 32-bit output word. The working is as follows:

$f(i;\ B,\ C,\ D) = (B\ AND\ C)\ OR\ ((NOT\ B)\ AND\ D)\ (0 <= i <= 19)$

$f(i;\ B,\ C,\ D) = B\ XOR\ C\ XOR\ D\ (20 <= i <= 39)$

$f(i;\ B,\ C,\ D) = (B\ AND\ C)\ OR\ (B\ AND\ D)\ OR\ (C\ AND\ D)\ (40 <= i <= 59)$

$f(i;\ B,\ C,\ D) = B\ XOR\ C\ XOR\ D\ (60 <= i <= 79)$.

$Const(i) = 5A827999\ (0 <= i <= 19)$

$Const(i) = 6ED9EBA1\ (20 <= i <= 39)$

$Const(i) = 8F1BBCDC\ (40 <= i <= 59)$

$Const(i) = CA62C1D6\ (60 <= i <= 79)$.

Generation of the Hash Value (Message Digest)

There are many methods for the generation of the message digest. Here we discuss two methods for the generation of message digest. The execution time requires for second method is more as compared to first method.

Method 1: The message is prepared as above by appending padding bits and length. Two buffers are used. Each buffer has five 32-bit words in addition of a sequence of 80 words. The words are labelled as A, B, C, D and E for the first buffer and H_0 to H_4 for the second buffer. The sequence of 80 words is labelled from W_0 to W_{79}. A temporary buffer is also used called TEMP.

Before processing any blocks, the H words are initialised in hexadecimal as:

$H_0 = 67452301$

$H_1 = EFCDAB89$

$H_2 = 98BADCFE$

$H_3 = 10325476$

$H_4 = C3D2E1F0$

The 16-word blocks $B_1, B_2,..., B_n$ are processed in order. This is shown in Figure 9.7. The processing of each B_n involves 80 steps.

(a) B_n is divided into 16 words W_0 to W_{15} where W_0 is the left-most word.
(b) For $n = 16$ to 79, let $W_n = S^1(W_{(n-3)}\ XOR\ W_{(n-8)}\ XOR\ W_{(n-14)}\ XOR\ W_{(n-16)})$.
(c) Let $A = H_0$, $B = H_1$, $C = H_2$, $D = H_3$, $E = H_4$.
(d) For $n = 0$ to 79 do

```
TEMP = S^5 (A) + f(n; B,C,D) + E + W_n + C_n;
E = D; D = C; C = S^30(B); B = A; A = TEMP;
```

(e) Let $H_0 = H_0 + A$, $H_1 = H_1 + B$, $H_2 = H_2 + C$, $H_3 = H_3 + D$, $H_4 = H_4 + E$.

After processing B_n, the 160-bit message digest is generated as:

$$H_0\ H_1\ H_2\ H_3\ H_4.$$

Method 2: In the above method an array is used to implement the sequence $W_0, \ldots, W_{79}$. This reduces the execution time. But it occupies more space. To reduce the space, one has to use a circular queue using an array of 16, 32-bit words from W_0 to W_{15}. Let M stands for masking bits.

M = 0000000F. Then processing of B_n is as follows:

(a) Split B_n into 16 words W_0 to W_{15}, where W_0 represents the leftmost word.
(b) Let $A = H_0$, $B = H_1$, $C = H_2$, $D = H_3$, $E = H_4$.
(c) For n = 0 to 79 do
```
s = n AND M;
if (n >= 16) W[s] = S¹(W[(s + 13) AND M] XOR W[(s + 8) AND M] XOR
W[(s + 2) AND M] XOR W[s]);
TEMP = S⁵(A) + f(n; B, C, D) + E + W[s] + C(n);
E = D; D = C; C = S³⁰(B); B = A; A = TEMP;
```
(d) Let $H_0 = H_0 + A$, $H_1 = H_1 + B$, $H_2 = H_2 + C$, $H_3 = H_3 + D$, $H_4 = H_4 + E$.

After processing B_n, the 160-bit message digest is generated as:

$$H_0\ H_1\ H_2\ H_3\ H_4.$$

Comparison of various SHA is given in Table 9.4.

Table 9.4 Comparison of various SHA

Algorithm	SHA-0	SHA-1	SHA-256/224	SHA-512/384
Size of message digest in bits	160	160	256/224	512/384
Size of internal state in bits	160	160	256	512
Size of block in bits	512	512	512	1024
Length of message	$2^{64} - 1$	$2^{64} - 1$	$2^{64} - 1$	$2^{128} - 1$
Size of word	32	32	32	64
Number of steps	80	80	64	80
Collision	Yes	2^{63} attack	None yet	None yet

A comparison of SHA-1 and MD5 is given in Table 9.5.

Table 9.5 Comparison between SHA-1 and MD5

Algorithm	SHA-1	MD5
Size of message digest in bits	160	128
Cryptanalysis attack	Vulnerable to attack	Not yet vulnerable
Speed	Slow	Fast
Number of steps	80	64
Buffer size in bits	160	128

9.3.5 HMAC

Message authentication code (MAC) allows the receiver to check the integrity of the message. Suppose user A sends a message to receiver B. At the receiving end how user B knows that it is the same message send by user A or it is a modified message by a third party. With the help of MAC receiver can check the message and decide whether it is the same message sent by user A or not. This is called *integrity checking*. MAC is used to check the integrity of the message. At the same time MAC helps to check the authentication of the sender. To provide the security hash function is used along with the encryption techniques. This is called *hash message authentication code* (HMAC). Hash function is used basically to check the integrity of the message and also makes digital signature technique more efficient. It also concerned about the non-repudiation of origin and validating identity of originator. The hash value of a message is indicated by $h(m)$. The requirements of hash functions are as follows:

- It can be applied to a message M of any size.
- It produces fixed-length output message digest or hash value h.
- For any message M, one can easily compute $h = H(M)$
- The hash value h is public and if someone knows the value of h, it is infeasible to find the original message from hash value such that $H(x) = h$, i.e., it works one way.
- If the value of x is given, it is infeasible to find y such that $H(y) = H(x)$, this shows weak collision resistance.
- It is not possible to find any messages x and y such that. $H(y) = H(x)$, this shows strong collision resistance.

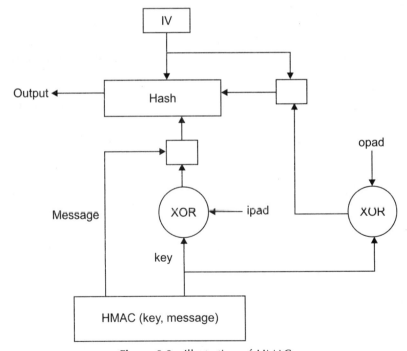

Figure 9.9 Illustration of HMAC.

A keyed-hash message authentication code, or HMAC, is a type of message authentication code (MAC) calculated using a cryptographic hash function in combination with a secret key. As with any MAC, HMAC may be used to verify simultaneously both the integrity and the authenticity of a message. One can use any message digest algorithm such as MD5 or SHA-1, for the calculation of hash value in an HMAC. If we use MD5 then the resulting MAC algorithm is called HMAC-MD5. If we use SHA-1 then the resulting MAC algorithm is called HMAC-SHA-1. The security provided by the HMAC depends upon the strength of the hashing algorithm used in addition to the size and quality of the key.

An iterative hash function splits up a given message into a block of fixed size and process them with a compression function. This is shown in Figure 9.9. For example, MD5 and SHA-1 operate on 512-bit blocks. The size of the output of HMAC is the same as that of the underlying hash function (128 or 160 bits in the case of MD5 and SHA-1). It can be truncated if desired but it reduces the security of the MAC.

$$HMAC_{key} (message) = HASH((key \oplus opad) || HASH((key \oplus ipad) || message))$$

where HASH is an iterated hash function, key is a secret key padded with extra zeroes to equalise it with the block size of the hash function, message is the message to be authenticated, || denotes concatenation, $\oplus$ denotes exclusive OR, and the outer padding opad = 01011100 or 0 X5c5c5c...5c5c (5c in hexadecimal repeated for b/8 times) and inner padding ipad = 00110110 or 0 X 363636.......3636(36 in Hexadecimal repeated for b/8 times) are two one-block–long hexadecimal constants.

9.3.6 RIPEMD-160

RIPEMD-160 (RACE Integrity Primitives Evaluation Message Digest) is a message digest algorithm developed by Hans Dobbertin, Antoon Bosselaers and Bart Preneel in 1996. It generates the hash value of 160-bit. It is somewhat similar to MD5 and SHA. It gives the performance similar to SHA-1.

There are different variants of RIPEMD such as RIPEMD-128, RIPEMD-256 and RIPEMD-320 having hash value 128-bit, 256-bit, and 320-bit, respectively. The 128-bit version was the replacement for the original RIPEMD. Its hash value was 128-bit which is same as RIPEMD and it is not secure. RIPEMD-128 and RIPEMD-160 provide more security as compared to RIPEMD-256 and RIPEMD-320-bit versions.

The overviews of RIPEMD-160 are given as follows:

1. *Padding*: Padding procedure is similar to MD5. The length of the message after padding should be equal to 448 modulo 512. The padding is always required though the length of the original message is multiples of 512 bits. The number of padding bits is from minimum 1 to maximum 512. The padding consists of a single 1-bit and remaining number of 0 bits.
2. *Append:* The message is always appended by 64-bit block to indicate the length of the message. It is an unsigned 64-bit integer and contains the length modulo 2^{64} of the original message.
3. *Initialisation:* Initialise 5-word buffer A, B, C, D and E as:

    A = 67452301
    B = efcdab89
    C = 98badcfe

D = 10325476

E = c3d2e1f0

These values are same as used for SHA-1 algorithm.

4. *Message processing:* There are 10 rounds of 16 operations each. The structure of all the rounds is similar, but each round uses different primitive logical function. Each round makes use of an additive constant. The output of the fifth round is added to the chaining variable input to the first round.

5. *Output:* The final value of the buffer is the output. It is 160-bit message digest.

Comparison of RIPEMD-160 with SHA-1 and MD5

Let us summarise the hashing algorithms about their differences and similarities between them. MD5, SHA-1 and RIPEMD-160 are invulnerable to attacks against weak collision resistance. Cryptanalysis of RIPEMD-160 is more difficult than SHA-1. RIPEMD-160 and SHA-1 are slower than MD5. A comparison of these algorithms are given in Table 9.6.

Table 9.6 Comparison of RIPEMD-160 with SHA-1 and MD5

Algorithm	RIPEMD-160	SHA-1	MD5
Message digest	160-bits	160-bits	128-bits
Cryptanalysis attack	Vulnerable to attack	Vulnerable to attack	Not to be vulnerable
Speed	Slow	Slower	Fast
Rounds	5	4	4
Operations	160	80	64
Buffer size (bits)	160	160	128
Endian architecture	Little endian	Big endian	Little endian

9.4 KERBEROS

Authentication of the user is very important to provide the security to any application. Under project Athena at MIT, an authentication system is developed known as *Kerberos*. The objective of this project was to provide a huge network of computer workstations so that undergraduate students can access their files stored on any workstation easily from anywhere in the campus.

For this project, a symmetric encryption is used to provide authentication and security. These authenticate and identify the users and the services in the network to each other. The most common way of authentication is the use of password. The server has a database of userid and password. When any user wants the service in the network, he has first log in by giving his user id and password. The server verifies the user id and password from the database available with it. Once it matches with the database, the user is permitted to use the necessary service. But as we already studied about the security issues of password authentication, they thought about some new system for authentication. So, they developed Kerberos, which address the security issues using a password for authentication.

The key innovation in Kerberos is that there is no need of reveal the secret about the key by the user. They can identify without revealing the secret. Users can prove their identity without sending the secret or password over the network. In Kerberos, an encryption key is used. Timestamp helps to prove that when the request is sent, the user created a timestamp and encrypted with shared secret, the request is sent to service. The service decrypts the request a with shared secret key and recovers the timestamp. Then authentication successes and the necessary service is provided to the user. If the user uses wrong key and encrypt the timestamp with that key, then the timestamp will not decrypt properly and authentication fails. In this case, the service rejects the request of the user. This system is secure as shared secret key is not transmitted over the network. Kerberos architecture is more complex due to the use of a secret key in more convenient manner and to patch some of the problems.

9.4.1 Basics of Kerberos

As discussed above, Kerberos is designed for authentication in client server architecture. In this architecture, server is not only dependent on the information given by the client but it also verifies the same from its database. The components of Kerberos are: a server, clients, an authentication server and a ticket-granting server.

Suppose there is no secret key shared by the client and the server. In this case identifying the client is done using Kerberos protocol and a session key is generated for a communication between the server and a client. The Kerberos working is shown in Figure 9.10.

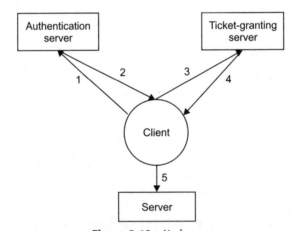

Figure 9.10 Kerberos.

The client sends his requests for a ticket to the ticket-granting service from the authentication server. The authentication server (AS) has a database of user id and password information for all the clients. Authentication server returns an encrypted ticket to the client. The client decrypts the ticket using his secret key. Now, client would like to use the service from the server. But before this, client must be allowed to communicate with the server. So, client submits the ticket to the ticket-granting server. The ticket-granting server verifies the ticket for identifying client and after verification gives a new ticket to client. This ticket will allow the client to make use of service. Client now submits the ticket to the server. He sends the service ticket and an authentication credential to the server. Server checks the ticket and the authentication credential to make sure whether it is a valid client or not. After verification, server will provide the service to client.

The main objective of Kerberos is authentication. So, there is no need to store the password by the client. The AS serves as an introducer for them. Both the client and the service must have a shared secret key which is stored with the AS. Such keys are used for long time. Figure 9.11 shows the Kerberos authentication.

Authentication can be done using the following steps:

Step 1 The user sends a request to the authentication server for a service.

Step 2 Authentication server generates a secret key that will be shared only by the user and the service. This key is called the *session key*. Authentication server replies to the user's request by sending a message. The message has two parts. The first part contains the secret key along with the service's name which is encrypted with the user's key. The other part contains that same secret key along with the user id encrypted with the server's key. In Kerberos phrasing, the first part is called the *user's credentials* and the second part is called *ticket*.

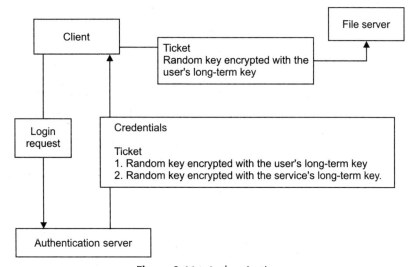

Figure 9.11 Authentication.

Step 3 Then the user generates a timestamp, and encrypts it with the secret key. User sends the timestamp called *authenticator* along with the ticket, to the service. The service decrypts the ticket with its secret key, recovers the session key. This key is then used to decrypt the authenticator. The service trusts the authentication server for the authentication of the user. So, at the service no further authentication process of the user takes place. Sometimes, the user may want the authentication of the service so the service takes the timestamp from the authenticator, adds the service's own name to it, and encrypts it with the session key. This encrypted message is sent to the user.

For every service if the user contacts the authentication server, the load on AS is increased and it takes time for authentication of the users. To reduce the load on the authentication server, one more server is introduced called *ticket-granting server* (TGS). Now, in this case the user requests his first service is for TGS, which then grants additional tickets for other services. Thus, the database of user id and password is located with authentication server and the trust is with TGS.

9.4.2 Kerberos Ticket-granting Approach

Here, the term "client" refers to a user or to a client-side application program operating on behalf of a user. The term "application" server refers to a remote computer which provides a shared service. The term "password" refers to the user's password or to a cryptographic key derived from it. The term "session" key refers to a cryptographic key issued for use in communication between a client and an application server, which is valid for some defined interval of time.

A ticket and an authenticator are the two basic credentials used in Kerberos. Both the credentials are based on private key but both use different private key. When the client or user login on a computer, he has to enter his password. He gets a ticket from the authentication server and send this ticket to the application server as a part of the request for a service. Then the client sends an authenticator to the application server along with the ticket. The application server uses the authenticator and the ticket to verify that the request was sent by the client to whom the ticket was issued.

To achieve these objectives, after the initial exchange with the authentication server, the AS issues a "ticket-granting ticket" (TGT) to the user. TGT contains a session key to be used for subsequent ticket requests. Each TGT have fixed life span generally it is set to 8 hours. The use of TGT reduces the load on AS and also there is no need for the user to authenticate himself every time for different services in a network.

The initial message was sent automatically at the time of login from the client to the authentication server. The initial message contains the user's identification number and request for a TGT as shown in Figure 9.12. The authentication server

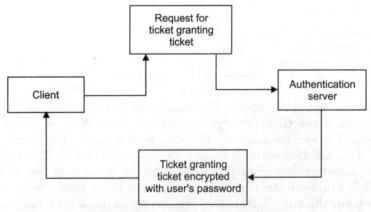

Figure 9.12 Ticket-granting ticket.

replies back with a message encrypted with the user's password and containing a TGT encrypted with the user's password (Figure 9.11). After receiving the message, the client decrypts the TGT message to get the session key. The user uses this session key for subsequent ticket requests. This session key for ticket-granting requests is referred to as the TG key.

9.4.3 Ticket-Granting Server

To reduce the load on the authentication server, one more server is introduced called *ticket-granting server* (TGS). TGS resolves the problem of password re-entry every time for new service requests. The TGS is located on the same server where authentication server located but logically it is different from AS. The purpose of the TGS is to provide the ticket and session key so that user has to enter his password only once and obtained additional services in the network by the use of ticket and session key.

Initially, the user sends the request for a ticket from the AS to talk to the TGS. This ticket is called the *ticket-granting ticket*, or TGT. The session key is encrypted using the user's secret key. After receiving the TGT and the session key, the user requests a TGS for a ticket. This can be done at any time if he wants to use any service. The reply from TGS is encrypted with the session key. The user already has a session key, so there is no need of his own secret key. It is sort of like when you visit some industry or organisation. You have to show your regular ID to the receptionist at the counter to get a guest ID (visitor card) for visit the industry or organisation. This is work like client's request to AS. After verifying the user ID, the receptionist issue a guest ID or visitor card just like AS replies to the user by sending TGT and the session key. Now, when you want to enter various rooms in the industry or organisation, instead of showing your regular ID over and over again, which might make it vulnerable to be dropped or stolen, you have to show your guest ID, which is only valid for a short time anyway. This is like user does not have to use his password once AS gives him the TGT and the session key. If it was stolen, you could get it invalidated and be issued a new one quickly and easily, something that you could not do with your regular ID.

The advantage of above scheme is that session key and ticket are used instead of user's secret key. Therefore, if the session key is captured by the attacker, less damage is happened as session key and TGT are valid only for a limited time period. But if the user has to use his secret key and the key is captured by the attacker, then the more damage is happened than session key and the TGT as the life of secret key is more. This TGT, as well as any tickets that you obtain using it, is stored in the credentials cache. The term "credentials" actually refers to both the ticket and the session key in conjunction.

Once the client gets a TG key, then the client requests for a specific service. This is shown in Figure 9.13. The client sends a request to the TGS to obtain a ticket for the service. The TGS can verify the client identification information encrypted in the message with its database of the TG key. Each ticket has a timestamp. The timestamp protects from reuse of the message.

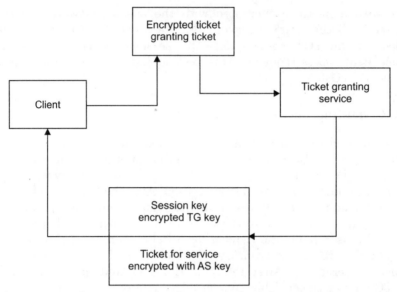

Figure 9.13 Subsequent requests for services from the ticket-granting service.

After checking the client's identity, the ticket-granting service sends a ticket to the user. The ticket contains information about the identity of the client and the newly generated session key. The information with the ticket cannot be changed or altered by the client. He can only forward it to the authentication server.

The client then sends a message to the application server. This message contains the ticket and an authenticator as shown in Figure 9.14. As noted above, the authenticator is constructed by the client, and contains identifying information and a timestamp. After receiving the message, the application server can decrypt the ticket, because it is encrypted with the authentication server's own key. The ticket contains the session key which is used to decrypt the authenticator. For the valid request, the data embedded in the authenticator must match that in the ticket. Further messages between the client and the application server may be encrypted using the session key.

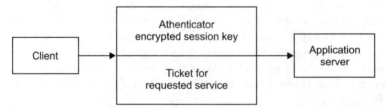

Figure 9.14 Communication between the client and the application server.

9.4.4 Kerberos Third-party Authentication Model

In the Kerberos system, one or more trusted *authentication servers* may be used (termed KDCs or key distribution servers). This is used to provide third-party authentication services which are helpful for cooperating systems and applications. Client acquires *tickets* from the trusted authentication server(s) which can be used to provide the proof of identification for subsequent request for service and applications. This ticket is encrypted so it is secured in transmission. The detail of the Kerberos authentication is as follows:

1. The user wants some service so he first sends his request to an authenticate server. This request contains the user's name and the name of the service granting server that he will use.
2. The user login on the client and requests for a ticket-granting ticket.
3. After authentication using password and username, the initial authentication ticket is granted by the AS to the client.
4. The client then submits this ticket to the ticket-granting service for a particular service.
5. The ticket-granting service issues a ticket to the client.
6. The client now submits the ticket to the particular server for the desired service.

The details of the communications between a client, the KDCs, and the various services used by the client are rather complex. Figure 9.15 graphically illustrates the interactions between different systems involved in the Kerberos network.

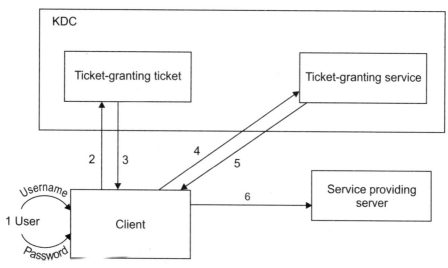

Figure 9.15 Authentication model.

9.4.5 Kerberos Authentication Model: Definitions and Notational Conventions

Some terms and notational conventions used in Kerberos authentication model are:

1. Authentication ticket: It is a record of authentication issued by an authentication server to a client system as a proof of that client's user being authentic.

2. Authenticated service: A service which is only provided to authenticated users via Kerberos and whose clients can present valid authentication tickets as proof of authentication.

3. Target service: The service for which a client is requesting a ticket or to which the client is presenting a ticket.

4. Initial ticketing service: It is the service by which the clients receive their initial tickets.

5. Ticket-granting service: The service by which clients receive tickets to specific target services.

6. Ticket-granting ticket: A ticket provided on demand by the initial ticketing service which must be presented to the ticket-granting service in order to request a service ticket.

9.4.6 Kerberos Authentication Model

The Kerberos authentication model uses a symmetric key encryption technique. Kerberos IV uses DES algorithm and Kerberos V uses DES and IDEA algorithms. To provide more security, double encryption technique is used. For encryption two keys are used, i.e., user password and the session key. The user password have a long life span and used only for initial authentication whereas session key has a life span of 8 to 10 hours and used for requesting different services after initial authentication.

The user first login on the client by using his user id and password. Client sends the request for a ticket to the authentication server for the particular user by providing his user id to AS and not the password. The authentication server verifies the user id and sends the encrypted ticket to the client. If the user is able to decrypt the ticket by his password then the user is considered as authenticate. Then the user sends the ticket to the service, he wants to use. If a service is able to decrypt a ticket using its own secret key, the service may presume that the user is authentic.

In this way, without passing the password information over the insecure channel, the authentication takes place in Kerberos environment. So, it is difficult for the attacker to capture the secret information about the user. The authentication in Kerberos takes place in 6 steps as shown in Figure 9.16.

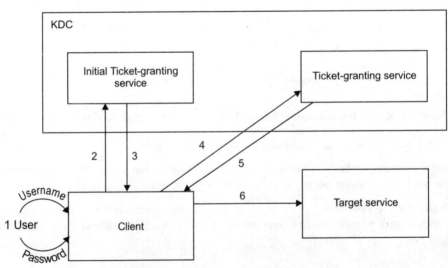

Figure 9.16 Kerberos authentication model.

Step 1 The user first login on the client by using his user id and password.

Step 2 The client sends a request to the AS requesting a ticket for the user. This request is totally unauthenticated and it contains only user id and not the password of the user.

Step 3 The ticketing service verifies the user's name in its database. If user name is in the database then he is an authenticate user and ticketing service generates a unique session key for later use during the user's authenticated session. This ticket sends to the client a double-encrypted ticket-granting ticket and the session key in the form:

$$Kuser\{Ks, Ktgs \{Ttgs, Ks\}\}$$

The client then decrypts the ticket-granting ticket using the user's password. If the client successfully decrypts the ticket using the user's password, then user is authentic. Then the client stores the ticket TGT(Ktgs {Ttgs, Ks}) for later use.

Step 4 Then the client sends a ticket request to ticket-granting service (TGS) for a particular service requested by the user. This request for ticket is in the form:

$$\{TGT, Ks\{request, client\text{-}IP, timestamp\}\}$$

(where TGT = Ktgs{Ttgs, Ks})

Step 5 The ticket-granting service decrypts the TGT using its own secret key (Ktgs) and the rest of the part of the message is decrypted by using the session key. If the ticket-granting service successfully decrypts the ticket, it gets the following information:
- The TGT was issued by authenticate ticketing service.
- The request for the service is from the authenticate user.

Once the authentication is completed the TGS generates a session key and the ticket for a requested service. The TGS sends the session key and the ticket to the client machine in the form:

$$K_S\{Ksession, Kser\{Tservice, Ksession\}\}$$

Step 6 The client machine decrypts the service ticket using the session key (Ks) and yield the session key (Ksession) and an encrypted service ticket (Kser{Tservice, Ksession}).

The client then submits the encrypted ticket to the requested service. The service decrypts the ticket using its own secret key (Kser). If the decryption is successful, the target service authenticates the user. The communication between the client and the service now start. They can use the session key for secure communication.

User can access other services in the Kerberos using steps 4, 5 and 6 repeatedly from the client machine.

9.4.7 Cross-Realm Authentication

So far we have discussed the client using the service in one Kerberos environment. If the user from one Kerberos environment wants to use the services from other

Kerberos environment, the authentication of that user should be done by the Kerberos which the user belongs is called *cross-realm authentication*. So, the user can use the services from other Kerberos environment without authentication by that other Kerberos environment. The users or clients of one realm use Kerberos to authenticate to services which belong to a realm other than their own. This property known as *cross-authentication*. It is based on a trust between the Kerberos involved. This relationship may be mono-directional, or bi-directional. *Mono-directional* means the users of Kerberos environment A can access the services of Kerberos environment B but not vice-versa. *Bi-directional* means the users of Kerberos environment A can access the services of Kerberos environment B and vice-versa.

We discuss the case where there is only one authentication server and only one ticket-granting server. These servers may or may not be installed on the same machine. This can work well if the requests are small. If the number of clients is more on the network, there are more number of requests to the AS and TGS. This deteriorates the performance of AS and TGS. If the AS or TGS fails, the whole system fails. Therefore, single KDC cannot work properly for the whole network. This is just like to work in a small group which always give better performance. In the same way, the large Kerberos environment divides into distinct small realms. Each realm has its own authentication server and ticket-granting server. This helps to improve the performance and also avoid the failure problem due to single AS and TGS.

To allow the user from one Kerberos environment to access the service in another Kerberos environment, the user should first register with TGS in the service's realm. In some cases, if there are many Kerberos realms, it is difficult for the user to register each realm in every other realm. Instead of above method, there is a network of realms, so that, the user sometimes contact to the RTGS in one or more intermediate realm. These realms are called the *transited realms*. Also the names of the realms are included in the ticket. Due to this, the end service knows all of the intermediate realms that were transited, and can decide whether or not to accept the authentication. Kerberos version 4 had only peer to peer realm authentication while Kerberos version 5 support for scaling.

There are three types of cross-realm authentication based on trust: direct, transitive and hierarchical.

1. *Direct relationship*: It occurs when the KDC of one realm has direct trust in the KDC of another realm (Figure 9.17). It allows the users of the latter realm to access its services. This can be done by using a shared key.

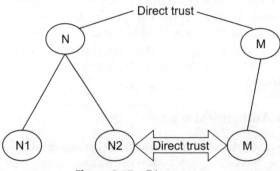

Figure 9.17 Direct trust.

2. Transitive trust relationship: In the above case, if the number of realms increases, the shared secret keys also increased. Transitivity trust relationship solves this problem. Here if realm A has a trust on realm B, and realm B has a trust on realm C, then realm A has a trust on realm C. This helps to reduce the number of shared secret keys required.

3. Hierarchical trust relationship: If, within organisations, the convention of naming realms uses upper case letters with the name of DNS domains and it belongs to a hierarchy, then Kerberos version 5 will support adjacent realms having a trust relationship.

Steps follows by cross-realm authentication are:

Step 1 Client requests to local KDC for a cross-realm ticket.

Step 2 Client submits a cross-realm ticket to the another KDC for a service ticket for the target service.

Step 3 Client submits the service ticket to the another AS server.

9.4.8 Kerberos and Public Key Cryptography

Kerberos uses symmetric key encryption techniques. But as we know that asymmetric key encryption techniques are more powerful than symmetric key encryption can be used for authentication, key distribution and non-repudiation. In this case, the public key is available for all the users in the Kerberos realms whereas the private key is known only by the owner user. KDC also not knows about the user's private key.

When the KDC generates the ticket after authentication, it encrypts the session key with the random key generated by the KDC. Again it encrypts it with user's public key. While at the user end the user can decrypt it using his private key and then obtains the random key, which he decrypts the message and get the session key. We can use one of the methods of public key cryptography as discussed earlier in this chapter.

9.4.9 Advantages of Kerberos

The Kerberos authentication model offers a number of advantages over more traditional authentication schemes.

1. User login on the client machine with his id and password. His passwords are never transmitted across the network in any form, i.e., encrypted or plaintext form. Only shared secret key is transmitted across the network in the encrypted form. This provides more security.
2. Client machine and server mutually authenticate each other during each communication.
3. Kerberos authentication model use timestamp and lifetime information in the ticket which limit the duration of their users' authentication. After specific lifetime, ticket is invalid for authentication.
4. Once the authentication of the user takes place, he can use different services across the Kerberos network without re-entering his personal information like password.

5. The shared secret may be used for encrypting the communication between the client and the service. This improves the security in Kerberos environment.
6. Kerberos is entirely based on open Internet standards.

9.4.10 Weaknesses of Kerberos

The weaknesses of Kerberos authentication model are as follows:

1. In Kerberos IV, DES algorithm is used for encryption. But DES is not a secure algorithm today. So in Kerberos V, 3DES or IDEA is used for encryption which is more secure.
2. For a multi-user client system, the Kerberos authentication scheme fails due to variety of ticket-stealing and replay attacks.
3. The AS model is vulnerable to brute-force attacks.

9.4.11 Attacks on Kerberos

Many attacks are successfully carried out against Kerberos. These attacks include: replay attacks, password guessing attacks, and inter-session chosen plaintext attacks.

1. Replay attacks: A replay attack occurs when an attacker captures a packet from the network and sends that packet to a service as a user of that service. When the packet is authenticated by the service, then the attacker can use the replay on behalf of other user and access other user's resources. Use of authenticator in Kerberos helps to prevent replay attack.

2. Password-guessing attacks: The reply to the request of a user, the ticket-granting ticket is sent in encrypted form. To decrypt the reply user's password is required. If user's password is not strong, then it is possible for the attacker to guess the password and attacker is able to decrypt the message.

3. Inter-session chosen plaintext attacks: As per Kerberos version 5 draft, inter-session chosen plaintext attacks are possible against it.

9.4.12 Applications and Limitations of Kerberos

To provide authentication, authorisation and confidentiality within a network or small set of networks, Kerberos is used. However, one cannot use Kerberos for generating digital signature.

The main assumptions about the Kerberos environment is that there should be trust on the hosts. But if the host is compromised, the attack can occur and the security of the Kerberos may be broken. Ticket is stored in host's cache may be used for such attack. But there is less possibility of such attacks. Dictionary attack is possible if the user password is guessable. Timestamp prevents such attacks. If the user needs more time for using the different services, then the small timestamp creates problem and again authentication is required. In Kerberos 4, for long processes, tickets having small timestamp can have this problem. Kerberos version 5 solved this problem by renewing the ticket after the end of time span allotted to a ticket.

9.4.13 Comparisons of Kerberos with SSL

Secure socket layer protocol (SSL) is also used for authentication. Table 9.7 shows the comparison between Kerberos and SSL.

Table 9.7 Comparison between Kerberos and SSL

SSL	Kerberos
Encryption is done using public key.	Encryption is done using private key.
Authentication is based on certificate.	Authentication is based on a trusted third party.
Ideal for secure communications with a large, variable user base that is not known in advance.	Ideal for networked environments where all services and users are known in advance.
Key revocation must be achieved either by sending certificates to all related servers or by having a centralised sever.	Key revocation can be achieved by disabling a user at the KDC.
Probability of cracking the certificates is more as it is stored in user's hard-disk.	Probability of cracking the password is less as it is not stored in written form.
One has to pay for the service as it is patented.	Freely available as Kerberos has open source.

9.5 X.509 AUTHENTICATION SERVICE

ITU-T recommends X.509, the authentication service. It specifies the authentication service for X.500 directories. It also specifies syntax for X.509 certificate. The first version of X.509 was published in 1988. The second version was published in 1993. The third version was proposed in 1994 and considered for approval in 1995. There were some security issues in the first two versions of X.509. These issues are addressed in version 3. Secret key or public key is used for directory authentication. The standard does not specify about the algorithms used for certificates but RSA is the most popular choice for this. In this, every user has a certificate whose validity depends on a chain of trust.

An X.509 certificate consists of the following fields:

1. *Version:* This gives information about the version of the X.509 standard applies to the certificate. Currently three versions of X.509 certificates are available. Version indicates the information available with the certificate.
2. *Serial number:* A serial number of the certificate distinguishes it from other certificates issued by the same party. Certificate's serial number is placed in a certificate revocation list (CRL) when a certificate is revoked.
3. *Signature:* This identifies the algorithm used to compute the signature on the certificate.
4. *Issuer name:* It is X.500 name of the entity who signed the certificate. Generally, it is a certificate authority (CA). Using issuer name certificate implies trusting the entity who signed the certificate.
5. *Validity:* Each certificate has its life span. Validity gives the information about this life span. The life span can be as short as a few seconds or almost as long as a century. This contains two types of information: a start date and

time, and an end date and time. The validity period chosen depends on a number of factors: the private key used or the amount one is willing to pay for a certificate. This is the expected period that entities can rely on the public value, if the associated private key has not been compromised.

6. *Subject:* The name of the user whose public key the certificate identifies. This name uses the X.500 standard, so it is intended to be unique across the Internet. This is the Distinguished Name (DN) of the entity, for example,

$$CN = Ram, OU = COEP, O = PIET, C = INDIA$$

CN: Subject's Common Name, OU: Organisational Unit, O: Organisation, and C: Country.

7. *Subject public key information:* This contains two types of information: the public key and an algorithm identifier which specifies which public key cryptosystem this key belongs to and any associated key parameters.

8. *Issuer unique identifier (versions 2 and 3 only):* This is an optional bit string field used to identify uniquely the issuing CA in the event the X.500 name has been reused for different entities.

9. *Subject unique identifier (versions 2 and 3 only):* Each user has one number which is unique across the internet. This provides the unique identity of the user.

10. *Extensions:* It is a set of one or more extension fields. Extensions were added in version 3.

11. *Signature on the above fields:* Covers all of the other fields of the certificate; it contains the hash code of the other fields, encrypted with the CA's private key. This field includes the signature algorithm identifier.

Most generic version of X.509 is version 1. X.509 version 2 introduced the concept of subject and issuer unique identifiers are introduced in version 2. These concepts help to handle the possibility of reuse of subject and/or issuer names over time. Most certificate profile documents strongly recommend that names not be reused, and that certificate should not make use of unique identifiers. Version 2 certificates are not widely used.

The most recent version of X.509 is version 3. It supports the notion of extensions, whereby anyone can define an extension and include it in the certificate. The most common extension in use is: KeyUsage. It restricts extension in use is: AlternativeNames. It allows other identities to also be associated with this public key. e.g., DNS names, E-mail addresses, IP addresses. Extensions can be marked critical to indicate that the extension should be checked and enforced/used. For example, if a certificate has the KeyUsage extension marked critical and set to "keyCertSign" then if this certificate is presented during SSL communication, it should be rejected, as the certificate extension indicates that the associated private key should only be used for signing certificates and not for SSL use. This certificate is signed by the issuer to authenticate the binding between the subject (user's) name and the user's public key. The major difference between versions 2 and 3 is the addition of the extensions field. This field grants more flexibility as it can convey additional information. Standard extensions include subject and issuer attributes, certification policy information, and key usage restrictions, among others. X.509 also defines syntax for certificate revocation lists (CRLs).

SUMMARY

Authentication is one of the key aspects of cryptography. It can be used to guarantee that communication end-points, i.e., sender and receiver are the parties who they claim. The main objectives of authentication requirement are to ensure that the claimants are really what they claim to be, and avoid compromising security to an impostor. Authorisation is the mechanism through which a system determines what level of access to a particular authenticated user should have. It is used to secure the resources controlled by the system. The password-based authentication method refers to a secret information which the user has to prove that he knows it. In two-factor authentication system, identification and authentication of the user take place in two different ways to establish his identity and privileges. Biometric authentication method uses thumb impression, iris or voices for authentication. Integrity of a message is checked by using the hash value or message digest calculated from the message. The hash value of the message is derived from the message which remains same if the message is unaltered. There are various algorithms available which can generate the hash value of the message. Two of them are message digest and secure hash algorithm.

MD5 generates message digest with a 128-bit hash value. The possible attacks against MD5 are possible. The more secure hash algorithm is SHA (secure hash algorithm).

Authentication of the user is very important to provide the security to any application. Under project Athena at MIT, an authentication system is developed known as Kerberos. The key innovation in Kerberos is that there is no need of user should reveal the secret. They can identify without revealing the secret. If the user from one Kerberos environment wants to use the services from other Kerberos environment, the authentication of that user should be done by the Kerberos which the user belongs is called cross-realm authentication.

EXERCISES

9.1 What is authentication? What are the objectives of authentication?
9.2 What is the difference between authentication and authorisation?
9.3 List the different methods of authentication. Explain each in brief.
9.4 Explain the password-based authentication method.
9.5 What are the guidelines for choosing a password or setting up a password?
9.6 Discuss the weaknesses of the password-based authentication method.
9.7 Explain the two-factor authentication method.
9.8 Compare the password-based authentication with the two-factor authentication methods.
9.9 Explain the fingerprint authentication method.
9.10 Discuss the weaknesses of the two-factor authentication method.
9.11 What is Kerberos? How TGS works?

9.12 With respect to Kerberos, give the three basic steps involved in authenticating a user to an end service.
9.13 Explain authentication in Kerberos with block diagram.
9.14 Explain the working of ticket-granting server.
9.15 Describe the third party authentication model in Kerberos.
9.16 Explain Kerberos authentication model with a diagram.
9.17 Explain cross-realm authentication.
9.18 What are the advantages of Kerberos?
9.19 What are the weaknesses of Kerberos?
9.20 Explain the different attacks on Kerberos.
9.21 Give the applications of Kerberos.
9.22 Discuss the limitations of Kerberos.
9.23 Compare Kerberos with SSL.
9.24 Explain the various fields included in X.509 certificate.
9.25 Explain the X.509 certificate.
9.26 Explain the difference between little-endian and big-endian format.
9.27 Compare SHA-1, MD5 and RIPEMD.
9.28 What are basic arithmetic and logical functions used in MD5 and SHA-1?
9.29 Discuss the role of ticket-granting server in inter realm operations of Kerberos?

MULTIPLE CHOICE QUESTIONS

9.1 Kerberos is considered secure because it
    (a) Uses AES for encryption
    (b) Has no single point of failure
    (c) Uses public key cryptography
    (d) None of the above

9.2 In Kerberos, a client sends a ticket $\{T_{cs}\}K_s$ to a server. The server is convinced that the ticket is genuine because
    (a) It came from the client
    (b) It can decode it
    (c) It came from the KDC
    (d) It is new

9.3 Kerberos does not addressed .... issues.
    (a) Availability
    (b) Privacy
    (c) Authentication
    (d) Integrity

9.4 A message sent with .... is authentic and digitally signed.
    (a) A message digest/hash encrypted with the receiver's public key
    (b) A message digest/hash encrypted with the receiver's private key
    (c) A message digest/hash encrypted with the sender's public key
    (d) A message digest/hash encrypted with the sender's private key

9.5 MD5 and SHA are ....
    (a) Asymmetric block ciphers
    (b) Message signing algorithms
    (c) Stream ciphers
    (d) Symmetric block ciphers

Answers

9.1 (b)   **9.2** (c)   **9.3** (d)   **9.4** (d)   **9.5** (b)

CHAPTER 10

Digital Signatures

10.1 INTRODUCTION

In our day-to-day life, we use signature for various purposes. Every person has his own style of doing signature. Signature indicates the identity of the person. It helps in proving the authentication of a particular person. Use of signature in various forms for identification of documents is a practice from ancient times. In the middle age, wax imprint of insignia was used by the noblemen to seal the documents, which proved their authentication. In the history, every kingdom had its own flags, which was synonymous with signature, as it also used for authentication. Artists use to do their signatures on their paintings, which helps in authenticating the owner of the painting. Nowadays, after using the credit cards for the purpose of paying bills, we have to sign a slip which is supposed to be verified by the salesperson by comparing the same with the signature on the card. But due to advanced technology such as online trading, all these methods of authentication are of no use. The new method of authentication in electronic form has emerged. This new technique is called *digital signature*. Digital signature may be in the form of text, symbol, image or audio.

In our discussion, we use digital signature, a term encompassing only cryptographic signature. Digital signature is a strong method for authentication used today. This includes message authentication code (MAC), hash value of a message and digital pen pad devices. It also includes cryptographically-based signature protocols. All these different techniques ensure that no unauthorised person of some document or record could have done so. Therefore, digital signature is used for authentication of the message and the sender and to verify the integrity of the message. Many schemes have been proposed for generation of digital signature. Some of these schemes are patented. Some are freely available and some are failed to pass the security test. In today's world of electronic transaction, digital signature plays a major role in authentication. For example, one can fill his income tax return online using his digital signature, which avoids the use of paper and makes the process faster.

Asymmetric key encryption techniques and public key infrastructure are used for digital signature. Digital signature algorithms are generally divided into two parts—signing part and verification part. The first part, i.e., signing part allows the sender to create his digital signature. The second part of the signature is used by the receiver for verifying the signature after receiving the message. Digital signature is different from electronic signature. Electronic signature is not necessarily cryptographic-based for identification of the sender. Sometimes, phone, fax transmission and telephone addresses are treated as electronic signatures. Many electronic signatures use digital signature technology to ensure that the legal intent is also cryptographically secure.

The requirements for a digital signature are as follows:

1. It must be in the form of pattern of bits.
2. Information unique to the sender should be used for the generation of signature. This information helps in preventing forgery and denial.

Digital signature is used for communications to verify

1. Authentication of the sender
2. Integrity of the message received
3. Non-repudiation

We will discuss all these in brief below:

1. *Authentication:* Authentication, as we have discussed in the last chapter, is the most important part of security. There are two issues related to authentication—confidentiality and time-span. Confidentiality of the secret key is the most important issue as the security of the communication between two parties depends on it. So, we first take a look on this issue.

In the public key infrastructure, each user has two keys—private key and public key. The private key is used for encryption of the message by the sender. The decryption of the received message is done using sender's public key. But in this scheme, recipient is not sure whether the sender has himself signed the message or somebody else has used sender's private key for encrypting the message. This may happen if the private key of the sender is captured by the attacker and used it to send the message on the sender's name using his private key.

The second issue is time-span. This is related to the hazard of message replay attacks. There are replay attacks which allow the attackers to compromise a session key. In financial communication, confidentiality and integrity of the message is very important. Small time-span helps in protecting the replay attacks. If the time-span is more and the sender's key is compromised, then replay attack is possible.

2. *Integrity:* It helps in checking whether the message is the same message as sent by the sender or a modified message. This can be achieved by the use of message digest techniques. Encryption provides the confidentiality to the message and protects it from the cryptanalyst to read. If the key gets compromised, then it is possible for the cryptanalyst to modify the message. This can be done perhaps maliciously, without actually reading it. Integrity of the message can be verified with the help of message digest. Initially, the message digest or hash value of the message is generated using any message digest algorithm (such as MD5 or SHA-1). Then, the sender uses his private key to encrypt the ciphertext and the message digest of the message. Then, the sender sends the encrypted message to the receiver. If the attacker or third party captures the message and modifies it, then due to hash value or message digest, the receiver can easily know about it because it is not possible to modify the message digest or hash value and no two messages can have the same hash value. The receiver decrypts the message digest using the public key of the sender. He also calculates the message digest of the message received. The receiver compares the two message digests. If the two messages digests match, then it proves that the message is unaltered and it is the same as sent by the sender.

3. *Non-repudiation:* Repudiation means that a person, who signs a document, is always able to disclaim a signature that has been credited to him or her. After receiving the message, the recipient asks the sender to attach his signature with the message so that it makes later repudiation more difficult. If the sender refuses that he is not the sender of the message, then the recipient can show the signed message to a third party (e.g., a court) to reinforce a claim that the message is sent by the signatories and not anybody else. However, if the sender's private key is compromised that means somebody else (i.e. attacker) know that key then all digital signatures generated using such private key may be generated by the attacker. In this case such digital signature cannot be helpful for non-repudiation. Notice that compromising the key is not the drawback of any cryptographic algorithm, but it is a human space and is unsolved. Digital signatures alone cannot provide inherent non-repudiation.

10.1.1 Implementation of Digital Signatures

Digital signature schemes have the following three algorithms:

1. A key generation algorithm
2. A signing algorithm
3. A verification algorithm

For example, user A wants to communicate with user B by sending him a message. User B wants to verify if the message has surely come from user A. User A signs her message and then sends to user B. For this, user A has generated the digital signature for the said message using her private key. Digital signature is in the form of a string of bits. After receiving the message, user B wants to know that whether the message has really been sent by user A or somebody else. For this, user B uses the verification algorithm. She uses the message and the digital signature as input for the verification algorithm and decrypts the message using user A's public key. If the digital signature matches, then user B can be confident that the message has really been sent by user A.

10.1.2 Association of Digital Signatures and Encryption

Message digest is used to generate the signature. The message digest (MD) is calculated from the plaintext or message. The message digests for two different messages are never same. The message digest is encrypted using user's private key. Then, the sender sends this encrypted message digest with the plaintext or message to the receiver.

The receiver calculates the message digest from the plaintext or message he received. He decrypts the encrypted message digest using the sender's public key. If both the MDs are not same, then the plaintext or message is modified after signing. This is explained in Figure 10.1.

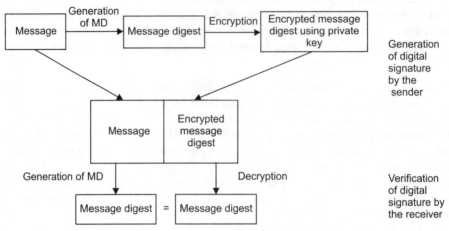

Figure 10.1 Generation and verification of digital signatures.

In digital signatures, the signature or hash value of the message is encrypted using encryption techniques. But the signature or hash value is small. In digital signature, the encryption techniques cannot be used for large messages. As compared to digital signature, more efficient methods are available. Signed document may be sent after encryption over an insecure channel like any ciphertext.

Generally, user A first uses a message digest algorithm like MD5 or SHA-1 and generates the hash value (MD) of the message. Then, he digitally signs the resulting MD (see Figure 10.1). An insecure MD can compromise the digital signature. For example, if it is possible to generate MD collisions (it is really difficult), it might be feasible to forge digital signatures.

In digital signature a message digest is signed instead of the complete message. This has the following advantages:

1. *Efficiency:* The size of digital signature is small, and thus, it improves the performance of the algorithm.

2. *The document is intended to be read by others:* The document includes degree certificates, birth date certificates, driving licenses of the users, rent agreement, contract agreement, etc. These documents are in the plaintext form. The accompanying digital signatures are in encrypted form and these can be used to verify that the documents are neither forged nor modified.

3. *Integrity:* Without the MD, the message 'to be signed' must be divided into a number of blocks. The blocks size should be smaller than the length of the private key. Then, each block is signed separately and sent to the receiver. The receiver can verify the individual block with the signature, but he would not be able to verify if all the blocks are received or not. If a block (or blocks) is lost during transmission, the receiver cannot know it. To know about this loss, the message digest should be computed for a complete message and not for individual blocks.

10.1.3 Using Different Key Pairs for Signing and Encryption

Nowadays, digital signature is the most common tool for verification. In several countries, digital signature is accepted like traditional signature methods. These provisions mean that a person cannot deny the responsibility of the ownership of the message or the documents. Due to this, one should take care to protect one's message and digital signature through proper encryption techniques using proper public key and private key. This makes it difficult to the attacker to modify the message and also to change the digital signature. Digital signature can be protected using following measures.

1. *Use of time stamp with digital signatures:* There are different digital signature algorithms for the generation of digital signature. But these algorithms do not provide any information about the date and time of signature generation. If the user includes a date and time with the message, then also it is not sufficient to check whether the signature is generated by the user or the attacker. To avoid the misuse, as above mentioned, we can use time stamp in addition to digital signatures.

2. *Additional security precautions:* The security of digital signature is based on the private key used for encryption of the signature. If this private key is compromised, the attacker may be able to capture the digital signature. It can be stored on the user's computer/laptop or notebook, and protected by a password, but it has two disadvantages—only the documents on that particular computer/laptop or notebook can be signed and the private key is secure if the computer/laptop or notebook is secure from threat. To provide security to the local computers is difficult due to hardware or operating systems.

So, better option for the security of private key is store it on a smart card. Smart cards are designed so that the data remain safe if, by mistake, it is tampered. The message digest calculated from the message is sent to the smart card. The smart card is connected to some computer, which encrypts the message digest using the user's private key and sends it back. Personal identification number (PIN) is required to activate the smart card. If the smart card is stolen, and the user's private key is located on the smart card, then also it does not make any harm, as PIN is needed to activate the smart card. So, without PIN, digital signature cannot be generated.

3. *Use of smart card readers:* To activate the smart card, PIN is entered using a numeric keypad. Some card readers have their own keypad, while some card readers are integrated into a computer. Sometimes, the PIN may be captured by the attacker. Nowadays, attackers use scanner machine with smart card reader so that when the smart card is swiped through the smart card reader, complete data on the card is copied, and later on, it is used by the attacker.

10.2 ALGORITHMS FOR DIGITAL SIGNATURE

There are many digital signature algorithms. Some of them are listed below:
1. Full Domain Hash, RSA-PSS, etc. based on RSA

2. Digital Signature Algorithm (DSA)
3. Elliptic Curve Digital Signature Algorithm (ECDSA)
4. ElGamal signature scheme
5. Undeniable signature
6. SHA (typically SHA-1) with RSA
7. Rabin signature algorithm
8. Pointcheval–Stern signature algorithm
9. Schnorr signature

10.2.1 Digital Signature Algorithm (DSA)

To generate the digital signature, the most widely used algorithm is Digital Signature Algorithm (DSA). In 1991, the National Institute of Standards and Technology (NIST) proposed the Digital Signature Algorithm to use it in their Digital Signature Standard (DSS). DSA was adopted as a standard in 1994. In 1996, a minor revision in DSA was issued. DSA standard was expanded further in 2000. DSA generates the message digest of length 160 bits. The algorithm is split into three steps—key generation, signing and verification. Now, we discuss all these steps of DSA.

Key Generation

1. Select a prime number q, which is 160-bit long. Select a prime number p, which is L-bit long such that $512 \leq L \leq 1024$, and L is divisible by 64, and $p = qk + 1$ for some integer number k.
2. Select h, where $1 < h < p - 1$ and generate g such that $g = h^k \bmod p > 1$.
3. Select private key x, where $0 < x < q$ and compute $y = g^x \bmod p$ (x should be kept secret).
4. The public key is (p, q, g, y).
5. p, q, g should be shared by different users.

Signature Generation

1. Select a secret integer number k, where $0 < k < q$.
2. Compute r and s such that

$$r = (g^k \bmod p) \bmod q \text{ and}$$

$$s = (k^{-1}(\text{SHA-1}(m) + x * r)) \bmod q,$$

where SHA-1(m) is the message digest of the message m using SHA-1 algorithm.
3. If $r = 0$ or $s = 0$, repeat the above procedure.
4. The digital signature for the message m is (r, s).

Signature Verification

1. If either $0 < r < q$ or $0 < s < q$ is not satisfied, reject the signature.
2. Compute $w = (s)^{-1} \bmod q$.

3. Compute $u_1 = (\text{SHA-1}(m) * w) \mod q$.
4. Compute $u_2 = (r * w) \mod q$.
5. Compute $v = ((g^{u_1} * y^{u_2}) \mod p) \mod q$.
6. If $v = r$, then the signature is valid.

Correctness: The DSA scheme is correct, as the verifier always accepts genuine signatures. This can be illustrated as below:

We know that $g = h^k \mod p$ and suppose $g^q \mod p \equiv h^{qk} \mod p$. Applying Fermat's little theorem, we get $g^q = h^{qk} \equiv h^{p-1} \equiv 1 \pmod{p}$. Since $g > 1$ and q is prime, it follows that g has order q.

The signer computes

$$s = (k^{-1}(\text{SHA-1}(m) + x * r)) \mod q$$

Thus,

$$k = \text{SHA-1}(m)s^{-1} + xrs^{-1}$$
$$= \text{SHA-1}(m)w + xrw \pmod{q}$$

Since g has order q, we have

$$g^k = g^{\text{SHA-1}(m)w} g^{xrw}$$
$$= g^{\text{SHA-1}(m)w} y^{rw}$$
$$= g^{u_1} g^{u_2} \pmod{p}$$

The correctness of DSA algorithm is checked as below:

$$r = (g^k \mod p) \mod q = (g^{u_1} g^{u_2} \mod p) \mod q = v$$

Digital signature algorithms have a number of prior requirements (mentioned below). Without these requirements signatures do not have any meaning.

1. Quality algorithms: Quality of the digital algorithm also depends on the quality of public key algorithms used.

2. Implementations: Implementation of any algorithm is very important. If a very good algorithm is implemented with some mistake, it will never work properly.

3. Private key: The security of any algorithm depends on the secrecy of private key. If the private key of a user compromises (known by the attacker), then the attacker also generates the same digital signature irrespective of how strong the algorithm can be used for the generation of signature.

4. Distribution of public keys: In public key cryptography, the distribution of public key is also very important. For this, there exist different key distribution methods. The distribution of public key is commonly done using a public key infrastructure (PKI) and certificate authority (CA). During distribution, if the public key of a user is given to non-authenticate user, i.e., attacker, then it compromises with the security.

5. Handling of signature protocol: Signature algorithms should be used properly by the users.

If all the above conditions are satisfied by any digital signature scheme, then the digital signature will have the information regarding the sender of the message and user's consent about the message.

10.2.2 ElGamal Signature

One more digital signature scheme described by Taher ElGamal in 1984 is the ElGamal signature. It is based on discrete logarithms. A variant of ElGamal signature is the Digital Signature Algorithm, which is much more widely used. There are several other variants of ElGamal signature. The ElGamal signature scheme is different from ElGamal encryption technique. The main feature of ElGamal signature scheme is that there are many different signatures, which are valid for a given message.

The ElGamal signature scheme allows a verifier that he can confirm the authenticity of a message m sent by the signer to him over an insecure channel.

The user should select parameters p and g as below:

1. Select a large prime p such that the discrete log problem in F_p is infeasible.
2. Recommended size of p is 1024 bits.
3. g is generator of the multiplicative group F_p.

Key Generation

1. Select private key x as $1 < x < p - 1$.
2. Compute $y = g^x \bmod p$.
3. Public key is (p, g, y).
4. Private key is x. 　　　　　　　　　　(Recommended size of x is 160 bits.)

Signature Generation

The signature for message m is calculated as below:

1. Select a secret integer number k, where $0 < k < p - 1$ and $\gcd(k, p - 1) = 1$.
2. Compute $r = g^k \pmod{p}$.
3. Compute hash value of the message as $s = (H(m) - xr)k^{-1} \pmod{p - 1}$.
4. If $s = 0$, repeat the above procedure.
5. The digital signature is (r, s).

Signature Verification

The digital signature for the message m is (r, s) and it is verified as follows:

$$0 < r < p \text{ and } 0 < s < p - 1$$
$$G^{H(m)} = y^r r^s \pmod{p}$$

If all conditions are satisfied, the verifier accepts a signature and rejects it otherwise.

Correctness: The above scheme is correct, as the verifier always accepts genuine signatures. The signature generation implies

$$H(m) = xr + sk \pmod{p - 1}$$

Applying Fermat's little theorem,

$$\begin{aligned} G^{H(m)} &= g^{xr} g^{ks} \\ &= (g^x)^r (g^k)^s \\ &= (y)^r (r)^s \pmod{p} \end{aligned}$$

Security: An attacker can forge signatures either by capturing the signer's private key x or by finding collisions in the hash function $H(m) = H(M) \pmod{p - 1}$. Capturing either of this information is believed to be difficult.

For each signature, the signer must select the value of k very carefully. Also, he should keep the value of k secret. If the value of k compromises, an attacker may be able to deduce the private key x with reduced difficulty. The practical attack is possible using the value of k. If two messages are sent using the same value of k and the same key, then an attacker can compute x directly.

10.2.3 Elliptic Curve Digital Signature Algorithm (ECDSA)

A variant of the Digital Signature Algorithm (DSA) is Elliptic Curve Digital Signature Algorithm (ECDSA). It is based on elliptic curve groups. The use of elliptic curve provides smaller key sizes for the same security level, with roughly, the same execution time. It also generates the signature of exactly the same size.

Signature Generation

Suppose there are two users A and B, user A wants to send a digitally signed message m to user B. Both should agree for some curve parameters such as q, FR, a, b, G, n, h. Also, user A selects two keys such as private key d_A and a public key Q_A. These keys are suitable for elliptic curve cryptography.

User A signs a message m as below:

1. Calculate $e = H(m)$, where H is a message digest or hash value of message m, MD can be calculated using secure hash algorithm SHA-1.
2. Select a secret integer number k, where k is from $1 \leq k \; k \; n - 1]$.
3. Calculate $kG = (x_1, y_1)$.
4. Calculate $r = x_1 \mod n$. If $r = 0$, go to step 2.
5. Calculate $s = k^{-1}(e + d_A r) \mod n$. If $s = 0$, go to step 2.
6. The signature of message m is (r, s).

Signature Verification

Using user A's public key Q_A, user B verifies user A's signature as below:

If r and s are integers in $[1, n - 1]$, signature is said to be valid, otherwise it is invalid.

1. Compute $e = H(m)$, where H is the same hash function used in the signature generation.
2. Compute $w = s^{-1} \pmod{n}$.
3. Compute $u_1 = ew \mod n$ and $u_2 = rw \mod n$.
4. Compute $(x_1, y_1) = u_1 G + u_2 Q_A$.
5. The signature is valid if $x_1 = r \mod n$, otherwise invalid.

10.3 DIGITAL SIGNATURE STANDARD (DSS)

For performing digital signature of any message or documents, some standard is required. This standard is called *Digital Signature Standard* (DSS). The NIST published this standard (i.e., DSS) in 1991. One should note that DSS is a standard, whereas DSA is an algorithm. It has been developed for performing digital signatures. For different digital applications, this standard specifies an appropriate Digital Signature Algorithm (DSA). As per this standard, the message digest of a document is calculated using secure hash algorithm-1 (SHA-1).

Using this algorithm, a signature is generated, which includes a pair of large number which is represented in the form of strings of binary digits. A set of rules and parameters are used to compute the signature. The DSA algorithm has three parts—key generation, signature generation and signature verification. Using user's private key, a signature is generated. Sender's public key is used for the verification of signature. Anyone can verify the signature of a sender.

In signature generation, the message digest of a message is computed using secure hash algorithm, as shown in Figure 10.2. Then, the signature is generated using this message digest. After that, the sender sends the signature with the message to the receiver. The receiver is first intended to verify the signature using sender's public key. The recipient should use the same hash function to calculate the message digest of the received message. The hash function is specified in a separate standard, the Secure Hash Standard (SHS), FIPS 180.

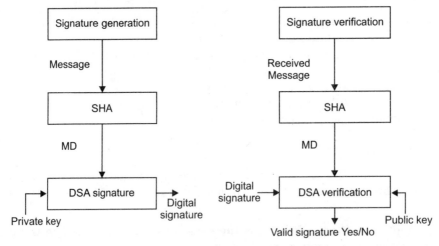

Figure 10.2 Using the SHA with the DSA.

10.3.1 Applications of Digital Signature

Digital signature provides the integrity and the authentication. Third party also verifies the authentication of the sender using digital signature. The applications of digital signature is intended in various areas such as in e-mail, online transactions, e-commerce, e-billing, interchanging the data electronically, and applications where data integration, and authentication of data origin are required. Nowadays, e-registration of flats and other properties also use digital signature for authentications. Even one can file income tax return using his/her digital signature.

10.4 AUTHENTICATION PROTOCOLS

There are various authentication protocols. Some of them are listed below:

1. *Challenge Handshake Authentication Protocol (CHAP)*: It is a three-way handshake protocol and it is much secure than PAP.

2. *Extensible Authentication Protocol (EAP)*: It is used as a dial-in between the client and the server. It is used to determine what authentication protocol will be used.

3. *Password Authentication Protocol (PAP):* It is a two-way handshake protocol. It is used with point to point protocol (*PPP*). It uses a plaintext password like older SLIP systems. It is not secure.

4. *Shiva PAP (SPAP):* Only NT RAS server supports this for clients dialing in.

5. *Data Encryption Standard (DES):* It is used for older clients and servers.

6. *Remote Authentication Dial-In User Service (RADIUS):* It is used in organisation's network to authenticate users dialing in remotely to servers.

7. *S/Key:* It is a RFC 2289 Authentication Protocol. It is secure against replays attacks. It is a one-time password system.

8. *Terminal Access Controller Access Control System (TACACS):* It is used for authentication, accounting and authorisation.

9. *MS-CHAP (MD4):* It is used to authenticate remote workstations and developed by Microsoft. It uses MD4 for computing the message digest and DES for encryption.

10. *SKID-SKID2* **and** *SKID3:* It uses symmetric encryption technique. Privacy of the users are not maintained and a man-in-the-middle attack is possible against it.

SUMMARY

Digital signature is a strong method for authentication used today. Digital signature includes message authentication codes (MAC), hash value of a message and digital pen pad devices. The Digital Signature Algorithm (DSA) is the standard algorithm for digital signatures. The algorithm is split into three parts—key generation, signing and verification. One more digital signature scheme described by Taher ElGamal in 1984 is the ElGamal signature. It is based on discrete logarithms. A variant of the Digital Signature Algorithm (DSA) is Elliptic Curve Digital Signature Algorithm (ECDSA). It is based on elliptic curve groups. The use of elliptic curve provides smaller key sizes for the same security level, with roughly, the same execution time. It also generates the signature of exactly the same size. The NIST published the standard for digital signature, called *DSS*, in 1991. One should note that DSS is a standard, whereas DSA is an algorithm. It has been developed for performing digital signatures. The applications of DSA are intended in various areas such as in e-mail, online transactions, e-commerce, e-billing. There are various authentication protocols. Some of them are CHAP, MS-CHAP (MD4), etc.

EXERCISES

10.1 What are the different components associated with a direct digital signature scheme?
10.2 Describe the properties of digital signature.
10.3 What is replay attack?
10.4 What is digital signature?
10.5 Why is the digital signature needed?
10.6 Explain the benefits of the digital signature.
10.7 Explain the following algorithms for digital signature schemes:
  (a) A key generation algorithm
  (b) A signing algorithm
  (c) A verification algorithm
10.8 Write and explain the Digital Signature Algorithm (DSA).
10.9 What is the ElGamal signature scheme?
10.10 Explain the Elliptic Curve Digital Signature Algorithm (ECDSA).
10.11 List various authentication protocols.
10.12 What happens if a k value used in creating a DSA signature is compromised?

MULTIPLE CHOICE QUESTIONS

10.1 Digital signature does not provide
  (a) Confidentiality of the message
  (b) Authentication of the sender
  (c) Integrity of the message
  (d) Authentication of the message
10.2 The strong method for authentication is
  (a) Message digest algorithms
  (b) Encryption techniques
  (c) Digital signature
  (d) None of the above
10.3 Digital signature includes
  (a) Message Authentication Code (MAC)
  (b) Hash value of a message
  (c) Both (a) and (b)
  (d) None of the above

Answers
10.1 (a)   10.2 (c)   10.3 (c)

Chapter 11

Electronic Mail Security

11.1 INTRODUCTION

We learn about various encryption techniques which secure data. Most of today's communication is performed through e-mail. The message is in the form of plaintext. So, if somebody captures this message, it may cause harm to the sender and the recipient. So, there is a need to provide security to this message. Pretty Good Privacy (PGP) is used to protect the message, which we can send securely through e-mail. In this chapter, we are going to discuss Pretty Good Privacy (PGP), Multipurpose Internet Mail Extensions (MIME) and Secure/Multipurpose Internet Mail Extensions (S/MIME).

11.2 PRETTY GOOD PRIVACY (PGP)

Today most of the personal communication is done using e-mail through internet. We know that internet is very insecure medium of transmission. If we send the message as plaintext using e-mail, the attacker can easily capture our message. So, there is a need to protect our message. One can use Pretty Good Privacy (PGP) to protect the message. It is used to encrypt and decrypt e-mail message over the Internet. PGP uses a combination of symmetric and asymmetric encryption algorithms for encryption and decryption of the message. It was developed in the late 1980s and early 1990s by Phil Zimmermann. An encrypted digital signature can be sent to the receiver using PGP. This helps the receiver in verifying the sender's identity and also in checking the integrity of the message. PGP is the most popular program used by individuals and for commercial applications. It is available as freeware and also in a low-cost commercial version. For e-mail security, now PGP has become a de facto standard. We can store our files in encrypted form using PGP to protect it from the attackers or unauthorised person. In PGP, each user has his certificate, but there is no certificate authority. The authentication of certificate is verified by the other users.

PGP is used for authentication of the sender. It is also used for encrypting documents. This secures the documents, as only intended recipients can decrypt the files. The public keys of the users are distributed so that the other users can use these keys for communication to a particular user. The sender encrypts the message using the public key of the recipient. This encrypted message is decrypted using the private key of the recipient's private key. The private key is a secret key and known to the owner only. The private key is used for encrypting the digital signature of the user. In this, the recipient uses sender's public key for decryption. For encrypting e-mails, PGP is useful. Any individual can use PGP to protect his/her message. PGP helps in providing privacy to the people.

11.2.1 Need of PGP

Privacy is the most important factor, which is needed by every user. PGP empowers users to maintain their privacy by their own. Some important conditions are given below in which encryption is required to protect the data:

1. Suppose two friends are exchanging encrypted messages via e-mail. For these friends, the messages may seem only passionate. If the messages are not encrypted, other people may read then, and for those people, they may be erotic messages. In such case, if the messages are encrypted, other people may not be able to read them.
2. The development team of a company's new product definitely wants to keep all the communication between the members of the team to be secret. For this, the e-mail regarding the product shared among them should be encrypted. This communication should be kept secret not only till the product becomes patented but also till the launching of the product in the market. In this case, not only the e-mails but also the data files need to be encrypted.
3. A wife and husband share a laptop/notepad and also their personal e-mail accounts. They also share e-mail passwords with each other. Now, they can access each other's mail accounts. Now, suppose as the wife can access husband's e-mail account, her husband keeps his passphrase secret. He wants to make her happy by giving a surprise birthday party. But he is anxious that she might know about the party. So, he uses encrypted e-mails for planning the party.
4. On the computer system at our office, if we store some important personal data, credit card numbers, personal scanned documents, family photos, etc., then this data should be kept in encrypted form.

PGP should be used in the following cases:

1. Financial data which we want to send through e-mail
2. Some data related to trade
3. Personal information
4. Information related to some product before its commercial launching

These are very limited examples. The list includes any information which causes us any type of loss. We use locker to protect our valuables; in the same way, PGP provides security to the documents electronically. Nothing is wrong if someone wants to secure his personal information. Taking proper care, PGP is stronger than your locker.

11.2.2 Working of PGP

PGP provides some important services such as:

1. Authentication
2. Confidentiality
3. Confidentiality and authentication
4. Compression
5. E-mail compatibility
6. Segmentation and reassembly

Now, we will see in brief how these services work.

1. *Authentication:* When the sender sends message, the receiver wants to authenticate the message. So, the sender uses digital signature for authentication. The authentication carries out as given below:

(a) The sender creates the message.
(b) The message digest or hash value of the message is generated by the sender.
(c) Message digest is encrypted using sender's private key. The encrypted message digest is the digital signature. RSA algorithm is used for this encryption. The message is attached to the digital signature.
(d) The receiver decrypts the message using sender's public key.
(e) The message digest or hash value of the received message is generated by the receiver.
(f) If the two message digests match, then the received message is accepted as authentic.

2. *Confidentiality:* PGP is also used to provide confidentiality. For providing confidentiality to the message, any encryption algorithm can be used. PGP suggests CAST-128 or IDEA or 3DES for encryption. These algorithms work on the block of fixed size. But the length of the message is an arbitrary and not the multiple of the size of the block. So there may be less number of bits in the last block, the cipher feedback mode is used. The PGP uses a symmetric key encryption. The session key is bound to the message and transmitted with it. The confidentiality is provided as given below:

(a) The sender creates the message and a 128-bit session key.
(b) Using CAST-128 encryption algorithm and a session key, the message is encrypted.
(b) The session key is encrypted using receiver's public key. For this, RSA algorithm is used. The encrypted session key is prepended to the message
(d) The receiver recovers the session key by decrypting the message using his private key. For this, he uses RSA algorithm.
(e) Using session key, the message is decrypted,

PGP provides Diffie–Hellman algorithm as an option to RSA algorithm for encryption.

3. **Confidentiality and authentication:** To provide more security, we can combine authentication and confidentiality.

   (a) The sender creates the message and a 128-bit session key.
   (b) The message digest or hash value of the message is generated using SHA-1 by the sender.
   (c) Message digest is encrypted using sender's private key. The encrypted message digest is the digital signature. RSA algorithm is used for this encryption. The message is attached to the digital signature.
   (d) The session key is encrypted using receiver's public key. For this, RSA algorithm is used. The encrypted session key is prepended to the message.
   (e) The receiver decrypts the message using his private key and recovers the session key. For this, he uses RSA algorithm.
   (f) The receiver decrypts the message using session key.
   (g) The receiver decrypts the message using sender's public key.
   (h) The message digest or hash value of the received message is generated by the receiver.
   (i) If the two message digests match, then the received message is accepted as authentic.

4. **Compression:** Compression means compact or reduce the size of the message. To reduce the size of the final message, PGP uses compression technique. Compression of the message is done after the generation of digital signature, but before encryption of the message. Compression provides advantages like saving of space for transmission and storage. The digital signature is generated before compression so that one can store only the uncompressed message, together with the digital signature for future verification. Encryption of the message is done after compression. This provides strong security because it has less redundancy than the original message. So, the cryptanalysis of the message is more difficult.

5. **E-mail compatibility:** When the PGP is used, at least the part of the block that needs encryption should be encrypted. For example, if authentication is needed, then the message digest is encrypted. If confidentiality is needed, the message and digital signature both are encrypted. Thus, the resulting block consists of a stream of arbitrary 8-bit octets. For the e-mail, where the block must have ASCII characters, PGP provides the service of converting the raw 8-bit binary stream into ASCII. This conversion is done using radix-64. Due to this conversion, the size of a message is increased by 33%. Generally, the sizes of digital signature and message digest are very small and PGP uses compression technique which reduces the size of the message. This compensates the above problem. Also, radix-64 converts the input, irrespective of the contents.

6. **Segmentation and reassembly:** We cannot send large messages through e-mail. If the message is very large, we have to divide the message into smaller parts and then e-mail the smaller segments separately. PGP automatically subdivides the larger message into smaller parts so that it can be sent through e-mail. When all the processes i.e., digital signature, message digest or compression on the original message are completed, then before sending it through e-mail segmentation is done on the message, so that the message digest or the key is in only one segment, other segments do not contain it. At the receiving end, PGP collects all the e-mail headers and reassembles

the original segments or parts of the message before decryption, compression, etc. The transmission diagram for PGP message is shown in Figure 11.1. The reception diagram for PGP message is shown in Figure 11.2.

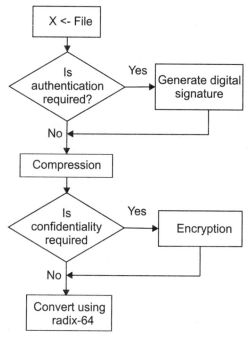

Figure 11.1 Generic transmission diagram of PGP messages.

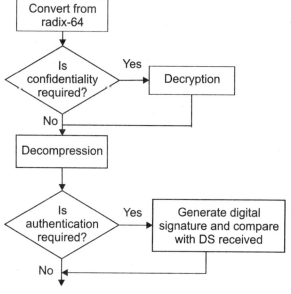

Figure 11.2 Generic reception diagram of PGP messages.

Radix-64 Conversion

We have to follow the following steps for radix conversion:

Step 1 Read the binary number. Then, split it into blocks of size 24-bits (3 bytes).
Step 2 Each block of 24-bit is then divided into four groups of 6-bit each.
Step 3 Each group will have a value between 0 and 2^6-1 (=63).
Step 4 This value is encoded into a printable character.

Table 11.1 gives the radix-64 encoding

Table 11.1 Radix-64 encoding

6-bit value	Character encoding	6-bit value	Character encoding	6-bit value	Character encoding	6-bit value	Character encoding
0	A	16	Q	32	g	48	w
1	B	17	R	33	h	49	x
2	C	18	S	34	i	50	y
3	D	19	T	35	j	51	z
4	E	20	U	36	k	52	0
5	F	21	V	37	l	53	1
6	G	22	W	38	m	54	2
7	H	23	X	39	n	55	3
8	I	24	Y	40	o	56	4
9	J	25	Z	41	p	57	5
10	K	26	a	42	q	58	6
11	L	27	b	43	r	59	7
12	M	28	c	44	s	60	8
13	N	29	d	45	t	61	9
14	O	30	e	46	u	62	+
15	P	31	f	47	v	63	/
						(pad)	=

Processing the message includes various steps. First, the message is encrypted. Then, ZIP algorithm is used to compress the message. The compressed message is converted to radix-64 format. Converting ASCII to radix-64 format is done by substituting 6-bit values for 8-bit ASCII characters. At a time, three bytes are converted into four characters. If the last group size is less than three bytes, append zeroes at the end of the 6-bit value. This is called *padding*. "=" sign is used if the padding bits are equal to one character. Following examples explain this process:

1. If there are 3 bytes in the last group, no processing is required.
2. If there are 2 bytes in the last group, the first two groups are processed in the normal way. The two zero-value bits are added to the third (incomplete) group and are converted. A pad character (=) is added to the output.
3. If the last data group has 1 byte, then the first 6-bit group is processed in the normal way. The four zero-value bits are added to second (incomplete) data group and are converted. Two pad characters (=) are added to the output. Finally, a 24-bit checksum is computed to detect errors after conversion. The checksum is lead by the equals sign (=).

Format of PGP message is shown in Figure 11.3.

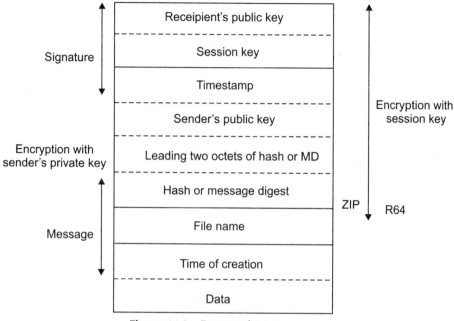

Figure 11.3 Format of PGP message.

11.2.3 PGP Encryption Applications

The messages sent by e-mail are encrypted using PGP. Since 2002, the applications of PGP have been diversified. Digital signatures, laptop hard disk encryption, file and folder security, protection, batch file transfer encryption, and protection for files and folders stored on network servers can be encrypted using PGP.

11.2.4 PGP: Backdoors and Key Escrow

Backdoors

PGP has many features, which may affect its performance. One of such features is backdoor. It allows an outside user to decrypt the encrypted message. How does the sender know whether someone has intentionally planted his own security hole in PGP? Suppose that the government induces PGP Corporation to insert a backdoor feature, which allows the police department to decrypt public messages and files easily.

Now, when somebody purchases the PGP product for which the source code is unavailable, then the outside inspection of the product will be impossible for the user. Due to this, old users of PGP would lose confidence in newer versions of the product. So, to restore confidence in the user, the PGP Corporation makes an attempt. The source code for various versions of PGP is available publically. Cryptanalyst can attack suddenly on each new version and examine the source code carefully. After finding out that the source code contains no backdoors, he can compile that source code. He compares the result with the executable program obtained from the PGP Corporation. Alarm has not been raised for a single time, which indicates that intentionally, no weakness has been inserted into PGP by the PGP Corporation. The same is true for other versions of the PGP.

Every time, source code examination does not prove fruitful. It has its limitation. This is because each newer version of PGP has much larger source code than its predecessors. This makes code examination more difficult. To overcome this drawback, digital signature is used by PGP with its own key.

Key Escrow

It is a key exchange process. In this, an encryption key is stored by a third party. This system provides the backup for the keys. A key, which is lost by its original user, may be used to decrypt the ciphertext. This allows the original message be retained in its original form. But key escrow system is sometimes risky, as third party is involved for storing the keys.

PGP makes use of four types of keys:

1. One-time session symmetric keys
2. Public keys
3. Private keys
4. Passphrase-based symmetric keys

With respect to these keys, three separate requirements can be identified.

1. Session key should be generated randomly and difficult to guess.
2. User can use multiple pairs of public-key/private-key. As a result, there is not one-to-one mapping between the users and their public keys. Thus, it is difficult to identify particular keys.
3. Each PGP entity should maintain a directory of its own public/private key pairs as well as a directory of public keys of other users.

Problems

Backdoors and key escrow have certain problems, which are discussed below:

1. The PGP design and algorithms are available to all. If the commercial sources have backdoors, then a cryptanalyst can simply implement his own PGP. If the personal PGP is made illegal, it does not mean that the cryptanalyst will bother.
2. Non-backdoor versions of PGP will remain available at the border of the country.
3. There is no guarantee that the government keeps our data secret after using backdoors and key escrow.

Suppose the government implements a backdoor. It makes mandatory to use the additional decryption key (ADK), which belongs to the government for all PGP users. If ADK is compromised or leaked, it affects all the confidential data of individuals. If the private key of the individual user is compromised or leaked, it will affect the security of that individual, but if the ADK is compromised, it will affect the security of everyone.

11.2.5 PGP Security Quality

PGP is more secure and is not possible for the cryptanalyst to break it by any mean. SSL secures our data in transit only, whereas PGP protects the data while in storage.

The security of PGP depends on the assumption that the PGP algorithms used are difficult for cryptanalysis using current hardware and techniques. In the original version of PGP, the session key is encrypted using RSA algorithm. Cryptanalyst is able to break the RSA algorithm, then he captures the session key. In the same way IDEA is used for symmetric encryption in PGP. After some time, if the security flaws are detected with IDEA algorithm one cannot use IDEA algorithm for encryption in PGP. So, to add more security, some additional encryption algorithm can be used to make it difficult for cryptanalyst to break it and provide more security.

11.3 MIME

MIME is defined by an Internet standard document, called RFC1521. MIME stands for Multipurpose Internet Mail Extensions. MIME adds some additional fields to the old standard. It provides new standard for e-mail. This includes some new fields for headers of the message. Initially, e-mail systems are used to send only text messages. However, nowadays, use of e-mail is done not only to send the text messages but also the audio, video and multimedia files. Also, e-mail is used to send images, documents in various formats, etc. Large message can split into different parts while sending by e-mail. Each part has its header, which gives information about that part.

Using MIME, messages can be sent through e-mail. The messages may contain:

1. Text with additional fields such as special headers and formatted sections
2. A number of parts
3. Any size
4. Other than English characters
5. Text having different fonts
6. Binary files
7. Images, audio, video and multimedia files
8. Application specific files

The improvement in MIME is done to provide more security to the message. This new version of MIME is known as *Secure MIME* or *SMIME*.

11.3.1 MIME Headers

There are different headers provided by the e-mail system. These headers include From, To, Date, Subject, etc. Some new header fields of MIME are as given below:

1. *MIME-Version:* Time to time, standards are updated and new standards are introduced. These new standards should support the old standards. The same is happened in case of MIME. MIME takes care of the old standard by making itself compatible with the older Internet mail standards. It has added some new fields. One such field is a version number. It is used to declare that a message matches with the MIME standard. For a single message, only one version field is used and it lies at the top of a message. If the message has more than one part, then in that case also, header has only one version field.

2. *Content-Type:* Another new field has been added, called *Content-Type*. The message contains data having different types and subtypes. This new field, i.e., Content-Type specifies the type and subtype of data. It also provides information about the encoding of data.

Content-Type header field is written as

```
Content-Type: = type "/" subtype [";" parameter]
```

Subtypes of Content-Type header are as follows:

- *Value text:* Textual information in the message is represented using value text field. Types of value text are plaintext, and enriched text. Plaintext allows a string of ASCII characters and enriched text allows greater formatting flexibility.
- *Value multipart:* If the message has more than one part, then the field value multipart indicates the information that there are multiple parts. It can be used to combine several parts of different types of data into a single message.
- *Value application:* It is used for transmission of binary or application data.
- *Value video:* This is used for transmitting video data.
- *Value image:* It is used for transmitting still images.
- *Value audio:* It is used for transmitting audio or sound data.
- *Value message:* This is used for encapsulating a message.

3. *Transfer encoding:* It specifies the encoding mechanism for the message.

4. *ID:* This refers to unique identification of entities with reference to multiple contexts.

5. *Description:* It gives more information about the data (video data) in a message.

In the MIME standard, the content-type values, subtypes and parameter names are case-insensitive; however, many parameter values are case-sensitive.

MIME standard is extensible such that new header fields and parameters can be added with time. Other MIME fields are likely to have new values defined over time. All such enhancements in MIME should be introduced in a proper manner. MIME has a registration process that uses the Internet Assigned Numbers Authority (IANA) as a central authority for registration.

The MIME has defined following content types:

1. ***Audio:*** This content type indicates that the data is audio data.
   (a) *Audio/Basic:* The audio is encoded using 8-bit ISDN u-law. The requirement for this type is a single channel and a sample rate of 8000 Hz.

2. *Image:* This content type indicates that the data is image data. The requirement for this type is a display device. The image may be in *jpeg* or *gif* format.

3. *Message:* This content type indicates the complete message.
  (a) *Message/RFC822:* It indicates message with an RFC822 syntax. It is used for transmitting the message digest of a message.
  (b) *Message/Partial:* It indicates a segment of message. It allows to transmit the message in parts or segments.
   There are three parameters in this content type—*ID*, *Number* and *Total*.
   (i) *ID* indicates the unique number for each message. For a message, there is only one ID. All the segments of a message have the same ID.
   (ii) When the message is split into number of parts/segments, each part/segment has a *number*, which indicates the sequence of that part/segment. It is an integer value.
   (iii) *Total* indicates the total number of parts or segments in a message. It is also an integer value. It is compulsory for the final part/segment, whereas for other parts it is optional.
  (c) *Message/External-body:* This content type is used to show the reference and not the actual message. It indicates the parameters for accessing the external data.

For a message, a complete message or part/segment of message or external body consists of a header, a blank line and the message header for complete message. To end the message header, another blank line should be added.

Consider the following message:

```
Content-Type: message/external-body;
   Access-Type=local;
   Name="/c/abc/photo.gif"

Content-Type: image/gif (gif shows the file is *.gif format)
Content-ID: 12345
Content-Transfer-Encoding: binary
```

Access-Type is mandatory to mention; other fields are optional or mandatory depending on the value of Access-Type.
  In addition to Access-Type, some parameters are optional, which are given below:
  (i) *Expiration date* gives the last date for valid data. After this date, there is no guarantee about the existence of data.
  (ii) The *size* of the data is specified.

4. *Multipart:* If the message is split into number of parts and each part is having its own data type, then this parameter is used. It gives the information about the start and end of each part using an *encapsulation boundary*; the end of last part is followed by a closing boundary.

A multipart Content-Type header field syntax is as follows:

```
Content-Type: multipart/mixed; boundary= abc09qw56as
```

The above syntax shows that a message has several parts. Each part has identical structure like to an RFC822 message. The header may be empty and each part is preceded by—

    abc09qw56as

The closing boundary is shown as—

    abc09qw56as

There are spaces to add more additional information before the first encapsulation boundary and following the final boundary. These spaces are often blank. Anything appearing before the first or after the last boundary is ignored.

Consider a multipart message, which has two parts. Both the parts are text, one is explicitly typed and the other is implicitly typed. The message syntax is shown below:

```
From: Ram Vyasan
To: Shyam Dhur
Subject: Hellow Message
MIME-Version: 1.0
Content-Type: multipart/mixed;
  boundary="simple boundary"

This is called the preamble of a message and may be ignored.
—simple boundary
This is implicitly typed ASCII text.
—simple boundary
Content-Type: text/plain; charset= ASCII
to end this part use
—simple boundary—
```

One can use a Content-Type of multipart in a body part within another multipart entity. Care should be taken to use a different boundary delimiter. In some cases, multipart Content-Type with only a single body part may be useful.

5. *Multipart/Mixed:* It is used to view multiple parts of a message sequentially.

Multipart/Alternative: There is an "alternative" version of the information of each part of the message.

```
From: Ram Vyasan
To: Shyam Dhur
Subject: Hello Text Message in formatted form
MIME-Version: 1.0
Content-Type: multipart/alternative;
  boundary=boundary25

—boundary25
Content-Type: text/plain; charset=ASCII

... plain text version...
```

```
—boundary25
Content-Type: text/richtext

... richtext version ...
—boundary25
Content-Type: text/x

... formatted version...
—boundary25—
```

In the above example, users whose e-mail system support for text/x format would be able to read the formatted version. Other users would see only the richtext or plain text version.

6. *Multipart/Parallel:* Its syntax is similar to Multipart/Mixed format. Here, all the parts of a message are presented simultaneously for processing. It is basically used to send multimedia messages.

7. *Multipart/Digest:* It shows that each part is an RFC822 mail message.

8. *Text:* If the message is in text form, then text Content-type is used to send the message. The syntax for text Content-type used for Internet mail is

```
Content-type: text/plain; Charset=US-ASCII
```

9. *Text/Plain:* It shows that the message is in the plain text form.

10. *Text/Richtext:* It shows that the message is in the word processing format, as per MIME standard.

11. *Video:* It shows that the message contains image or picture.

12. *Video/MPEG:* It shows that the message is video encoded as per MPEG standard.

13. *X-TypeName:* This is any type name that begins with X-.
   The mechanisms for defining new Content-Type subtypes are as follows:
   (a) Private values (starting with X-) are defined between cooperating mail composing and reading programs. No outside registration is required. This is useful to the reader to correctly identify the type of the content.
   (b) New standard values must be registered with IANA.
      Syntax for user agents is

```
Content-Type: Text/plain; Charset = US-ASCII
```

14. *Application:* It shows data which is not represented in any category.

15. *Application/Octet-Stream:* This shows uninterpreted binary data. The parameters used are
   (a) *Name:* This shows name of binary data
   (b) *Type:* This shows type of binary data.
   (c) *Padding:* It shows the number of bits used for padding.

16. *Application/PostScript:* This shows a message having a postscript document.

11.3.2 MIME Transfer-Encoding Header Field

Many Content-Types are usefully represented as 8-bit character or binary data. Some transport protocols such as SMTP are not supported for such data transmission. SMTP supports 7-bit ASCII data and message up to 1000 characters per line. MIME converts the data into 7-bit format and the mechanism used for conversion is shown in Content-Transfer-Encoding header field.

The Content-Transfer-Encoding field are as follows:

1. BASE64
2. QUOTED-PRINTABLE
3. 8BIT
4. 7BIT
5. BINARY
6. x-EncodingName

Message should be in a 7-bit mail-ready format. The syntax is

```
Content-Transfer-Encoding: 7bit
```

There are maximum 76 ASCII characters per line for BASE64 and QUOTED-PRINTABLE fields. For the data that consists of printable ASCII characters, QUOTED-PRINTABLE is the most appropriate encoding method. The equal's sign (=) is used for any character, which is not a printable ASCII character. To show extended line greater than 76 characters, equal sign is used.

The advantages of the QUOTED-PRINTABLE format are mentioned below:

1. Additional characters required are less.
2. The message is in readable form.

Non-standard values are represented by starting with x. It syntax is

```
Content-Transfer-Encoding: x-new message.
```

If the header of a message contains a Content-Transfer-Encoding field, then it applies to the complete message. If it is included in the header of a part, then it applies to that part of a message. If a message Multipart or Message type, then the Content-Transfer-Encoding must be 7-bit, 8-bit or binary.

The syntax for header of a message or part of a message is

```
Content-Type: text/plain, charset=ISO-8859-1
Content-transfer-encoding: base64
```

This means that the part of a data, which is a Base64 ASCII, was originally in ISO-8859-1.

Optional Content-ID Header Field

It allows one part to reference another part of a message.

Optional Content-Description Header Field

The descriptive information is indicated using this header.

11.4 S/MIME

S/MIME stands for Secure/Multipurpose Internet Mail Extensions. It is a standard for public key encryption and digital signing of e-mail encapsulated in MIME. Apart from text data, there are some other data, which are also important. MIME specifies to encrypt those data which look like a text data to the third party in communication.

The standards for Internet e-mail were established in 1982. These standards put some restrictions on the e-mail messages. Some of the restrictions are as follows:

1. The message contains only ASCII characters.
2. The message contains maximum 1000 characters in one line.
3. The message does not exceed a certain length.

Since EDI messages can violate all of these restrictions, the 1982 standards, do not allow EDI to be reliably transmitted through Internet e-mail. There are some new standards which support to send different types of messages and services. A new Internet mail standard was approved in June, 1992. The new standard is called *MIME*. Before S/MIME, e-mail administrators used a widely accepted e-mail protocol, called *Simple Mail Transfer Protocol* (*SMTP*). It was inherently not secure. S/MIME provides a solution for e-mail administrator that is more secure and also widely accepted. S/MIME is as important as SMTP because it brings SMTP to the next level. It allows widespread e-mail connectivity, with strong security.

11.4.1 History of S/MIME

The first version of S/MIME was proposed by RSA data security, Inc. in 1995. At that time, for security of message, no recognised standard existed, but many contending standards existed.

In 1998, the second version of S/MIME was submitted to IETF to be considered as Internet standard. In 1999, to improve the performance of S/MIME, IETF proposed the third version of S/MIME. RFC 2632 built on the work of RFC 2311 in specifying the standards for S/MIME messages, and RFC 2633 enhanced RFC 2312 specification of certificate handling. RFC 2634 added some additional services to S/MIME, which include labels, receipts and triple-wrapping.

Following two security services are provided by S/MIME:

1. Digital signatures
2. Encryption

S/MIME improves the security of e-mail by providing digital analogs. It also provides the integrity of a message. We have already discussed more about integrity in message digest and hashing algorithms. Privacy is another factor in e-mail communication. S/MIME makes messaging cheap, the software is user-friendly and reduces the cost. Due to all these factors, the commercial community attracts towards S/MIME. The first example of this community is the Electronic Data Interchange (EDI). It has been made over value-added networks (VANs). VANs provide trustworthy and secure service, but these are costly. S/MIME helps in reducing the cost of this service, and at the same time, improves the security, makes user-friendly connectivity and reduces the response time.

11.4.2 Working of S/MIME

S/MIME uses symmetric encryption algorithms, public key cryptography, message digest algorithms, and certificates for authentication and message integrity. This improves the efficiency of S/MIME. S/MIME uses RC2 and Triple-DES as symmetric encryption algorithms, RSA as key generation algorithm and SHA-1 or MD5 as message digest algorithm. We will see how different services such as secrecy and authentication are provided in S/MIME.

Secrecy

Suppose Ram wants to send a secret message to Shyam so that only Shyam can read it. Ram and Shyam has to take some steps to provide security to the message as below:

(a) A random key, called *session*, is generated. It is used to encrypt for only one session of the e-mail. Then, the e-mail program uses symmetric encryption algorithm and the session key to encrypt the message.
(b) The session key is also encrypted using Shyam's public key.
(c) The e-mail program creates folder, which contains encrypted message, encrypted session key, Ram's x.509 certificate, and information of the encryption algorithms used.
(d) The folder is transmitted to Shyam. This is an S/MIME e-mail message. This encrypted message is called *digital envelope*.
(e) When Shyam receives the message, his private key is used to decrypt the session key. He also gets the information about the encryption algorithm used for the encryption of message.
(f) Using this session key, Shyam's e-mail program decrypts the message.

Authentication

Suppose Ram wants to send a message to Shyam. He wants to prove (i.e., authenticate) that the mail is really sent by him and not by someone else. Ram and Shyam have to take some steps to provide authentication of the sender as below:

(a) A message digest algorithm is used to create a message digest of the message.
(b) The e-mail program encrypts the message digest using Ram's private key.
(c) The e-mail program creates folder that contains the original message, encrypted message digest, Ram's x.509 certificate, and information of the encryption algorithms used.
(d) The folder is transmitted to Shyam. This is an S/MIME e-mail message. This encrypted message is called *digital envelope*.
(e) When Shyam receives the message, first, his e-mail program verifies whether x.509 certificate is valid or not. If it is valid, then he retrieves Ram's public key from the certificate.
(f) Ram's public key is used to decrypt the message digest. He also gets the information about the message digest algorithm used by Ram.

(g) Shyam's e-mail program computes the message digest of the message received.
(h) Two message digest values are compared. If the values match, then Shyam authenticate Ram as the originator of the e-mail received.

Secrecy and Authentication

To provide secrecy and authentication to a message, we should use the combination of the above two approaches. For this, one has to follow the following steps:
Use authentication technique to the message such as calculate message digest.
The authenticated folder is encrypted using receiver's public key.
Transmit the folder to the recipient.
The recipient decrypts the folder by using his/her private key. He gets the session key.
Using session key, he decrypts message. The result is a signed S/MIME message.

11.4.3 Applications of S/MIME

S/MIME is useful for transmitting the data securely through e-mail. So, many companies and organisations use S/MIME to securely exchange their data. In software companies, part of code can be securely transmitted using S/MIME. Government organisations and stock market data can be securely transmitted using S/MIME. Many hospitals use to send patient's information confidentialy to the authorised persons only.

11.5 COMPARISON OF PGP AND S/MIME

A comparison of PGP and S/MIME is given in Table 11.2.

Table 11.2 Comparison of PGP and S/MIME

Class	PGP	S/MIME
Authentication	Distributed authentication	Hierarchical authentication
Key storage	Key ring	Key certificate
Standard	–	IETF
Commercialisation	No compatibility test, small products	Compatibility test, many commercial products
Applications Summary	Personal	Company, enterprise

SUMMARY

PGP was developed in late 1980s and early 1990s by Phil Zimmermann. PGP is used for encrypting and digitally signing the data. It is used for authentication of the sender and also for encryption applications such as e-mail and attachments, digital signatures, laptop hard disk encryption, file and folder security, protection. The security of PGP depends on the assumption that the PGP algorithms used are difficult for cryptanalysis using current hardware and techniques. S/MIME stands for Secure/Multipurpose Internet Mail Extensions. It is a standard for public key encryption and digital signing of e-mail encapsulated in MIME. S/MIME uses symmetric encryption algorithms, public key cryptography, message digest algorithms and certificates for authentication and message integrity. It is useful for transmitting the data securely through e-mail.

EXERCISES

11.1 What is PGP? What are the different applications of PGP?
11.2 What is the importance of PGP?
11.3 Why is PGP used in security?
11.4 Explain the working of PGP.
11.5 Discuss the applications of PGP.
11.6 Explain the backdoor feature in PGP.
11.7 What is key escrow?
11.8 Give the problems with backdoor and key escrow.
11.9 Explain the security issue related with PGP.
11.10 What is S/MIME?
11.11 What is MIME?
11.12 Explain the different header fields included in MIME.
11.13 Explain the security services provided by S/MIME.
11.14 Explain the working of S/MIME.
11.15 Explain, with example, how the secrecy can work in S/MIME.
11.16 Explain authentication in S/MIME with example.
11.17 Discuss different applications of S/MIME.
11.18 Compare PGP with S/MIME.
11.19 List the services provided by PGP.
11.20 In the PGP scheme, what is the expected number of session keys generated before a previously created session key is produced?

MULTIPLE CHOICE QUESTIONS

11.1 Which is not true about PGP?
 (a) PGP stands for Pretty Good Privacy.
 (b) It is used for secure transmission of message through e-mail.
 (c) It is used to encrypt and decrypt e-mail message over the Internet.
 (d) All of the above.
11.2 PGP does not provide
 (a) Authentication
 (b) Confidentiality

(c) Access control
(d) Compression

11.3 S/MIME provide--------
(a) Digital signature
(b) Encryption
(c) Integrity
(d) All of the above

Answers

11.1 (d)   **11.2** (c)   **11.3** (d)

CHAPTER 12

IP Security

12.1 INTRODUCTION

As the use of Internet is increasing rapidly, there is a need to secure the network infrastructure from unauthorised persons, who try to monitor and control the network traffic. Therefore, authentication and encryption mechanisms are required to secure end-user-to-end-user traffic. One of the attacks on the network infrastructure is IP spoofing. In IP spoofing, attackers create packets with false IP addresses and then exploit applications, which use authentication based on IP address. Also, there are some other attacks like eavesdropping and packet sniffing, in which attackers read the confidential information which is transmitted through the insecure channel. This chapter provides details about IP security architecture, IPv4, IPv6, authentication protocols, ISAKMP, OAKLEY Key Determination Protocol and Virtual Private Network.

12.2 IP SECURITY ARCHITECTURE

To guarantee the security services like integrity, confidentiality and authentication of information or data during transmission over the insecure channel like Internet, some security mechanism should be used. This mechanism is called *IP security*. This security mechanism is implemented at the Internet Protocol layer. Currently, researchers work to improve the toughness of the security algorithms, which can work at IP layer. This helps in providing more security at IP layer for the users who request security. To provide security for individual applications as well as for virtual private networks, the security should be added at the network layer.

12.2.1 Strengths of IPsec

IPsec is an Internet standard for network layer security. IP security provides additional security to the applications. Some of the strengths of IPsec are given as:

1. *Multivendor:* There are many vendors whose products support IPsec framework. Users should have the freedom to select the product of any vendor as per their requirement.

2. *Scalability:* Scalability is the important feature of any network. So, IPsec should support the scalability criteria of any network environment.

The design of IPsec protocol is complicated; so, most of the users avoid using this protocol. Virtual private network (VPN) products widely use IPsec protocols. IPsec scenario is well explained in Figure 12.1.

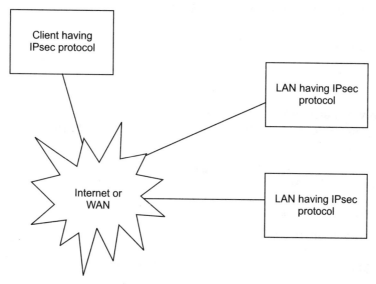

Figure 12.1 IP security scenario.

IPsec uses cryptographic algorithms to provide security to the message. Encryption and hashing techniques are used for securing transmission of data. Confidentiality to the message is provided using encryption and authentication and integrity is provided using hashing algorithms.

Now, we will take a look on different services which are provided by IPsec.

1. Data authentication
2. Data origin authentication
3. Integrity using hash function
4. Data encryption to provide privacy
5. Protection against replay attacks
6. Provide confidentiality to the traffic flow
7. Transport and tunnel modes to meet different network needs

12.2.2 Applications of IPsec

IPsec has a wide range of application areas. Some applications are given as:

1. VPN can be built in the wide campus of a large institute. This is helpful in providing secure communications among the different departments of the Institute. This makes the management of the network easy and also reduces the cost and overhead of the network management.
2. Due to IP security, it is possible to call any person through the computer system. IP security allows remote access over the Internet.
3. It provides authentication and confidentiality to the connection.
4. In banking sector, IPsec provides services like secure communication.
5. IPsec is useful to encrypt or authenticate the entire traffic at the IP level.
6. IPsec is useful in distributed applications.

12.2.3 Benefits of IPsec

IPsec has the following benefits:

1. In firewall, IPsec restricts the bypass of all the traffic.
2. It provides strong security to the traffics within the intranet or extranet.
3. It is transparent to applications as well as to the end-users.
4. It also provides security to the end-users.

12.2.4 Overview of IPsec

The components of IPsec are

1. Authentication Header (AH)
2. Encapsulating Security Payload (ESP) header
3. Key Management Protocol (ISAKMP/OAKLEY)

To achieve strong security such as authentication and confidentiality, AH and ESP headers can be attached to IP packet. Authentication Header (AH) can provide security and integrity to the IP packet, whereas Encapsulating Security Payload (ESP) provides encryption in addition to integrity to the IP packet. The IP security protocol can be used for host-host, host-gateway or gateway-gateway communications. Considering the security aspect, host-host communication is the most secure communication. In other two cases, the security attacks will be more because behind the gateway, the trusted hosts become untrusted. Then, it is difficult for the untrusted systems to attack in any kind of implementation.

Integrity, authentication and confidentiality are provided to the IP packets using the Encapsulating Security Payload (ESP) header. For this, ESP header can be used alone or in combination with AH or in a nested way by using tunnel mode. The ESP header can be implemented as host to host, host to gateway or gateway to gateway. The IP packet first contains the IP header, then the ESP header, and then, a higher-level protocol header (if we use transport mode) or the encapsulated IP header (if we use tunnel mode). Gateway-to-gateway ESP implementation is dangerous for VPN. For IPv4, IPsec is optional but for IPv6, IPsec is mandatory.

Important RFCs are as follows:

1. RFC 2401: Overview of IPsec architecture
2. RFC 2402: AH specification

3. RFC 2406: ESP specification
4. RFC 2408: ISAKMP specification
5. RFC 2412: OAKLEY specification

12.2.5 Working of IPsec

IPsec is a set of protocols and services, which provides a complete security to the network. It provides security using the Authentication Header (AH) and the Encapsulating Security Payload (ESP). IPsec protocols define IP header options (for IPv4) or header extensions (for IPv6). There is Security Parameter Index (SPI) in both the header. The combination of SPI, AH or ESP and the identity (the other end) forms the Security Association (SA). There are two types of databases—Security Policy Database (SPD) and Security Association Database (SAD). The security database contains the information about security policies. This database is known as *Security Policy Database (SPD)*. The sender machine uses SPD and decides about the security provided to the packet. This security is decided depending on destination IP address or transport layer port number.

Another database contains security parameters, called *Security Association Database (SAD)*. These parameters are associated with all active Security Association. The sender machine checks the appropriate selector to determine the SPD for that referenced destination IP address or transport layer port number. Then, the host looks up the SA in SAD to select the security parameters for that packet. One more aspect of IPsec is the key management. It consists of the issues of key selection and distribution. IPsec has two protocols for these issues—the Internet Security Association and Key Management Protocol (ISAKMP) and OAKLEY Key Determination Protocol. We will discuss both these protocols later on in this chapter.

12.3 IPv6

There was less number of addresses provided by IPv4. As the use of Internet spread rapidly, this address space got vanished rapidly. IPv6 provides flexibility for further growth and expansion. Let us discuss the address and header features of IPv6 in detail.

Address

1. It supports 128-bit address space.
2. There are two parts in an address—a network address and a host address. High order bits indicates the network address and low order bits indicate the host address. For example, the IP address is 227.45. 62.122 to indicate that the network address is 227.45 and the host address is 62.122.
3. Three types of addresses are—unicast, multicast and anycast.
4. A unicast address acts as an identifier for a single interface.
5. A multicast address acts as an identifier for a group of interfaces that may belong to the different nodes.

6. Anycast addresses acts as an identifier for a set of interfaces that may belong to the different nodes.

Figure 12.2 shows the comparison of address length for IPv6 and IPv4.

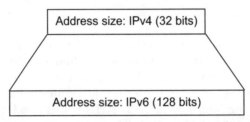

Figure 12.2 Address length for IPv6 and IPv4.

In IPv6, the address size is large as compared to IPv4. It is 128-bit in IPv6 as compared to 32-bit of IPv4. Therefore, the address space is increased significantly for IPv6. The size of address space is huge, as for every single bit of size address length, the available number of addresses are double. For IPv4, 2^{32} addresses are available, whereas for IPv6, 2^{128} addresses are available. IPv6 addresses are represented in hexadecimal number; so, there are 32 hexadecimal digits (each hexadecimal digit is represented by four bit binary; so, $32 \times 4 = 128$ bits). In each address, there are eight groups and each group has 4 hexadecimal digits. These groups are separated by colons in between them. This improves the readability of the address.

The IPv6 address looks like

2014:0110:0000:0000:0010:09C5:523A:2341

DNS plays an important role, as manually it is difficult for typing these addresses. To make it easy, some abbreviations are allowed, which help in shortening the address length. The above address can be written as:

2014:110: 0: 0: 10:9C5:523A:2341

If there is a sequence of all-zero groups in the IP address, then each group is reduced to zero and separated by colons in between them. For example,

0:0:0:0:0:0:0:1 may be written as ::1

0:0:0:0:0:0:0:0 ->:: (unspecified address)

This helps in reducing the size of an address and also in making it readable. The initial bits of an address form the prefix. In a network prefix, the size of bits is separated with '/' (back slash). The format to write prefix is given below:

prefix::/size of the bits

For example, 2014:110:2345:1234::/64.

It denotes the network address as 2014:110:2345:1234 and it contains the addresses from 2014:110:2345:1234:: to 2014:110:2345:1234:: ffff.ffff.ffff.ffff

Special addresses in IPv6 are given below:

1. *::/96*: The prefix zero shows the addresses compatible with the IPv4 protocol.

2. ::/128: An address with all zeroes is referred to as an unspecified address. It is used in the software for addressing

3. ::1/128: It is used to refer to the local host.

4. 2001:db8::/32: It is a documentation prefix. This is used to indicate an example.

5. *fec0::/10*: This is a site-local prefix. This address is valid within the local addressing.

6. *c00::/7*: It is used for routing within a group of cooperating sites. It provides a 40-bit pseudorandom number to reduce the risk of address conflicts.

7. *ff00::/8*: It is used to indicate the multicast addresses.

8. *fe80::/10*: This is link-local prefix. It denotes that the address is valid only in the local network.

Header

IPv6 uses the datagram format defined in RFC 2460 [RFC2460]. The header size for IPv6 is fixed so that it can increase the processing speed. This helps in improving the performance of IPv6 over IPv4. The IPv4 header format has a number of fields. In addition to the fixed fields, some unpredictable optional fields are also present. This leads to variable header sizes. The size of IPv6 is double than that of IPv4 header. IPv6 header has different approaches. First approach is that the basic header is minimised and the second approach is that the header has a constant size. In the first approach only essential fields are included in the header. Remaining fields are stored in the extension header. This extension header is attached with the packets, if required.

Version	Traffic class	Flow label	
Payload length		Next header	Hop limit
Source address			
Destination address			

Figure 12.3 IPv6 header format.

The IPv6 header format is shown in Figure 12.3. Each header has a number of fields. The contents of individual fields are given below:

Version: It is the identification of version of protocol use. The version field has value 6 to identify IPv6.

Traffic class: This field is used for the Quality of Service (QoS). This is used to set priorities to different addresses for processing.

Flow label: This field indicates that a flow is related to a particular group of datagrams.

Payload length: This field indicates the size of the datagram payload. The size includes all the contents of header and extension header. The size is in bytes and maximum size of payload is 64 KB.

Next header: This field indicates the header of the next protocol. It indicates the data of the next header.

Hop limit: This field indicates the life time of a datagram. The initiator node assigns some value to this field. This indicates for how much time a datagram is valid in communication. After reaching to every new node, the value decreases by 1. When the value reaches zero, the datagram is dropped, i.e., the destination is reached and an ICMP message is sent to the sender. If the datagram hops in a loop, then due to hop limit the datagram circulates only for a limited time. This protects the traffic deadlock in IPv6.

Source address: This field indicates the identification of the sender of the datagram. It contains the address of the source node from where the datagram is originated.

Destination address: This field indicates the identification of the receiver of the datagram. It contains the address of the destination node. It indicates the address at which the datagram is to be delivered.

Extension headers: Datagram has some additional information which is not that much important. This additional information should be placed in optional fields at the end of header. These additional fields are called *extension headers*. These fields are added only if required, i.e., these are optional fields. These are appended after the main header. There are any number of extension headers to a datagram. To identify these headers, some mechanism is necessary, called *header chaining*. It is implemented using the next header field in the basic header. The next header field is used to determine the next extension header or the header of the datagram of the next layer protocol. Many datagrams have only basic header and there is no need for extension header. Every extension header has next header field, which identifies the following data. This helps in header chaining. The last header contains the information about the protocol it belongs.

Routing header: This field indicates the routing information of the datagram. There are two types of routing header—type 0 (used to allow an arbitrary checkpoint sequence) and type 1 (used for mobility purposes). Type of routing header is given in a field inside the extension header. The routing header contains two types of information:

1. Addresses for the checkpoint sequence
2. Counter which indicates the number of checkpoints remained to visit

The sender, who wants the above features in the datagram, adds the routing header to the datagram. The address of first checkpoint is placed into the basic header under the destination address field. The sequences of remaining checkpoints are placed in the router header. The last sequence is the address of the next protocol.

Fragmentation: IPv6 packet size is large and many technologies cannot support transport of these packets. They have some limitations for transmission of these packages, called *Maximum Transmission Unit* (*MTU*). If the IPv6 header is smaller than the MTU, then the packets are transmitted as usual, but if it is larger than MTU, then it is divided into smaller headers. This process is called *fragmentation*. Each fragment is transported individually and integrated by the receiver to generate the original header. Every fragment contains part of the original data. Each fragment contains a fragment extension header, containing the following three fields:

Identification: It is unique for every original header and used to detect fragments of the same header.

Offset: It gives the position of data carried by current fragment in the original header.

More fragments flag: It announces if this is the last fragment or another fragment follows.

The receiving node collects all the fragments and groups them using identification values. The proper ordering of the fragments is possible using the offsets. More fragment flag gives the information that there are no more fragments left; it is able to reconstruct the original header. In this way, fragmentation allows the larger header to be transmitted using the lower layer technology. The drawback is that the performance is reduced due to overhead added. At the receiver's side, the collection and assembling the header in proper order require some buffer for temporary storage as well as some timer. These reduce the reliability of the header connection. If there is loss of one or more fragments, the assembly of original header is affected because each header contains part of original information. Therefore, minimum use of fragmentation is recommended. Contrary to IPv4, IPv6 tries to minimise fragmentation by applying some restrictions:

1. IPv6 restricts the MTU only up to 1280 bytes which decreases the need for fragmentation.
2. IPv6 permits to fragment a datagram only by the sender node and not the intermediate node.
3. For all the parties, each node has to keep the track of the path MTU. This improves the communication.

Options: Header has some additional information which is given in the option field. Option field is of two types—options committed to every in-between node those forwarding the datagram, and options intended for the destination host only.

12.4 IPSEC, IPv4, AND IPv6

IPsec provides security services to IPv4 and IPv6. The ways to provide these services are different for IPv4 and IPv6.

Every IP packet contains 40 octets. There are various fields in the header. We will discuss this in detail later on.

If any option is there, it can be accommodated in the extension headers that follow the IPv6 header. IPv6 has an extension header through which IPsec services are provided.

The order of header in IPsec within IPv4 and IPv6 is important. For example, suppose encryption of the payload is required first, and then, the integrity of the payload. In this case, AH is used first to provide integrity, and then, ESP header is used to provide confidentiality. If integrity is required first, and then, the confidentiality, then in such case, ESP should be used first and then AH. This order basically depends on the application and services required.

Internet Protocol

A set of rules, which defines the communication process of the computers over the network, is called *Internet Protocol*. Every computer in the network should follow these rules. There are two versions of Internet Protocol—IP version 4 (IPv4) and IP version 6 (IPv6). IPv4 has many drawbacks. IPv6 removes these drawbacks and supports global networking.

IPv4

The first version of Internet Protocol is IPv4 and was set up in 1981. It widely supports the Internet traffic but there were only 4 billion IP addresses. These addresses were not sufficient to last this version for long time. The address size of IPv4 is 32 bits.

IPv6

The next version of Internet Protocol is IPv6 and was deployed in 1999. It provides a much larger address pool as compared to IPv4. The address size of IPv6 is 128 bits.

Difference between IPv4 and IPv6

The major difference between these two versions of Internet Protocol is the number of IP addresses provided. IPv6 has a large number of addresses as compared to IPv4. But the functioning of both the versions is same. Today's most networks use IPv6 and also support the addresses of IPv4 and IPv6. Table 12.1 gives the comparison between IPv4 and IPv6.

Table 12.1 Comparison between IPv4 and IPv6

	IPv4	IPv6
Deployed	1981	1999
Address size	32-bit	128-bit
Address format	Dotted decimal notation is used 192.149.252.76	Hexadecimal notation is used 3FFE:F200:0234:AB00: 0123:4567:8901:ABCD
Prefix notation	192.149.0.0/24	3FFE:F200:0234::/48
Number of addresses	2^{32} = ~4,294,967,296	2^{128} = ~340,282,366, 920,938,463,463,374, 607,431,768,211,456

12.5 IPSEC PROTOCOLS AND OPERATIONS

Security Association (SA)

IPsec has many important components. One of the basic components is Security Association (SA). It is one-way relation between sender system and receiver system. It is a logical bond between the two computers in communication. It provides protection to the data for unidirectional traffic by using IPsec protocols. It describes how the parties in communication will utilise the security. It is a relationship or contract between these entities which all parties must agree upon. These services are provided by SA using either AH or ESP. AH and ESP cannot be used at a time by one SA. If there are two or more SAs, then some SAs may use AH and some may use ESP. For typical IP traffic, two SAs are used—one for source and the other for host—for the traffic flows in each direction. SA is considered as unidirectional. Security Association (SA) is required for the execution of AH and ESP header.

The parameters of Security Association (SA) are as follows:

1. Security Parameter Index (SPI)
2. Destination address
3. Protocol (AH or ESP) identifier

The SPI contains the information for identifying the SA. It is a bit string assigned to SA. AH and ESP contain SPI to allow the responder to select an SA for communication. Destination address contents is the address of end system, e.g., router. Protocol identifier indicates whether the SA is in AH or ESP.

An SA is normally unidirectional. There should be two SPIs for communication between two hosts, one for each direction. In IPsec, two modes are used for secure transmission of data. These modes of operations are transport mode and tunnel mode these are described below:

Transport mode: Transport mode is used to protect the upper layer protocols. Protection is applied only to the payload of a packet. The IP header remains unchanged. In this mode the IPsec information is added between the IP header and the remainder of the packet. It is used between the end nodes and it allows end-to-end security. The packet sent by the source host also secures it and the destination host can verify the security. This authentication can be done either by decrypting the packet or by certifying the authentication.

Tunnel mode: Tunnel mode is used to protect all the contents of the IP packets. In this mode, the original packet remains unchanged. Additional header and information are appended to the packet. The gateway accepts the packets and encapsulates the set of IPsec headers and then forwarded this encapsulated headers to the other end of tunnel At the other end, the original packets are extracted and sent to their destination. Tunnel mode provides security to the packet by encapsulating it only inside the tunnel, but these packets are already secured by the sender.

For the communication between the two users, transport mode is good, whereas for VPN, tunnel mode is good. If gateways are used for secure communication, then tunnel mode is useful. Tunnel mode is mostly used for firewall-to-firewall communications.

12.6 AUTHENTICATION HEADER (AH) PROTOCOL

The Authentication Header (AH) protocol provides connectionless data integrity and authentication of data origin for IP packets. Sometimes, AH can provide protection against replays attacks. We know that data integrity ensures that the contents of the packet remain unchanged in transit. The authentication enables receiving node to authenticate the sender or packet and filter the packet, if it is not authenticated.

The authentication for AH and ESP is a little different. ESP generally authenticates the packet payload. AH authenticates roughly the complete packet with its headers. The different fields of authentication header are next header, payload length, reserved field, Security Parameter Index (SPI), sequence number. Authentication Header with its fields is shown in Figure 12.4.

Next header (8 bits)	Payload length (8 bits)	Reserved field (16 bits)
SPI		
Sequence number field		
Authentication data		

Figure 12.4 Authentication Header.

The next header field gives the address of the header immediately after this header. Payload length gives the length of AH. SPI indicates the SA used to generate the header. Sequence number gives the sequence number of the packet. For all AH and ESP headers, the sequence number field is mandatory. It provides security against replays attacks. The sequence number for each packet is assigned by SA and it is unique for each packet. The first packet has sequence number 1 and it is incremented sequentially. The receiving host checks the sequence number to use the anti-replay service for the respective SA. If the receiving host receives a packet with a sequence number which it has already received, then that packet is discarded.

There are two modes—transport mode or tunnel mode—which are used to secure transmission of packets. AH may use any one of the two modes. In transport mode, AH is tagged before the IP header of a datagram. It is used only for end-to-end communications. It provides security to the higher layer protocols and only selected header fields. In tunnel mode, AH is appended after the IP header and before a high layer protocol. Tunnel mode provides gateway security. In tunnel mode, AH protects the complete inner IP packets and the IP header. Some authentication algorithms use AH to provide non-repudiation. But AH cannot support confidentiality of the packets.

12.6.1 AH Transport Mode

The default mode for IPsec is transport mode. It is used only for end-to-end communications. Transport mode provides security only to the IP payload by encrypting it. This mode protects the upper layer protocols, including TCP segments, a UDP message, and an ICMP message. The details of transport mode are shown in Figure 12.5.

IP header	TCP/UDP header		Data
IP header	AH	TCP/UDP header	Data

Figure 12.5 Transport mode.

AH provides security services, which include authentication, integrity and anti-replay protection for the entire packet. AH protects the complete inner IP packets and the IP header. Sometimes, AH is used to provide non-repudiation, but it cannot be used to provide confidentiality.

For example, two users A and B communicate to each other. User A sends the data from his computer to user B on his computer. The packet transmitted by user A's computer contains the IP header, the AH, and the data. This means user B can be sure that the data is sent by user A and it is received as it is.

12.6.2 AH Tunnel Mode

In tunnel mode with IP payload, IP header is also encrypted. Tunnel mode protects the entire IP packet. The packet is encapsulated with an AH or ESP header and an additional IP header. The address of the outer IP header indicates the end of the tunnel. The addresses of the encapsulated IP header are the source and destination addresses.

Tunnel mode protects the traffic flow between different networks. Tunnel mode provides security for the traffic, which flows through untrusted network.

As shown in Figure 12.6, AH tunnel mode encapsulates an IP packet, with an AH and IP header, and digitally signs the complete packet for integrity and authentication.

New IP header	AH	Original IP header	TCP/UDP header	Data

Figure 12.6 Tunnel mode.

12.7 ENCAPSULATING SECURITY PAYLOAD (ESP) PROTOCOL

ESP is similar to AH, but it can be used to provide more security. ESP is used to provide confidentiality and authentication. This includes confidentiality of message and traffic flow. These services can be provided between the two hosts, two gateways or between a host and a gateway. ESP supports IPv4 and IPv6.

Like AH, ESP also has two modes—tunnel mode and transport mode. We can use only ESP or combinations of ESP with AH.

The ESP provides the following services:

1. Confidentiality using encryption
2. Authentication
3. Integrity using message digest
4. Replay attack protection
5. Limited traffic flow confidentiality

The confidentiality is provided using encryption technique. Authentication is provided using public key cryptosystem and integrity is provided using hashing or message digest algorithms such as SHA-1 and MD5. ESP uses sequence number for each packet. This is helpful in identifying the duplications in the packets as well as in avoiding the replay attacks. ESP also provides traffic flow confidentiality, but this is only when the tunnel mode is used. These services are provided depending on the options selected during Security Association (SA) establishment and on the network topology.

The ESP header is inserted in the packet after the IP header and before the next layer protocol header in transport mode or before an encapsulated IP header in tunnel mode. The ESP header contains different fields. These fields are—Security Parameter Index (SPI) of size 32 bits, sequence number of size 32 bits, payload data of variable length, padding which uses minimum 0 byte and maximum 255 bytes, pad length of size 8 bits, next header of size 8 bits, and authentication data of variable bit length. ESP header is shown in Figure 12.7. Each of the fields is discussed here.

SPI (32 bits)		
Sequence number (32 bits)		
Payload data (variable)		
Padding (0 to 255 bytes)	Pad length (8 bits)	Next header (8 bits)
Authentication data (variable)		

Figure 12.7 ESP header.

Security Parameters Index (SPI)

This is a mandatory field, with 32-bit size. It is a random value generated from the combination of destination IP address and security protocol (ESP). It is used to uniquely identify the SA used to generate this encrypted packet. The SPI values from 1 to 255 are reserved and may be used in future. These values are normally not assigned to any packet by IANA. Reserved values are used only if these are is specified in an RFC. It is normally selected by the destination node after the selection of an SA. The zero value of SPI is reserved for the local hosts for implementation-specific use and must not be transmitted on the wire.

Sequence Number

This is a mandatory field, with 32-bit size. This field is always present. This is used as a counter and for every new packet, its value is incremented sequentially like counter. Sequence number is used to prevent the replay attacks. Though the sender always transmits this field with a packet, it is decided by the receiver whether to use this field or not. When the SA is established between the two users, both the sender and the receiver should initialise their counters to zero. The packets sent by SA and the sequence number assigned to the first packet are represented as 1. For subsequent packets, the sequence numbers are 2, 3, 4,..., respectively. If anti-replay is enabled, the transmitted sequence number must never be reused. In this case, both the counters (sender's and receiver's counters) must be reset. This can be done by establishing a new SA and using a new key. This is done before the transmission of the $2^{32\text{nd}}$ packet (i.e., the last packet) on an SA.

Payload Data

This is a mandatory field with variable size. The contents of this field are the data described by the next header field.

Padding

The size of this field is variable. Padding is always required, irrespective of the algorithm used for encryption. Minimum 0 byte and maximum 255 bytes are used as padding.

Pad Length

The size of this field is 8 bits. The length of the padding bytes used is given by this field.

Next Header

The size of this field is 8 bits. The payload format is described using this field.

Authentication Data

This is an optional field with variable size. The size is decided by the authentication function.

ESP header uses two modes—transport mode and tunnel mode. In transport mode, higher-layer protocol (e.g. TCP or UDP) is encapsulated inside ESP and a new IP header is appended. This makes an impact on the performance of the systems in SA, but not on the routers or the systems outside SA. In tunnel mode, the complete IP datagram is encapsulated within the ESP header. ESP processing is more complex than AH processing.

The ESP header may be used in combination with the AH to provide strong security. Using AH in the datagram and before encapsulating, ESP header provides integrity, authentication, and confidentiality to the packet.

12.7.1 ESP Transport Mode

In transport mode, only the payload is protected and not the complete packet, i.e., the header is not protected in ESP transport mode. ESP can be used alone or in combination with AH, as shown in Figure 12.8.

For example, two users A and B communicate with each other. User A sends data from his computer to user B on his computer. User A's computer encrypts the payload and signs the datagram to provide integrity. Upon receipt, user B's computer verifies the integrity of the packet first, and then, decrypts that payload data. Now, user B is sure that the data is sent by user A and the same data is received as sent by user A.

Figure 12.8 Transport mode.

12.7.2 ESP Tunnel Mode

In tunnel mode, an IP packet is encapsulated with both an ESP and IP headers and an ESP authentication trailer. This is shown in Figure 12.9.

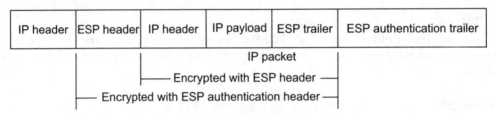

Figure 12.9 Tunnel mode.

Some part of the packet is digitally signed to provide integrity and authentication. Some part of the packet is encrypted to provide confidentiality. In tunnel mode, a new header is added with the packet. This header is also encrypted with the part of the packet. After the ESP header, the original header is attached, followed by ESP trailer. Then, the total packet is encrypted except ESP authentication trailer. The complete ESP payload is then encapsulated within a new tunnel header. There is no need to encrypt this new tunnel header because this information is used only to show the traffic path (route) to the packet from origin to the endpoint of the tunnel.

When the packet is sent across a public network, it selects the destination path using IP address of the gateway. The gateway decrypts the packet and discards the ESP header. The gateway now uses the original IP header to get the address of the receiving node. In the tunnel mode, we can use the combination of ESP and AH protocol so that authentication, integrity and confidentiality for the packet can be achieved.

IPsec tunnel mode secures IP traffic between either two IP addresses or two IP subnets. If the tunnel is used between two computers systems, then there is same IP address outside and inside the AH or ESP payload.

12.7.3 Cryptographic Algorithms

IPsec provides confidentiality, authentication and integrity using encryption and authentication algorithms. The selection of algorithms is based on the security required for the application. IPsec decides the layer of security using ISAKMP and SA protocols.

12.7.4 Usage

The strength of IPsec depends on the encryption algorithm, the strength of the key and the key management protocol. The security of the implementation depends on the security of the operating system. The AH and ESP header can be used in many scenarios. Here, we will discuss some of them.

Use with Firewalls

Firewalls used with IP frequently require to parse the headers and options. Its use determines whether the transport protocol is UDP or TCP with their port number. If the firewall is not attached with SA, then also it can be used with the AH. But in this case, firewall is not be able to decrypt the higher layer protocol. So, it is not be able to read the information about the protocol or port number. If the firewall is attached with SA, then it can decrypt the higher layer protocol and can be able to get the information about the protocol and port number. This information is used by firewall to perform per-packet filtering and also to verify whether its data used for access control and authentication is correct or not.

Depending on the application, the firewall is selected. For example, suppose some company has more than one campus. These campuses are connected with each other using IP service. This IP service may use limited encrypting firewall, as it is used only for internal communications.

Use with IP Multicast

The Security Parameters Indices (SPIs) are receiver-oriented. Therefore, it is useful for multicasting.

Use to Provide Quality of Service (QoS) Protection

Nowadays, Quality of Service has gained more importance and it is user-oriented. The user wants authentication about the origin of the data. Therefore, authentication of the packet should be provided by the sender of the packet along with the packet. This information for authentication is given in Authentication Header. Within router, for packet classification, this authentication is important. In this case, the IPv6 traffic flow identifier may act as a low level identifier.

Use in Multilevel Networks

In a multilevel network, to communicate data at different levels, a single network is used. It requires strong access control so that unauthorised users cannot access it. In this case of strong access control, the AH secures the multilevel networks. If the packet contains sensitivity labels related to IP, then such packet is authenticated using AH. Generally, IPv6 uses hidden information related to SA. But this information is not attached with each packet during transmission. ESP key management uses different keys. For each sensitivity information, separate key is used so that security is provided to multilevel networks. Also, there are different keys for AH header. Selection of key depends on the information contained in the packet. IPsec provides different services using AH and ESP header. This is summarised in Table 12.2.

Table 12.2 IPsec services

	AH	ESP (encryption and authentication)	ESP (encryption only)
Data origin authentication	✓	✓	
Integrity	✓	✓	
Confidentiality		✓	✓
Limited traffic flow confidentiality		✓	✓
Replay detection	✓	✓	✓

12.8 ISAKMP PROTOCOL

ISAKMP stands for Internet Security Association and Key Management Protocol (ISAKMP). It is defined in RFC2408. It was developed by the IETF Network Working Group. The use of Internet is increased rapidly. Therefore, the security requirements of Internet users also are increased. Number of cryptographic algorithms and other security mechanisms provide security required by these users. First, we will see an overview of ISAKMP. It is intended to support the SA management for security protocols at all layers. It centralises the SA management and reduces the amount of duplicate functionality.

12.8.1 Overview

ISAKMP is separated into two points—Security Association (SA) and key management, key exchange protocol. ISAKMP defines procedures and packet formats for the SA. It helps the SA to establish, negotiate, modify and delete the associations. An SA is a contract between different parties in communication that they are agreed upon certain rules. Key management handles the key generation and key exchange between different parties. These techniques decides the security in the communication. As we know, authentication enables the two parties to trust on each other. ISAKMP provides a structure for establishing security associations between the parties in communication and use of keys. ISAKMP implementation is shown in Figure 12.10.

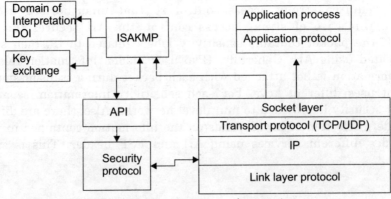

Figure 12.10 ISAKMP implementation.

12.8.2 Terms and Definitions

1. *Security protocol:* It is a protocol which provides different security services to secure transmission of data. Examples of security protocols are IPsec, ESP and AH.

2. *Protection suite:* It is a list of security services provided by using different security protocols. For example, DES algorithm to provide confidentiality can be used by ESP and message digest algorithm, MD5 for digital signature can be used by AH.

3. *Security association:* It is a set of rules used to secure communication. It is based on a protocol selected.

4. *Security Parameter Index (SPI):* It is an identifier for an SA within a protocol.

5. *Domain of Interpretation (DOI):* It defines the format for different fields such as payload, situation, exchange types, and naming conventions for security policies, or encryption algorithms.

6. *Situation:* It is a set of all security-related information. A party selects the service using it.

7. *Proposal:* It contains a list of services with priorities.

8. *Payload:* It is used to transfer data.

9. *Exchange type:* It defines the number and order of message exchange in ISAKMP.

12.8.3 Security Association Negotiation

Before the start of data exchange, the entities in communication must negotiate an SA. In ISAKMP, there are two steps of SA negotiation. Negotiations during second step reduces the effort for the first step negotiations. In the first step, one SA is established for one security protocol. This provides protection for the following traffic. In the second step, for different security protocols, more SAs can be bargained and established. As there are two steps for SA establishment, it is costly at the beginning. But it has some advantages also. Many times, second step bargaining can take place again and again, which increases the cost. Some security services provided by the first step SA may be used in the second step. This reduces the effort for second step negotiations. If some error occurs, the reauthentication of the entities is not required, as two-step SA negotiation is used. This is the second advantage of the two-step SA.

Once a security association is established between the two parties, any party can start negotiation. A cookie is generated by each party. These requirements for cookies are given below:

1. The cookie should depend on the communication parties.
2. The generating party generates cookies acceptable to it.
3. The cookie generation process should be fast.

These conditions help in protecting against the attacks. For every new SA establishment, new cookies are generated. The SA provides security service as per the order of message payload.

12.8.4 ISAKMP Payloads

A number of payloads are there in an ISAKMP message. Payload always starts with an ISAKMP header of fixed format. This ISAKMP header format is shown in

Figure 12.11. The header contains information about state, payloads and is useful to prevent attacks.

Initiator cookie (64 bits)				
Responder cookie (64 bits)				
Next payload (8 bits)	Major version (4 bits)	Minor version (4 bits)	Exchange type (8 bits)	Flags (8 bits)
Message ID (32 bits)				
Length (32 bits)				

Figure 12.11 ISAKMP message header.

These are described below:

1. *Initiator cookie:* It initiates establishment, notification or deletion of SA.

2. *Responder cookie:* For the first message, it is null. It gives response to the establishment of request, notification or deletion of SA.

3. *Next payload:* It shows the type of the first payload in the message. The value with its description and reference is shown in Table 12.3.

Table 12.3 Values of next Payload with Description

Value	Description	Reference
0	None	
1	SA	
2	Proposal	
3	Transform	
4	Key exchange	
5	ID	
6	Certificate	RFC 2408
7	Certificate request	
8	MD	
9	Sign	
10	Nonce	
11	Notification	
12	Delete	
13	Vendor ID	
14		
15	SAK, SA KEK Payload	
16	SAT, SA TEK payload	
17	Key download	RFC 3547
18	Sequence number	
19	Proof of possession	
20	NAT-D, NAT discovery	RFC 3947
21	NAT-OA, NAT original address	
22 to 127		
128 to 255	Private use	

IP Security

4. **Major version:** It shows the major version of protocol.
5. **Minor version:** It shows the minor version of protocol.
6. **Exchange type:** It shows the exchange type. It gives the order of payload.
7. **Flags:** It shows the options that are set for the ISAKMP exchange. The format of flag field is shown in Figure 12.12.

0	1	2	3	4	5	6	7
Reserved					A	C	E

Figure 12.12 Formats for Flag Field for the ISAKMP.

Here, bits 1 to 4 are reserved and bits 5, 6 and 7 are used to show the status for authentication, commit and encryption, respectively.

(a) *A–Authentication only:* It checks the integrity of the data and allows transmission. Encryption is not used.
(b) *C–Commit:* It is used for synchronisation of signal key exchange.
(c) *E–Encryption:* All the payloads after the header are encrypted.

8. **Message ID:** It is a unique message identifier. It is generated by the initiator.
9. **Length:** It gives the size of the total message. It includes header and payloads size.

Figure 12.13 shows the format for a payload header.

Next payload	Reserved	Payload length
(8 bits)	(8 bits)	(16 bits)

Figure 12.13 Payload header.

(a) *Next payload:* This shows the type of the next payload in the message.
(b) *Reserved:* This field is unused, and it is set to 0.
(c) *Payload length:* It gives the size of the payload including header.

The next payload field allows chaining so that a payload can easily be appended and verified.

Security Association Payload

The SA payload is used to negotiate security elements. It shows DOI and the situation. The negotiation takes place using DOI and security elements. Figure 12.14 shows the payload fields.

Next payload	Reserved	Payload length
Domain of Interpretation (DOI)		
Situation		

Figure 12.14 Security Association payload.

Proposal Payload

It consists of security methods or transforms. It is used to secure communications. The list of transforms is called *proposal*. It specifies the security protocol and the related transforms. The Transform # shows the number of transforms will trail for the current security protocol. Figure 12.15 shows the payload fields.

Next payload	Reserved	Payload length	
Proposal #	Protocol-ID	SPI size	Transform #
SPI (variable)			

Figure 12.15 Proposal payload.

Transform Payload

A transform is a method used for the security protocol mentioned in the proposal payload. Figure 12.16 shows the fields of the transform payload. It defines the DOI-specific transforms and the attributes of SA.

Next payload	Reserved	Payload length
Transform #	Transform-ID	Reserved2
SA Attributes		

Figure 12.16 Transform payload.

Key Exchange Payload

The key exchange payload supports key exchange algorithms, e.g., RSA, OAKLEY and Diffie–Hellman. Figure 12.17 shows the payload fields.

Next payload	Reserved	Payload length
Key exchange data		

Figure 12.17 Key exchange payload.

We will see the payload type in brief below:

1. ***Signature payload:*** It is used for verifying integrity of the message.

2. ***Identification payload:*** It is used for exchanging identification information between the communication parties. It contains DOI specific data.

3. ***Certificate payload:*** It is used to transport certificates or certificate-related information. It supports different certificate types, e.g., DNS Signed Key, X.509, PGP or Kerberos. These can appear in any ISAKMP message.

4. ***Certificate request payload:*** It is used when an entity requests one or more certificates via ISAKMP.

5. ***Hash payload:*** It contains hash value for the message generated by hashing algorithm. The hash algorithm is selected during SA establishment. The integrity of a

data is verified using the hash value. A hash function is applied to part of a message or ISAKMP state.

6. *Nonce payload:* It contains random value. It is also used to prevent replay attack using current date and time.

7. *Notification payload:* It is used to notify about error or status information to the entities.

8. *Delete payload:* Using this, an initiator can remove the SA identifier from its database. It shows that the communication between the sender and the receiver has been ended. It is the intimation given by the initiator to the responder.

9. *Vendor ID payload:* It contains constant defined by the vendor for identification of remote experiments of the vendor. This allows to maintain backward compatibility with the previous versions.

12.8.5 ISAKMP Exchange Types

ISAKMP agrees to create exchanges for the SA establishment and keying material. For ISAKMP, there are five exchange types. These provide one or more security services to exchange itself and the information transmit through the communication channel. It includes only the necessary messages and payloads. New exchange types can be created and have to be defined in the SA payload's DOI. The following notations (Table 12.4) are used to exchange message and payload between the initiating and responding entities.

Table 12.4 Notations for ISAKMP Exchange Types

Notations	Descriptions
H	An ISAKMP header whose exchange type is the mode, when written as HDR*, it indicates payload encryption
SA	An SA negotiation payload that embeds one or more proposal and transform payloads
KE	Key exchange payload
HASH	Hash value payload
SIG	Signature payload
A_{UTH}	Used in authentication algorithm
Nx	Nonce payload. x can be I for initiator and R for responder
ID_I	Identity information of the initiator
ID_R	Identity information of the responder
*	Shows that from here, all payloads are encrypted

Base Exchange

It allows key exchange and authentication data transmission in one message. Figure 12.18 shows the message communication for base exchange.

Msg	Initiator		Responder
1	H,SA,N_I	→	
2		←	H,SA,N_R
3	H,KE,ID_I,A_{UTH}	→	
4		←	H,KE,ID_R,A_{UTH}

Figure 12.18 Base exchange.

Initially, the initiator transmits a ISAKMP header, SA payload and the nonce to the responder. SA payload contains protection suites and transform payloads. Nonce prevents the replay attack. The responder sends the next message to the initiator. It contains the header, the protection suit selected and the nonce generated by the responder. Third message is sent by the initiator to the responder. It contains information related to key exchange and identification of the sender and the data required for authentication. Fourth message is sent by the responder. It contains the key information on which the responder agrees, identification of the responder and the data required for authentication. All the messages are secured using digital signature or hashing algorithms.

Identity Protection Exchange

It separates the key exchange from the information related to identity and authentication. Therefore, two additional messages are required. The shared secret key is used to encrypt the identity information. Figure 12.19 shows the used messages and payloads.

Msg	Initiator		Responder
1	H, SA	→	
2		←	H, SA
3	H, KE, N_I	→	
4		←	H, KE, N_R
5	H*, ID_I, A_{UTH}	→	
6		←	H*, ID_R, A_{UTH}

Figure 12.19 Identity protection exchange.

The first and second messages are worked as above. To share a secret key, the keying material is exchanged using third and fourth messages. The replay attack is used to avoid nonce payload. The fifth and sixth messages are used to encrypt and decrypt the messages using shared secret key.

Authentication Only Exchange

It exchanges only the information related to authentication. Therefore, no encryption is needed, and thus, no encryption key is required. This saves the time for key computing and encryption. Figure 12.20 shows the authentication exchange.

Msg	Initiator	Responder
1	H, SA, N_I →	
2		← H, SA, N_R, ID_R, A_{UTH}
3	H, ID_I, A_{UTH} →	

Figure 12.20 Authentication only exchange.

The first message contains a list of acceptable protection suites. The second message contains the chosen protection suite, a nonce payload, and identity information. The third message contains identity information and is protected by the authentication function. This message is sent by the initiator to the responder. So, there are only three messages.

Aggressive Exchange

It allows transmitting information related to security association, key exchange and authentication, together with the nonce generated by the initiator with his identification information. Therefore, identities are protected. Figure 12.21 shows the messages for aggressive exchange.

Msg	Initiator	Responder
1	H, SA, KE, $N_I ID_I$ →	
2		← H, SA, N_R, ID_R, A_{UTH}
3	H, ID_I, A_{UTH} →	

Figure 12.21 Aggressive exchange.

The first message is sent by the initiator to the responder. It contains one protection suite, keying material, ID information and nonce. The second message contains keying material, nonce and ID information protected by authentication function. This message is sent by the responder to the initiator. The third message is sent by the initiator to the responder again. It contains authentication function encrypted with shared secret key.

Informational Exchange

It is an exchange and not a message. It is used only for the management purpose. It is one-way transmission to inform other party about a notification or delete payload. Figure 12.22 shows the information exchange format.

Msg	Initiator	Responder
1	H*,N/D →	

Figure 12.22   Informational exchange.

If the information exchange takes place before the transmission of keying material, then the information is not protected. This happens in the first step of negotiation. If this transmission takes place after the transmission of keying material or establishment of SA, then the information is protected. In an ISAKMP information exchange, we can use any payload.

12.9   OAKLEY KEY DETERMINATION PROTOCOL

For secure communication, transmission of shared secure key should be transmitted securely. So, the establishment of secret keying material between the communication parties is very important. OAKLEY is a key determination protocol used for keying material establishment securely.

12.9.1   Overview

OAKLEY is a key determination protocol based on the Diffie–Hellman key exchange algorithm. It provides additional security in communication. It allows two authenticated parties to exchange and establish secret keying material. The two parties negotiate for encryption, key generation and authentication.

OAKLEY allows the following features.

1. Cookies exchange
2. Authenticates the Diffie–Hellman exchange to thwart man-in-the-middle attack
3. Uses nounces to detect replay attacks
4. Enables the parties to negotiate Diffie–Hellman public key values

The following abbreviations/notations are used for the OAKLEY Key Exchange Protocol.

C-I: Initiator Cookie
C-R: Responder Cookie
KID: Identification of the key
sKID: Keying material identified by KID
OK_KEYX: Message type is OAKLEY exchange
EID: Material is encrypted
NEID: Material is not encrypted
GR: Group

g^x, g^y: An element of a group is g, and x and y are random numbers generated by the entities

LEHA: List of encryption, hash and authentication algorithm selected

OEHA: One encryption, one hash and one authentication algorithm the responder has accepted

ID(I): Identities of the initiator

ID(R): Identities of the responder

E(x)Ki: Encryption of the material x using initiator's public key

S(x)Ki: Digital signature of the material x using initiator's private key

prf(a, b): Result of a pseudo random function applied to the material b; a is an index to choose one function out of a set of different pseudorandom functions

Ni: Nonces generated by the initiator

Nr: Nonces generated by the responder

These notations are used to describe the key exchange with OAKLEY.

12.10 KEY EXCHANGE PROTOCOL

An aggressive exchange between the initiator and the responder is shown in Figure 12.23.

Initiator								Responder
→								
C-I	0	OK_KEYX	GR	g^x	LEHA	NEID	ID(I)	
ID(R)	Ni	0 | S(ID(I))	| ID(R)	| Ni | 0 | GR	| g^x	| 0 | EHAO)Ki		
←								
C-I	C-R	OK_KEYX	GR	g^y	OEHA	NEID	ID(R)	
ID(I)	Nr	Ni | S(ID(R))	| ID(I)	| Nr | Ni | GR	| g^y	| g^x | OEHA)Kr		
→								
C-I	C-R	OK_KEYX	GR	g^x	OEHA	NEID	ID(I)	
ID(R)	Ni	Nr | S(ID(I))	| ID(R)	| Ni | Nr | GR	| g^x	| g^y | OEHA)Ki		

Figure 12.23 Key Exchange–An Aggressive example.

The first message is sent by the initiator to the responder. The message contains a cookie (C-I) generated by the initiator. The initiator chooses a random value x and calculates g^x, which is included in the message. The message again contains a list of algorithms for encryption, hash, and authentication (LEHA).

The responder collects the information from the message received and selects an appropriate algorithm and generates the digital signature. It verifies the signature, then generates a cookie and calculates the KID as C-I concatenates with C-R. The responder selects the value of y and calculates g^y. Then, the responder sends a message to the initiator, which contains the information digitally signed by the responder. After receiving the message, the initiator verifies the signature and collects the necessary data for key generation and authentication. The established key has the KID = C-I | C-R. The value of the key is sKID = prf(Ni | Nr, g^{xy} | C-I | C-R), with index Ni | Nr and the material g^{xy} | C-I | C-R. For signing the message, both the initiator and the responder have their public key and private key pair. The public keys can be established with ISAKMP before the OAKLEY protocol is used or they are obtained from a trusted third party.

12.11 VIRTUAL PRIVATE NETWORK

In the past, the term *Virtual Private Network* (*VPN*) was used with remote connectivity services such as Public Switched Telephone Network (PSTN). Nowadays, VPNs are linked with IP-based data networking. It is a network which uses public network (Internet) and also preserves the security of private networks.

Virtual: Virtual means not real. In a VPN, public network is used for private communication between two or more systems. Here, the communication takes place virtually.

Private: Private means to hide the information from the general public. In this communication, third party is not able to capture or modify the information.

Network: A group of two or more computer systems, which can communicate with each other is called *network*. A VPN is a network used to transport the information effectively over a long distance.

VPN uses private network to connect remote sites or users together. It gives the same capability to the organisation as private leased lines. The cost of VPN is less due to the use of public network.

Some important VPN technologies are as under:

1. *Trusted VPN:* A customer blindly depends on the leased circuits of a vendor and uses it to communicate without interruption. It is not secure.

2. *Secure VPN:* Encryption and decryption techniques are used by sender and receiver to secure the information passed to and fro. The networks which use encryption techniques are called *secure VPNs*.

3. *Hybrid VPN:* It is a combination of secure VPN and trusted VPN. A customer controls the secure parts of the VPN or the service provider, who controls the trusted part.

4. *Provider-provisioned VPN:* It is VPN that is managed by a service provider.

Advantages of VPN

1. VPNs are inexpensive.
2. VPNs provide framework for intranets and extranets.
3. VPNs enable legacy applications for the use of intranet.
4. Due to VPNs, use of private IP addresses has increased significantly.

Limitations of VPN

1. Detailed understanding of network security issue is required. One should take proper care for installation to protect the information on a public network (Internet).
2. There is no direct control of organisation on the VPN for reliability and performance.
3. There are compatibility issues with VPN products and solutions from different vendors. This is due to VPN technology standards.

Types of VPN

There are three types of VPN.

1. Remote access VPN: Remote access is also called *Virtual Private Dial-up Network* (*VPDN*). It is mainly used where remote access to a network becomes essential. It is used to allow remote access from an external location to a physical layer 2 network. It allows to connect to a LAN of an organisation from outside the campus. It allows to access the data between an organisation's private network and the remote users through a third party service provider. Figure 12.24 shows the remote access VPN architecture.

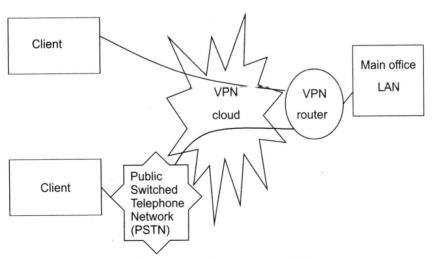

Figure 12.24 Remote access VPN.

The main advantages of remote access VPN are as follows:
(a) It reduces the cost of infrastructure such as modem and terminal server equipment.
(b) It provides scalability so that new users can be added easily.

2. *Intranet VPNs:* Intranet VPN is also called *site-to-site VPN*. It provides virtual circuits between different offices of an organisation over the Internet. It can be used when multiple remote locations can be made to join to a single network. Figure 12.25 shows the intranet VPN architecture.

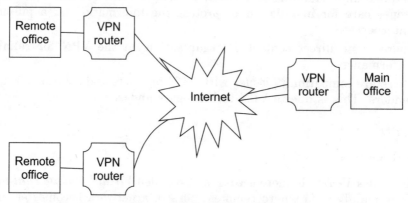

Figure 12.25 Intranet VPN.

The following are the main advantages of Intranet VPN:
(a) It reduces the cost of WAN bandwidth by effective use of bandwidth.
(b) Topologies are flexible.
(c) It uses bandwidth management traffic shaping to avoid congestion.

3. *Extranet VPN:* Extranet VPN can be used when different organizations work in a shared environment. It is more manageable and reliable. Figure 12.26 shows the extranet VPN architecture. It allows the partners, the suppliers and the customers to access the intranet securely.

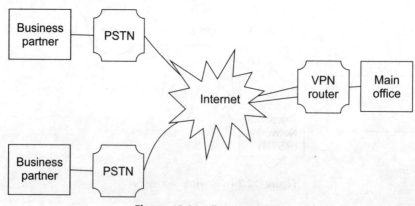

Figure 12.26 Extranet VPN.

VPN Security

In VPN, confidentiality is provided using encryption techniques. VPN uses tunneling process to transmit the encrypted data across the Internet. Tunnelling is a method for encapsulating one protocol in another protocol. In VPN, data integrity is provided using message digest techniques. By default, there is no strong authentication provided by VPN. To maintain the connection and data security VPN applies several measures. Some of the measures are as follows:

1. Firewall: VPN go hand-in-hand with firewall. Firewall provides a strong barrier between the private network and the Internet. It controls the access to private network resources and establishes trust between the user and the network. Earlier, firewall products provided only firewall security service, but nowadays, many firewall products support VPN functionality. To establish strong security, both VPN and firewall functionality are required.

2. Encryption: A VPN uses encryption and decryption techniques to protect the data from unauthorised users. It ensures that the data cannot be changed without detection as it flows through the Internet.

3. Internet Protocol Security (IPsec): IPsec provides strong security using strong authentication and encryption techniques. Systems with IPsec compliant can take advantage of this protocol. IPsec can encrypt data between router to router, computer to router, firewall to router and computer to server.

4. Authentication, Authorisation and Accounting (AAA): The access in a VPN environment is controlled by three servers—Authentication server, Authorisation server and Accounting server. They are known as *AAA servers*. To establish a session, a dial-up client sends a request. This request stands into the AAA server. AAA then checks the following:
  (a) Authentication of the sender
  (b) Authorisation of the sender
  (c) Accounting of the sender

Secure VPN Requirements

1. VPN must encrypt and authenticate all traffic to provide security.
2. All parties in the VPN must be agreed upon the security properties of the VPN
3. Outside the VPN, no one can affect the security properties of the VPN.

SUMMARY

IPsec is an Internet standard for network layer security used to provide additional security to the applications. To achieve strong security such as authentication and confidentiality, AH and ESP headers can be attached to IP packet. Authentication Header (AH) can provide security and integrity to the IP packet, whereas Encapsulating Security Payload (ESP) provides encryption in addition to integrity to the IP packet. A set of rules which defines the communication process of the computers over the network is called *Internet Protocol*. IPsec has IPv4 and IPv6 as the two versions. IPv6 provides huge number of addresses as compared to IPv4. ISAKMP is a combination of the concepts of security association, key management and authentication. OAKLEY is a key determination protocol based on the Diffie–Hellman key exchange algorithm. Virtual Private Network (VPN) is a private network, which makes use of public infrastructure or network, maintaining privacy using tunnelling protocol and security procedures.

EXERCISES

12.1 Discuss the strengths of IPsec.
12.2 What are the different security services offered by IPsec?
12.3 Describe the applications of IPsec.
12.4 What are the benefits of IPsec?
12.5 Discuss the working of IPsec.
12.6 What is security association in IPsec? How can it work?
12.7 Discuss the IPsec transport mode and tunnel mode.
12.8 Why is Authentication Header used?
12.9 Which security services are provided by Encapsulating Security Payload (ESP) protocol?
12.10 What is the basic difference between ESP and AH authentication services?
12.11 How do the AH transport mode and tunnel mode work?
12.12 Describe the transport and tunnel mode in ESP.
12.13 Discuss ESP header.
12.14 Describe the working of ISAKMP payloads.
12.15 Discuss the various fields in the ISAKMP header.
12.16 Discuss the various types of payload.
12.17 Discuss the OAKLEY Key Determination Protocol.
12.18 Explain different types of VPN.
12.19 Differentiate between IPv4 and IPv6.
12.20 Explain the addressing in IPv6.
12.21 Explain the header format for IPv6.

MULTIPLE CHOICE QUESTIONS

12.1 In IPsec, integrity to the message is provided using
   (a) Encryption algorithm
   (b) Digital signature
   (c) Hashing algorithm
   (d) None of the above
12.2 Which of the following standard represents the overview of IPsec security architecture?
   (a) RFC 2401
   (b) RFC 2402

(c) RFC 2406
(d) RFC 2408

12.3 The address size of IPv6 is
(a) 32 bits
(b) 64 bits
(c) 128 bits
(d) 256 bits

12.4 The address size of IPv4 is
(a) 32 bits
(b) 64 bits
(c) 128 bits
(d) 256 bits

12.5 In IPv6, the total number of addresses available are
(a) 2^{32}
(b) 2^{64}
(c) 2^{128}
(d) 2^{256}

Answers

12.1 (c)   **12.2** (a)   **12.3** (c)   **12.4** (a)   **12.5** (c)

Chapter 13

Web Security

13.1 INTRODUCTION

Nowadays, most of the companies and organisations use web services for their business and other applications. For these applications, security is the most important part. One can secure his/her web site by understanding and implementing proper security measures. This provides a secure environment in which the users of that web site work comfortably with that application. This chapter provides an overview of Secure Socket Layer (SSL) and secure electronic transactions.

13.2 SECURE SOCKET LAYER

Secure Socket Layer (SSL) is a certificate-based general purpose protocol. It has been developed by Netscape. SSL is used for managing the encryption of information that is transmitted over the Internet. SSL uses public key infrastructure. So, encryption is done by using a public key. This encrypted data is transferred over the SSL connection. Nowadays, SSL is the most widely used protocol for e-commerce.

The transmission and routing of data on Internet is controlled using TCP/IP protocol. The SSL protocol executes above the TCP/IP and below higher level protocols such as HTTP or IMAP. On behalf of higher level protocol, SSL uses TCP/IP protocol. In the process, SSL allows the server to authenticate the client by showing its certificate. The client is authenticated by using user id and password. Authentication enables the client and the server to communicate securely. There is an issuing authority, which is responsible for distribution of SSL key and certificate. On the server, SSL makes these keys and certificates available and broadcasts the same using protocol exchanges between the server and the client. Client and server exchange the information regarding encryption using SSL handshake protocol. After successful handshaking, both the server and the client know about the encryption algorithm used and each other's public key for encryption and decryption. Then, server and client share their information in encrypted form so that third party is not able to read the information. If the attacker tries to capture and read this information, long time is required to decrypt it before he is able to get any meaningful information from it. The time required for the attacker to decrypt the information depends on the length of the key used for generating the certificate. Nowadays, SSL is also popular as *Transport Layer Security (TLS)*.

SSL is a set of protocols, which are given below:

1. *Record Protocol:* It is used to ensure security and integrity to the data. It defines the format used to transmit the data.

2. *ChangeCipher SpecProtocol:* This message is sent by both the server and client to inform the other party (receiver) that subsequent records will be protected under the just-negotiated CipherSpec and keys.

3. *Alert Protocol:* This protocol is used to inform SSL-related alerts to the communication parties. These messages are encrypted and compressed.

4. *Handshake Protocol:* This protocol is responsible for establishing an SSL connection. To establish the connection for the first time, it uses Record Protocol to exchange the messages between the server and the client. There are three protocols—Handshake Protocol, Cipher Change Protocol and Alert Protocol.

The main objectives of SSL are as follows:

1. *Authentication:* The SSL protocol supports the authentication of the server and the client to each other. For authentication, SSL uses public key cryptography. Generally, certificate is used for authentication and SSL also uses the same method.

2. *Data integrity:* Whatever the data transmitted by the sender, it should be received as it is (without modification) at the receiving end. Data integrity ensures that the data received is the same data sent by the sender without any modification.

3. *Data privacy:* During transmission of information between the server and client, the data should be protected from the attacker such that only authorised users can read it. This is the prerequisite for the application data and the data related with the protocol itself. The *application data* is the data that is sent during the session itself and the *data related with the protocol* is the data used for securing traffic during negotiations.

The SSL protocol stack is illustrated in Figure 13.1.

Handshake Protocol	Cipher Change Protocol	Alert Protocol	Application Protocol
SSL Record Protocol			
TCP			
IP			

Figure 13.1 SSL protocol stack.

The SSL Record Protocol is used to define the format for the message. It provides encryption and integrity to the data. It is also used to encapsulate data sent by the other SSL protocols. So, it is also involved in the tasks associated with the SSL check data. The other three protocols, i.e., Handshake Protocol is concerned with session management, Cipher Change Protocol is related to cryptographic parameter management and Alert Protocol is involved in transferring of SSL messages between the client and the server.

13.3 SSL SESSION AND CONNECTION

Let us discuss how the connection is established and the session starts in more detail.

1. The first step in SSL protocol is establishing the connection between the server and the client. It is a logical link between them. It is done so that the client can use the services available with the server. SSL connection should be between two network nodes and it is peer-to-peer type.
2. An association between a server and a client is called *session*. Session defines different parameters used in communication. It includes session number, different algorithms used, etc. Handshake Protocol is used to create the SSL session. When the connection is established and the session starts, the Handshake Protocol is used for sharing the parameters. If there is a request for new connection, session is not allowed for such request. So, there is a single session shared by multiple connections, but single connection cannot have multiple sessions.
3. Parameters used in communications are given below:
    (a) *Session identifier:* The identifier is generated by the server and it is used for identifying a session with a client.
    (b) *Peer certificate:* X.509 certificate is used for authentication.
    (c) *Compression method:* It gives the method used to compress the data. Compression of data is done before its encryption.
    (d) *Algorithm specification:* It gives the encryption algorithm and the message digest or hashing algorithm used during the session.
    (e) *Master secret:* The client and the server share secrete data of length 384 bits.
    (f) *"is resumable":* It is a flag indicating whether the session can be used to initiate new connections.
4. The *connection state* is defined by the following parameters:
    (a) *Server and client random:* For each connection, both the client and the server generate a random data.
    (b) *Server write MAC secret:* It indicates the secret key used by the server for data written
    (c) *Client write MAC secret:* This indicates the secret key used by the client for data written
    (d) *Server write key:* This indicates the key used by the server for encryption and by the client for decryption.

(e) ***Client write key:*** This indicates the key used by the client for encryption and by the server for decryption.

(f) ***Sequence number:*** Server maintains sequence numbers separately for each message transmitted and received during the data session.

13.4 SSL RECORD PROTOCOL

The SSL has different layers such as Handshake Protocol, Record Layer Protocol, ChangeCipher SpecProtocol and Alert Protocol. SSL uses these protocols for different purposes. The SSL Record Protocol provides integrity service to the data in SSL. SSL Record Layer Protocol takes the data from the application layer and divides the data into different parts of fixed length. If the size of any individual part is not equal to the expected size of the part, then the required number of padding bits are added at the end of the message. Then, the data is compressed using appropriate compression algorithm/technique. After that, the MAC value is calculated for the respective part using the secret key. The secret key may be Server write MAC secret key or client write MAC secret key depending on who prepares the packet. MAC is used for the verification of the integrity of the message. MAC is calculated using message digest algorithms such as MD5 or SHA-1. The MAC is then appended to the part message, followed by encrypting the packet of fixed length. Then, headers are added to the packet. The object created is called *record*. This record is transmitted using TCP protocol. The header contents are protocol definition of length 1 byte, protocol version of length 2 bytes, and length of 2 bytes. The length includes the length of the message part and the length of the padding bits used. The possible values for protocol definition are ChangeCipher Spec, Alert, Handshake, and application data related to the appropriate protocols. Protocol version indicates major version and minor version. For SSL 3.0, the value of major version is 3 and minor version is 0.

The detailed procedure of formation of records is given below:

1. *Fragmentation:* Divide the message into number of parts or fragments of fixed size. If the part size is less than the requisite size, then necessary numbers of padding bits are added at the end of the message.

2. *Compression:* Compress the message part.

3. *Append MAC:* Calculate the MAC.

MAC = Hash function [secret key, message part, padding bits, sequence number]
Append the MAC value to each part of a message.

4. *Encryption:* Encrypt the complete part with MAC using symmetric key encryption algorithm.

5. *Attach header:* Attach the header to the packet.

Now, the record is prepared and made ready for transmission. This complete process of record preparation is shown in Figure 13.2.

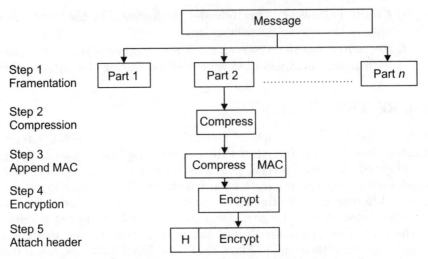

Figure 13.2 Creating a packet under SSL Record Protocol.

The SSL Record Protocol is used to provide confidentiality applying encryption and integrity using MAC value to the message, which is transferred within a session.

13.5 CHANGECIPHER SPECPROTOCOL

The ChangeCipher SpecProtocol is the simplest SSL protocol. This message is sent by both the server and the client to inform the other party (receiver) that subsequent records will be protected under the just-negotiated CipherSpec and keys. It consists of a single message. The message consists of a single byte value of 1. The message is encrypted and compressed under the current CipherSpec. The main objective of this message is to cause the pending read/write state to be established as a current read/write state. The client sends a ChangeCipher Spec message followed by the key exchange and certificate to the server and the server sends a value one after successfully processing the key exchange message.

13.6 ALERT PROTOCOL

The Alert Protocol is used to inform SSL-related alerts to the communication parties. These messages are encrypted and compressed. There are two bytes in each message in the Alert Protocol. The first byte indicates the severity of a message. If its value is 1, then it is a warning and if it is 2, then it is fatal, which terminates the connection immediately. The second byte of the message contains preset error codes. Error code may occur during an SSL communication session.

13.7 HANDSHAKE PROTOCOL

The Handshake Protocol is used to establish a session between the server and the client. It provides information about key and cryptographic algorithms to SSL Record Protocol.

The server and the client optionally authenticate each other using this protocol. This protocol allows the server and the client to negotiate for various encryption algorithms and share secret key for encryption.

The process of negotiations between the client and the server is illustrated in Figure 13.3. The Handshake Protocol is divided into four phases.

1. *Establish security capabilities:* In this phase, a logical connection is initiated among the client and the server. Once the logical connection is established, the negotiation on the connection parameters takes place between the server and the client. For this phase, the client sends a client_hello message to the server and the server replies back by sending server_hello message.

The client_hello message contains the following fields:

(a) *Version*: This field indicates the highest SSL version supported by the client.

(b) *Random*: It consists of 32-bit timestamp and randomly generated value (nonce) of length 28 bytes. This information is used to secure the key exchange session between the server and the client.

(c) *Session ID:* It is a number (variable length) used to define the session identifier. Non-zero value of this field indicates that the client wants to update the parameters of an existing connection or wants to establish a new connection on the existing session. If the value of this field is zero, then it indicates that the client wishes to establish a new connection on a new session.

(d) *CipherSuite list:* A list of different encryption algorithms in decreasing order of priorities and key exchange method supported by the client is given.

(e) *Compression method:* This field gives the list of methods supported by client. The server_hello message contains the same set of fields as the client message:

(f) *Version*: This field indicates the lowest SSL version supported by the server.

(g) *Random value*: It follows the same fashion as used by the client, but the data generated is completely independent.

(h) *Session ID*: The same value is sent back to the client if the field value is non-zero, otherwise the value for a new session is sent.

(i) *CipherSuite*: The encryption algorithm and key exchange method selected by the server from the list received from the client is given. The first element of this field indicates the key exchange method and the next element indicates the encryption algorithm and hash functions along with all specific parameters.

The first phase establishes the following three components:

(a) Method of key exchange
(b) Encryption algorithm
(c) A hash function

2. *Server authentication and key exchange:* The server replies by sending its certificate, key exchange and the request certificate to the client. The certificate may be of format X.509, which is used for authentication. If required, the server may send server_key_exchange message. If the key exchange method is fixed, then there is no need of this additional message. Moreover, the server may request for a certificate from the client by sending certificate_request. The server sends the server_done message to end the negotiation phase and it waits for the reply from the client.

3. *Client authentication and key exchange:* After receiving the message, the client should verify that the certificate provided by the server is valid. For verification, if required, the client may check the validation data and path and also check whether any other parameters sent by the server are acceptable or not.

The client may verify the following information:

(a) Validity date of the certificate to know whether the certificate is still valid or not.

(b) Check whether the certifying authority (CA) is present in the list of trusted certifying authorities which the client possesses. If that CA is not in the present list, then the client tries to verify the signature of the CA. If the client fails to get any information about the CA, then he terminates the identification procedure.

(c) In the same way, the client verifies the public key of the CA for the authenticity of the certifying authority.

(d) It verifies whether it is the same domain name used in the certificate, as shown in the server's certificate.

Upon satisfactory completion of all of the above steps, the client sends a message to the server. If requested, the client should send his certificate to the server for authentication. At the end of this phase, the client sends the client_key_exchange message. This is required to deliver the keys.

4. *Finish:* The secure connection is now set up and handshaking is completed. This phase is to confirm that the client and server may start their communication. They may exchange their application layer data. This phase sends a message for confirmation of the messages so far received and also for the verification of any pending data. The client sends a change_cipher_spec message to the server with the pending parameters. At the end, the client sends the finished message to the server. This last message is secured using encryption algorithm and one of the key from public key–private key pair upon which both parties, i.e., server and client agree. This message is sent by the client to confirm parameters and data are as per the negotiations. The server uses the other key from public key–private key pair and decrypts the message. Then, the server replies by sending the same message sequence.

Phases 2 and 3 are used for authentication of the communicating parties.

Figure 13.3 shows the procedure to establish SSL session between the client and the server.

There are many applications where SSL is used. But it is widely used for protecting web browser session. Therefore, it is seen as associated only with WWW pages. SSL is also used for e-mail application to send and receive e-mail messages securely.

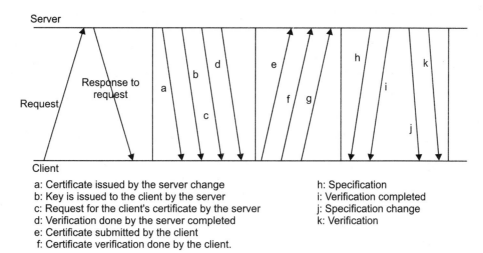

a: Certificate issued by the server change
b: Key is issued to the client by the server
c: Request for the client's certificate by the server
d: Verification done by the server completed
e: Certificate submitted by the client
f: Certificate verification done by the client.
h: Specification
i: Verification completed
j: Specification change
k: Verification

Figure 13.3 Establishing the SSL session between the client and the server.

13.8 SECURE ELECTRONIC TRANSACTIONS

The users of Internet are increased rapidly, and at the same time, the usage of Internet for different applications and purposes is also increased. Initially, people use Internet to get some information or to send e-mails. But nowadays, use of Internet is not limited to any particular application area. Now, we can use Internet for banking transaction, to pay the bill of electricity/telephone or to purchase something online. So, there was a need to provide security for these online transactions. Secure Electronic Transaction (SET) is emerged to support all these online transactions. It is an open encryption and specification design which has the potential for securing online transactions over the Internet. SET protocol was jointly developed by Visa and MasterCard, in cooperation with IBM, GTE, Microsoft, Netscape, SAIC, Terisa, Verisign and American Express. We know that privacy and authentication are very important for online transactions. SET is used to protect the privacy and confirm the authenticity of online transactions.

Cryptography is used for strong Secure Electronic Transactions (SET) protocol. In SET protocol, both the symmetric and asymmetric encryption techniques are used. For the encryption of data, symmetric encryption is used, whereas for the exchange of shared secret key, asymmetric key is used. Data Encryption Standard (DES) is used as symmetric encryption algorithm and the key used for DES encryption is sent to the receiver using asymmetric encryption technique. The computational cost for execution using asymmetric encryption technique is more. So, this technique is applied only for transmitting the key used for symmetric encryption and the message is encrypted using symmetric encryption. Asymmetric encryption is also used for authentication.

13.8.1 Importance of SET

Today, most of the Internet users use Internet for online banking transaction, to pay their electric/telephone bills or to purchase online. For all these applications, SET plays an important role in securing communications. It provides privacy and authentications to the customer as well as to the merchant. The security of SET protocol depends on the strength of encryption algorithm as well as on the length of the key. For large scale use of e-commerce, SET is very important. The data integrity relies on the ability to resolve the identities to a particular individual, merchant or payment gateway.

SET has the following requirements:

1. It should provide confidentiality of payment information and the order given by the customer.
2. It should ensure the integrity of all data transmitted between the customer and the merchant.
3. It should provide authentication to the customer as well as to the merchant.
4. It should ensure that the techniques used are sufficient to protect an electronic commerce transaction between the two parties.
5. It should create a protocol, which works independent of transport security systems.
6. It should assist and support interfacing between the software and network service providers.

SET should have the following features:

1. Confidentiality of information
2. Integrity of data
3. Cardholder account authentication
4. Merchant authentication

13.8.2 SET Mechanism

The success of SET operation depends on the different algorithms used and the software required for the execution of these algorithms. In SET, many participants are involved such as merchant, cardholder, payment issuer and certification authorities (CA).

- *Merchant:* A merchant may be a person or an organisation that has goods and services to sell using web sites.
- *Cardholder:* In e-commerce, the customers or purchasers interact with the merchants through mobile phones, note books, laptops or computers over the Internet. A cardholder is an authorised holder of the payment card (credit card or debit card) that has been issued by an issuer.
- *Payment issuer:* It is the issuer of the payment card. It maybe a bank or any financial institution.

- **Certification authority (CA):** It is the trusted party which issues X.509 certificates to the merchants, cardholders, and payment issuer. The security of SET depends on CA.

- **Acquirer:** It is an organisation which provides card authorisation and payment capture for merchants.

In the working of e-commerce, multiple countries, multiple service providers, multiple parties (customers and merchants) are involved. So, SET working is a complex processing of authentication.

13.8.3 Key Elements of SET

SET has two key elements.

1. Framework establishment
2. Payment transaction

Framework Establishment

We know that SET uses asymmetric encryption technique for transmitting the shared secret key. So, each participant should have a pair of keys—public key and private key. He can broadcast his public key so that it is available to the parties who want to communicate with him. He should keep his private secret. The integrity and security of transaction depends on public key and the certificate. The certificate for a particular user is generated using his identification number and the public key. Using this information, the CA verifies the information and binds the identification number and the public key together. Then, the digital signature is generated on the result. Any person who wants to verify the certificate should have a trusted copy of CA's public key.

The security of SET depends on the existence of CA infrastructure available for this purpose.

1. Credit card account: The basic requirement of online transaction is a credit card. So, the customer should obtain a credit card account.

2. Issue of certificate to the customer: After verification of the information of the customer, the bank issues a certificate to the customer. For this, generally X.509 certificate format is used.

3. Merchants certificates: A merchant has also own his certificates, one for signing the messages and other for key exchange. He is also having a copy of the payment gateway's public-key certificate.

The generation and distribution of certificates are done using hierarchical approach. This is shown in Figure 13.4. The root certificate authority is at the top of the hierarchy maintained by SET. The root certificate authority issues public key certificates to the various payment brands. These payment brands now work as certificate authorities and can issue certificates to their members.

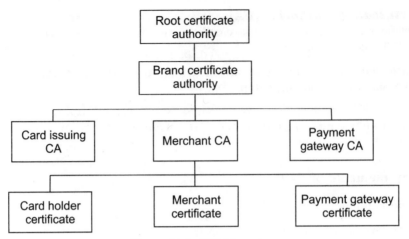

Figure 13.4 SET hierarchy.

Payment Transaction

To purchase online, the customer has to pay online. For this, the following steps should be followed:

1. The customer sends a message that he wants to make a payment.
2. The merchant responds to the request of the customer.
3. The customer provides details of the payment to be paid with a copy of certificate.
4. The merchant sends a request of the customer for authorisation to the payment processing organisation.
5. Authorisation is verified using offered processes.
6. After verification of authorisation, the authorisation certificate is sent to the merchant.
7. The merchant sends a message about customer payment transaction.
8. The merchant receives confirmation about the transaction.
9. The merchant sends confirmation message to the customer about the successful transaction of payment.

13.8.4 Strengths of SET

SET provides high level of security and privacy to the users. This is due to the uses of technologies such as public key encryption, digital signatures and certificates and established protocols such as SHA, RSA, DES and X.509. Initially, the SET has been designed for credit card transactions so it does not support the use of PINs. Debit card transaction needs PIN; so, early versions of SET cannot support debit card transactions.

13.8.5 Weaknesses of SET

The performance of SET depends on the number of users meeting the requirements of specification. There is a problem of securing the private keys. SET does not mention anything about the losses happened in the transaction. But the cardholders/customers are considered responsible for any loss in the transaction, as the private key belongs to the customer. To provide more security to the smart card, RSA algorithm can be implemented on the card. This increases the cost of card. In addition, there are problems of bandwidth and processing speed when the customer uses cell phone or personal digital assistant (PDA) for online transactions.

SUMMARY

Secure Socket Layer (SSL) is a certificate-based general purpose protocol. SSL is used for managing the encryption of information that is transmitted over the Internet. SSL is the most widely used protocol for e-commerce. The main objectives of SSL are authentication, data integrity and data privacy. SSL is a set of protocols, which includes Record Protocol, ChangeCipher SpecProtocol, Alert Protocol, Handshake Protocol. Secure electronic transaction is an open encryption and specification design, which has the potential for securing online transactions over the Internet. SET is used to protect privacy and to confirm the authenticity of online transactions. The security of SET protocol depends on the strength of encryption algorithm as well as on the length of the key.

EXERCISES

13.1 What is SSL? What are the different protocols used in SSL?
13.2 What are the objectives of SSL?
13.3 Explain SSL protocol stack.
13.4 Explain SSL connection and session.
13.5 Discuss the parameters which define the session state.
13.6 What is MAC? Why is MAC used in SSL?
13.7 Explain the working of SSL Record Protocol.
13.8 Explain the working of Handshake Protocol.
13.9 Explain how SSL can be protected from different attacks.
13.10 What are the weaknesses of SSL?
13.11 What is SET?
13.12 What is the importance of SET?
13.13 Explain the operation of SET.
13.14 What are the strengths of SET?
13.15 What are the weaknesses of SET?
13.16 What are the requirements and the key features of the SET?

MULTIPLE CHOICE QUESTIONS

13.1 Which of the following protocol is not a part of a set of SSL Protocol?
  (a) Record Protocol
  (b) ChangeCipher SpecProtocol
  (c) ESP Protocol
  (d) Alert Protocol

13.2 The SSL protocol does not provide
  (a) Data confidentiality
  (b) Authentication
  (c) Data privacy
  (d) Data integrity

13.3 The first phase of Handshake Protocol does not establish ------------------component.
  (a) Method of key exchange
  (b) Digital signature algorithm
  (c) Encryption algorithm
  (d) Hashing algorithm

Answers

13.1 (c)   **13.2** (a)   **13.3** (b)

CHAPTER 14

Intrusion

14.1 INTRODUCTION

Network security is becoming increasingly important in the modern systems, where Internet is an essential part of human life. The evolution of the Internet along with its use in day-to-day life has increased the need for network security systems. With the development of networking and interoperation on public networks, the number and the severity of security threats have increased significantly. Internet has changed the life of human being completely. Applications of computer using Internet are unlimited. Unfortunately, due to large scale use of Internet, the risks and chances of attacks are also increased. So, it is essential to protect our system from different attacks. The system which is used to protect our system from different attacks is called *intrusion detection systems* (*IDS*). The process of identifying the attacks in a system or network is called *intrusion detection*. An *intrusion* is a deliberate or unauthorised activity or action that attempts to access or manipulate the information or compromise the security of the systems to make them unreliable or unusable. An *intruder* is a person who is responsible for intrusions. He may be a person from inside the network, i.e., legitimate user of the network or from outside the network.

It is a well-known thought that prevention is better than cure. Same is applicable to computer systems and networks. Generally, firewall is used to prevent attacks on the network. Firewall is having a set of rules and it protects those attacks, which are defined in advance as a rule. So, firewall cannot protect the new attack, as the rule is not defined. In this case, IDS is useful to detect new attacks. But it is unrealistic to prevent all the attacks. An IDS collects the information from inside as well as from outside the network and analyses this information to identify whether there is intrusion or not.

Intrusion detection is different from intrusion prevention. *Intrusion detection* means the process of observing the incoming and outgoing traffic and it collects the data. Then, it analyses the data for possible attacks. *Intrusion prevention* is the process of identifying the attacks and it endeavours to block the detected possible incidents. *Intruders* are the person, who have unauthorised access the network.

There are different types of intruders.

1. Masquerader: This refers to the unauthorised user of the computer system, who penetrates the security of computer system by using legitimate user account. Generally, masquerader is an outsider.

*2. Misfeasor***:** It refers to a legitimate user who accesses the resources that he is not authorized to access, or the user who is an authorised user of a system, but misuses his privileges. Generally, misfeasor is an insider.

3. Clandestine user: It refers to a user who gains supervisory control over the system.Clandestine may be either an insider or outsider.

Anderson, first time in 1980, introduced the concept of intrusion detection. He defined an *intrusion* is an attempt or a threat to be the potential possibility of a deliberate unauthorised attempt to

1. Access information
2. Manipulate information, or
3. Render a system unreliable or unusable

After 1980, many techniques for intrusion detections have been studied.

14.2 INTRUSION DETECTION

Intrusion detection means to detect the vulnerabilities exploited against the computer system or against any application. Intrusion detection system helps in providing the information about such vulnerabilities to the network administrator and helps him in preparing some system to protect such attacks or deal with such vulnerabilities. It includes collection of information by monitoring the network traffic and the suspicious activities in the network. It also collects the information about these vulnerabilities from different sources and analyses the same. Many people think that firewall is sufficient to protect their network and can recognise the attacks on the network and block the intrusions. But the fact is that the firewall works just like a fence to our home. It restricts the access only to the designated points on the network, but the whole network cannot be secured using firewall. Firewall cannot detect the new attacks on the network. This detection of new attacks is done by IDS.

Intrusion detection provides the following functions:

1. Monitoring and analysing both the user and the system activities
2. Analysing system configurations and vulnerabilities
3. Assessing the integrity of system and files
4. Analysing the traffic pattern based on knowing attack patterns
5. Analysing abnormal activity patterns
6. Tracking the policy violations by the user
7. Doing audit of the operating system

Today, it is more difficult to provide 100% security to any network. This is because the technologies for attacks are very user-friendly and many free tools are easily available to perform such attack. No prior technical knowledge is required to attack any system. This helps a novice attacker in making the attack with more ease.

The intrusion detection system can be divided into following two types depending on the architecture:

1. Network intrusion detection system (NIDS): It works on the network and performs an analysis of all the traffic passing on the entire subnet. Every packet is monitored and if the attack is identified or some abnormal behaviour is observed, then the alert can be sent to the administrator.

2. Host intrusion detection system (HIDS): It works off the host, monitors the system events and audits the event logs. It then takes a snap shot of the existing system files and compares it with the previous snap shot available. If any of these files are found modified or deleted, then the alert is sent to the administrator.

14.3 INTRUSION DETECTION SYSTEM

An *intrusion detection system* (*IDS*) is a security system that monitors the network traffic and analyses the data for possible attacks from outside the network or from inside the network.

IDS can be categorised depending on the method of detection attacks. Following are the categories of IDS:

1. Misuse-based detection versus anomaly-based detection: The misuse-based intrusion detection systems (IDS) uses a database of previous attack patterns and known vulnerabilities as a reference. Each intrusion have some specific pattern. This pattern is called *signature*. This pattern or signature is used to identify the attacks on the computer system or on the network. So, this system is also called *signature-based IDS*. The drawback of misuse-based IDS is that there is a need of frequently updation of the database. If there are some unique attacks, this IDS may fail to identify such attacks.

In anomaly-based intrusion detection systems (IDS), a baseline or learned pattern of normal system activity is used as references to identify intrusion. Using this information, an alarm is to be triggered. The drawback of this method is that it has higher false alarm rate.

2. Network-based system versus host-based systems: Network-based intrusion detection system monitor the packets that flow over the network. These packets are compared with the reference data present and then analysed. Then, it is verified whether the said packet is malicious or benign. It is responsible to control the vulnerabilities in the networks, so, it is distributed IDS. Network-based IDS uses packet-sniffing technique to collect the packets along the network. The architecture for Network-based IDS is shown in Figure 14.1.

In a host-based system, the activity on each individual computer or host is examined by the IDS. It is installed on an individual computer to detect the attack on that computer. There are two drawbacks of this method. The first drawback is that the system compromises with security; therefore, the log files of the system are corrupt or inaccurate. The same corrupted or inaccurate files are reported by the IDS, which makes it unreliable. The second drawback is that in host-based IDS, the IDS has to be deployed on each computer, which increases the administrative overload.

3. Passive system versus active system: A passive IDS is configured to only monitor and analyse the network traffic and if vulnerability or attack is found, it sends an alert to the network administrator. It is not able to protect or correct any actions by itself. An active IDS is used to block the suspected attacks automatically. There is no intervention required from the network administrator. It is also known as *intrusion detection and prevention system*. The advantage of this method is that it takes real time corrective action.

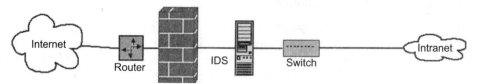

Figure 14.1 Network-based IDS.

14.3.1 Need for Intrusion Detection Systems

Out of the total security attacks that occur on a network, up to 85% attacks come from the users inside the network. These users may be authorised users of the system. The remaining attacks come from outside the network. It consists of mainly denial of service attacks or attacks to penetrate the infrastructure of the network. To protect the network from all these types of attacks, IDS is an integral part of the network or information security. It is helpful for complete supervision of the network. IDS is used to

1. Prevent problem like behaviours of the system
2. Detect various attacks and vulnerabilities in the network
3. Detect new attacks and identify its signature
4. Protect the network from internal as well as external users

Nowadays, due to the availability of tools for making attacks, it is very easy to make attack on any computer system or network. There are different methods to protect the system or network from these attacks. Firstly, develop a fully secure computer system or network. For this, the system is accessible only to the authenticated and authorised users. Secondly, use of cryptographic methods to protect the data applies tight access control. But in real life, all these solutions are feasible due to the following reasons:

1. In actual practice, to develop a completely secure system is not possible. Designing and implementing a totally secure system is an extremely difficult task.
2. Use of cryptographic methods to protect the information has its own limitations. The security of these methods depends on the secret key. If the attacker is able to capture this secret key, then he can read, change or modify the data and the entire system can be broken.
3. Many times, the protective measures are applied to prevent the external attacks. But as discussed above, approximately 85% of the total attacks are

from internal users. This happens because the internal legitimate users misuse their privileges and create the attacks internally.
4. If we tight the access control, the efficiency of the system reduces.

When an attack is detected, the IDS first alarms the network administrator. IDS works as a reactive system, instead of preventative one. It works as an informative system.

14.3.2 Intrusion Detection Method

Intrusion detection can be done using the following strategies:

1. Define the rules for the normal behaviour of the computer system or network and then search for the traffic, which is responsible for the change in behaviour of the system or computer.
2. Define the patterns of the attack and then search for the occurrence of an attack.

The first strategy is called *anomaly-based IDS* and the second strategy is called *misuse-based IDS*. We will now discuss about these methods in the subsequent sections.

Anomaly-based Detection

Anomaly-based detection techniques are based on the assumption that all intrusive activities are malicious. Therefore, we have to build a system, with a normal activity profile of the computer system and then wait for the anomalous activities to happen. That is, we identify the system states which have different behaviour from the normal established profile. Such activities are identified as intrusive activities and flagged as intrusion. However, if we assume that the rules for intrusive activities and the rules of anomalous activities are not exactly the same, but there are some matches among them, then there are chances like

1. Some activities, which are anomalous, but not intrusive activities, are also flagged as intrusion. This results in false positives.
2. Some activities are intrusive activities, but not anomalous. Such activities are not flagged and treated as normal activities. This results in false negatives.

False negative is a serious problem, as malicious packets are allowed to enter in the network or system as a normal packet. It may harm the system. This reduces the accuracy of the IDS and deteriorates the performance of the IDS. To reduce the false negatives in the system, generally the threshold is used. In anomaly-based IDS, there is a need to keep track of system profile and also updating of system profile is required. Therefore, this method is computationally expensive. The advantage of this method is that it is able to detect the new or unknown attacks.

A block diagram of anomaly-based detection system is shown in Figure 14.2.

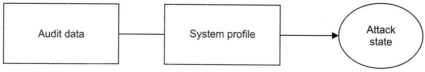

Figure 14.2 Anomaly-based detection system.

The main advantages of anamaly-based detection system are as follows:

1. It is possible to detect the new or unknown attacks.
2. Accuracy is more.
3. Internal attacks can be detected easily.

Disadvantages of anamaly-based detection system are given below:

1. False negatives are more.
2. It is expensive.
3. Accuracy is less.

Misuse-based Detection

In misuse-based detection method, the patterns or signatures are used to detect the attacks. If there are variations in the same attack, then it is possible to detect those attacks by using pattern or signature. Misuse-based detection systems use a database of information that has a number of patterns. The system collects audit data and compares this data with the stored patterns in its database. If any match is found, then the alarm is generated. If the match is not found, then it is considered as legitimate activity. The success of misuse-based detection method depends on the database of signatures or patterns. The database should include all possible patterns with the variations for different attacks and also for normal activities. How to generate these patterns or signatures is the main issue of this approach.

A block diagram of a misuse-based detection system is shown in Figure 14.3.

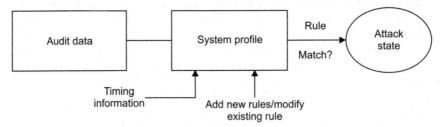

Figure 14.3 Misuse-based detection system.

The only advantages of misuse-based detection system is that it generally produces very few false positives.

Disadvantages of misuse-based detection system are as under:

1. A lot of effort is required for the generation of pattern or signature database.
2. It cannot detect new attacks.

14.4 ANOMALY-BASED INTRUSION DETECTION SYSTEMS

Anomaly-based intrusion detection systems have few major approaches to detect the intrusions. Some of these approaches are described here.

14.4.1 Statistical Approach

Statistical approach is the earliest method used for intrusion detection. It is assumed that the normal behaviour and malicious behaviour are different. So, statistical approach can be used to differentiate the normal user from the intruder. In this approach, the behaviour profiles are generated. Its variances are generated from the present profile. This approach is adaptive; so, the performance of this approach is good. The drawback of this method is that the intruders are trained gradually so the intrusions are treated as normal. The performance of this approach depend on the threshold. If the threshold is set too low or too high, then it affects false negatives and false positives.

Denning suggested a number of statistical parameters for IDS. Some of them are as follows:

1. Threshold: It is the heuristic limit to occur an event or count of events occurs within a specific interval. For example, logging into user account is not allowed after a specific number attempts of failed log in.

2. Mean and standard deviation: The confidence interval for the abnormality is computed using the comparison of event measures and the mean and standard of a profile deviation.

3. Multivariate model: This model considers computing the correlation between different event measures with respect to the profile expectations.

4. Markov process model: This model considers the types of events with respect to the state variables in a state transition matrix.

Limitations

1. The performance of statistics-based IDS depends on the data representation. If it contains some irrelevant data, then IDS may fail to identify an unknown attack.
2. The performance of this approach depends on the threshold. If the threshold is set too low or too high, then it affects false negatives and false positives.

14.4.2 Immune System Approach

This approach provides a model of normal behaviour in the form of application code paths. For a variety of different conditions, the applications are modelled in terms of sequences of system calls. These conditions include normal behaviour, error conditions and attempted exploits. These models are compared with the event observed and then classify them as normal or attack. This approach detects a number of typical attacks, but cannot detect the attacks which are based on race conditions, policy violations or masquerading.

14.5 MISUSE-BASED INTRUSION DETECTION SYSTEMS

Misuse-based intrusion detection systems have few major approaches to detect the intrusions. Some of these approaches are described below. In misuse-based detection, it is checked whether a pattern being executed violates the security policy of the system. If this happens, then set the alarm for an intrusion.

14.5.1 Expression Matching

It is the simplest form of misuse-based IDS. It uses techniques like matching of expression, searches for various event patterns. For this model, we can define the signatures/patterns easily.

14.5.2 State Transition Analysis

This model uses matching events to find out the attacks. Every observed event is compared with the finite state machine patterns and causes the transitions. If the machine reaches the final state, that means it is an attack. Complex intrusions can be detected using this model. It is used to detect distributed attacks.

14.5.3 Genetic Algorithm

Genetic algorithm can be used to identify the known attacks. In this, the patterns of the observed event are compared with the available patterns and the best match is found out. Then, a hypothesis vector is evaluated depending on the risk associated with the attacks involved. If a mismatch occurs, a quadratic penalty function is used to give the details. In each turn, the best hypotheses of the current set are mutated and retested again. This reduces the false positives and false negatives to zero. The performance of this approach is good.

14.6 DISTRIBUTED INTRUSION DETECTION SYSTEM

With the widespread growth of internet, there is an increase in malicious activity against the network. Current IDS technology is sufficient to protect the global network infrastructure from attacks. So, there is a need of an IDS, which can support global network. Distributed IDS (dIDS) increases the identifying power and scope of single IDS by using an attack correlation with database obtained from geographically different networks. A distributed IDS consists of multiple intrusion detection systems over a large network. All these IDSs are communicated with each other, or with a central server. This allows them to monitor different advanced networks, help for analysis and find out the attack data. There are different agents which coordinate with each other and are distributed across a network. This gives the detailed pictures of different events that take place in the network to the network administrators. It allows maintaining the records related to attacks at the central place so that it is easily available to the analyst easily. There is a centralised analysis engine and on each system, there is an agent which monitors the network traffic. Current dIDS has the following limitations:

1. Observing a single site is not sufficient to detect the existence of attacks by the single attacker.

2. When a single attack is generated by a group of attackers, then to protect such attack, the global scope for assessment is required.
3. If there is a change in the system and attack behaviour, then false negatives are generated.
4. For prevention of attacks, the intention behind these attacks is required.
5. Due to advances in technology the attacks are automated. Also, these attacks are autonomous. To prevent these attacks, quick analysis and mitigation of these attacks are required.
6. The total volume of notifications about the attacks received by internet service providers (ISPs) and host systems is becoming overwhelming. If collective details about the attacks are provided to the responsible party, then the possibility of a positive response increases.

Thus, in nutshell, distributed intrusion detection system has a number of IDSs, which are spread over a global network (Internet). All these IDSs are interconnected and communicate with each other or with a central server. This allows it to monitor the network, help for analysis of the incident and find out the data related to attacks.

14.6.1 Overview

There are various components of dIDS. These components are discussed below:

Central Analysis Server

The core part of dIDS is central analysis server. It consists of a database, reporting engine and the web server. It collects the responses from the agents to permit attack correlation. It allows analysis to perform aggregation of attack, collect statistical information, recognise the pattern of attack and report the incident details.

Cooperative Agent Network

The most important components of the dIDS is the cooperative agent network. An *agent* is a software or a device which is responsible for collecting and inspecting the data. Agent might be a firewall, or host-based IDS or network-based IDS. Agent reports the information related to the attack on the central analysis server. There are multiple agents across a single network. It gives a broad view of the network than a single IDS.

Generally, these agents are located on separate network segments. They are also located on different geographical locations, as shown in Figure 14.4. The agents can also be distributed across multiple physical locations. Due to this, a single incident analysis team can view attack data across multiple corporate locations.

Attack Aggregation

Another important part of dIDS is attack aggregation. It is located in the central server. It is the method in which the information is gathered from the agent network. An example is collecting the information according to IP address of the attacker, putting together all attacks from an IP address, together with the other attacks from the same IP address. Another example is to collect the data of attacks according to destination port or put them by date and time.

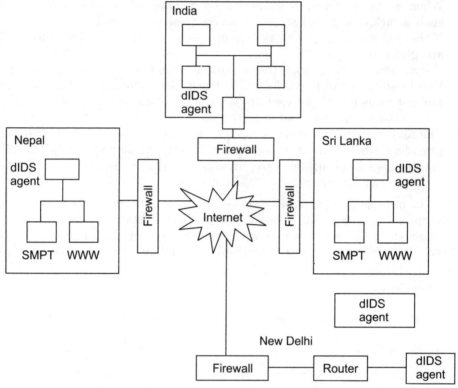

Figure 14.4 Agent network.

Data Sources

The agent reports about the internal network traffic to the perimeter or an organisation or both. This depends on where the agent resides. For dIDS, both the locations are useful because some malicious software behaves differently for inside the network than for outside the network. To get useful information about the internal attacks, the agent located inside the organisation is useful.

14.6.2 Advantages of a dIDS

The dIDS has many advantages over a single IDS. It can detect attack patterns across the entire network of the organisation, with physical locations having different time zones or even in different continents. Therefore, the attacks can be detected early and this protects the system from damage. The offending IPs are prohibited to access. Another advantage of dIDS is to allow early detection of Internet worm through the global network. The major advantage of dIDS is that a single team can analyse the attack information of places located at different places, whereas a single IDS system requires several analysis teams for the same. So, it reduces the cost of analysis. It also reduces the time required to collect the information from different places. Many times, the attacks are generated by people within the network. With the help of analysis server, the incident analyst is able to keep track of such attacks within the organisation and provide evidence against such internal people. This helps in protecting the system or network internally.

14.6.3 Incident Analysis with dIDS

The important part of dIDS is incident analysis. The main command, strength and flexibility of the dIDS lie with incident analysis. The analysis of incidence of attack helps in protecting the system. So, while designing dIDS, the designer mainly focusses on this part.

14.6.4 Analysis Using Aggregation

Aggregation is helpful for the analysis of attack incidence across the multiple segments of a network. By aggregating the similar or related data from multiple physical locations using multiple agents, the analyst, using dIDS, is able to examine how an attack has progressed across multiple network segments through different stages. Incident analyst also gets the information about time frame in which the attacker is working. He also correlates other attack attempts against the networks and decides about the attacker's working, i.e., whether he is working in multiple cooperative groups. The most common methods of aggregation are source IP, destination port, agent ID, date, time, protocol, or attack type. These are discussed below:

1. Aggregating by source IP: It allows an incident analyst to follow an attacker's attempt from start to finish across the multiple segments of a network.

2. Aggregating by destination port: It permits an incident analyst to look new trends in attack types and methods. Using this method, dIDS is able to identify several new attacks.

3. Aggregating by agent ID: It allows an analyst to see the variety of attacks and different attempts made by the attackers on a specific segment network, where the agent is located. The analyst can find out whether the attackers are working in group in cooperation with each other or they target some specific network segments for attacks. This analysis is helpful to the security team to concentrate on providing the security.

4. Aggregating by date and time: It allows the analyst to look the pattern of new attack. So, new worms or viruses can be identified easily. These worms or viruses are only triggered at certain times.

5. Aggregating by protocol: It works in a statistical manner. The analyst can identify new attacks in particular protocols or identify protocols on a network segment using aggregating by protocol.

6. Aggregating by attack type: It is useful for matching the attack pattern and also correlates the coordinated attacks against multiple network segments.

Using the above aggregation methods, an analyst can get a variety of data to correlate against other attacks. Therefore, a variety of data is available to the analyst. He can identify the attacks by correlating this data against other attacks. It is possible to detect coordinated distributed attacks, attacks within the network and new exploits and vulnerabilities. Use of dIDS gives a guarantee of minimum false positives and false negatives.

14.7 BASE RATE FALLACY

The main aim of analyst is to make the detection rate of intrusion detection system high, with minimum false negatives. This can be achieved using the base rate fallacy phenomenon. For assessment, two types of information are available with the analyst. One is the specific information about the individual case at hand, and second is in terms of numerical data that summarises information about many similar cases. This type of numerical information is called *base rate or prior probability*. For IDS, we can apply base rate fallacy by first finding the different probabilities or if such probabilities cannot be found, then necessary assumptions are made regarding these probabilities.

14.7.1 Basic Frequency Assumptions

We have to install the network consists of few workstations and some servers. This installation produces 10,00,000 audit records per day used to test data for intrusion detection. Suppose there are very few actual intrusion attempts per day. But it is difficult to know the exact number of real attack attempts per day. If we assume that only one person can analyse the data that react to a relatively low number of alarms, especially when the false alarm rate is high, then in this case, there is a possibility that an intrusion could affect only one audit record; it is likely, on an average, that it will affect a few more than that.

14.7.2 Honeypots

A *honeypot* is an information system on the Internet. It is a virtual machine used mainly to attract and trap people, who make an attempt to penetrate other users of the computer systems. A honeypot makes fool of attackers by enabling them to believe that it is a legitimate system. The attacker attempts the attack on the honeypot assuming that it is a system. These attempts are observed, but the attacker does not know about it. At the same time, the information related to attack is collected by the system, which includes the IP address of the attacker. This information is useful to trace back the attacker. When many honeypots are connected to a system on a subnet, it is called a *honeynet*. Honeypots can be used for multiple applications such as for detection, prevention or information gathering.

The objectives of honeypot designs are given below:
1. It diverts the attacker from accessing some specific systems.
2. It is useful to collect the information regarding the attacks.
3. It motivates the attacker to use the system for more time so that the administrator gets more time to collect the information about the intruder.

Types of Honeypots

Honeypots are classified into two types.

1. Production honeypots: These honeypots are easy to use. It captures only limited information and uses it for risk mitigation. Most of these honeypots are emulations of specific operating systems. The attacks generated by automated tools are random and can be identified by these honeypots. Some of these honeypots can shut down attacks altogether. They send an acknowledgement of zero size to them. The attack waits to increase the size of window so that it could send the data when the window size increases.

2. Research honeypots: These honeypots are real operating systems and services. The attackers interact with these operating systems (honeypots); therefore, there is high risk with these honeypots. These honeypots are used to collect detailed information regarding new methods and techniques used for attacks. All these information provide an accurate picture of the types of attacks being penetrated. They also provide more information from the log files. The information provided by honeypots is used for intrusion detection and prevention.

Advantages

1. Honeypots attract and trap attackers and can be diverted them to target that they cannot damage.
2. Administrators have sufficient time to respond to an attacker.
3. The activities of the attackers' can be monitored through it. It captures valuable information about the attacks and uses this information for analysing attacking techniques and improves the threat models.
4. It can capture internal attacks efficiently and provides information about internal attackers.
5. It docs not add extra burden on the existing bandwidth of the network.

Disadvantages

1. Honeypots cannot detect attacks against the other systems in the network because they only track and capture activity that directly interacts with them
2. If honeypots are deployed without planning and thought, then they may introduce risks to the existing network.

14.8 PASSWORD MANAGEMENT PRACTICES

One of the important security services is authentication. Password is the most common mechanism for authentication. So, there should be a password management policy. The policy contains the procedure for selecting the passwords, validity of the password, distribution rules. There are different types of password management practices. Some of them are discussed here.

User Authentication and Passwords

It describes the objectives of authentication of the user and alternative mechanism for authentication. It also describes the importance of the passwords for the authentication of the user. In many applications, identification of user depends on authentication. For authentication, different methods are used. These methods are classified below:

1. Secrets (e.g. a password or PIN)
2. Tokens (e.g. a token card or smart card)
3. Biometrics (e.g. fingerprint, iris, voice or face)

The cost of secrets using password is less as compared to the other methods. So, password is the most popular method for authentication.

Security Threats

Using passwords or PIN for authentication is the most knowledge-based authentication method. Today, the use of computer for day-to-day life is increasing. This results in increasing the number of user IDs and passwords. For any individual, there are many user IDs and passwords. To remember all these user IDs and passwords is difficult for any user without keeping any record of it. If any individual user uses the same user ID and password for all his accounts and if the password is compromised, then huge damage may happen to the user. Because an intruder may gain access to all the accounts of that individual user using a single password. If the user selects different passwords and user IDs for different systems, then there is a tendency to select the passwords which he can easily remember. Secondly, there is a chance that the user may forget the passwords. This increases overload on the system to provide new passwords.

The most convenient and easy method of authentication is password method. It can be easily implemented. At the same time, there are a number of risk factors associated with this method. Some common risk factors are given below:

1. As an individual can have a number of passwords, there is a tendency to write down or share the password. Therefore, the password does not remain secret.
2. When the individual uses his password, the evesdropper may be able to know the password. This can be done by observing the typing of the keys or from the camera.
3. Attackers may guess the password using brute force method. If the length of the password is small, it is very easy for the attacker to apply brute force method and find out the password.
4. Password can be captured using sniffing attack. When the passwords are transmitted over a network either in plaintext or in poor encrypted form, then sniffing tool is used to get the password.
5. Attacker creates a fake log in screen looking similar to the original screen. When the user logins to the fake screen, immediately his password is captured and informed to the attacker.

Using one of the above techniques, an attacker is able to get the password of the users. There is no method which ensures whether the holder of the password is a valid user or somebody else.

Human Factors

In a large organisation, each user may have different passwords for accessing different computer systems. To provide security, some rules are framed for selecting the password. But in general, it is difficult for any individual to remember all these passwords and a particular password for a particular computer system. For the users, it is difficult to remember

1. Complicated passwords
2. Number of passwords
3. Frequently changing passwords
4. Rarely used passwords

For any one of the above case, it is troublesome for the user to remember the passwords. So, they select one of the following options.

1. Users may note down their passwords on a paper. This reduces the security of the password and also the security of the computer system.
2. Many people forget their passwords and request the network administrator for a new password. This increases the overhead on the network administrator.
3. Many users use a single password for all the computer systems. If the password is compromised, then the attacker may access all the computer systems.
4. Many times, users select very simple and easy-to-remember passwords. But these passwords can easily be compromised.
5. Sometimes, users select old password and reuse it again and again.

There should be some strong password management system which helps in avoiding the above practices of users.

Composition Rules

The main weakness of the password authentication method is that the password can be easily guessed. Using software like Crack and L0phtCrack attacker can guess millions of passwords combinations easily. So, it is necessary to prevent password guessing attack by selecting a strong password. Password strength is decided by the length and complexity of a password. Complexity depends on the unpredictability of the characters used in the password. For strong password, select a long password. The strong password can be generated using the following guidelines:

1. Password should be a passphrase having multiple words or acronyms.
2. It should be a combination of both upper and lowercase characters (e.g., a–z, A–Z).
3. It should have some digits and punctuation characters as well as letters (e.g., 0–9, !@#$%^&*()_+|~-=\`{}[]:";'<>?,./).
4. The length of the password should be at least 6 alphanumeric characters long.
5. The password should not be a word in any language, slang, dialect, jargon, etc.
6. It should not be based on some personal information such as names or family or pets name, etc.

The strength of password for some likely combinations using the above rules are shown in Table 14.1.

Table 14.1 Password strength

Legal characters	5	6	7	8	9	10
0 to 9	$1.00e^{05}$	$1.00e^{06}$	$1.00e^{07}$	$1.00e^{08}$	$1.00e^{09}$	$1.00e^{10}$
a to z	$1.00e^{06}$	$3.09e^{08}$	$8.03e^{09}$	$2.09e^{11}$	$5.43e^{12}$	$1.41e^{14}$
a to z and 0 to 9	$6.05e^{07}$	$2.18e^{09}$	$7.84e^{10}$	$2.82e^{12}$	$1.02e^{14}$	$3.66e^{15}$
a to z, 0 to 9, 3 punct	$9.02e^{07}$	$3.52e^{09}$	$1.37e^{11}$	$5.35e^{12}$	$2.09e^{14}$	$8.14e^{15}$
a to z, A to Z	$3.80e^{08}$	$1.98e^{10}$	$1.03e^{12}$	$5.35e^{13}$	$2.78e^{15}$	$1.45e^{17}$
a to z, A to Z, 0 to 9	$9.16e^{08}$	$5.68e^{10}$	$3.52e^{12}$	$2.18e^{14}$	$1.35e^{16}$	$8.39e^{17}$
a to z, A to Z, 0 to 9, 32 punct	$7.34e^{09}$	$6.90e^{11}$	$6.48e^{13}$	$6.10e^{15}$	$5.73e^{17}$	$5.39e^{19}$

As per the system restrictions, user has to select his passwords. For example, some systems are not case-sensitive and treat uppercase and lowercase letters as same. So, there is a need to design the password policies which ensure that the search space for all possible combinations of password is reasonably large. Such passwords are difficult to guess.

Changing and Reusing Passwords

For better security, the passwords should be changed periodically. But many users do not follow this rule and use the same password for long time. Such passwords can be compromised. Some of the ways in which password may be compromised are given below:

1. Passwords shared with the other users
2. Passwords noted down on some paper
3. Password transmitted via insecure manner
4. Use of social engineering by the intruders to capture the password

To avoid the compromises of the password, the best solution is to change the password regularly. Many systems force the users to change their passwords after some fixed time period. Also, another precaution the user should take is that avoid the use of old password again. To avoid the reuse of passwords, many systems keep track of passwords previously used by the particular users. This may keep record of some limited attempt of changing passwords. So, some users who do not wish to change their passwords may take advantage of these criteria. Some users change their passwords to the required times in a day, and then, again use their current password. To prevent such users from doing this, all the previous passwords of the users should be stored so that in any case, user's old password is not permitted.

Secrecy

To identify a user uniquely, a password is used because it is secret to each user. Many times, users are not serious for keeping their passwords secret. As a result, other person may know the password. This is happened as the users:

1. Select passwords which are easy to guess
2. Share the passwords with the other persons
3. Note down passwords on paper or store in the computer file

Intruder Detection

If the user tries to log in using wrong password, in many systems, there is a provision to detect such attempts. If there are too many such attempts within a short period of time, then it is assumed that somebody tries to log in some other user's account by guessing the passwords. To protect the system from such an attempt, many systems allow the user some fixed attempt to feed the password and after that the user account is locked. For example, if the user tries to log in the SBI account, after attempting three times with wrong password, the system locks that account for a day and not allowed to use that account for that day for a valid password also. This method is effective to protect the attack against a single user account. This method cannot be useful to prevent the attacker from guessing the passwords of multiple user accounts simultaneously. In order to guess the password, attackers makes some number of attempts to login through a particular account which will cause locking of the account for some pre-decided period. This may lead to denial of service attack for the genuine user of that account.

To avoid this attack, the best practices are as follows:

1. Apply the wrong log in attempt limit only to the users account. There should not be any limit for wrong log in attempt to the administrator log in.
2. Apply some high threshold value for intruder detection, e.g., 10 wrong log in attempts within 10 minutes.
3. Automatically allow the user to log in after some time, e.g., after 30 minutes.

Encryption

Generally, user passwords are stored on the workstations or the server and during his first log in, the password is transmitted from the workstation to the server in encrypted form. But the best method is to use the hashing algorithms like MD5 or SHA algorithms to check the integrity of the password with the encryption of the password. This provides more security to the password. The password transmission from workstation to server is based on the server's protocol used. Mainframe or Unix servers have no default encryption method used for the transmission of passwords. Some computer systems may cache password and when the user wants to log in, the passwords automatically transmitted to the server. This transmission of password also requires strong protection. So, if security is not guaranteed, then avoid such methods.

Synchronisation

Generally, users have different user accounts on different systems for which they have different passwords. So, there should be some mechanism to help the users in keeping the passwords same that they can use for their different accounts on different systems. This process is called *password synchronisation*, which helps the users to log in different user accounts with same passwords. It is questionable whether such technique is really secure or not. There is some debate as to whether password synchronisation makes systems more secure, or less. The questions may be as follows:

1. Compromise the security: A user has same password for a number of accounts on different systems in the same network. If any system compromises the security, then the attacker/intruder is able to log in all the accounts of the same user. To avoid such attack, the user should use different passwords for different accounts in the same network.

2. Synchronisation improves security: As discussed earlier, a single user may have different passwords for different systems. But there is a problem of remembering all these passwords. Many users write their passwords on paper or store on their notepads, laptops, etc. This reduces the security or there is almost no security. So, synchronised password avoids this need of remembering the password and improves the security.

Some guidelines for using synchronised passwords are mentioned below:
1. Only strong security systems should be involved in this synchronisation system.
2. Users should change their passwords periodically.
3. The passwords should be strong enough so that it cannot be compromised easily.

It is better to use a single, but strong password rather than using multiple passwords. The password should be changed periodically.

User Support

Nowadays, there are a number of user accounts for a single user on different systems. So, the user may forget his password for a particular system. In this situation, he tries to log in with a wrong password and this leads to lock his account. If this happens, the help desk provides help to solve the problem of log in. The process is given below:
1. There is a log in problem to the user.
2. The user requests the help desk for necessary action.
3. The member of help desk team asks the username and details about the problem faced.
4. To authenticate, the member of help desk asks the user's information.
5. For authentication, he compares the information given by the user with the information available with him.
6. Once authentication is completed, the member of help desk either resets the password or forwards the user request to the respective member of help desk, who has the tools and privileges to reset the user's password.
7. Once the password is assigned to the user, he tries to log in.
8. The user should change the password and enter his new password immediately.

But the above process has a number of security loop holes. Some of these loop holes are as under:
1. The authentication of the user is not carried out.
2. For any particular user, the information for authentication may not be available.
3. The information for authentication may be compromised easily.
4. From the members of help desk, anybody may change the password and there is no record of this. The member, who changes the password, knows the user's password. So, the password is no longer truly secret.

The above problem can be solved by ensuring that there should be authentication information available for all the users. The member of help desk logs in the server and then changes the password. Some systems allow the users to reset their own forgotten passwords after reasonable authentication. For this, they have to select a secret question. If the user forgets his password, he has to give the answer of the question selected by him and then the system allows the user to reset his password.

14.9 LIMITATIONS OF INTRUSION DETECTION SYSTEMS

1. Similar IDSs have identical vulnerabilities. So, they cannot detect similar attacks. Thus, the selection of proper IDS model is a serious issue.

2. No IDS has 100% accuracy. It is difficult to measure the sensitivity of IDS. So, making the balance between sensitivity and accuracy of an IDS is critical.
3. For working of IDS, human interference and monitoring are required.
4. Many times, IDS compromises with its security policies.
5. IDS is unable to instantaneous detect, report and respond to an attack.

14.10 CHALLENGES OF INTRUSION DETECTION

Theoretically, IDS looks like a defense tool used to secure our network from the attackers. Speed, accuracy and adaptability are the basic requirements of every IDS. If the attack is not identified in specific time, then the damage caused by the intrusion is large. So, speed is the important requirement of any IDS. IDS should correctly identify the attack. For this, more analysis is required and this increases the computational overhead. If the false alarm rate is more, then many normal attacks are treated as attacks and the alarm is triggered. This blocks normal traffic to enter into the network. The last requirement is adaptability, which means that the IDS should be able to adapt to the new environment and to detect the new attacks. However, IDS has some challenges. The most relevant challenges in the area of intrusion detection that motivate the research work in this area can be summarised as follows:

1. False alarms: One of the most important challenges in intrusion detection is detection accuracy. The high rate of false positives and false negatives intrusion detection tools generated does not help system administrators in simplifying their daily tasks. On the contrary, they may eventually opt for disabling these tools rather than interpreting the alarms reported by the security system that may, in fact, not be reflecting the truth.

2. Performance: Data filtering and screening is a computationally demanding task that is central to intrusion detection. Providing a system with real-time monitoring capabilities implies good search and pattern matching algorithms as well as very fast processing of network traffic, audit trails, etc. that guarantees no data element goes through without being scrutinised. Given the detailed checking needed for intrusion detection, a lot of resources are consumed and the performance of the hosting system ends up being severely affected. As a consequence, the detection task is moved to run offline where its benefits are considerably reduced.

3. Amount of data: The amount of data available within a single host may render the intrusion detection problem intractable. For network-based intrusion detection systems, the amount of traffic going through a gateway, for instance, can be immensely large, making it practically impossible for a security scanner to check every single packet. Similarly, audit trail facilities can generate huge log files, which also limit the possibility of real-time detection. Intrusion detection is a needle-in-the-haystack problem, as the amount of normal activity information may be huge as compared to the pieces of irregular activity that need to be found.

4. Switched networks: Modern networks utilise more intelligent devices to route packets. Many intrusion detection prototypes are based on the ability to configure a network device in promiscuous mode in order to observe a large number of packets. With the modern network technology, this monitoring approach may no longer be successful. A network switch only forwards a packet to its intended recipient to optimise the bandwidth use. Network-based intrusion detection systems need to be strategically placed in order to protect as many hosts as possible inside a LAN. The filtering functions of a switch, which represent performance advantage, are, in fact, a challenge to the security of networked systems.

5. Encryption: Encrypted data cannot be easily interpreted unless the decryption key is available. The evolution of the Internet has witnessed the development of cryptographic protocols and tools that protect the privacy of data. Encrypted file transfers, encrypted interactive sessions, and encrypted e-mail—all eliminate the possibility of meticulous security analysis. As more companies have become security-conscious, the use of encryption is increasing and will certainly increase even more. Intrusion detection tools are currently unable to deal with this problem, as they are blind to the encrypted information.

6. Security of intrusion detection technologies: By definition, a security tool must be secure; otherwise, it cannot be trusted and its results are worthless. As software products, intrusion detection systems face the same security challenges that the other applications do (e.g., poor implementation and a weak design). In fact, not much attention has been put on the secure design of this type of software. Only a few systems can be considered moderately secure, but the vast majority is prone to many types of security attacks.

7. Reaction to incidents: Although it is not a part of the traditional definition of intrusion detection, response to incidents is a very desirable feature that a few intrusion detection systems have actually tried to implement. Taking action based on incorrect information can have serious consequences and the problem of automated response has remained unexplored due to the low levels of detection accuracy which intrusion detection tools currently display.

Many current approaches have been suggested by the researchers for intrusion detection. They have many advantages. But at the same time, there are some problems with these approaches. Some of the problems with these approaches are given below:

1. These new approaches have high detection rate. But at the same time, they have relatively high false alarm rates. Therefore, most of the normal packets are treated as attacks and alarms are generated for the same. Checking all these normal packets for attacks consumes the resources.
2. The computational complexities of these new approaches are very high. Therefore, practical implementations of these approaches are difficult.
3. Updating the signature database is very important for signature-based intrusion detection systems. If a new attack occurs, the pattern of that attack is not present in the signature database. So, in this case, detection of this new attack is difficult.

SUMMARY

The system which is used to protect our system from different attacks is called *intrusion detection systems* (*IDS*). The process of identifying the attacks in a system or network is called *intrusion detection*. An *intrusion* is a deliberate or unauthorised activity or action that attempts to access or manipulate the information or compromise the security of the systems to make them unreliable or unusable. An *intruder* is a person who is responsible for intrusions. There are different types of intruders—masquerader, misfeasor, clandestine user. The intrusion detection system can be divided into two types depending on the architecture—network intrusion detection system (NIDS), and host intrusion detection system (HIDS). Anomaly-based detection techniques are based on the assumption that all intrusive activities are malicious. In misuse-based method, the patterns or signatures are used to detect the attacks. A distributed IDS (dIDS) consists of multiple intrusion detection systems (IDS) over a large network. All these IDSs are communicated with each other, or with a central server. A honeypot is a virtual machine used mainly to attract and trap people, who make an attempt to penetrate other users of the computer systems. Password is the most common mechanism for authentication.

EXERCISES

14.1 What is intrusion?
14.2 What are the different types of intruders? Explain in brief.
14.3 What are the different functions included in intrusion detection?
14.4 Explain the different categories of intrusion detection system in brief.
14.5 Why is intrusion detection system required?
14.6 Define the following terms:
   (a) Risk   (b) Vulnerability
   (c) Attack   (d) Penetration
14.7 Classify the intrusion detection system.
14.8 Explain anomaly detection.
14.9 What is misuse-based detection? Explain in brief.
14.10 Explain model-based intrusion detection.
14.11 Explain rule-based intrusion detection system.
14.12 Describe distributed intrusion detection.
14.13 Explain the attack aggregation in distributed intrusion detection.
14.14 What are the advantages of distributed intrusion detection?
14.15 What is base rate fallacy in intrusion detection system?
14.16 What is honeypot? Explain different types of honeypots.
14.17 Explain the different types of password management best practices.

MULTIPLE CHOICE QUESTIONS

14.1 An advantage of anomaly detection system is
   (a) Rules are simple and easy to define

(b) The engine can scale as the rule set grows
(c) Protocols can be analysed easily
(d) Its false positive rate is lower

14.2. A false positive rate can be defined as
(a) An alarm that indicates an attempt of an attack on a system, which is actually a legitimate network traffic or behavior.
(b) An alarm that indicates an attempt of an attack on a system, which is not running on the network.
(c) The lack of an alarm for an attack.
(d) Both (a) and (b)

14.3 Which of the following is not a type of an IDS ?
(a) anomaly-based detection
(b) signature-based detection
(c) Zone-based detection
(d) Misuse-based detection

14.4 Which of the following is the weakness of the host-based IDS?
(a) Less accuracy
(b) System specific activity
(c) Requirement of more hardware
(d) Very slow at detection

14.5. Which of the following is the weakness of the network-based IDS ?
(a) Increased cost of ownership
(b) Malicious intent detection
(c) Additional hardware is required
(d) Poor real time detection and response

Answers

14.1 (b)   **14.2** (d)   **14.3** (c)   **14.4** (d)   **14.5** (c)

CHAPTER 15

Malicious Software

15.1 INTRODUCTION

To have a high specification computer or laptop with all modern application software is not sufficient today. The most important thing is whether it is secure and virus-free. The malicious software is one of the major issue for the security of the computer or laptop. These malicious software have the ability to disrupt the conduct of our computing work. So, to protect our computer from all these malicious code we have to install an antivirus on the computer and update it regularly. This chapter provides the overview of malicious code, introduction of various malwares such as viruses, worms, Trojans, spyware, bots and the countermeasures for these malwares. It also discusses the digital immune system and different type of attacks.

15.2 MALICIOUS CODE

Malicious software is often called as *malware* or *malicious code*. It is a software purposely designed to damage the computer system or the data stored in that system. Sometimes, malicious software is used to prevent the computer system to perform its regular function in the normal manner. Computer viruses, worms, Trojans, spyware are the main types of malicious software. These programs are specially written to spy the traffic flow through the network. It is used to record the communications between two parties, execute some unauthorised commands, and steal and distribute the information, which is private and confidential. The most common types of malware are viruses, worms, Trojans, bots, back doors, spyware, and adware. The damage caused by these malware is also not same. There may be a damage like causing minor irritation, destroying data from the storage devices, capturing confidential data, for example, user's net banking user account and password, and compromising the systems and networks. It cannot damage the hardware or the network and the software installed on the computer system.

The various types of malicious programs are as follows:
1. Viruses
2. Worms
3. Trojans
4. Spyware
5. Bots

Now, we will discuss these in the subsequent sections.

15.3 VIRUSES

The software which intends to damage the computer system is called *virus*. It is a piece of software which damages the software residing on the computer or any storage. The damage may be in terms of deletion, modification or corruption of the software.

In the last few years, there is a dramatic increase in the threat of virus infections. This mainly happens due to the spread of Internet and e-mail. As the e-mail born viruses have increased, the damage caused by the viruses has also increased on a very large scale. Previously, viruses spread through physical devices such as floppy disk, and therefore, the damage is also on a small scale. But, nowadays, due to increase in the use of Internet, spread of viruses is faster and it causes more damage as compared to past. Viruses have the ability to replicate themselves, and thus, spread rapidly.

15.3.1 Types of Viruses

Viruses can be classified according to their origin, techniques used, damage caused, platforms they use for attack and the types of files they mainly select for damage. Types of viruses are discussed below:

1. *Parasitic virus:* This type of virus is propagated by attaching itself to particular program or a file. It is also known as *executable*. It generally resides at the start or at the end of the file, called *prepending virus* or *appending virus*, respectively. The files with extension .COM and EXE files are easiest to infect because these types of files are directly loaded into the memory and their execution always starts at the first instruction. For example, Jerusalem, a famous parasitic virus, has a payload, which slows down the system and deletes the program that the user tries to execute.

2. *Boot sector virus:* This type of virus spreads when the infected floppy disks or pen drives are used to boot the computers. This type of virus affects the boot sector of the hard disk. Examples are Polyboot. B, Disk Killer, Michelangelo, and Stone virus, AntiEXE.

3. *Polymorphic virus:* This type of virus changes itself with each infection and it creates multiple copies. This makes it difficult for antivirus software to detect it. Examples are Involuntary, Stimulate, Elkern, Cascade, Phoenix, Marburg, Evil, Satan Bug Proud, Virus 101, Tuareg.

4. *Memory resident virus:* This is a virus which installs code in the computer memory. It gets activated when the operating system runs and it damage all the files opened at that time. Examples are Randex, CMJ, Meve.

5. *Stealth virus:* This type of virus hides its path after it infects the computer system. After infection, the virus modifies itself so it is difficult for the antivirus software to identify it. It masks the size of the infected file. Examples are Frodo, Joshi, Whale.

6. *Macro virus:* This type of virus infects the files that are created using some applications, which contain macros. This virus activates when the .docx or .xls files are opened by the user and then infect the normal templates, i.e., every document we open. This virus is attached with the documents; so, it spreads with the infected documents only. When such infected documents are opened on some other computer, it spreads on that computer. Examples are DMV, Melissa. A, Relax, Nuclear, Word Concept.

The damage done by the viruses are not same, it depends on the type of virus. During the design of a virus, a precaution is taken so that it cannot be detected easily and remain undetected until it infects any file or program on the computer. Some viruses are activated on a specific date and at specific time. This type of virus is called *time bomb*. Some viruses are activated by a certain sequence of events and for some specific number of times, it can produce its replicates or the infected program runs automatically for some specific number of times. This type of virus is called *logic bomb*.

7. *Hybrids:* Many times, features of different types of viruses are combined to form a more dangerous virus, called *hybrid virus*. For example, Happy99 virus. It causes e-mail attack. This virus is sent with the e-mail attachment.

8. *E-mail viruses:* Earlier, e-mail was considered to be a pretty safe communication medium. For those still using PINE or some other text-only mail client, it is still safe. But for the rest of us, who want to take advantage of all the advanced features of modern e-mail client software, opening an e-mail message can be a scary experience.

Nowadays, e-mail is the easier way through which viruses can be spread in a very easy manner. Generally, the e-mail attachment is used for this purpose. The virus is sent with the attachment. When the attachment is downloaded, immediately the virus program runs and infects the files stored on the computer. Sometimes, these viruses use the address book of the e-mail holder and send the messages to all the e-mail addresses. So, everybody should take the precaution not to open the attachment of the e-mail sent by any unknown person. Examples of these viruses are Melissa and Klez.

Though the above solution of not opening the attachment is simple, but it does not work always. Many times, the virus creator uses different extensions to the attached file to fool the people so that they open the file.

To protect from e-mail virus, one should take the following precautionary measures:

1. Use licensed antivirus software.
2. Do not open e-mail attachments directly.
3. Use a document viewer.
4. Enable virus protection.

15.3.2 Working of Antivirus Software

A user can protect himself from the virus by installing a licensed copy of antivirus software. It is a program which is used to scan files and identify and eliminate the viruses and other malicious software such as Trojan horses or worms.

The antivirus software uses different approaches to detect the viruses. Two major approaches are signature or pattern-based approach and behaviour-based approach. The approaches are discussed below:

1. *Signature or pattern-based approach:* In this approach, the dictionary has a database containing the signature or pattern of viruses. Then, the information from the file is checked with the signature or pattern from the dictionary. If there is a match found, then the antivirus program can either delete the file or quarantine it so that the other programs cannot access it. This helps in stopping the spread of viruses to the other files. It also tries to remove the virus from the infected file and recover the original documents. For making this approach even more better, the database should be updated periodically. Sometimes, the polymorphic viruses, which hide their identity, are difficult to detect using this approach.

2. *Behaviour-based approach:* The drawback of the above approach is that new viruses cannot be detected, as the signature or pattern is not available in the database of the dictionary. In this approach, this drawback is removed, as it does not use any database of the known viruses. The detection of viruses depends on the suspicious behaviour of the computer programs. It monitors the behaviour of all programs. If some program, tries to modify an executable program, then this behaviour is treated as suspicious and it sends an alert to the user. Therefore, using this approach, new attack can be identified, which is not possible using the first approach. But the drawback of this approach is that it creates large number of false positives. This limits the use of this approach for the design of antivirus software.

3. *Other approaches for detecting viruses:* Here, for each new executable program that is being executed, the antivirus software initially tries to emulate the beginning of the code. This is done before transferring control to the executable program. If it is observed that the program is using self-modifying code or otherwise appears as a virus, then it means that the executable program has been infected with a virus. The drawback of this method is that false positive rate is large.

Another approach is a sandbox method. In this approach, the sandbox emulates the OS and executable runs on this simulation. Then, the sandbox is analysed for any changes. Then, the conclusion is made about the virus. The drawback of this approach is poor performance. So, generally, it is used for on-demand scans.

Prevention

All of us know about the popular maxim 'prevention is better than cure'. For computer security, this maxim is effectively applicable. To protect the computer system from viruses, installation of antivirus software is required. This software helps in detecting and eradicating viruses. But only installation of the antivirus software is not sufficient, as a number of new viruses emerge everyday. For this, there is a need of updating the antivirus software. This modifies the database of the signatures or patterns in the dictionary. Second precautionary measure is one should update his/her internet browsers periodically. Third precautionary measure is that not to open or download the e-mail attachment sent by unknown person.

Detection

For detection of viruses, run the antivirus software to scan the computer system everyday. This helps in detecting the virus and the infected files.

Eradication

The most important measure is to use real-time antivirus software. When the virus is detected, immediately, the alarm is given and the warning is displayed on the screen. The virus protection program counters the virus by either repairing the infecting file or deleting it.

15.3.3 Methods to Avoid Detection

Some viruses apply different kinds of deception so that the user could not detect them. On the MS-DOS platform, some old viruses keep the date of last modification same so that the antivirus software cannot detect it. Some viruses infect the file without changing the file size or damaging the file. This can be done by overwriting some unused part of the executable files. These types of viruses are called *cavity viruses*. Some viruses hide themselves by killing the tasks associated with antivirus software before they can detect them. These techniques are useless for new antivirus software; so, new techniques always emerge for this.

Avoiding Bait Files and Other Undesirable Hosts

To propagate further, a virus needs to infect hosts program. Sometimes, it may be a bad idea. Suppose, many antivirus programs check their performance by doing integrity check of their own program code. This increases the probability of the detection of the virus. Therefore, some viruses are programmed in such a way that they do not infect the part of the antivirus software. Also, virus program should not infect the bait files. The files which are created by the antivirus software or antivirus professionals so that the virus could infect such files are called *bait files*. These files are used to detect the viruses. Bait files are affected by the virus, and then these files are used to collect the signature or pattern of the virus, which is used by the antivirus professionals to modify the signature database in the dictionary. These bait files are also used to know the behaviour of the virus and this helps in developing the method for detection of the virus. This technique is most useful for polymorphic viruses. We know that polymorphic viruses infect many files, particularly bait files. Now, for experimentation and analysis, a large number of bait files are available, which are helpful for getting the detailed features of the virus. The virus programs also try to avoid these bait files, particularly small programs. Baiting can be made difficult by using sparse infection but this is not happened always. Sometimes, sparse infectors do not infect a host file. For example, a virus selects the files for infection randomly. Secondly, the host files are infected on some particular day of a week or some particular date of a month or year.

Stealth

Some viruses trap the antivirus software by interrupting its request to the operating system and hide it. Therefore, the request sent by antivirus software to the operating system for reading the file is captured by the virus. Actually, this file is infected; so, to hide this, virus program sends the non-infected version of the file to the antivirus software. So, the antivirus software assumes that the file is clean. This mechanism is called *stealth mechanism*. To protect from this stealth mechanism, modern antivirus software uses different techniques. The most reliable technique is to boot from a clean medium.

Self-modification

We learn that there are two approaches for detecting viruses—signature or pattern-based approach and behavior-based approach. Antivirus programs scan the files for virus signatures or patterns. These signatures or patterns are then compared with the signature database in the dictionary. If the match is found, the virus is detected and the user knows that the file is infected. The user may delete or clean such infected files. To make this detection more difficult, viruses use different techniques such as modifying the program code after each infection so that the signature or pattern changes. So, different files infected by the same virus have different signatures or patterns.

Simple Self-modifications

Some computer viruses modify themselves by exchanging their subroutines. But antivirus software identifies such viruses.

Encryption with a Variable Key

As encryption is useful for protecting the message, it is also used to protect the virus code. A virus has a copy of code encrypted with a key and a decrypting module. Generally, encryption means simple XOR operations are used so that the encryption and decryption algorithm is same. For each infected file, a virus is encrypted using different key. The decrypting module remains unchanged and is appended at the end of the file. For the use of different encryption key, the ciphertext for the virus is changed. This produces different signatures for the same virus and makes it difficult for the antivirus software to identify the virus. But advance antivirus software can detect such viruses, as the decrypting module remains unchanged.

Polymorphic Code

Polymorphic virus uses an encrypted copy of its code for infection to a file and decryption module is used for decryption. Here, not only the encryption module but also decryption module is modified after each infection. So, after each infection, both the parts of a virus are changed. This makes it difficult to get the same signature for the same virus. So, signature-based approach cannot be useful for polymorphic viruses. In this case, an emulator is used by the antivirus software to detect the virus. Sometimes, polymorphic viruses reduce their rate of mutation so that it makes difficult for the antivirus software to obtain a sample of signature of the viruses. Generally, antivirus professions make use of bait files to capture the signature of the virus. As the polymorphic viruses make their rate of infection slow, the number of bait files are infected in one run is also small. This makes it difficult to get the signature of the virus to the antivirus professionals.

Metamorphic Code

Some viruses rewrite themselves after each infection so that it is difficult to detect such viruses using emulation. Such viruses which use this technique are called *metamorphic viruses*. The code of these viruses is large in size and complex. They use a metamorphic engine for metamorphism.

Antivirus Software and Other Countermeasures

A large number of new viruses emerge everyday. Protecting the computer system from such new viruses is the most important part of security. Antivirus software provides necessary security to our computer. The important thing is that it should be updated so that new viruses can be detected. For the detection of viruses, two approaches are used—signature or pattern-based approach and behaviour-based approach. The first approach uses the signature of the viruses, whereas in the second approach, the detection of viruses depends on the suspicious behaviour of the computer programs. It monitors the behaviour of all programs. If some program tries to modify an executable program, then this behaviour is treated as suspicious and an alert is sent to the user. This approach can detect the new virus for which the signature is not created yet by the antivirus professionals. The drawback of the signature-based approach is that the new virus cannot be detected, as the signature or pattern is not available in the database of the dictionary. The drawback of behaviour-based approach is that it creates large number of false positives. Antivirus software checks the contents of heuristics of RAM, the boot sectors and the storage devices. Then, it compares these against the signature from the database present in the antivirus software. Some antivirus software also scan the opened files in the same way, called *on-access scanning*. To capture the new viruses, the antivirus software should be updated periodically.

To prevent data loss by the viruses, precautions should be taken by the user. One of the most important precautions is to keep backup of the important data in regular intervals. If the backup is taken of optical devices like CD or DVD, it becomes read only, and then, the viruses cannot infect it. This backup is useful if the data is lost due to virus, i.e., one can use backup data to recover the loss. Second method is to use different operating systems on different file systems. In this case, the virus cannot infect both the files.

15.4 WORMS

A *worm* is a small piece of software different from a virus. It can execute and spread itself, whereas virus needs host program for its execution and spread. Some modern worms also hide inside a file. It uses security loop holes within networks to reproduce itself. It is self-replicating and it does not make any change in the files or documents. It resides in active memory and replicates itself. It scans the network for another computer, which has security loop hole. It copies itself to the new computer system and then replicates itself. It affects the performance of the computer by using its resources and shuts down the computer. It expands quickly and uses all the available memory available to a computer.

15.4.1 Historical Background

In 1975, John Brunner first time used the word *worm* in his novel. John Shoch and John Hupp first time implemented a worm in 1978 at Xerox PARC. They designed this worm to find out the idle processor on the network so that they can assign some work to that processor and improve the utilisation of the systems in the network. The purpose of this worm was to share the load and improve the efficiency of the entire network. The first worm on the worldwide network is the Christmas Tree. This worm spreads across the IBM's own international network and BITNET and affects the performance of both the networks. Morris worm is the first worm, which attracts the attentions of the researchers related to computer field.

15.4.2 Different Types of Computer Worms

1. *E-mail worm:* It is a type of worm that spreads through infected e-mail attachments. It distributes copies of itself by attaching to the fake e-mail messages. The link to an infected web site is sent in any form of attachment or link in an e-mail. When the user opens the attachment immediately, the worm activates. If the user clicks the link, then also worm activates. One can prevent the infection by worm simply by not opening an attachment.

2. *Instant messaging worm:* It is a type of worm which spread via instant messaging applications. It spreads in instant messaging network using the loop holes in the network. It spreads by sending links to the infected web sites to each user on the local address list. In 2001, the first instant messaging worm is identified. Thereafter, many more worms of this type are in news. These worms infect a user's account and find out the addresses from the contact list and try to send themselves to all the users in the address list.

3. *Internet worm:* An internet worm spreads across the internet through network connections. For this, it scans all the resources using operating system services as well as scans for vulnerable computer systems. Then, it tries to access these computer systems. Also, this type of worm tries to locate those computer systems which are still open for exploitation.

4. *Internet Relay Chat (IRC) worm:* This type of worm spreads via IRC channels. It transfers infected files or links to the infected web sites.

5. *File-sharing networks worm:* File-sharing networks worm places a copy of itself in a shared folder. It spreads through P2P network.

6. *Payloads:* The purpose of many worms is to spread and not to alter any configurations of the system. But the worms like Morris and Mydoom cause an effect on the network traffic. Payload is optional but commonly used component of the computer worm. Most popular payload is DoS attack against a specific web site. A *payload* is a code which is designed to do some more such as delete or encrypt files or send the files through e-mail, rather than only spreading the worm. A very common payload is to install a backdoor in the computer. This allows creating a zombie computer. This infected computer is then under the control of the attacker, who creates the worm. The network of such computer systems is called *botnet*. The senders of spam messages use these botnets for sending junk mails. They may use them to cloak the web site's address. They overload the network router. They have a side effect like attack on network printer. They can be used to compromise the systems as supercomputer. There is a planned interaction between the two worms as a payload. Many antiworms have been created with the purpose of killing other worms and also installing patches against the vulnerabilities they exploit. A Simple Mail Transfer Protocol (SMTP) can be installed as spam relay server to use it as the payload of a worm.

7. *Worms with good intent:* Some worms can be used for good intentions. For example, the Nachi worms are used to download and install the patches from Microsoft's web site. This is useful to fix various vulnerabilities in the host system. This makes the system more secure, but the drawback is that the traffic generated more deteriorates the performance of the network. It also reboots the computer system and performs all these activities without the consent of administrator of the system.

15.4.3 Protecting against Computer Worms

The main intention of computer worm is to exploit the vulnerabilities in the operating systems. To protect and identify the worm, periodical updation of the software is needed. One can take precaution while opening the e-mail attachment sent by unknown senders.

Steps to make a computer system secure from worms are given below:
1. Use the update and license copy of operating system and other software. Because these updated software contain patches for security, which help in protecting the computer system from worms.
2. Do not open the e-mails sent by unknown sources.
3. Avoid opening the attachments or using links from unknown parties.
4. Use license copy of antivirus software and firewall.

15.4.4 Symptoms of a Computer Worm

Some of the symptoms of the computer worms are as follows:
1. The performance of the computer becomes slow.
2. Sometimes, the computer may crash.
3. Some programs automatically open and execute.
4. The performance of the web browser is affected.
5. Some of the files may be modified or missing.
6. There are some errors in the operating system.
7. On the desktop, some unknown icons appear.
8. E-mails from the user account may be sent automatically.

15.5 TROJANS OR TROJAN HORSES

Trojan horse or Trojan programs are named for the famous hollow wooden horse filled with enemy soldiers used by ancient Greece to gain entry of their soldiers into the city of Troy. It is a program that conceals its purpose. Trojan horse program claims to do one thing, but in reality, it performs another thing. Most of the times, it appears as attachment in the e-mail and it is a non-replicating program. Many times, Trojan horse program is used to install virus program on the computer system. Using Trojan horse, the attacker could gain access to a computer system. A specific type of Trojan horse program is a *logic bomb*, which executes when some specific events occur. It is a program that hides inside some useful application program and when it invokes it performs some harmful function. For example, a Trojan horse program is attached with the interest calculator program of a bank. The interest calculator program is executed after some specific period by a bank such as after every six months. When this program runs, the Trojan horse program invokes and performs the activity defined. Suppose the attacker designs the Trojan horse in such a way that when the interest calculator program runs, the Trojan horse program automatically invokes and transfers the fractional part of the interest of each bank account holder to some specific account. This account may be the attacker's account. Suppose the total number of accounts in a bank is 10,00,000, and suppose the fractional part of interest of each account holder ranges from 0.01 to 0.99 rupees. We assume that the average fraction part per account holder is 0.25, so approximately ₹2.5 Lakh will be transferred to the attacker's account after every six months, and as each user loses the amount, which is less than ₹1, nobody knows about this and the damage may continue until somebody knows it.

15.5.1 Features of Trojan Horse Virus

The Trojan horse and virus are different. Trojan horse program does not replicate or spread itself. It spreads through downloading either an infected file from Internet or payload of some other virus. It is used to steal information from the infected computer system and also to download other malicious codes to a computer system. One can protect his/her system by using updated licensed copy of antivirus software and by using firewall. But this is not sufficient, as antivirus software cannot detect the Trojan horse in the computer system. This happens because Trojan horse program is active only when specific event occur. Therefore, manual method should be used to remove Trojan horse program from the computer system.

Manual Removal of Trojan Horse

To identify the Trojan horse the following steps may be followed:

Step 1   The first step is to locate the file infected by Trojan horse. When the computer system gives DLL error, then there is a possibility of Trojan horse attack. Copy the error and search online for the affected .EXE file.

Step 2   The next step is to stop the system restore function so that any deleted file cannot be restored again.

Step 3 Then, restart the computer system in the safe mode.

Step 4 Go to control panel and select 'Add or Remove Programs' from the control panel. Then, remove the programs infected with Trojan horse.

Step 5 Delete all files from system folder.

After completion of the above steps, restart the computer system in normal mode.

Alternative Method for Removing Trojan Horse

To remove Trojan horse, edit the system registry and complete the following steps:

1. Go in the folder options and display all the hidden folders.
2. Then, restart the computer system in the safe mode.
3. Then, stop all the processes associated with Trojan horse.

For removing the affected files from the registry, first search the file in RUN folder. Then, delete the DLL and .EXE files those are related to the Trojan horse. At the end, delete the value. Now, restart the computer system and go to the Startups and check which programs are automatically loaded. For this method, knowledge of registry is needed.

15.6 SPYWARE

One more malware program is spyware. Without the knowledge of the owner of the computer, it is installed on the computer. It is used to gather the secret and private information about the user from the computer system. Then, this information is used for advertising purpose. Spyware can be used to collect personal information and also to change the configuration of the targeted system. The performance of the computer is affected by the spyware. This can be done by installing additional software, redirecting the web browser search, changing the settings of the computer, reducing the speed of the internet, changing the home page. It can be used as a type of adware. In this, the software delivers unsolicited pop-up ads in addition to tracking the behaviour of the user. When the user installs some free software from the internet, spyware is installed with it. It starts collecting the personal information from the computer system. It is also installed with Trojan horse and also with some free antivirus software.

15.7 BOTS

It is derived from the word *robot*. It is an automated process which interacts with the other network services. It automates the tasks and provides information or services that would otherwise be conducted by a human being. It is used to collect the information, or interact automatically with instant messaging, Internet Relay Chat (IRC), or other web interfaces. It may also be used to interact dynamically with web sites. The intention to use bot may be good or malicious. The malicious bot is designed to infect the host and connect back to a server, which acts as a command and control centre for the whole network of these compromised systems, called *botnet*. Attackers use this botnet to launch different attacks. Bots can replicate themselves like worms. They have the ability to log keystrokes, capture and analyse the packets, collect passwords, and information related to various applications. Bots are more versatile in their infection as compared to worms.

15.8 BEST PRACTICES

1. Install a license copy of the antivirus software and update it regularly.
2. The antivirus software should always run and it automatically scans the entire computer everyday.
3. Do not open the e-mail attachment sent by unknown person. Scan the attachment before opening it.
4. All the removal devices are scanned by antivirus software before using.
5. Configure the antivirus software for maximum protection.
6. Download files only from trusted sites.
7. Take the backup of important files regularly.
8. Directories should be password protected.
9. Make use of licensed copy of the operating system and other software.
10. Install available patches of the software.

15.9 DIGITAL IMMUNE SYSTEM

The biggest weakness of the antivirus software is that they are not able to detect most of the new viruses. Due to the vast use of Internet, the viruses are spread all over the world in a day. To cure the human disease, the solution is cure spreading faster than the disease. The first digital immune system for computers was developed by IBM in early 1990. It provides the general purpose emulations and virus detection. The purpose of digital immune system is to identify the virus as soon as it introduces into the system. When the new virus enters in the computer, the digital immune system automatically detects it, analyses it and modifies the database by adding its signature to protect the system by detecting and removing the virus. It also provides information to the antivirus software so that it can detect the virus and protect the computer system. The efficiency of digital immune system response depends on the ability of the system to differentiate normal packets from abnormal packets.

Following are the features of digital immune system:

1. The detection rate for new or unknown threats is high.
2. It makes the system highly scalable.
3. It provides secure submission of virus signature and secure distribution of new definitions.
4. It provides intelligent filtering of submissions.
5. It provides fast analysis of the threats.
6. It helps in reducing false positives in the system.
7. It detects the threat automatically, analyses it and distributes the signature of this new threat.

15.9.1 Behaviour Blocking

Behaviour blocking monitors the file activities, prevents certain modifications to the operating system or related files. It is a protective mechanism and is also known as *sandboxing*. It observes the behaviour of the running program and if some misbehaviour is found, then it blocks it. It blocks the actions of malicious software. It is more effective than an antivirus software, as it blocks the malicious programs. An antivirus software compares the signature of any malicious activity with the signature from the database, whereas behaviour blocking monitors the actual functions of the malicious program. As the signatures of new viruses are not present in the database, the antivirus software cannot detect these new viruses, whereas behaviour blocking stops these new viruses from causing harm to the system. Figure 15.1 shows the block diagram of digital immune system.

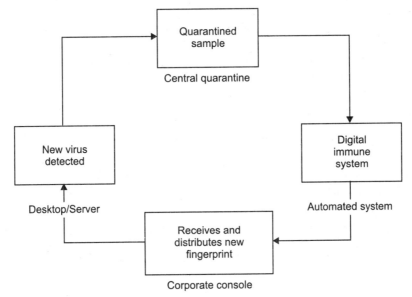

Figure 15.1 Digital immune system.

15.10 ATTACKS

In the last 35 years, use of computers and Internet have increased significantly which result in increase in threats to the security of the computer system. A number of tools are easily available for attackers, which make it easy to create new vulnerabilities. These tools require very little or no prior knowledge to use. An *attack* can be defined as any action that compromises the security of computer systems or the information. There are different types of attacks, which can damage the computer system as well as the network. Some of these attacks are discussed in the subsequent sections.

15.10.1 Hoax

A *hoax* is an attempt to give false warning about the virus. It may consist of instructions or advices to delete an important file under the pretence to avoid virus infection.

Characteristics of Hoaxes

Hoaxes are not always created, initiated or sourced in the same way. Hoax can be classified into different classes as below:

1. Hoax by tradition
2. Hoax by design (such as in war)
3. Hoax originating in legitimate non-hoax use (e-mail hoax)
4. Hoax by scare tactics (virus hoaxes)
5. Urban legend

15.10.2 Backdoor Attack

A *backdoor* is a means of remotely access to a computer program that bypasses the normal authentication process. A backdoor program may be used for troubleshooting or for other purposes by the programmer before deploying the same. But the attacker uses it to exploit the system. Backdoors permit the attackers to establish a connection with their target network while escaping recognition. In fact, a research has made it public that many of the backdoors used in attacks have been designed with the ability to bypass intrusion detection system (IDS).

15.10.3 Brute Force Attack

A *brute force attack* consists of trying all possible combinations, code or the password until we get the correct one. It is simple attack. It is difficult to protect from this attack. As it is trial and error method, it is time-consuming. To protect the algorithms from this attack, following factors make it difficult for brute force attack:

1. The length of the key should be long.
2. Possible values for each components of the key should be more.
3. Time required to check for the validity of each key should be large.
4. There should be some restrictions on the number of incorrect attempts to log in.

For example, for DES algorithm, the key size is 64 bits. The possible number of keys are 2^{64}. Suppose the key size is 4 bits, the possible number of keys are 2^4, i.e., 16. Now, one can easily guess manually 16 keys of 4 bits within a short time. So for better security, the key length should be large. The same rule is applied for the password. If the password is large enough and if it is a combination of alphabets and numbers and special characters, then brute force attack is difficult.

Giving sufficient time, brute force attack always succeeds. But if the key size is large, it takes billions of years to find out the key. Therefore, brute force attack is successful against DES, but not against AES or triple DES due to long key size.

15.10.4 Dictionary Attack

A *dictionary attack* is a technique of breaking a password of a computer or server by using every word in a dictionary as a password. It is also used to find the key of the encryption algorithm. It is more efficient than brute force attack, but there is no guarantee of success of dictionary attack to find out the password successfully. Generally, user selects poor password, which can be easily broken using this attack. If the password contains passphrases, then it is difficult to find out the password using dictionary attack. In the dictionary attack, the attacker collects some information that is derived from the user's password. This information may be a hash value of the password, which is stored in the database of the user's computer or it may be encrypted responses produced by a challenge response authentication protocol. The attacker tries to generate the computation that should have the same value which he has collected from user's computer. This is done by using successive words stored in the dictionary. If one of the word produces a matching result with the collected information, then it can be used to masquerade that user. This complete process works offline, and the user and the computer system do not know about all this process. Therefore, it is difficult for the user to interpret that the attack is taking place. The performance of this method depends on the size of the dictionary and the computing power used for matching the information. To make the process faster, sometimes, the attacker computes the hash value of each dictionary word in advance so that he can directly compare with the information collected.

Improve the Performance of Dictionary Attacks

The performance of dictionary attack can be improved using the following methods:

1. Use one or more large dictionaries. It may include technical words and phrases from foreign language. This increases the chances of obtaining the correct password.
2. Another method is the use of string manipulation on the dictionary. For example, the dictionary may have the word *himalaya* in it. Using string manipulation techniques, this word reverses which will give the word *ayalamih*. Alternatively, we can use common number-letter replacements like h23a5aya (where 2, 3 and 5 gives the position of missing letters) or we can use different capitalisation such as *Himalaya*.

If the dictionary attack fails, use brute force attack.

15.10.5 Spoofing Attack

In spoofing attack, one person or program masquerades as another person or program by hiding his own identity and giving false information and thereby gaining an illegitimate advantage. This is an access attack.

Man-in-the-middle Attack and Internet Protocol Spoofing

In this attack, an attacker spoofs, for example, the attacker enables Ram to believe that he is Shyam, and spoofs Shyam by making him believe that he is Ram. In this way, he gains access to all messages in both the directions, thereby modifying any information. The attacker monitors the packets and guesses the sequence number of the packets sent from Ram to Shyam. Then, the attacker sends a SYN attack to Ram and adds his own packets, claiming to have the address of Ram. A firewall having all the IP addresses is able to defend spoofing attack.

URL Spoofing and Phishing

A fake attempt to steal the personal information of the user made by an attacker is called *phishing*. Phishing is generally made using e-mail. Web page spoofing is also known as *phishing*. In web site spoofing, forged sites appear nearly identical to their legitimate web sites. In this attack, a legitimate web page is created through which an e-mail is sent requesting the personal information. The web page looks identical to the original web page. So, the user believes that it is the original web page and enters his username and password on this web page. This fake web page is controlled by the attacker so he captures all this information. URL spoofing is used to perform this attack. When the user enters his password, the password error displays and then it redirect the user to the legitimate site.

Referer Spoofing

When user visits some web page, the web server collects information about the user's browser. The most important information collected is web URL. The HTTP header field which identifies the address of the web page that gives the link of the previously requested resources. This is called referer. This is used by the attacker to see where the request originated. Referer spoofing is the sending of incorrect referer information which is helpful to prevent a web site from obtaining accurate identities of the address of the web page that gives the link of the previously requested resources by the user. It is used to protect data privacy.

Poisoning of File-sharing Networks

The copyright holder uses spoofing to protect the material from downloading. The distorted or unlistenable versions of the original copyrighted work are available on the file-sharing network. Due to this version, people avoid to download from such sources.

Caller ID Spoofing

When the user calls either on a landline or on a mobile phone the caller ID information is displayed on the receivers end. This information about the caller is transmitted with the call. Nowadays, there are new technologies that allow the caller to hide his identity from the receiver and display false information about the caller, including false caller name and number. This technique could be used to harass or defraud somebody. There are different services and gateways which interconnect VoIP with other phones or mobile phones on the globe. These gateways and services are used to transmit false information about the caller. Therefore, the purpose of callerID is useless. Calls using VoIP can be generated from anywhere or any country. Due to legal problems between the different countries, it is difficult to control the attackers who use false caller ID.

15.10.6 Denial-of-Service Attack (DoS Attack)

The attack is made by flooding the network with some useless traffic. This type of attack is called *Denial-of-Service (DoS) attack*. This attack makes memory resources too busy to serve legitimate networking requests, and hence, denying access to legitimate users. Different types of DoS attacks are back, neptune, ping of death, land, pod, smurf, teardrop. The ping of death and teardrop attacks make use of the limitations in the TCP/IP protocols. DoS attacks are 80% of the total attacks attempted on the network. There are software available to fix and limit the damage by the known DoS attacks. But new DoS attacks are constantly developed by the attackers.

Working of Denial-of-Service Attacks

To establish the connection in a network, the authentication of the users takes place. For this authentication, the user sends a request message to the server for authentication. The server sends the response to the user after authenticating the user and gives the approval to the user. The user again sends the acknowledgement message to the server and then starts the communication.

The attackers use this authentication method and generate the Denial-of-Service attack. For this, the user sends several request messages for authentication to the server. This floods the network. The addresses of all these requests are false. So, it is not possible for the server to send responses about authentication approval to the user. Before closing the connection, the server tries to send the reply. Sometimes, it may wait for this more than a minute. When the server closes the connection, the new requests are sent by the attacker and the process is repeated again and again, which makes the server busy to find the address for responding. As this process continues indefinite times, the server remains busy to give the response and it denies its service for other requests. Using ping command in infinite loop can generate the DoS attack. This prevents legitimate or authorised users of the server to use the system resources or services of the server.

Blocking A Denial-of-Service Attack

We can protect the server from DoS attack by using filter or sniffer. This helps in blocking the DoS attack. This sniffer or filter is installed on a network. It blocks the stream of information on a network before it reaches the servers. The filter observes the incoming request for pattern. If the requests come from the same address, then the pattern remains same. If the same pattern comes frequently, then the filter blocks the requests coming from that address. In this way, DoS attack is avoided and the servers are protected.

15.10.7 Distributed Denial-of-Service Attack

A multitude of compromised systems attacks a single system, resulting in Denial-of-Service for users of that system. This type of attack is called *Distributed Denial-of-Service attack (DDoS)*. The number of requests coming to the target system shuts down it forcefully. This prevents legitimate or authorised users of the target system to use the system resources or services of the server. DDoS attack is done through distributed network, Internet for attack. It first breaks number of computers all over the Internet. Then, installs Distributed Denial-of-Service attack software on these computers. This makes the distributed network of all these computers. This allows them to control all these computers for launching coordinated attacks. This attack overloads the bandwidth, the router and the stack resources. This completely breaks down the network connectivity. Then, the attacker launches the DDoS attack by exploiting the vulnerability in one of the computers and making it the master for DDoS. Then, the attacker uses this master computer to identify and communicate with other computers in the network, which can be compromised. Then, the attacker installs tools for cracking on number of compromised computers on the Internet. Using single command, the attacker uses these machines and launches flood attacks against a specific computer. This causes Denial-of-Service on that computer.

15.10.8 Man-in-the-middle Attack

A *man-in-the-middle attack* is an attack in which an attacker intercepts a communication between two parties. The attacker is able to read, modify and insert at will, messages between two parties without either party in communication knowing that the communication channel between them has been compromised. The attacker controls the complete communication between the two parties. It is a form of eavesdropping.

This attack is related to key transmission. Suppose two parties A and B are trying to communicate to each other. In this attack, the attacker places himself between the two parties A and B. Then, the attacker captures the data which A and B transfer to each other. Then, he (the attacker) performs key exchange separately with A and B. A and B uses the different keys sent by the attacker. The attacker is now able to decrypt any message sent by the two parties A and B.

15.10.9 Spam

Many copies of the same message flood the Internet in an attempt to force the message on the users, who would not otherwise wish to receive it. Spam is used generally for advertising the product. Sender has to pay less for spam as compared to recipient. Spam is categorised into two types—cancellable Usenet spam and e-mail spam. We can send a single message to 20 or more Usenet groups using cancellable Usenet spam. Individual users are targeted with direct mail messages using e-mail spam. The e-mail address lists are created by scanning the Usenet postings, searching the addresses on the web, and stealing the Internet mailing.

15.10.10 E-mail Bombing and Spamming

E-mail bombing is an attack by repeatedly sending the message through e-mail to a particular address at a specific target computer. Many times, the messages will be large and have meaningless data. It sends to consume system and network resources. Multiple accounts at the target site may be abused. This results in the Denial-of-Service. The variant of bombing is e-mail spamming.

15.10.11 Sniffer

A *sniffer* is software that captures all of the traffic flowing in both the directions, i.e., into and out of a computer attached to a network. It is also known as *network protocol analyser*. It is used as a network troubleshooting tool. The attackers use sniffers to capture the packets flowing across the network to get the information. With the help of sniffer, one can read the data from the captured packets if the data is not in encrypted form. Sniffers are available in both commercial and open-source variations. Some of the well-known packet sniffers are wireshark, Dsniff, sniffit. Intrusion detection system uses sniffers to capture the packets and analyse the packets against the defined rules for normal or abnormal behaviour. Sniffers are also used to check the performance of network by monitoring and analysing the network traffic. Sniffers are used to capture the packets, inspecting and analysing the contents of the packet on a TCP/IP network. Attackers use sniffers to steal the information like user ID, password, PIN, credit card number, etc. As the attacker only observes the information, this attack is referred to as *passive attack*; so, it is difficult to detect.

Working of a Sniffer

When the computers are connected with each other via network, they communicate with each other by sending packets. When the users perform some tasks such as web surfing and messaging, user's computers are constantly communicating with other computers by sending and receiving packets. For a non-switched network, every computer on the network is able to see the traffic flowing across the network.

Every computer has a network interfacing card (NIC) through which it is connected to the other computer. Sniffer allows the NIC to observe all the traffic across the network. This can be done by putting NIC in a promiscuous mode. This mode gives all the administrative privileges to the computer so that it can observe all the information transmitted across the network. Then, the sniffer program, which is installed on that computer, reads the contents of all the packets coming to that computer. The packet contains the information related to source address, destination address, port number, payload, etc. All this information is collected using sniffers.

Sniffer can be used for both legitimate and illegitimate purposes. The network administrator can use sniffer to monitor the flow of traffic across the network. This is useful to improve the performance of the network. However, attackers can use sniffers to capture the valuable information related to the users such as user ID, password, etc. So, to protect the user from attackers is an essential task for network administrator. The first option for this security is to uninstall the sniffer software if it is there on any computer on any network. The NIC in promiscuous mode is responsible for capturing all the packets on the network. Another option is install antisniff tools, which give the information whether the NIC is running in promiscuous mode or not. This tool should run regularly so that the network administrator sends the alarm if the NIC in promiscuous mode and sniffer is working. One more option is the use of switched network. In non-switched network, all the traffic is visible to every computer on the network. In the switched network, the packets are delivered only to the destination address, so, other computers cannot see the packets. As the packets are delivered only to the destination address, NIC in promiscuous mode of any other computers can not be able to capture the packets for other computers.

15.10.12 Timing Attack

In a timing attack, the attackers analyse the time taken by the cryptographic algorithm for its execution. Using this analysis, the attackers try to break the algorithm. This attack is also known as *side channel attack*. The information about execution time taken by a particular algorithm or program is collected from the response time of the computer to certain queries. This information depends on the design of the cryptosystem, the speed of the CPU, the algorithms used for implementation, protective measures used to prevent timing attack and the accuracy in the measurement of timing. This attack depends on the implementation; so, in design phase, nothing can be done to prevent the timing attack.

A timing attack is a practical attack. In this, the attacker tries to exploit the implementation of the algorithm rather than the algorithm itself. If the same algorithm is implemented in such a way that no information is leak about time for execution, then timing attack is difficult for such implementations of the same algorithm.

SUMMARY

Malware is software purposely designed to damage the computer system or the data store in that system. Sometimes, malicious software is used to prevent the computer system to perform its regular function in the normal manner. Computer viruses, worms, Trojans, spyware are the main types of malicious software. It is a piece of software which damages the software residing on the computer or any storage. The damage may be in terms of deletion, modification or corruption of software. Worm can execute itself, whereas virus needs host program for its execution. It is self-replicating and it does not make any change in the files or documents. Trojan horse program claims to do one thing, but in reality, it performs another thing. Trojan horse program does not replicate or spread itself. It spreads through downloading either as an infected file from internet or as payload of some other virus. It is used to steal information from the infected computer system.

An attack is any action that compromises the security of computer systems or the information. There are different types of attacks, which can damage the computer system as well as the network. A hoax is an attempt to give the false warning about the virus. A backdoor is a means of remotely access to a computer program that bypasses the normal authentication process. A brute force attack consists of trying all possible combinations, code or the password until we get the correct one. A dictionary attack is a technique of breaking a password of a computer or server by using every word in a dictionary as a password. In spoofing attack, one person or program masquerades as another person or program by hiding his own identity and giving false information and thereby gaining an illegitimate advantage. The attack is made by flooding the network with some useless traffic. This type of attack is called Denial-of-Service (DoS) attack. A man-in-the-middle attack is an attack in which an attacker intercepts a communication between the two parties. A sniffer is a software that captures all of the traffic flowing in both directions, i.e., into and out of a computer attached to a network. In timing attack, the attackers analyse the time taken by the cryptographic algorithm for its execution. Using this analysis, the attackers try to break the algorithm.

EXERCISES

15.1 What is a malicious program? List the various types of malicious programs.
15.2 List the various types of viruses. Explain each in detail.
15.3 Explain the working of e-mail viruses.

15.4 How does antivirus software work?

15.5 What is worm? What are the different types of worms? Explain the working of worm.

15.6 What is Trojan horse? What is the difference between Trojan horse and the virus?

15.7 Explain spyware.

15.8 Explain digital immune system.

15.9 What are the different types of attack? Explain each in brief.

MULTIPLE CHOICE QUESTIONS

15.1 In denial of service attacks, typically against the targeted web sites ----------------is used.
  (a) Zombie
  (b) Trojan
  (c) Virus
  (d) Worm

15.2 A .... attaches itself to executable files. When the infected program is executed, it replicates itself by finding other executable files to infect.
  (a) Macro virus
  (b) Stealth virus
  (c) Polymorphic virus
  (d) Parasitic virus

15.3 A type of virus explicitly designed to hide itself from detection by antivirus software is
  (a) Macro virus
  (b) Parasitic virus
  (c) Stealth virus
  (d) Polymorphic virus

15.4 A .... is a malicious code that is installed secretly on another Internet-attached computer and then attacks are launched using that computer.
  (a) Zombie
  (b) Virus
  (c) Trap doors
  (d) Worm

15.5 Bots have the ability to
  (a) Log keystrokes
  (b) Capture and analyse the packets
  (c) Collect passwords
  (d) All of the above

15.6 Which of the following is not true about digital immune system?
  (a) It makes the system highly scalable.
  (b) It helps in reducing false positives in the system.
  (c) It provides fast analysis of the threats.
  (d) The detection rate for new or unknown threats is low.

15.7 Which of the following is not true about e-mail bombing?
   (i) It is sent to consume system and network resources.
   (ii) It results in the Denial-of-Service.
   (iii) Multiple accounts at the target site may be abused.
   (a) (i) and (ii)
   (b) (ii) and (iii)
   (c) (i) and (iii)
   (d) (i), (ii) and (iii)

15.8 Which of the following statements is true about a worm?
   (a) It is a program that never copies itself into a computer's memory until no more space is left.
   (b) It is a program that replicates itself.
   (c) It attaches itself to e-mails.
   (d) It corrupts boot sector instructions.

Answers

15.1 (a)   15.2 (d)   15.3 (c)   15.4 (a)   15.5 (d)   15.6 (d)   15.7 (d)   15.8 (b)

Chapter 16

Firewall

16.1 INTRODUCTION

Today, the use of Internet is increasing rapidly. Internet is the main medium of attack to the computer system or network. To protect the computer or the network is the main intention of the network administrator. Firewall plays an important and major role in protecting the system. It prevents the unauthorised access to and from the network. Firewall is an effective tool used to protect the network from the attackers. It also allows the internal users to access the outside network via Internet and WAN. The walls of our home restrict the access to any body to enter in our home. In the same way, firewall protects our network. It is a first line of defense. Firewalls are of two types—software and hardware or combinations of both. Firewall observes each and every packet coming inside and going outside the intranet and allows only authenticated packets to do the same. If the packets are not authenticated, then the firewall blocks such packets to cross the firewall. In short, firewall isolates one network from the other network.

To protect the message in communication, different measures are applied. These include encryption of the message, password protection. These measures are not sufficient to prevent the attackers to send different malwares to the computer systems and steal data from the computers. Firewall makes the security strong enough by performing centralised access control and protects the network as well as computers in the network. Routers are used to filter the packets using the IP address of the packets, whereas a firewall stops all packets and filters up through the application layer. Firewalls are generally installed between the network and the Internet. It is also installed in an Intranet to protect one internal network such as one LAN from other LAN.

Firewall performs different security functions as follows:
1. It blocks unauthorised traffic.
2. It forwards the incoming traffic to more reliable internal computer systems.

3. It hides internal computers or networks, which are vulnerable.
4. It hides the information about internal network such as names of the computer system, network topology used, types of network device, etc.
5. It provides strong user authentication.
6. It can serve as a platform for IPSec.

16.2 CHARACTERISTICS OF A FIREWALL

Firewall has the following characteristic:
1. Firewall must act as a gateway for all traffic between the two networks.
2. It allows to pass only authorised traffic that is permitted by local security policy.
3. The firewall itself is protected from any type of penetration.
4. It cannot give assurance about protection from attacks coming from outside network.
5. Risk analysis helps in defining the level of protection for firewall implementation.
6. Firewall implements different local security policy. It
   (a) defines what type of protection is to be expected from the firewall.
   (b) specifies the cases when the exceptions are considered.
   (c) defines the rule for determining authorised and unauthorised traffic.

Firewalls works on simple rules given below:
1. All traffic is denied except that which is specifically authorised.
2. All traffic is allowed except that which is specifically denied.

Firewalls use four techniques to control access and enforce the security policies. These techniques are service control, direction control, user control and behaviour control.

1. *Service control:* The access to any specific types of Internet Services is controlled by this technique. It filters the traffic on the basis of port number, protocol or IP address.

2. *Direction control:* It decides from where the particular service requests should be initiated. It decides whether to allow the request to flow through the firewall or not.

3. *User control:* Depending on the user access, it controls the access to a service.

4. *Behaviour control:* It controls the behaviour of a particular service.

16.3 TYPES OF FIREWALL

Firewalls are categorised into three types—packet filtering firewall, application level gateway and circuit level (proxies) gateways.

16.3.1 Packet Filtering Firewall

The first generation of firewalls is the packet filtering firewalls. It works on the rule and allows the IP packets for incoming and outgoing. Using this rule, the packets are forwarded or discarded. This firewall works at OSI layers 3 and 4. It is generally designed to filter packets going in both the directions. It tracks the source address and destination address of the packets and TCP/UDP port numbers. The contents of a packet are not analysed by this firewall. The detailed architecture of packet filtering firewall is shown in Figure 16.1.

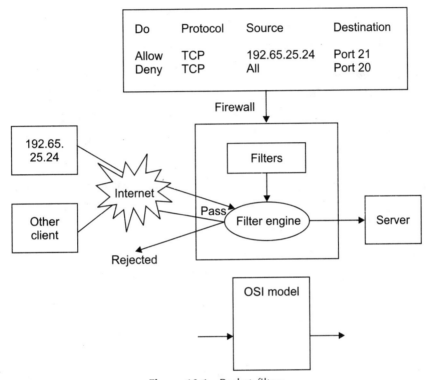

Figure 16.1 Packet filters.

There are various strategies for implementing packet filters. These strategies are based on information contained in a network packet. Some of them are as follows:
1. Source IP address
2. Destination IP address
3. Source and destination port number
4. IP protocol field
5. Interface

Advantages: Its advantages are as follows:
1. Its performance is good.
2. It is very fast.
3. Packet filters are relatively inexpensive.
4. It is transparent to users.
5. The traffic management is good.
6. It is simple.

Disadvantages: Its disadvantages are as follows:
1. Direct connections are allowed between untrusted and trusted hosts.
2. It is vulnerable to spoofing attacks.
3. It has poor scalability.
4. Large port ranges may be opened.
5. Most of these firewalls do not support advanced user authentication schemes.
6. Due to improper configuration, it is susceptible to security breaches.

Some of the attacks against packet filtering firewalls are discussed below:

IP Address Spoofing

The attacker sends the packets from outside the firewall. The packets have different fields. One of the fields is IP address of the source. It gives the address information of the source of the IP packet. But the attacker puts the internal address as a source address. He believes that due to this spoof address, the firewall assumes that this packet is from trusted internal host and allows to pass that packet.

Countermeasure: If the packet coming from outside and has the IP address of the internal host, then discard such packet. This is implemented at the router, which is external to the firewall.

Source Routing Attacks

The attacker assumes that the source routing information is not analysed. So, the route of a packet across the Internet is specified by the source.

Countermeasure: Discard the packets which use this option

Tiny Fragment Attacks

The attacker creates small fragments using the IP fragmentation option. The separate fragment is used for the TCP header information. This design helps in avoiding the filtering rules based on TCP header information. The filtering decision is taken from the first fragment, of a packet and on the basis of this first fragment subsequent fragments, of that packet are allowed or discarded. The attacker takes the advantage of this strategy that only the first fragment of the packet is examined for forwarding the complete packet.

Countermeasure: The preventive measure for this attack is to enforce a rule that the first fragment must hold a predefined minimum amount of the transport header. The filter should remember the packet if the first fragment of the packet is rejected. Then, discard the remaining fragments of the packet.

16.3.2 Application Level Gateways

Packet filtering firewalls is based on address information, so it examines the lower layers of the OSI model. To provide more security, all layers of the OSI model should be examined simultaneously. Application level gateway firewall is useful which provides this security. It uses server-based programs, known as *proxy server* or *bastion host*. It forwards or rejects the packets by ensuring that the protocol specification is correct.

Proxies accept requests from the external side, examine the request, and then forward the legitimate and trusted requests to the destination host on the other side. This type of firewall makes decisions at all the seven layers of the OSI model. It acts as a mediator for different applications such as e-mail, FTP, etc. It does not permit the client to directly connect to the destination node.

Advantages: Its advantages are as follows:
1. It is configured so that firewall is the only host address that is visible to an outside network.
2. For separate services, separate proxy servers are used.
3. Application gateways support strong user authentication.
4. It provides strong security at the application level.
5. At the application level, it is easy to log and audit all the incoming traffic.
6. It provides strong access control.
7. It is more secure than packet filtering firewall.

Disadvantages: Its disadvantages are as follows:
1. For each application, special proxy is required.
2. Performance is slow.
3. On each connection, there is an additional processing overhead.
4. Sometimes, it is inconvenient for the users.
5. There is a lack of transparency.

Demilitarised Zone (DMZ)

There are two types of firewall based on its locations in the network—Internal firewall and external firewall. An *internal firewall* protects the entire network of an organisation. An *external firewall* is installed at the boundary of local or organisation network. It is located inside the boundary router. The region between the two firewalls is called *demilitarised zone* or *DMZ*. Many network devices are located between these two firewalls. It includes devices which are allowed to access from external networks. These devices can be accessed externally, but protected from vulnerability. The systems which are located in DMZ require connectivity with the external network such as domain name server (DNS), an e-mail server or web sites. The protection and access control to these systems are provided by the external firewall. The external firewall provides basic security to the entire network. The internal firewall has strong filter capabilities as compared to external firewall. This provides strong security to the servers and workstations from the external attacks. The internal firewall also provides two-way protection. Initially, it protects the entire internal network from attacks launched from DMZ systems that originate from worms, bots or other malicious software. Then, the internal firewall protects system located at DMZ area from internal attack. To protect different portions of the large network from each other, multiple internal firewalls are used.

16.3.3 Circuit Level Gateways

Circuit level gateway is a type of firewall and it is a stand-alone system. It validates connections and then allows the exchange of data. It also works as per the defined rules similar to packet filter. Circuit level gateway cannot route the packets. The connections are allowed or discarded based on these rules. So, circuit level gateway establishes the connections between the source and the destinations. It focuses on the TCP/IP layer. It is more secure than packet filters. This firewall is installed between the router and the external network such as Internet. The actual address is hidden from the external users because only the address of the proxy is transmitted. Circuit level gateway provides services for many different protocols. It can be adapted as per the requirement to provide greater variety of communications.

Advantages: Its advantages are as follows:
1. It is transparent to the users.
2. This is excellent for relaying outbound traffic.

Disadvantages: Its disadvantages are as follows:
1. It is slower than packet filtering firewall.
2. Inbound traffic is risky.

16.4 BENEFITS OF A FIREWALL

1. Increased ability to enforce network security standards/policies (e.g. id. undocumented systems)
2. Centralisation of internetwork audit capability (audit of in/out-bound traffic)

16.5 LIMITATIONS OF A FIREWALL

1. It cannot protect those attacks that bypass the firewall.
2. It cannot protect the network against the internal attacks.
3. An internal firewall that separates the different parts of a network cannot protect against wireless communications among local computer systems on different sides of the internal firewall.
4. Different devices such as laptop or portable storage device may be used and infected outside the network, and then used internally.

16.6 FIREWALL ARCHITECTURES

Generally, firewall is implemented on a single machine. The stronger firewalls have multiple components. In this section, different firewall architectures are discussed.

16.6.1 Dual-Homed Host Architecture

The simple firewall architecture uses dual-homed host architecture. It is a computer system, which has separate network interfaces for minimum two networks. This host computer can act as a router between the networks. This routing function should be disabled when it is used in firewall architecture. Therefore, the host computer isolates the networks from each other, but it can see traffic on all the networks. Therefore, IP packets from one network, for example, external network or Internet are not directly routed to the other network, for example, internal network. Systems inside the firewall, i.e., internal network can communicate with the dual-homed host via one interface and systems outside the firewall, i.e., on the Internet can communicate with the dual-homed host via another interface. However, these systems cannot communicate directly with each other. The traffic between these two networks is completely blocked.

The dual-homed host firewall architecture is simple. The architecture for dual-homed host is shown in Figure 16.2.

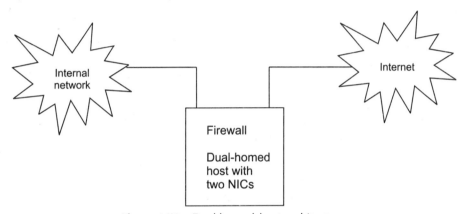

Figure 16.2 Dual-homed host architecture.

Dual-homed hosts can provide a very tight control on the traffic flowing on the network. Not a single packet is allowed without the consent of dual-homed hosts. If the rule is designed that does not allow the packets to flow between the internal and external network then all the packets are blocked by the dual-homed hosts. In this architecture, dual-homed host itself is critical for the network security. It provides services by only proxying them. Proxying is much less challenging, but it may not be available for all services the users are interested in.

16.6.2 Screened Host Architecture

The screened host architecture provides services from a host that is attached to the internal network only. For this, a separate router is used. In this architecture, packet filter is used to provide the main security. The screened host architecture is shown in Figure 16.3. The required applications are provided by the bastion host that sits on the internal network. The packet filtering rules are configured in such a way that the bastion host is the only host on the internal network that is accessible from the Internet. Even then, only certain types of connections are allowed. If any external computer wants access to the internal computer or wants to use some services, it has to first connect to this host. The bastion host is responsible to maintain a high level of security for the host.

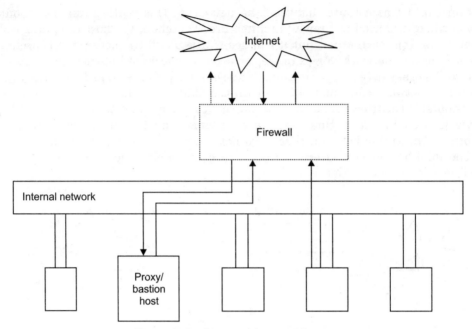

Figure 16.3 Screened host architecture.

The major disadvantage of the screened host architecture is that if an attacker becomes successful to attack into the bastion host then the network security between the bastion host and the rest of the internal hosts is completely collapsed. In screened host architecture, the router still works as the first line of defense. Filtering and access control for all the packets is performed at the router. The router allows entering only that traffic that the rules explicitly identify. It restricts other incoming connections to the host. Therefore, the router may also be a single point of failure. If the security of the router is compromised, the complete network is available to an attacker.

Nevertheless, screened host architecture is popular due to the following reasons:

1. It allows companies to easily enforce various security policies in different directions.
2. It is relatively easy to implement.

16.6.3 Screened Subnet Architecture

The screened subnet architecture is functionally similar to the screened host architecture. But it provides some extra security. It gives strength to the security of the firewall by adding a perimeter network, which helps in further isolating the internal network from the Internet. The most vulnerable computer in the network is bastion host. In screened host architecture, the internal network is wide open to attack through the bastion host. In this case, bastion host is a very attractive target for the attacker. If the attacker is able to successfully break the security of bastion host, then the complete internal network is open for the attacker. To reduce the impact of attack, the solution is to isolate the bastion host on perimeter network. In this case, the attacker may be able to get partial access, but the complete internal network is not available to the attacker.

In screened subnet architecture, two screening routers are used. Each of these routers are connected to the perimeter net. One router is installing between the internal network and the perimeter net, while the other router is to install between the external network and the perimeter net. So, there are two routers are used to protect the network. To break into the internal network, the attacker has to pass both the routers. If the attacker is able to break the bastion host (external router), then also due to the internal router, the internal network is not accessible to the attacker. And to compromise the internal network, there is no single point that will be vulnerable.

To provide more security, a number of perimeter nets can be used between the Internet or outside world and the interior network. The less trusted services are kept in the outer perimeter net so that if the attacker is able to break the outer systems, he has to work hard to break the internal systems. This can be achieved by using different configurations for each perimeter net. If all the systems have same rules, then this additional perimeter has no use to provide the additional security. The screened subnet architecture is shown in Figure 16.4.

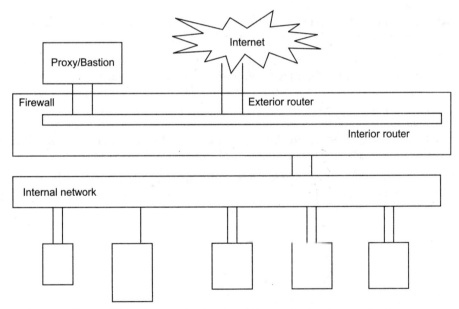

Figure 16.4 Screened subnet architecture (using two routers).

Perimeter Network

A *perimeter network* is a firewall, which is installed between a private network and Internet. It controls all the traffic between the private network and the Internet. The perimeter network is an additional network between the external network and the internal network. It provides additional security to the internal network. If an attacker is able to break the outer security of the firewall, then the perimeter net protects the internal network by providing an extra layer of security between the attacker and the internal network.

If the attacker breaks a bastion host on the perimeter net, then the use of perimeter net allows him to snoop only the traffic on that specific network. There are two types of traffic on the perimeter net.

1. To or from the bastion host
2. To or from the Internet

As the traffic from two internal hosts does not pass from the perimeter net, it is safe from the attacker, though the security of bastion is breakon. But the traffic to and from the bastion host or the traffic to and from the external world remains visible to the attacker. So, care should be taken during the configuration of the firewall because this traffic is not itself confidential enough. So, if the attacker is able to capture it, it does not make any harm to the network.

Bastion Host/Proxy

In the screened subnet architecture, a host is attached to the perimeter net. This host is called *bastion host*. Any connection from the external network is first contacted to this host. For example, for e-mail session coming from external network sessions to deliver electronic mail to the site

Outbound services, i.e., services from users on the internal network to any servers on the external network are handled in the following ways:

1. Install the packet filtering firewalls on both routers. This allows internal clients to establish direct connections with the external servers.
2. Install proxy servers to run on the bastion host. This allows internal clients to establish indirect connections with the external servers. Packet filtering firewall can be used to establish the connections between the internal clients with the proxy servers on the bastion host and vice versa. This prohibits direct communication between the internal clients and external network.

In any of the above case, the packet filtering firewall is used, which allows the bastion host to connect to the Internet. It also allows the bastion host to accept the connections from the hosts on outside world.

Interior Router

The interior router is also called *choke router*. It protects the internal network from the outside world or external network as well as from the perimeter net. It blocks most of the packets using packet filtering for the firewall. It allows selected services on the internal network to any servers on the external network. Selected services reduce the number of computers, which can be compromised from the bastion host. These services are provided using packet filtering rather than proxies. These services might include FTP, Telnet and others, as per needs. It is not necessary that the services are allowed by the interior router between the bastion host and the internal network, and the services between the internal network and the Internet are same.

Exterior Router

Theoretically, exterior router is also called *access router* in firewalls. It protects the perimeter net as well as the internal net from the outside world such as Internet.

Practically, exterior routers allow almost all packets outbound from the perimeter net. Exterior routers perform packet filtering on a small scale. There would be same rules for interior and exterior router. If any of the rule has an error, it allows the attacker to get access in the network. This error is present on both the routers.

The exterior router is provided by an Internet provider and it limits the access of the internal users. An Internet provider puts few general packet filtering rules. One of the special rules on the exterior router is related to protect the computers on the perimeter network. A user should not trust on this exterior router as one trusts on interior router. Many rules on the interior are put on the exterior router, which prevent insecure traffic between the internal host and the Internet. The interior router allows the internal hosts to send some protocols to talk to the bastion host. This is used to support the proxy services. The exterior router allows those protocols through as long as they come from the bastion host. It is expected that these rules on the exterior router provide an extra security, but theoretically, it does not happen. This is because these packets are already blocked by the interior router. If such packets do exist, that means the interior router has either failed or an unexpected host is connected to the perimeter network. The main task of the exterior router is not to allow the packets coming from the internet which have forged source addresses, i.e., the source address is shown as the address of the system within the internal network. For interior router, it is possible to do this, but cannot tell that the packets are forged.

A comparison between packet filtering firewalls and application level gateways is shown below:

Packet Filtering Firewalls	*Application Level Gateways*
It is the simplest firewalls.	It is complex firewalls.
No change in the software is required for performing its job.	No change in the software is required for performing its job, but it is visible to the user.
It can see only addresses and type of service protocol.	It can see full data of packet.
Auditing of this filter is difficult.	Auditing of this filter is simple.
Configuration is difficult due to complex rules.	Proxies can be used to substitute complex addressing rules.
Screen is based on connection rules.	Screen is based on behaviour of proxies.
It is less powerful.	It is more powerful.

16.7 TRUSTED SYSTEM

A system that you have no choice but to trust is known as *trusted system*. The security of the system depends on the success of the system. If the trusted system fails, then it will compromise the security of the entire system. Therefore, there should be minimum number of trusted components in a system. Trusted system should provide security, integrity, reliability and privacy.

16.7.1 Trusted Systems in Policy Analysis

In trusted systems, some conditional prediction about the behaviour of users or elements within the system has been determined prior to authorising access to resources within the system. Many systems are trusted systems if they have the following options:

1. The probability of threat or risk analysis is calculated, which is used to access trust for taking the decision before authorisation.
2. To insure the behaviour within the system, the deviation analysis is used.

16.8 ACCESS CONTROL

One of the security services is access control. In this service, users are identified and given certain privileges to computer systems or resources. The access to the data or computer is controlled. If the user misuses the privileges given to him, then the access to such user's is denied. For example, suppose you give access to your friend to your own computer by giving him separate user account. But you find out that your friend misuses your system by some other activities. Then, the administrator of the computer can delete that user account so that he cannot access your computer any more. Protecting the private and confidential information from the unauthorised users on the computer, which is connected to the network, particularly to the Internet, is most important. Access control mechanism allows to protect this private and confidential information from unauthorised users. In access control mechanism, identification of the users is carried out first using authentication algorithm. It includes keeping the records and timestamp of all the requests, which is helpful during the audit of the system.

16.8.1 Objectives of Access Control

Access control has different objectives, which include preserve and protect the confidentiality, availability and integrity of data or information, systems and resources.

Confidentiality is the process of protection of data or information from unauthorised disclosure. It ensures that information is accessible only to the authorised person. In cryptography and network security data, confidentiality is done by using encryption techniques.

Integrity means assurance that data received is same as it is sent by an authorised sender, i.e., in transmission, there is no change in the data. This modification or change includes deletion, modification and creation of new information in the data. We can use hashing algorithms like MD5, SHA to check the integrity of the message. Integrity protects the data from unauthorised modification.

Availability is the measure to which a system or information is accessible and usable upon request by an authorised user at any particular time. Availability means a functioning condition of a system at any particular instance. For example, access to a system or information should not be prevented to the legitimate users.

16.8.2 Types of Access Control

Access control can be categorised into four classes as follows:

1. Discretionary access control systems: In discretionary access control system, the owner of the information has the right to decide about who can read, write and execute the information. Using discretionary access control, users can create and modify files in their own directories.

2. Mandatory access control systems: In mandatory access control systems, the creator of the information has no right to decide about who can access or modify it. The access to any information is decided by the administrators and authorities. These systems are used in military applications, financial application, etc.

3. Role-based access control systems: In role-based access control systems, the users are permitted to access systems and information based on their role within the organisation. This type of access can be allowed to individuals or groups of people.

4. Rule-based access control systems: In rule-based access control systems, some rules are configured and predefined. The decisions about whom to allow the access to the systems and information are based on these rules. Rules are designed such that all the users from a particular network, host, domain or IP address are allowed to use the information or system or resources.

SUMMARY

In this chapter, we have discussed about the firewall and types of firewall. Firewall is an effective tool used to protect the network from the attackers. Dual-homed host architecture is a computer system, which has separate network interfaces for minimum two networks. This host computer can act as a router between the networks. Dual-homed hosts can provide a very tight control on the traffic flowing on the network. Not a single packet is allowed without the consent of dual homed hosts. The screened host architecture provides services from a host that is attached to the internal network only. For this, a separate router is used. The screened subnet architecture gives strength to the security of the firewall by adding a perimeter network which helps in further isolating the internal network from the Internet.

EXERCISES

16.1 What is a firewall?
16.2 What is the main function of a firewall?
16.3 List the protections associated with firewall systems.
16.4 Discuss the characteristics of a firewall.
16.5 What are the three main types of firewall?
16.6 Explain packet filtering firewalls.
16.7 Explain application level gateways.
16.8 Explain circuit level gateways.
16.9 List the advantages and disadvantages of application level gateways.
16.10 What are the benefits of firewalls?

16.11 What are the limitations of firewall?
16.12 Discuss dual-homed host architecture.
16.13 What is bastion host?
16.14 What is trusted system?
16.15 What is access control matrix?
16.16 Discuss the limitations of firewall? Why do corporate houses implement more than one firewall for security?

MULTIPLE CHOICE QUESTIONS

16.1 Firewall protect the network against
   (a) Virus
   (b) Fire
   (c) Unauthenticated interactive log ins from the outside world
   (d) Connecting to and from the outside world

16.2 Which of the following is not true about the firewall?
   (a) It blocks unauthorised traffic.
   (b) Traffic must only be allowed to pass from inside to outside the firewall.
   (c) The firewall, itself, should be immune to penetration.
   (d) It hides internal computers or networks, which are vulnerable.

16.3 Which of the following is not true about the firewall?
   (a) It cannot protect those attacks that bypass the firewall.
   (b) It cannot protect the network against the internal attacks.
   (c) An internal firewall that separates the different parts of a network cannot protect against wireless communications among the local computer systems on different sides of the internal firewall.
   (d) None of the above

Answers

16.1 (c)   16.2 (b)   16.3 (d)

CHAPTER 17

Computer Forensics

17.1 INTRODUCTION

A new emerging discipline in computer security is computer forensics. If any security incident happens, computer forensics focuses on the digital evidence findings. In computer forensics, the analysis of digital information related with the incident is done. This information is collected from the computer systems and the storage devices used in that incident. In the investigation, the focus is on what the incident was, when the incident happened, how the incident happened and what are the different parties/elements involved in the incident. Therefore, *computer forensics* is the process of investigating a computer system and related elements to find out the cause of an incident. Computer forensics relates to the application of technical knowledge to get the solutions to the legal problems. It is helpful to solve the crime related to computer systems. It helps in crime detection and in investigation of the various crimes done with the help of computer system. The main objectives of computer forensics is the preservation of the data, identification of the data, extraction of the information, documentation of the evidences found and interpretation of information collected. The primary objective of the computer forensics is the secure collection of data stored on the computer system. Then proper analysis of collected data so as to prepare strong evidence about the crime is the second objective of computer forensics. Due to advancement in technology, the same techniques can be applied to the crimes related to all digital devices such as digital cameras, mobile phones, USB hard disks, DVDs, PDAs, etc.

Computer forensics can be done by specialised trained persons, who are experts in different techniques related to data collections, preservations and in analysing the digital evidences. Though computer security and computer forensics are associated with each other there are two basic differences between them. The computer security is concerned with unauthorised access of the data as well as confidentiality, integrity and non-repudiation of the data, whereas computer forensic is concerned with acquisition, preservation and analysis of the digital evidences. The experts of computer forensics first investigate the use of particular computer systems for any illegible purpose or find out any unauthorised person who used that computer. This helps in collecting the evidences about the crime happened. Apart from computer systems, the experts investigate all the storage devices like pen drive, CD, DVD use for storage of data related to that computer system. Computer forensic experts use the following four phases (see Figure 17.1) during the investigation of the crime:

1. Identification
2. Preservation
3. Extraction
4. Interpretation

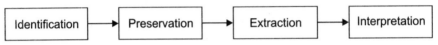

Figure 17.1 Computer forensic investigation phases.

1. *Identification*: The first phase of investigation is to identify the sources of documentary or other evidences. This includes the identification of the computer system, hard disks, pen drives, DVDs, CDs, log files, etc. From the given list of source, the computer system or hard drive cannot be considered as evidence because they themselves are not evidence but the evidence are related to these devices. This source is useful during the analysis phase to identify the data and the information, which are actually significant to the situation at hand.

2. *Preservation*: It is essential and very important to preserve the captured data. This data is required for the analysis phase. Preservation of data involves making the copy of the original data and store the original data in a secure manner such as sealed it. The seal should be signed by the authority who sealed the data. The seal should also have the information such as name of the authority, date and time of seal.

3. *Extraction*: The next phase is information extraction from the data at hand. This extracted information should be saved in some other form and also in the form of hard copy. The security of this extracted information is important, as it is used to prove the crime. If this extracted information is tempered by some attacker, then it is difficult to prove the crime.

4. *Interpretation*: The most challenging phase of computer forensics is interpretation of the extracted information. The interpretation of the collected information requires knowledge about different things such as operating system, etc. The wrong interpretation of information gives wrong output. So, to find out the correct evidence is one thing and interpret it correctly is another story. There are some GUI tools available for the analysis of the information that make it easy to interpret the information correctly and easily. During interpretations, any data should not be written, as it may destroy the evidence.

Documentation

Documentation is the important part of any investigation. Well documentation helps the investigator to cross-check the progress in the investigation as well as if the person is replaced by some other person, in that case, documentation is helpful to understand the complete process of investigation. As soon as the investigation starts, documentation should be prepared. It gives the information from beginning to end as soon as any person becomes involved in the case. This helps in keeping the log of every event occurred from the time of investigation. In many situations, it is not possible to keep track of events occurred in the investigation. In this case, documentation plays an important role. Documentation should contain the answer of the questions related to

1. The person who collected the evidence
2. The time and place of the evidence taken
3. The person/officer who is the custodian of the evidence
4. The person responsible for the handling and transporting of data
5. The information about the storage and security measures applied to the secure storage of evidence

The information about the user of the evidence with date, time, purpose and the name of the person

Evidence

It includes different documents, statements of different persons related to the case and the various elements which can be put as a supporting material in the court. Evidence can be of different types such as direct evidence, real evidence, demonstrative evidence and documentary evidence.

Legal Processes

After collecting the evidences, the next process is the procedure for search warrants, depositions, hearings, trials, etc.

Integrity of Evidence

This indicates that there should not be any alteration or change in the original evidences. This can be done by keeping secret of all the information related to investigation. It also includes not to share any information related to investigation, specifically with the people not involved in the investigation team.

Accurate Reporting of the Collected Information

The conclusions and reports prepared about the case from the collected information should be prepared using proven techniques and methodology. From the same information, the same conclusions and reports should be generated by any expert of forensics.

Opinion of Experts

Whatever be the conclusions drawn from the evidences, the expert has to put and prove them in front of the court of law.

Computer forensics can be used in different application areas to collect the evidence. This may include some of the areas as follows:

1. Piracy of software and movie CD, DVD
2. Violation of copyright
3. Industrial surveillance
4. Money laundering
5. Sexual harassment
6. Violation of intellectual property
7. Use of confidential information by unauthorised users
8. Destruction of information
9. Fraud
10. Child pornography

17.2 Computer Forensics Investigations

There are three main steps in computer forensics investigation. These steps are acquiring the data, authenticating the data and analying the collected data.

1. Acquiring the data: It consists of creating a copy of the data from the hard drive.

2. Authentication: It ensures that the copy is exact duplicate of the original data collected during investigation.

3. Analysis: This is the last step of investigation. It is the most time-consuming step. In this step, the evidence of wrongdoing is uncovered by the investigator.

Computer forensics investigations can be categorised into two types as given below:

1. In some cases, the crimes are committed using the computers. In this case, the hard disk or any storage devices can be used for investigation.
2. In some cases, the target for crime is the computer. This may include hacking the computer and stealing the personal information from it. In these cases, the investigation should start from that particular computer, specifically from RAM.

Irrespective of the cases, the forensics techniques and methodology used for investigation should always be same.

Types of Data

Nowadays, there are various types of data stored in the computer. Some of these data are active, whereas other may be residual or backup data. In the field of computer forensics, one should be concerned about three types of data—active data, archival data and latent data.

1. Active data: The data which is available and can be seen by anybody is called *active data*. It is created by the user. This includes programs, data files and files used by the operating system. This data can be collected easily.

2. Archival data: The data for which back up is taken and which is stored on some media is called *archival data*. For example, data stored on CDs, DVDs, pen drives or USB hard disks.

3. Latent data: The data that can be extracted using special tools is called *latent data*. Many times, the attackers delete the information or format the hard disk. Such information can be recovered using special tools. This is more time-consuming and costly process.

17.3 AREAS OF APPLICATION OF COMPUTER FORENSICS

Computer forensics is useful for investigation in both public and private sectors.

17.3.1 Public Sector

In public sector, computer forensics is used by the government and law enforcement personnel for investigation of different crimes. Nowadays, the use of computer and computer technology for criminal activities is increasing rapidly. Criminals use computers for breaking computer network and stealing the data. As the number of crimes using computer is increasing, the use of computer forensics by the police department and law people is also increasing. The evidence produced by computer forensics experts is used by the prosecutors to solve the criminal cases like terrorism, murder, hacking, fraud, etc.

17.3.2 Private Sector

In public sector, computer forensics is used by the people to investigate electronic frauds, stealing and misuse of computing resources by employees.

Forensic investigation is helpful to generate a number of evidences from the hard disks, pen drives, CDs and DVDs. The evidences may be in the form of image, printouts, password in the written form, software manuals, or logs of the computer. The experts of computer forensics must look for the evidences not only into the internal part of the computer but also around the computer to collect the evidence. The evidence should be collected systematically so that it can stand in court to prove the crime. For this, apart from technical aspect, legal aspect of the evidence should be considered.

17.4 UNDERSTANDING THE SUSPECTS

The forensics team should have expert members, who have complete understanding of the superiority of the suspect. Many times, the suspects use countermeasures to erase the information from the computer so that forensics team cannot get any information from it. In such case, the forensics team should use a proper software to recover the information from the computer.

17.4.1 Electronic Evidence

A criminal always leaves back some evidences. It is the forensics expert's job to find out the correct evidences for the crime. If these evidences are in the form of electronic, then it can be collected from a variety of sources. Criminal may use internal network of the organisation to transmit the data or store the data. So, to collect evidence, this network is useful. The workstation or the server also contains evidence; so, forensics experts should collect it through these resources. Some precautions should be taken by the experts while collecting the evidences, as evidence may be infected by viruses, there may be damage like electromagnetic or mechanical damage or sometimes, criminal may put some explosive devices hidden in the evidence. So, precautions should be taken so that the evidence should not be destroyed. These precautions are as follows:

1. Original evidence should be handled rarely to avoid any damage to it.
2. To protect the evidence, establish and maintain the chain of protection.
3. Maintain the documents of the complete process regularly.
4. Do not share the information with anybody not related to the case.

Apart from the above precautions, the following rules help in providing additional security to the evidence:

1. Select the proper time for collection of evidence
2. During investigation, some sensitive information may be discovered. Care should be taken to handle it properly.
3. Legal permission should be taken before investigation so that the owner of the computer or any electronic devices can permit the forensics team to investigate.
4. Use different computer to analyse the data.

For analysing the collected information, the following steps should be followed:

Secure Digital Card

The forensics team first starts its job from analysing the surrounding environment. The first step is to take the photographs of the surrounding environment before any of the hardware is dealt with. The next step is to collect all printouts, notes, CDs, DVDs, pen drives, USB devices, etc. The collected evidences must be kept securely so that only authorised members can access it. Then, observe the surrounding and try to find out any information related to password of the computer.

Note Down Information from the Computer

If the computer system is on and any application is running, then try to find out whether any information can be inferred from the working applications. If some information is gained, record it. Sometimes, the criminal deletes some of the information from the hard disk. In such case, before turning off the computer, collect such information from RAM, because after power off, the information from RAM may be lost.

Shut Down the Computer Carefully

If the forensics team finds out the computer in power on mode, then before shut down, care should be taken so that the minimum information loss will happen.

Inspect for Traps

Before opening the chassis of the computer system, care should be taken, as the criminal may place some intrusion detection mechanisms and self-destruct mechanisms for trapping. These destructive mechanisms are used to destroy a hard disk to the point so that it will not possible to recover the data at all. But this trapping cannot avoid recovery of data completely. To find out whether any such trap is present or not, one should look for a hole in the chassis so that without opening the chassis, the forensics team can find out such trap. The holes may be available from the position of fan or a better solution is to drill the chassis to inspect the inside body of the computer.

Fully Document Hardware Configuration

Take the photographs of the complete configuration of the computer system. Note down the serial numbers of the computer system. Study the booting sequence of the computer system. Give some time for this study of the configuration of the computer system. This is useful in the latter stage of investigation.

Duplicate the Hard Drives

To protect the original evidence like hard disk, it is better to take the duplicate of the entire hard disk. For this, hard drive duplicator may be used. The process of taking image, which is written protected is called *imaging* and it is less vulnerable for damage. This image can be stored for a longer time. Image of the hard disk helps in copying all the information correctly. So, the accuracy of copying is high. To verify the integrity of the copied data, secure hash algorithm (SHA-1) or message digest algorithm (MD5) can be used. To check the integrity of the data, the forensics team takes two images of the same hard disk and then calculates the message digest for both the images. If both the message digest values are same, then both the images are same. (It is very difficult to have the same message digest or hash value for two different messages).

17.4.2 E-mail Review

Nowadays, e-mail is the mostly used medium of communication. So, it is the most important source of evidence. Most of the e-mail clients save a copy of the outgoing messages. So, there are two copies of the same message, one with the sender and the other with the recipient. Each e-mail message has a header. This header has the information about the source and destination. Using this information, the location of the sender and the recipient can be easily identified by the investigation team. But many times, criminals use a malicious mail server to send the messages. This makes it difficult to identify the sender. Though theoretically, it is possible to review all e-mails, practically, it is very difficult due to the sheer volume of the e-mails.

17.5 EXAMPLES OF COMPUTER FORENSICS

Nowadays, many criminals use computer or mobile for criminal activities. For investigation of such frauds, computer forensics plays an important role. Some of the examples of computer forensics are discussed below:
   1. There have been a number of cases recently found in banking sectors, where the money from users' bank account are transferred to some unknown account

by the hackers. The investigation team uses computer forensics in such cases. Through the ability to track the transfer of money online, computer forensics investigators have been able to locate people involved in these crimes. Investigation team uses this information that is found on the computers as circumstantial evidence in court, allowing prosecution to occur.
2. Computer forensics is also useful to maintain the security in the workplace. In the large software companies, employees' computers/laptops are being monitored. This ensures that no illegal actions take place in the company. The company also protects their confidential data from unauthorised persons by using access control mechanism. If the attacker is able to break the security and capture the data, then computer forensics is used, which traces back information, including which computer is being tampered and what information has been extracted from it. This is helpful to know the parties involved in capturing the confidential information and it also allows the companies to take necessary security measures.

17.6 FREE SPACE AND SLACK SPACE

There are some free or unused clusters on a hard disk. These unused clusters are called free space. There is also a space between the end of a file and the end of the disk cluster where a file is stored in. This space is also called *free space* or *file slack*. Free space occurs because the size of the data and the fixed space for storage are not same. Computer forensics is used to examine the free space because it may contain meaningful data. We delete some file from the hard disk which is no more required. But the file is not actually deleted but the pointer to that file, which is used by an operating system to track down the file in a file allocation table, is deleted. So, the data is not removed from the disk. When some other file or data is stored in that location on the hard disk, the old data is overwritten. This new file or data does not completely occupy the space of the deleted file. Some of the data from the old file remains as it is on the hard disk. So, there is still a fragment of the original file. The sector that holds this fragment of the old file is referred to as *free space* because the operating system has marked it usable when needed. The area at the end of the space allocated to a file, which is not occupied by the data belonging to that file, is called *slack space*. When a file is saved to a storage media such as a hard drive, the operating system allocates space in blocks of a predefined fixed size. This is called *sector*. All the sectors on a given hard disk have equal size. So, if a file has only five characters, the operating system will allocate one complete sector. So, some space remains blank in the sector. This is called *slack space*. Attackers may hide malicious code, tools, or clues in the slack space as well as in the free space. It contains information from files that previously occupied that same physical sector on the drive. Therefore, forensic team should review slack space using utilities that can display the information stored in that area.

17.7 INCIDENT RESPONSE

If any institute or organisation becomes a victim of suspected computer crimes, instead of trying to search the criminal, the institute should first contact the computer forensics specialists without disturbing the computers and other related materials that can be used as evidence. Following precautions should be taken:

1. Keep the screen display as it is.
2. Do not delete system logs and access logs.
3. Do not shut down the computer and other devices.
4. Printouts and other documents should be kept as it is.
5. Do not use that computer for any other purpose.
6. Backup file restoration should not be carried.

17.8 WEAKNESSES

Though computer forensic is very useful for investigation, it also has some weaknesses. The main causes of these weaknesses are training, standards of working and international standardisation.

1. *Training:* Training is very important for the success of any technology. For computer forensics, as a new discipline, many private institutes are offering training in the form of organising seminars and workshops. As the computer crimes are increasing rapidly, training related to computer forensics is an investment for any institute. The question is whom should be given the training. There are many people involved in computer forensics investigation. These include experts from computer software, hardware as well as experts from law. To collect the evidence, computer experts are useful, while to produce and defense in front of the court, the law persons are useful. So, law person should require the training related to computer technology and computer experts should be trained and have knowledge about law. Computer experts should also have knowledge about network and intrusion detection. Training is useful to train all these people.

2. S*tandard of working:* Crimes done using computer is not limited to the boundary of any particular country. Many times, the criminal uses the server from some other country, generally, an enemy country, to make attack. So, some standard guidelines are required to collect the evidences. These guidelines may relate to planning, monitoring, reporting process, recording procedure, etc.

3. *International standardisation:* Each country has its own laws, methods, standards for computer forensics. Due to difference in laws, the same evidence, which is acceptable in one country, is not acceptable in another country. The criminals or attackers take the advantage of these laws. They use Internet for crimes, which have no country boundary. Criminals can use the system in one country to hack the system located in another country. The use of Internet may have no physical boundaries of countries, but the law enforcement does have. So, there are many issues for the collection of the evidence by the investigation team. These include the servers located in different countries, source and destination of the attack and victim from different countries and political and legal issues between different countries.

In some countries, where the computer networks are owned and controlled by the government agencies may allow the foreign governments to investigate a crime. In some countries, hacking is considered as lawful, whereas the same type of hacking is considered as crime. So, there is a need for some standardisation in procedure to collect evidences. For collection of evidences, G8 group has recommended the following six principles:

1. Evidences should be collected using standard computer forensics and procedural principles.
2. Provide strong security measures to protect the gathered evidences so that nobody can alter it.
3. The team members who access the evidences should have appropriate training.
4. Maintain proper documentations of the complete procedure.
5. Fix the responsibility and keep the evidence in that person's custody.
6. Any forensic team that is responsible for seizing, accessing, storing or transferring digital evidence is responsible for complying with these guidelines.

SUMMARY

Today, computer forensics is an emerging branch of engineering, which is helpful for solving many criminal cases related to computer. Computer forensics is the process of investigating a computer system and related elements to find out the cause of an incident. The main objectives of computer forensics are preservation of the data, identification of the data, extraction of the information, documentation of the evidences founds and interpretation of information collected. The person or team members, who are involved in solving any criminal cases related to computer crimes, should have the knowledge to acquire, authenticate and analyse the data stored in electronic devices. Further the team members should have knowledge about the latest technologies involved in tracing and detecting the actions of the particular computer users.

EXERCISES

17.1 What is computer forensics?

17.2 List the different phases for recovering evidence from computer systems. Explain each in detail.

17.3 Discuss the weaknesses of computer forensics.

17.4 What is free space and slack space?

17.5 You are training newly hired IT people on how to handle incidents and investigate a case. You want them to know exactly what to do and in what order, without wasting time on extraneous tasks. List the necessary steps of a forensic investigation.

17.6 A college of engineering is documenting the steps that should be taken if an intruder compromises data. The college wants to create a flow chart showing the steps that should be taken stepwise, with a particular emphasis on detailing the chain of custody. Which storage is suitable for storing a disk drive as evidence?

MULTIPLE CHOICE QUESTIONS

17.1 The main objective of computer forensics is
  (a) Preservation of the data
  (b) Identification of the data
  (c) Extraction of the information
  (d) All of the above

17.2 Which of the following statements is true about computer forensics?
  (i) It is concerned with confidentiality.
  (ii) It is concerned with integrity.
  (iii) It is concerned with acquisition, preservation and analysis of the digital evidences.
  (a) Only (i)
  (b) Only (i) and (ii)
  (c) (i), (ii) and (ii)
  (d) Only (iii)

17.3 During the investigation of the crime, the experts of computer forensics
  (i) Identification
  (ii) Preservation
  (iii) Extraction
  (iv) Interpretation
  (a) (i) and (ii)
  (b) (i) and (iii)
  (c) (i) and (iv)
  (d) All of the above

Answers
17.1 (d)   **17.2** (d)   **17.3** (d)

Bibliography

Bishop and Sathyanarayana, *Introduction to Computer Security*, Pearson Education, New Delhi, 2006.

Bragg, Rhodes-Ousley, Strassberg, *The Complete Reference Network Security*, Tata McGraw-Hill, New Delhi, 2004.

Conklin, et. al., *Principles of Computer Security*, International Edition, McGraw-Hill, Singapore, 2005.

Kahate, Atul, *Cryptography and Network Security*, 2nd ed., Tata McGraw-Hill, New Delhi, 2005.

Kaufman, Charlie, Perlman, Radia, and Speciner, Mike, *Network Security*, 2nd ed., Prentice-Hall of India, New Delhi, 2005.

Lehtinen, Russell, Gangemi Sr., *Computer Security Basics*, 2nd ed., O'Reilly, Navi Mumbai, 2006.

Merkow, Breithaupt, *Information Security*, Pearson Education, New Delhi, 2006.

Merkow, Breithaupt; *Information Security*, 2nd ed., Pearson Education, New Delhi, 2007.

Northcutt, et. al., *Inside Network Perimeter Security*, 2nd ed., Pearson Education, New Delhi, 2005.

Pfleeger, C.P. and Pfleeger, S.L., *Security in Computing*, 3rd ed., Pearson Education, New Delhi, 2006.

Ronald, Rivest, *The RC5 Encryption Algorithm*, MIT Laboratory for Computer Science, 1997.

Smith, *Internet Cryptography*, Pearson Education.

Stallings, William, *Cryptography and Network Security*, 4th ed., Prentice-Hall of India, New Delhi, 2007.

Tanenbaum, Andrew, *Computer Networks*, 4th ed., Prentice-Hall of India, New Delhi.

Trappe, *Introduction to Cryptography with Coding Theory*, 2nd ed., Pearson Education, New Delhi, 2006.

Whitman, Mattord, *Principles of Information Security*, Thomson, Chennai, 2007. www.networksorcery.com

Index

3DES, 57

Access control, 4, 7, 372
Access points (APs), 208
Access router, 370
Accurate reporting of the collected information, 377
Active attack, 10
Active data, 378
Active system, 320
Advanced encryption standard (AES), 57
Advantages of a dIDS, 326
Aggressive exchange, 295
Agrawal, Kayal and Saxena primality test, 153
AH transport mode, 282
AH tunnel mode, 283
AKS test, 153
Alert protocol, 308
Algorithms for digital signature, 245
Alternative names, 238
Analysis using aggregation, 327
Anomaly-based Detection, 321
Anomaly-based intrusion detection systems (IDS), 319, 322
Append, 224
Appending length, 214
Appending virus, 340
Application, 265
Application level gateways, 364
Application/Octet-stream, 265
Application/PostScript, 265

Application server, 228
Applications of DSS, 250
Applications of IPsec, 273
Applications of S/MIME, 269
Architecture of Blowfish algorithm for encryption, 100
Architecture of Blowfish for decryption, 101
Archival data, 378
Areas of application of computer forensics, 379
Association of digital signatures and encryption, 243
Asymmetric encryption, 163
Attack, 351
Attack aggregation, 325
Authenticated service, 231
Authentication, 7, 165, 202, 242, 255, 268
Authentication header (AH) protocol, 281
Authentication only exchange, 294
Authentication protocols, 251
Authentication server (AS), 226, 230
Authentication ticket, 231
Authenticator, 227
Availability, 7, 372
Avalanche effect, 66

Backdoor, 259, 352
Backdoor attack, 352
Backdoor program, 352
Backup of data, 4
Bait files, 343
Base exchange, 293

Bastion host, 365
Bastion host/Proxy, 370
Behaviour-based approach, 342
Behaviour blocking, 351
Benefits of a firewall, 366
Benefits of IPsec, 274
Best practices, 350
Bi-directional, 234
Biometric authentication, 206
Black hat, 8
Block cipher, 17, 47
Blocking a denial-of-service attack, 355
Blowfish algorithm, 97, 98
Blowfish architecture, 101
Blowfish's f-function, 101
Boot sector virus, 340
Botnet, 347
Bots, 349
Bruce Schneier, 97
Brute force attack, 217, 352
Bucket brigade attack, 185

Caesar cipher, 17
Caller ID spoofing, 354
Cave story, 196
Cavity viruses, 343
CBC pad mode, 105
Central analysis server, 325
Certificate, 182
Certificate revocation lists (CRLs), 239
Challenges of intrusion detection, 335
ChangeCipher SpecProtocol, 308
Changing and reusing passwords, 332
Characteristics of a Firewall, 362
Characteristics of Hoaxes, 352
Checksum, 210
Chinese remainder theorem, 154
Choke router, 370
Chosen-text, 198
Cipher block chaining (CBC), 105
Cipher block chaining (CBC) mode, 49
Cipher modes in RC5, 105
Ciphertext, 5
Circuit level gateways, 366
Clandestine user, 318
Client, 228
Comparison of PGP and S/MIME, 269
Completeness, 195
Composite numbers, 131
Composition rules, 331
Compression, 256

Computer forensics, 375
Computer forensics investigations, 378
Confidentiality, 2, 165, 166, 255, 372
   and authentication:, 256
Content-type, 262
Cooperative agent network, 325
Cross-authentication, 234
Cross-realm authentication, 233
Cross-realm ticket, 235
Cryptanalysis, 9, 32
   of Blowfish, 102
Cryptogram, 18
Cryptographic algorithms, 286
Cryptography, 5, 7, 17
CTS cipher mode, 105

Data confidentiality, 7
Data encryption standard (DES), 57
Data security, 5
Data sources, 326
Decryption, 8
Decryption algorithm, 16
Demilitarised zone (DMZ), 365
Denial of service attack, 2
Denial of service attacks (DoS), 11, 354
Description, 262
Deterministic test, 151
Dictionary attack, 33, 352
Difference between IPv4 and IPv6, 280
Differential cryptanalysis, 66
Different types of computer worms, 346
Digital envelope, 268
Digital immune system, 350
Digital signature, 241
Digital signature algorithm (DSA), 246, 251
Digital signature standard, 250
Digital signature standard (DSS), 246, 250
Direct relationship, 234
Discrete logarithms, 158
Discretionary access control systems, 373
Distributed denial-of-service attack, 355
Distributed intrusion detection system, 324
Distribution of public keys, 179
Documentation, 376
Double columnar transposition, 31
Doubling the point Q, 189
Dual-homed host architecture, 366

EAP infrastructure, 208
EAP method, 208

Electronic code book (ECB) mode, 48
Electronic evidence, 379
ElGamal signature, 248, 251
ElGamal Signature, 248
Elliptic curve, 186
Elliptic curve cryptography (ECC), 193
Elliptic curve Diffie–Hellman (ECDH), 193
Elliptic curve digital signature algorithm (ECDSA), 249
Elliptic curve groups, 190
Elliptic curve security, 194
E-mail bombing, 356
E-mail compatibility, 256
E-mail review, 381
E-mail viruses, 341
E-mail worm, 346
Encryption, 4, 5, 8, 97, 333
  with a variable key, 344
Error rates, 208
ESP transport mode, 285
ESP tunnel mode, 286
Euclidean algorithm, 143
Euler's theorem, 138
Euler totient function, 138
Evidence, 377
Examples of computer forensics, 381
Executable, 340
Expansion permutation, 62
Expression matching, 324
Extended euclidean algorithm, 145, 146
Extensible authentication protocol (EAP), 208
Extension, 238
Extension headers, 278
Exterior router, 370
External approach, 3
External firewall, 365
Extraction, 376
Extranet VPN, 300

Fail to enroll rate, 207
False accept ratio (FAR), 207
False reject ratio (FRR), 207
Feedback mode, 51
Feistel ciphers, 56
Fermat primality test, 152
Fermat's little theorem, 134
Fermat's theorem, 134
File-sharing networks worm, 346
Final permutation, 64
Fingerprint authentication, 207
Finite fields, 190

Firewall architectures, 366
Firewalls, 4
Forced delay, 198
Fragmentation, 278
Framework establishment, 313
Free space, 382
Fully document hardware configuration, 381

Genetic algorithm, 324
Greatest common divisor, 131
Grey hat, 8

Hacking, 8
Hamiltonian cycle, 197
Handshake protocol, 308
HASH, 224
Hash message authentication code (HMAC), 223
Hash value, 221
Header, 277
Header chaining, 278
Hierarchical trust relationship, 235
Hill Cipher, 22
History of S/MIME, 267
HMAC, 222
HMAC-MD5, 224
HMAC-SHA-1, 224
Hoax, 351
Honeypots, 328
Host-based systems, 319
Human factors, 330
Hybrids, 341

ID, 262
IDEA structure, 110
Identification, 376
Identity protection exchange, 294
Image, 263
Imaging, 381
Immune system approach, 323
Impersonation, 198
Implementation of digital signatures, 243
Importance of set, 312
Incident analysis with dIDS, 327
Incident response, 382
Index calculus algorithm, 159
Informational exchange, 295
Initialisation, 224
Initialising MD buffer, 214

Initial permutation, 60
Initial ticketing service, 232
Inspect for traps, 380
Instant messaging worms, 346
Integrity, 2, 7, 242, 372
Integrity checking, 223
Integrity of evidence, 377
Interior router, 370
Interleaving, 198
Internal approach, 3
Internal firewall, 365
International data encryption algorithm (IDEA), 66, 110
International standardisation, 383
Internet protocol, 280
   spoofing, 353
Internet relay chat (IRC) worms, 346
Internet worms, 346
Interpretation, 376
Inter-session chosen plaintext attacks, 236
Intranet VPNs, 300
Intruder detection, 332
Intruders, 318
Intrusion detection, 317, 318, 320
  method, 321
  system (IDS), 4, 317, 319
Intrusion prevention, 317
IP address spoofing, 364
IPsec protocols and operations, 280
IP security architecture, 272
IPv4, 280
IPv6, 275, 280
ISAKMP exchange types, 293
ISAKMP payloads, 289
ISAKMP protocol, 288
Issuer name, 237
Issuer unique identifier (versions 2 and 3 only), 238
ITU-T, 237

KDC, 235
KDCs, 230
Kerberos, 225, 226
  authentication model, 232
  ticket-granting approach, 228
Key, 16
  distribution, 162, 178
  distribution servers, 230
  elements of SET, 313
  escrow, 260
  establishment protocol, 193

exchange payload, 292
exchange protocol, 297
expansion, 97, 98
generation, 111
length, 172
management, 163
scheduling algorithm, 106
usage, 238

Latent data, 379
Legal processes, 377
Limitations of a firewall, 366
Linear cryptanalysis, 67
Logic bomb, 341, 348

Macro virus, 341
Malicious code, 339
Mandatory access control systems, 373
Man-in-the-middle attack, 9, 185, 353, 356
Manual removal of Trojan horse, 348
Masquerade, 11
Masquerader, 318
Maximum transmission unit (MTU), 278
MD2, 210
MD4, 211
MD5, 211, 212
Memory resident virus, 340
Message, 263
Message authentication code (MAC), 222
Message digest, 210, 243
  algorithm, 210
Metamorphic code, 345
Metamorphic viruses, 345
Miller–Rabin primality test, 153
MIME, 261
MIME Headers, 261
MIME transfer-encoding header field, 266
Misfeasor, 318
Misuse-based detection, 322
Misuse-based intrusion detection systems, 319, 323
Modular arithmetic, 131
Monoalphabetic ciphers, 17, 18
Mono-directional, 234
Multipart, 263
Multipart/digest, 265
Multipart/parallel, 265

Naïve methods, 151

Index

Need for intrusion detection systems, 320
Need of PGP, 254
Network-based system, 319
Network protocol analyser, 356
NIST, 246
Non-repudiation, 7, 243

OAKLEY key determination protocol, 296
Objectives of access control, 372
Objectives of SSL, 305
On-access scanning, 345
One-time pad, 28
Opinion of experts, 377
Optional content-description header field, 266
Optional content-ID header field, 266
OTP (one time password), 206
Overview of IPsec, 274

Packet filtering firewall, 362
Padding, 210, 213, 224
Parasitic virus, 340
Passive attack, 9, 357
Passive system, 320
Password, 204, 228
Password-based authentication method, 204
Password-guessing attacks, 236
Password synchronisation, 333
Password table, 205
Payloads, 346
P-box permutation, 63
Perimeter network, 369
PGP encryption applications, 259
PGP security quality, 261
Phishing, 354
Physical security layer, 1
PKI, 242
Plaintext, 5
Playfair cipher, 19
Point-to-point protocol (PPP), 208
Poisoning of file-sharing networks, 354
Polyalphabetic ciphers, 26
Polygraphic substitution ciphers, 17
Polymorphic code, 344
Polymorphic virus, 340
Preamble, 264
Prepending virus, 340
Preservation, 376
Pretty good privacy, 168, 179
PRETTY good privacy (PGP), 253
Prevention system, 320

Primality test, 151
Prime number, 130
Private sector, 379
Private security, 1
Probabilistic test, 151, 152
Processing message, 214
Production honeypots, 328
Project security, 1
Proposal payload, 292
Proxy server, 365
Pseudo-random generating algorithm, 107
Public announcement, 179
Public key authority, 180
Public key certificates, 181
    approach, 182
Public key cryptography, 163
Public key–private, 163
Publicly available directory, 179
Public sector, 379

Radix-64 conversion, 258
Raw block cipher mode, 105
RC4, 106
RC5, 103
RC6, 107, 109
RC6 encryption, 108
Receiver operating characteristic (ROC), 208
Referer spoofing, 354
Reflection, 198
Relative prime numbers, 131
Remote access VPN, 299
Replay, 198
    attacks, 236
Research honeypots, 329
RIPEMD, 224
RIPEMD-160, 224
Role-based access control systems, 373
Rounds 1 to 16, 61
RSA, 169
R-smooth, 159
Rule-based access control systems, 373

Sandboxing, 351
S-box substitution, 62
Screened host architecture, 367
Screened subnet architecture, 368
Secrecy, 165, 332
    and authentication, 269
Secure digital card, 380
Secure electronic transactions, 311

Secure hash algorithm (SHA), 210, 218
Secure MIME, 261
Secure socket layer (SSL), 164, 304
Secure VPN requirements, 301
Security, 172
Security association (SA), 280
   negotiation, 289
   payload, 291
Security threats, 330
Segmentation and reassembly, 256
Self-modification, 344
Serial number, 237
Series of confidence, 4
Session, 228
Session key, 227
SET mechanism, 312
SHA-1, 218
   algorithm, 219
Side channel attack, 358
Signature, 237, 319
Signature-based IDS, 319
Signature on the above fields, 238
Signature or pattern based approach, 342
Simple self-modifications, 344
Simple weak key, 67
Single columnar transposition, 30
Single round of IDEA, 113
Slack space, 382
S/MIME, 267
SMIME, 261
Smooth integer, 159
Sniffer, 356
Solovay–Strassen primality test, 153
Soundness, 195
   error, 196
Source routing attacks, 364
Spam, 356
Spoofing attack, 353
Spoofing MD5, 218
Spyware, 349
SSL communication, 238
SSL record protocol, 307
SSL session and connection, 306
Standard of working, 383
State transition analysis, 324
Static, 194
Statistical approach, 323
Stealth mechanism, 344
Stealth virus, 341
Steganography, 34
Stream cipher, 17, 47
Strengths of IPsec, 272

Strengths of SET, 314
Strong authentication method, 206
Subject, 238
Subject public key information, 238
Subject unique identifier (versions 2 and 3
   only), 238
Subkey, 59
Substitution ciphers, 17
Swapping, 63
Symmetric encryption, 15
Symptoms of a computer worm, 347
Synchronisation, 333

Target service, 232
TEMP, 221
Text, 265
Text/Plain, 265
Text/Richtext, 265
Thumb impression, 207
Ticket, 227
Ticket-granting server (TGS), 228, 229, 230,
   232
Ticket-granting ticket, 228, 229, 232
Time bomb, 341
Timestamp, 226
Timing attack, 357
Tiny fragment attacks, 364
Totient function, 139
Traditional authentication method, 205
Training, 383
Transfer encoding, 262
Transform payload, 292
Transited realms, 234
Transitive trust relationship, 235
Transport mode, 281
Transposition ciphers, 29
Triple CBC (Cipher Block Chaining), 65
Triple DES, 57, 64
Triple electronic code book (3ECB), 65
Trojan or TROJAN HORSES, 348
Trusted system, 371
   in policy analysis, 371
Tunnel mode, 281
Two-factor authentication method, 206
Types of data, 378
Types of firewall, 362
Types of viruses, 340

Understanding the suspects, 379
URL spoofing and phishing, 354

User authentication and passwords, 329
User id, 204
User's credentials, 227
User support, 334

Validity, 237
Vernam cipher, 28
Version, 237
Video, 265
Video/MPEG, 265
Vigenere cipher, 26
Vigenere square, 26
Virtual private network, 298
Viruses, 340
VPN security, 301

Weaknesses, 383
   of SET, 315

White hat, 8
Working of antivirus software, 341
Working of a sniffer, 357
Working of denial-of-service attacks, 355
Working of IPsec, 275
Working of PGP, 255
Worms, 345
   with good intent, 347

X.509, 237, 238, 239
X.509 authentication service, 237
XOR operation, 62, 63
X-TypeName, 265

Zero-knowledge, 195
   proof, 195, 202
   proof of knowledge, 196
   protocol, 195